GFI Network Security and PCI Compliance Power Tools

Brien Posey

Troy Thompson Technical Editor

Foreword by Laura Taylor
President and CEO, Relevant Technologies

PUBLISHED BY
Syngress Publishing, Inc.
Elsevier, Inc.
30 Corporate Drive
Burlington, MA 01803

GFI Network Security and PCI Compliance Power Tools

Publisher: Laura Colantoni
Acquisitions Editor: Andrew Williams
Developmental Editor: Matthew Cater
Technical Editor: Troy Thompson
Project Manager: Andre Cuello

Page Layout and Art: SPI
Copy Editor: Judith H. Eby, Michael McGee
Indexer: SPI
Cover Designer: Michael Kavish

For information on rights, translations, and bulk sales, contact Matt Pedersen, Senior Sales Manager, Corporate Sales, at Syngress Publishing; email m.pedersen@elsevier.com.

Technical Editor

Troy Thompson has worked in network administration for over 20 years, performing network monitoring and backup, Microsoft Exchange administration and training. Troy has written many technology articles, tutorials, and white papers, which have been published by leading technology publications and businesses including CNET, Microsoft, TechRepublic, and the Security Evaluation Center. Troy is a Cisco Certified Academy Instructor (CCAI), and has numerous other certifications including CCNA, MCSE+I, CCAI, Network+, Security+ and A+. Troy has also traveled the world playing music as the guitarist for Bride. Check out www.bridepub.com or view some videos on YouTube.

Lead Author

Brien Posey is a freelance technical writer who has received Microsoft's MVP award five times for his work with Windows Server, IIS, Exchange Server, and file system storage. Over the last thirteen years, Brien has published over 4,000 articles and whitepapers for a variety of technical publications and Websites including TechTarget, CNET, Windows IT Professional, ZDNET, Windows Networking, and many others. He has also written or contributed content to over 30 books.

In addition to his technical writing, Brien is the co-founder of Relevant Technologies (www.relevanttechnologies.com) and also serves the IT community through his own Web site at www.brienposey.com.

Prior to becoming a freelance author, Brien served as CIO for a nationwide chain of hospitals and healthcare facilities, and as a network administrator for the Department of Defense at Fort Knox. He has also worked as a network administrator for some of the nation's largest insurance companies.

When Brien isn't busy writing he enjoys exotic travel, racing speed boats, scuba diving, and pretty much anything else that's good for an adrenaline rush.

Foreword Contributor

Laura Taylor is Relevant Technologies' President and CEO. Her research has been used by the FDIC, the FBI, the IRS, various U.S. Federal Reserve Banks, U.S. Customs, the U.S. Treasury, the White House, and many publicly held Fortune 500 companies. Ms. Taylor specializes in security Certification and Accreditation (C&A) consulting and training, as well as audits of financial institutions. She has provided information security consulting services to some of the largest financial institutions in the world, including the U.S. Internal Revenue Service, the U.S. Treasury, the U.S. Governmentwide Accounting System, and National Westminster Bank—a division of the Royal Bank of Scotland. Ms. Taylor is the author of the bestselling FISMA Certification and Accreditation Handbook. In assisting her customers, Ms. Taylor has a 100-percent accreditation rate for FISMA compliance. Ms. Taylor has taught her FISMA 101 class for both SANS and for Yale University.

Before founding Relevant Technologies, Ms. Taylor was Director of Security Research at TEC. Ms. Taylor has also served as CIO of Schafer Corporation, Director of Information Security at Navisite, and Director of Certification and Accreditation for COACT. Earlier in her career, Ms. Taylor held various positions at Sun Microsystems where she was awarded several "Outstanding Performance" awards, and a CIS Security Award. Most recently, Ms. Taylor received an award from a division of the U.S. Financial Management Services Commissioner for her assistance with FISMA-compliant Security Certification & Accreditation of highly sensitive systems. Ms. Taylor is a Certified Information Security Manager (CISM).

Ms. Taylor has been featured in many media forums, including ABC-TV Business Now, CNET Radio, Boston Business Journal, Computer World, and The Montreal Gazette. Her research has been published on numerous Web portals and magazines, including Business Security Advisor, Forbes, SecurityWatch, eSecurityOnline, SecurityFocus, NetworkStorageForum, ZDNet, Datamation, MidRangeComputing, and Securify. Ms. Taylor has authored over 500 research articles and papers on information security topics and has contributed to multiple books. A graduate of Skidmore College, Ms. Taylor is a member of the Society of Professional Journalists, the IEEE Standards Association, the National Security Agency's IATFF Forum, and is the Chair of the FISMA Center's CCAP Exam Advisory Board.

Contents

Foreword

Today, all companies, U.S. federal agencies, and nonprofit organizations have valuable data on their servers that must be secured. One of the challenges for information technology (IT) experts is learning how to use new products in a time-efficient manner so new implementations can go quickly and smoothly. Learning how to set up sophisticated products is time-consuming and can be confusing. GFI's LANguard Network Security Scanner can report vulnerabilities so they can be mitigated before unauthorized intruders wreak havoc on your network. To take advantage of the best things LANguard Network Security Scanner has to offer, you'll want to configure it on your network so it captures key events and alerts you to potential vulnerabilities before they are exploited.

In understanding how to use this product most effectively, Brien Posey has pinpointed the most important concepts with examples and screenshots so systems administrators and security engineers can understand how to get the GFI security tools working quickly and effectively. Brien's straightforward no-nonsense writing style is devoid of difficult-to-understand technical jargon. His descriptive examples explain how GFI's security tools enhance the security controls already built into your server's operating system. Brien's ability to explain technology so just about anyone can understand it is what has made him today's most popular information technology author.

I have had the pleasure of working with Brien over the years, and his understanding of technology and his ability to explain it so that I can understand it, has made him my #1 go-to person when I need to know how something works. With *GFI Network Security and PCI Compliance Power Tools* now available for all, all IT professionals who want to take advantage of cutting-edge security tools can learn how to strengthen their security controls, and put in place best practice security management processes. Brien's skill at sharing his technical knowledge in a way that anyone can understand is a breath of fresh air in the world of pedantic, overly technical white papers that seem to purposely use pretentious language and knotty examples for a select exclusive audience. With this very cool product, it's nice to have a practical guidebook to help you make the most of it.

—Laura Taylor
President and CEO, Relevant Technologies

Acknowledgements

First and foremost, I want to thank my wife Taz for her patience and understanding while I was working on this book. Taz has constantly supported me in every way imaginable throughout my career. I only wish that words could truly express the love and gratitude that I have for her.

I would also like to thank Troy Thompson and Laura Taylor of Relevant Technologies (http://www.relevanttechnologies.com). Both Troy and Laura have put a lot of work into this book. More importantly, I have learned a lot from working with Laura and Troy on various IT projects over the years. They are both extremely talented individuals, and I attribute a high degree of my overall success to the experience that I have gained while working with them.

I also wish to express my gratitude to:

- Andrew Williams, Matthew Cater, David George, and the rest of the staff at Syngress.

- David Kelleher, Angelica Micallef Trigona, and Stephen Chetcuti Bonavita at GFI.

- Seth Oxhandler at Coolcat Inc. (http://coolcatinc.com)

- The staff at BigSecurityStore.com

- Shamir Dasgupta, Jeremy Broyles, and Billy Brown at Xpressions Interactive (www.xpressions.com)

Chapter 1

Installing GFI LANguard Network Security Scanner

Solutions in this chapter:

- **Installing GFI LANguard Network Security Scanner**

☑ **Summary**

☑ **Solutions Fast Track**

☑ **Frequently Asked Questions**

Introduction

When Syngress asked me to write a book on the various GFI security products, I wasn't quite sure what I was going to write. Most of the GFI products are fairly intuitive, and GFI always seems to do a good job on the instruction manuals for their products, all of which can be downloaded from the GFI Web site.

When I stopped and thought about it, I began to realize that although the various GFI instruction manuals are both comprehensive and well written, they tend to be a little bit bloated because they cover every feature that the various products have to offer. That's not necessarily a bad thing (especially for an instruction manual), but instruction manuals rarely reflect how people use the products in the real world.

Since GFI already offers such thorough instruction manuals, I decided to write this book as a guide to using the various products in a real-world environment. What that means is that I'm not going to waste your time by talking about the more obscure product features, or by showing you convoluted techniques that you would never use in practice. I'm also going to try to avoid using a lot of technical jargon. My goal is to write a book that's easy to read and that teaches you what you need to know, but without wasting your time in the process.

For each of the products that this book covers, I will walk you through the installation process, and then walk you through the most useful administrative tasks in a step-by-step manner. As I do, I will also share with you any hints or tricks that I have found for getting better results or for accomplishing your goals more quickly. I sincerely hope that you will find this book to be a useful reference.

Installing GFI LANguard Network Security Scanner

Installing GFI LANguard Network Security Scanner is pretty simple and straightforward, but I wanted to go ahead and walk you through the process just so there aren't any surprises later on.

GFI LANguard Network Security Scanner can be installed on any of the following operating systems:

- Windows 2000 (with SP4 or higher)

- Windows XP (with SP2 or higher)

- Windows Server 2003

- Windows Vista (with SP1 or higher)

- Windows Server 2008

Windows Vista and Windows Server 2008 can be running either the X86 version or the X64 version of Windows.

Are You Owned?

Checking for Infections

The whole point of installing GFI Network Security Scanner is to help you to secure your network. Using a security product like this one does you absolutely no good though, if the server that will be running it has already been compromised. I recommend scanning the server that you will be installing the product onto for malware prior to performing the installation.

GFI LANguard Network Security Scanner also requires you to be running Internet Explorer 5.1 or higher, and the Client for Microsoft Networks component, which is installed by default in every version of Windows since Windows 95. To install GFI LANguard Network Security Scanner, perform the following steps:

1. Download the languardnss8.exe file from the GFI Web site (www.gfi.com/downloads/downloads.aspx?pid=lanss&lid=EN), place the file into a temporary directory, and then double click on it.

2. Depending on the version of Windows that you are using, you may see a security warning that asks you if you want to run this file, as shown in Figure 1.1. If you receive such a warning, click the **Run** button.

Figure 1.1 If You Receive This Security Warning, Click the Run Button

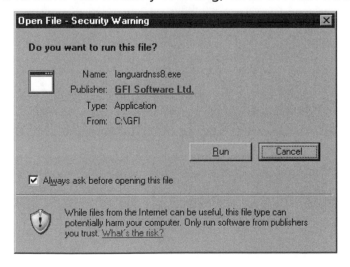

3. Windows will now launch the InstallShield Wizard, which will extract the various files used by the Setup process.

4. When the process completes, Windows will launch the Setup wizard, which will initially display a welcome screen. Click **Next** to bypass the welcome screen, and you will see a screen prompting you to accept the end user license agreement.

5. Choose the option to **accept the license agreement**, and click **Next**.

6. At this point, the Setup wizard will display the Customer Information screen that's shown in Figure 1.2. As you can see in the figure, you are prompted to enter a user name, a company name, and a license key. GFI LANguard Network Security Scanner allows you to enter the word **EVALUATION** (all caps) in place of a license key. If you choose to do so, you will be able to use all of the product's features for the next ten days. GFI offers this evaluation feature as a way of allowing you to test drive their products. If you have purchased a license for GFI LANguard Network Security Scanner, then the license key should be listed in the e-mail message that you receive from GFI.

Figure 1.2 You Have the Option of Entering the Word EVALUATION in Lieu of a License Key

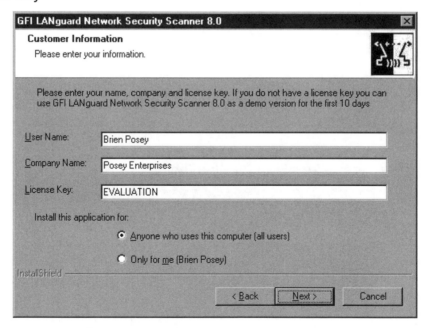

7. Click Next, and Setup will prompt you to choose an account to use for the Attendant Service to run under. Unlike many other services, the Attendant Service cannot run using

the Local System account. You can specify any account that you want, but the account needs to be a domain member, and it must have administrative privileges for the domain.

8. When you finish entering the service account credentials, click **Next,** and you will see a screen asking you if you want GFI LANguard Network Security Scanner to use a Microsoft Access Database, or a SQL Server database.

If you want to take the easy out, go with the Microsoft Access database option. If you choose this option, you don't even have to install Microsoft Access.

The down side to using a Microsoft Access database is that it does not offer the performance or scalability of a Structured Query Language (SQL) Server database. Using a Microsoft Access database will work fine if you have a small- to medium-sized network, or if you are just installing GFI LANguard Network Security Scanner for evaluation purposes. If you have a larger network, then performance is typically going to suffer if you try using a Microsoft Access Database.

If you choose the SQL Server option, then you have the option of using SQL Server 2000 or higher, or of using Microsoft Database Engine (MSDE). In case you are not familiar with MSDE, it is Microsoft's free version of SQL Server.

So why would Microsoft offer SQL Server for free? Well, from what I have heard, they did it because so many of their products (and so many third-party products) require a backend database, and in a lot of cases a full blown SQL Server would be overkill. MSDE provides you with a way of using products that require a SQL Server database, but without having to spend good money on SQL Server licenses or on the supporting hardware.

As great as MSDE sounds, you've got to remember that nobody in their right mind would buy SQL Server if MSDE was truly as good as SQL Server. Earlier I mentioned that MSDE stood for Microsoft Database Engine. MSDE is just that; a database engine. MSDE can host SQL databases, but it doesn't perform quite as well as a full blown SQL Server installation. It is also missing a lot of the management tools, and doesn't offer clustering or a lot of the other more advanced SQL Server capabilities. On the upside though, it is free!

So right about now, you might be wondering where you can get your hands on a copy of MSDE. Microsoft allows you to download it from their Web site for free. You can get the original version of MSDE, which is really a SQL 2000 database engine at: www.microsoft.com/downloads/details. aspx?familyid=413744D1-A0BC-479F-BAFA-E4B278EB9147&displaylang=en

There is also a SQL 2005 version of MSDE available at: www.microsoft.com/sql/editions/ express/default.mspx. Although this is technically the next version of MSDE, Microsoft has changed its name to Microsoft SQL Server Express Edition. The most important thing that you need to know about this release is that the original version of MSDE will not work with Windows Vista or with Windows Server 2008.

Since most of you who are going to be installing GFI LANguard Network Security Scanner will probably be using it in an enterprise environment, I'm going to go ahead and show you how to configure it for use with a true SQL Server database. If you want to use MSDE or Microsoft Access to host the database, you can easily do so by following the steps outlined in GFI's installation instructions. You can download a copy of the installation instructions (and a copy of the full blown instruction manual) at: www.gfi.com/downloads/downloads.aspx?pid=lanss&lid=EN.

In either case, I will continue guiding you through the Setup process after I show you how to prepare SQL Server.

TIP

SQL Server offers far better performance than MS Access or MSDE databases, but is also a lot more expensive. A lot of organizations start out using one of the less expensive database options, but eventually decide that they want to upgrade to SQL Server. Upgrading is not a simple proposition, so think long and hard about which database you want to use before you perform the installation.

Installing SQL Server

For demonstration purposes, I'm going to install SQL Server 2005 Developer Edition. Assuming that you are installing SQL Server in a production environment, you will probably be using a different version or different edition of SQL Server, so I'm not going to spend a lot of time talking about the installation process. At the same time, there are a couple of things that I want to point out, so I don't want to skip talking about the SQL Server installation process completely either.

TIP

You do not have to use a dedicated SQL Server, but you should use a dedicated SQL instance.

To install SQL Server 2005 Developer Edition, follow these steps:

1. Insert your installation media, and double click on the **Setup.exe** file.
2. After a brief delay, Windows will launch the Setup Wizard, which asks you to accept Microsoft's software license.
3. Accept the license agreement, and click **Next**.
4. You will see a message telling you that SQL Server Component Update is about to install a couple of components that are required for SQL Server Setup.
5. Click the **Install** button and the wizard will install these components.
6. When this initial component installation process completes, click **Next**, and Windows will launch the Microsoft SQL Server Installation Wizard.

7. Click **Next** to bypass the wizard's Welcome screen, and the wizard will perform a system configuration check. If you look at Figure 1.3, you can see that I received a warning message because Internet Information Server (IIS) is not installed. There are some SQL Server features that can't be installed unless IIS is also installed. In this case, it isn't a big deal because we won't be using those features.

Figure 1.3 Ignore Any Warnings about IIS Not Being Installed

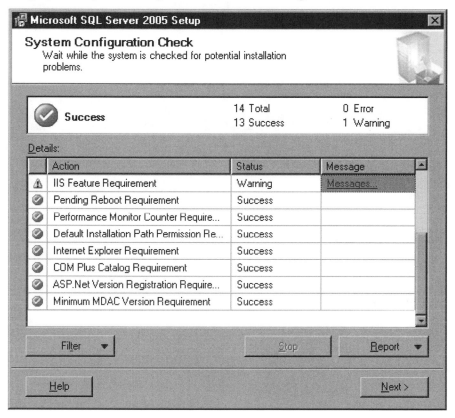

8. Click **Next,** and the wizard will prompt you to enter your **name, company name, and product key**.

9. Click **Next** again, and Setup will ask you which components you want to install. Just go ahead and select all of the available components (some will be grayed out), and click **Next**.

10. You will now see a screen asking you if you want to install SQL Server using a default instance or a named instance. I like using a named instance, because doing so helps to identify the purpose of the installation, and it reduces the temptation to use the installation for other purposes. I recommend creating a named instance called **GFI,** as shown in Figure 1.4.

Figure 1.4 Create a Named Instance Called GFI

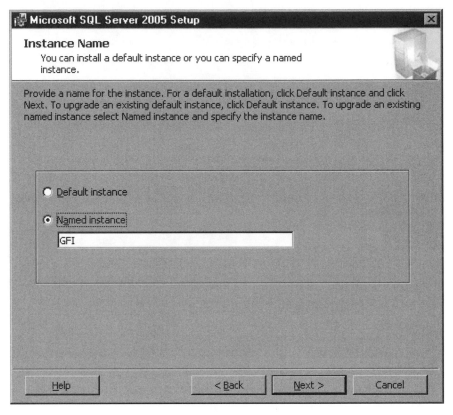

11. Click **Next and** you will see a screen that's similar to the one that's shown in Figure 1.5. As you can see in the figure, SQL Server requires the use of a service account. Setup gives you the choice of either using the built-in system account or using a domain account. We have already created a domain account that is to be used as a system account for GFI LANguard Network Security Scanner. I recommend going ahead and using this same service account for SQL Server. Keep in mind that this service account does have domain administrator privileges, so you will want to take the appropriate steps to keep your SQL Server secure.

Figure 1.5 Use the Service Account That You Created for GFI LANguard Network Security Scanner

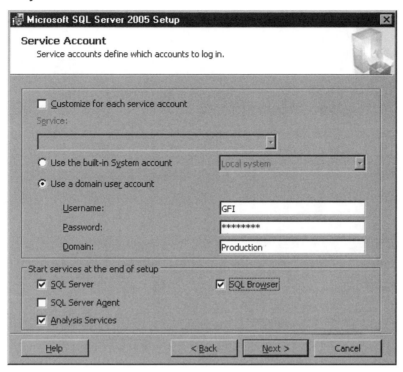

12. Make sure that all of the check boxes found in the Start Services at the End of Setup section are selected, except for the SQL Server Agent check box. You can see an example of this in Figure 1.5 above.

13. Click **Next**, and you will see a screen asking you if you want to use Windows Authentication Mode or Mixed Mode authentication. Choose the Windows Authentication Mode option and click **Next**.

14. When the Setup wizard displays the Collation Settings screen, click **Next** to accept the default settings.

15. The Setup wizard should now display the Error and Usage Report Settings screen. Again, click **Next** to go with the default settings.

16. You should now see a summary screen that shows you which components are being installed. Click the **Install** button to begin the installation process.

17. Verify that all of the components have installed correctly, as shown in Figure 1.6, and then click **Next**.

Figure 1.6 Verify That All of the SQL Server Components Have Installed Correctly, and Then Click Next

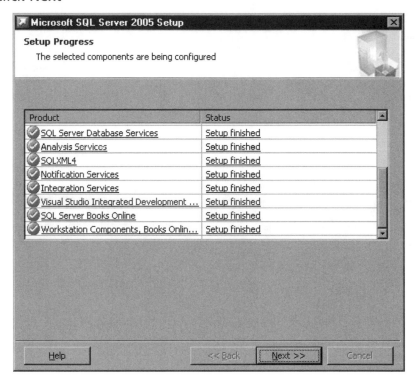

18.   Click **Finish** to complete the installation process.

19.   Install any necessary service packs or other patches.

It is important to note that when you apply SQL Server 2005 SP2, the security model changes a bit. Members of the domain administrator's group are no longer automatically granted permission to connect to SQL Server, nor are they automatically granted administrative privileges. When you apply the service pack, you will see a screen similar to the one that's shown in Figure 1.7 toward the end of the installation process. As you can see in the figure, this screen gives you the opportunity to specify which administrative accounts should have access to the SQL Server.

Figure 1.7 SQL Server 2005 SP2 Does Not Automatically Grant Domain Administrators Access to the SQL Server

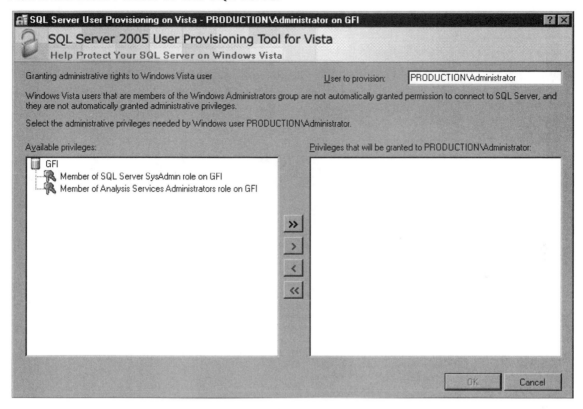

Continuing the GFI LANguard Network Security Scanner Setup Process

Now that I have talked about setting up SQL Server, I want to pick back up where I left off with setting up GFI LANguard Network Security Scanner. As I mentioned before, I will be using SQL Server for the backend database, but that doesn't mean that you have to. If you want to use Microsoft Access or MSDE, then your setup procedure will be slightly different than what I am about to show you, but you can always refer to GFI's installation instructions if you need help.

With that in mind, let's pick the installation procedure back up, starting with the Installation Type screen, shown in Figure 1.8.

Figure 1.8 You Must Tell the Setup Wizard Which Type of Backend Database You Want to Use

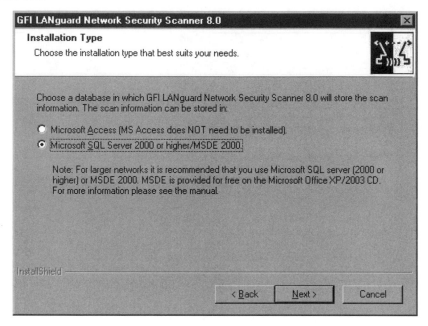

1. Choose the **Microsoft SQL Server 2000 or Higher/MSDE** option and click **Next**.

2. The following screen asks you to specify the database server that you are going to be using. You must enter the server name in UNC format (servername\SQL server instance name). If you installed SQL Server onto the same server that will be running GFI LANguard Network Security Scanner, then the database path will be [local]\GFI, as shown in Figure 1.9. [local] refers to the local server, and GFI is the name of the SQL Server instance that we installed earlier.

Figure 1.9 You Must Specify the Path of the Database That You Will Be Using

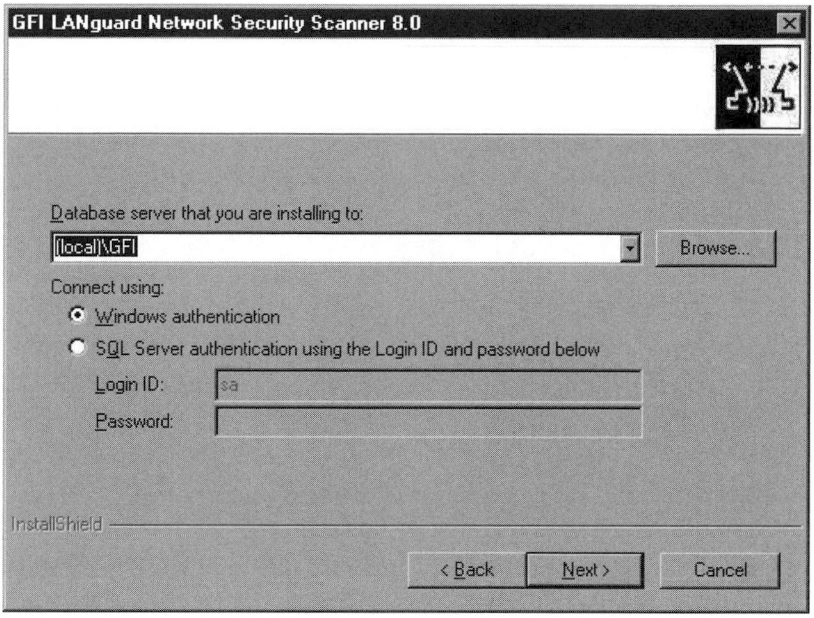

Installing GFI LANguard Network Security Scanner and SQL Server onto the same server is fine for smaller deployments, but if you work in a large enterprise environment, you will probably end up needing to use separate servers for performance reasons.

    3.   Verify that the Windows Authentication option is selected, and click **Next.**

Now it's time to configure the server's ability to transmit e-mail notifications. Since this is a somewhat involved procedure, I will cover it in its own section.

Configuring E-mail Notifications

GFI LANguard Network Security Scanner has the ability to send out e-mail notifications with scan reports. Ideally, you should configure the software to send these messages through your Exchange Server. If you don't have an Exchange Server, it isn't a big deal. You can just as easily configure your server to act as a standalone Simple Message Transfer Protocol (SMTP) server. I will show you both configuration methods.

Configuring a Standalone SMTP Server

If you don't have access to an Exchange Server, you can configure your GFI LANguard Network Security Scanner server to act as a standalone SMTP server. Windows ships with everything that you need, but the SMTP components are not installed by default. The exact method of installing the SMTP components varies depending on the version of Windows that you are using. For the purposes of this book, I will be using Windows Server 2003.

1. Begin the process by having whoever is in charge of your organization's e-mail create a dedicated mailbox for you that you can use for receiving server notifications. For demonstration purposes, I am going to be using a mailbox with an address of Security@production. com. I do not actually own the production.com domain, it is just the name of an internal Active Directory domain that I use. You should use an e-mail address that reflects the mail domain that you use in real life.

2. Once the new mailbox has been created, open the server's Control Panel, and select the **Add or Remove Programs** option.

3. When Windows displays the Add or Remove Programs dialog box, click the **Add\ Remove Windows Components** icon.

4. After a brief delay, Windows will launch the Windows Component Wizard. Choose the **Application Server** option from the list of available components. Don't click on the check box, just click on the words **Application Server**.

5. Click the **Details** button, and you will see the various Application Server components.

6. Click on the **Internet Information Services (IIS)** component. Once again, you should click on the words, not the check box.

7. Click the **Details** button, and Windows will display a list of the various IIS components that are available.

8. Scroll toward the bottom of the list of components, and then select the **SMTP Service** option. This time you are actually going to select the check box rather than just clicking on the words, as shown in Figure 1.10.

Figure 1.10 You Must Select the SMTP Service Option

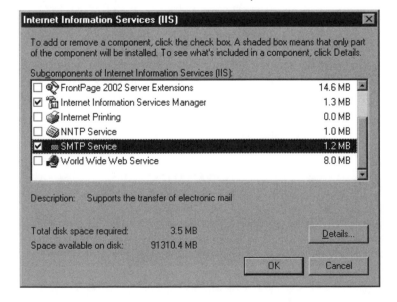

9. Click **OK**.

10. Click **OK**.

11. Click **Next** and Windows will begin installing the necessary files. Depending on how your server is configured, you may be prompted to insert your Windows Server 2003 installation media.

12. When the installation process completes, click the **Finish** button, and close the Control Panel.

13. Now that the SMTP Service is installed, we need to configure it. Fortunately, the configuration process is pretty simple.

14. Choose the **Internet Information Services (IIS)** option from the server's Administrative Tools menu.

15. When the IIS Manager opens, navigate through the console tree to **Internet Information Services | your server | Default SMTP Virtual Server | Domains**, as shown in Figure 1.11.

Figure 1.11 Navigate Through the Console Tree to Internet Information Services | your server | Default SMTP Virtual Server | Domains

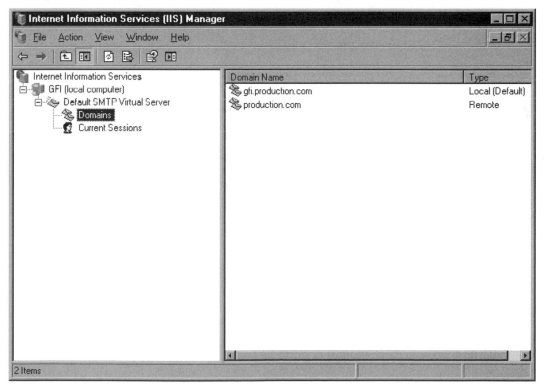

Notice in the screen capture above that when I selected the Domains container, that the pane on the right displays two domain names. The top domain name, in this case gfi.production.com, was placed there by default. Gfi.production.com is actually the server's fully qualified domain name (FQDN), but the SMTP service treats it as though it were an independent domain.

As it stands right now, the SMTP service is only capable of sending e-mail to recipients in the gfi.production.com domain. Of course there aren't any mailboxes in this domain, because the server that we are configuring isn't a full blown mail server. The SMTP component only allows us to send mail, it does not allow for the storage of mailboxes on the server.

That being the case, we must make the SMTP Service aware of the domain that we want to send e-mail to. In this case, we will be sending messages to an e-mail address named Security@production.com. Since this mailbox resides in the production.com domain (or at least in an internal domain named production.com), we need to make the SMTP Service aware of the domain's existence. I had already done that when I created the screen capture above. That's why you see the production.com domain listed in the console. Here's how it's done:

16. Right click on the **Domains** container, and choose the **New | Domain** options from the resulting shortcut menus.

17. Windows will now launch the New SMTP Domain Wizard. The wizard's initial screen asks you if you want to specify a remote domain or an alias. Choose the **Remote** option, and click **Next**.

18. Now enter the name of the domain that you want to send mail to, into the space provided.

19. Click **Finish**, and the domain that you have specified will be added to the list of domains.

20. Right click on the domain that you just added, and then select the **Properties** command from the resulting shortcut menu.

21. When the domain's properties sheet appears, select the **Allow Incoming Mail to be Relayed to this Domain** check box, as shown in Figure 1.12.

Figure 1.12 You Must Allow Incoming Mail to Be Relayed to the Domain That You Just Set Up

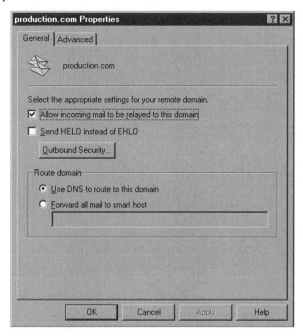

Now that we have configured Windows to act as an SMTP server, it's time to configure GFI LANguard Network Security Scanner to use the SMTP server to send mail. You can see the screen that Setup uses for this purpose in Figure 1.13.

Figure 1.13 You Must Configure the Mail Settings as a Part of Installing GFI LANguard Network Security Scanner

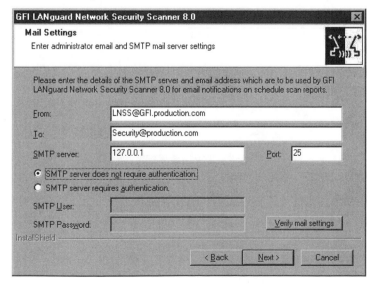

To configure the mail settings, follow these steps:

1. You can use any e-mail address in the From field, so long as the domain portion of the address reflects the server's FQDN. In this case, the server's FQDN is gfi.production.com.

2. You must enter the destination e-mail address into the To field. Remember that you can only send messages to e-mail addresses that use a domain that you have specified through the IIS Manager.

3. Verify that the SMTP Server field is set to **127.0.0.1**. In case you are wondering, this is the local loopback address. You are essentially telling the server that it is the SMTP server. As an alternative, you could enter the server's own Internet Protocol (IP) address into this field.

4. Make sure that the port number is set to **25**. Port 25 is the port that is normally used for SMTP traffic.

5. Select the **SMTP Server Does not Require Authentication** option.

6. Click the **Verify Mail Settings** button to make sure that your SMTP server is working correctly, and that GFI LANguard Network Security Scanner is configured properly. You can see what a properly configured server looks like in Figure 1.14.

Figure 1.14 Click the Verify Mail Settings Button to Make Sure That the Mail Settings are Configured Properly

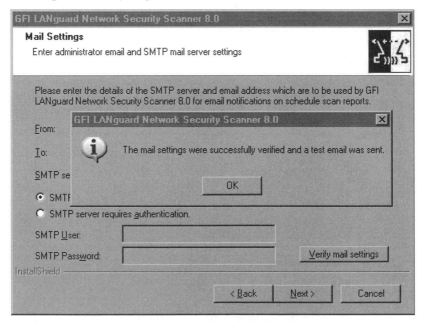

Notes from the Underground...

Mail Relay

You need to be careful about how you configure your SMTP server, and how it is used. As it is right now, your SMTP server can transmit mail without requiring authentication. Should this server become compromised, it could easily be turned into a "spam factory" and the resulting spam would be traced back to your IP address, which would likely get you blacklisted.

Configuring GFI LANguard for Use With Microsoft Exchange Server

Although I am writing this book on GFI security software, I am best known throughout the IT community for my work with Microsoft Exchange Server. That being the case, I wanted to show you an alternate mail settings configuration that you can use if you have an Exchange Server organization in place.

As I mentioned earlier, my internal domain name is production.com. I therefore created an Exchange Server mailbox with an e-mail address of Security@production.com. Since I don't actually own the production.com domain name, this e-mail address is only accessible from within my perimeter network.

I'm not going to go through the steps of creating an Exchange Server mailbox, because these steps are performed in a very different manner from one version of Exchange Server to the next. Besides, if your company has an Exchange Server organization in place, I would think that it would be a safe assumption that somebody in the company knows how to create a mailbox. I will tell you that my Security@production.com mailbox resides on an Exchange 2007 server.

If your company has an Exchange Server organization in place, then the process of configuring the mail settings for GFI LANguard Network Security Scanner will be a lot simpler than what you saw in the previous section. That's because in the previous section, we had to build an SMTP server from scratch. Exchange Server is natively equipped to handle SMTP mail, so we don't have to bother with most of those configuration steps. In fact, the entire configuration takes place through the GFI LANguard Network Security Scanner setup wizard. To do so, follow these steps:

1. You can enter any e-mail address that you want into the From field. For the sake of simplicity, I used the recipient's own e-mail address (security@production.com), as shown in Figure 1.15.

Figure 1.15 The From Address Should Reflect the Server's FQDN

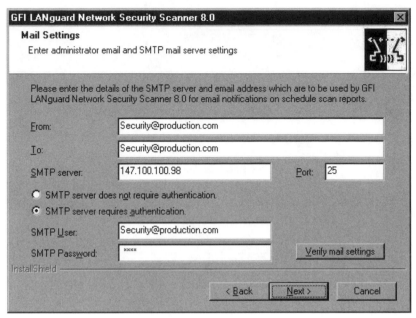

2. You must enter the e-mail address for the mailbox that you created earlier into the To field.

3. You must enter your Exchange Server's IP address into the SMTP Server field.

4. Make sure that the Port field is set to **25.**

5. Select the **SMTP Server Requires Authentication** option.

6. Enter the e-mail address of the recipient mailbox into the SMTP User field. Remember that Windows allows you to substitute an e-mail address for a login name.

7. Enter the recipient's account password into the SMTP Password field.

8. Click the **Verify Mail Settings** button to make sure that the mail settings are configured correctly, as shown in Figure 1.16.

Figure 1.16 Click the Verify Mail Settings Button to Make Sure That the Mail Settings Are Configured Correctly

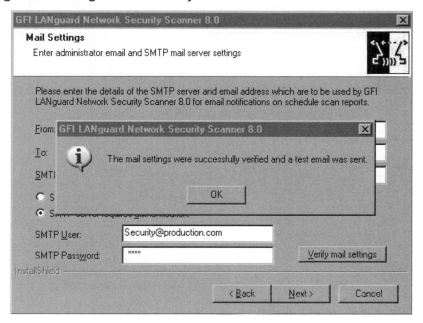

As you can see in the figure, GFI LANguard Network Security Scanner sends a test e-mail message to the address that you have specified. Therefore, before you move on, I recommend opening the recipient Inbox using either Outlook or Outlook Web Access (OWA) to make sure that the message has arrived, as shown in Figure 1.17.

Figure 1.17 You Should Receive a Test Message in the Recipient's Mailbox

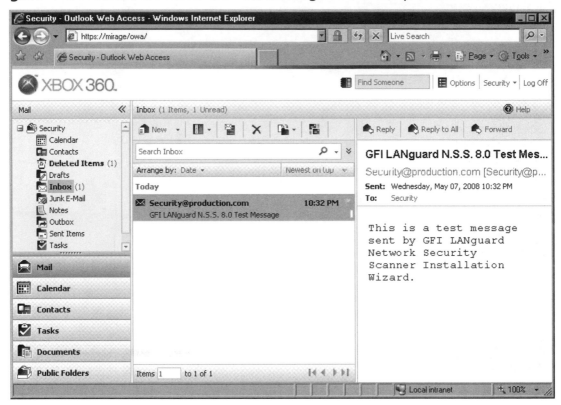

If you are using Exchange Server 2007, there may be one more thing that you need to do before you will be able to receive the test message. Exchange 2007 is designed so that the hub transport only allows secure, authenticated connections. This means that if you simply specify the IP address of a hub transport server, the Exchange Server is going to reject the test message.

There are two ways of getting around this problem. The best option is to use the IP address of an edge transport server as the SMTP server address. If you don't have an edge transport server, then you will need to allow anonymous connections to the transport pipeline. You can do this by opening the Exchange Management Shell and entering the following command:

```
set-ReceiveConnector "Default <Servername>" -permissiongroups:"ExchangeUsers,
ExchangeServers,ExchangeLegacyServers,AnonymousUsers"
```

As you can see in Figure 1.18, the command doesn't really appear to do anything when executed, but it should allow you to send messages from your GFI LANguard Network Security Scanner server to a mailbox on the Exchange 2007 mailbox server.

Figure 1.18 The Set-ReceiveConnector Command Doesn't Appear to Do Anything When It Is Executed

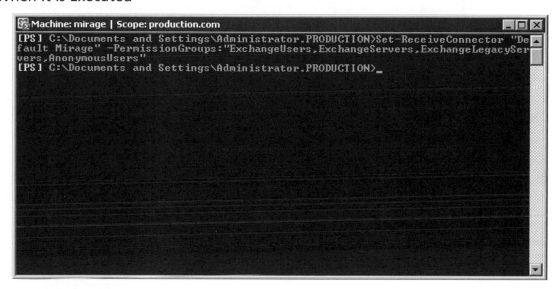

Continuing the Server Configuration Process

Now that you have gotten the mail server settings configured, it's time to finish configuring the GFI LANguard Network Security Server. The next screen that you should encounter asks you which localizations of the Microsoft security updates you want to apply. As you can see in Figure 1.19, English language updates are selected by default, but you also have the option of downloading updates in other languages.

Figure 1.19 You Have the Option of Downloading Updates in Other Languages

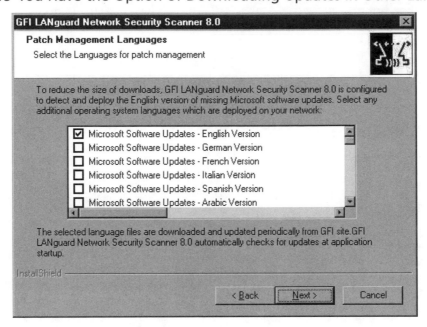

To complete the configuration process, follow these steps:

1. Click **Next**.

2. Accept the default installation path unless you have a compelling reason to change it.

3. Click **Next.**

4. Click the **Install** button. Setup will now begin copying the necessary files.

5. When the installation process completes, click **Finish**.

GFI LANguard Network Security Scanner should now be completely installed. In Chapter 2, I will introduce you to the management console that you will use for performing network security scans.

Summary

GFI LANguard Network Security Scanner isn't one of those applications that allow you to quickly point and click your way through the installation process. You are going to have to do some planning as to how you want to install the software. This is particularly true in regard to how the database will be used, and for the server's e-mail configuration.

Solutions Fast Track

Installing GFI LANguard Network Security Scanner

- ☑ Weigh your decision carefully as to which database type you want to use.

- ☑ If you decide to use an existing SQL server, make sure that the server has the performance and capacity necessary for hosting an additional database.

- ☑ If your organization has its own Exchange Server, it is better to use Exchange for e-mail alerts than to set up an SMTP server.

Frequently Asked Questions

Q: I don't have an Exchange Server, but I may want to use one later on. Is this possible?

A: Yes, the management console allows you to reconfigure your alerting options.

Q: How do I know if I need SQL Server?

A: Smaller organizations don't have to have SQL Server. However, if your organization has more than a hundred PCs that you will be scanning, I would recommend using SQL Server. Keep in mind that this is just my recommendation; not GFI's, and it certainly isn't a requirement.

Q: The installation process seems to be taking forever. Is this normal?

A: On my lab machines, the installation process was fairly quick. Keep in mind, however, that your server hardware has a lot to do with the speed of the installation.

Q: Can I piggyback GFI LANguard Network Security Scanner onto a server that is running other applications?

A: It is possible, but I would recommend using a dedicated server if possible for security and performance reasons.

Q: Can I install a SQL Server database onto the same server that is going to be running GFI LANguard Network Security Scanner?

A: Assuming that your server has the resources to run both, then yes.

Chapter 2

An Introduction to the GFI LANguard Network Security Scanner Management Console

Solutions in this chapter:

- **The Main Console Screen**
- **The Configuration Screen**
- **The Tools Screen**

☑ **Summary**

☑ **Solutions Fast Track**

☑ **Frequently Asked Questions**

Introduction

Now that we have worked through the installation process, I want to teach you how to use GFI LANguard Network Security Scanner to secure your network. However, before we get started, I want to give you a crash course in using the GFI LANguard Network Security Scanner management console. I will be spending a lot of time on this portion of the book showing you how to perform various tasks using the management console, so I think that it makes sense to take some time up front to familiarize you with the console.

The Main Console Screen

You can access the management console by choosing the LANguard Network Security Scanner command from the **Start | All Programs | GFI LANguard Network Security Scanner 8.0** menu. When the management console first opens, you will see a screen similar to the one that's shown in Figure 2.1, asking if you want to perform a local computer scan, a complete network scan, or a custom scan. Since we're not quite ready to scan anything yet, click the **Cancel** button. You might also have noticed in the figure, that this screen contains a check box that you can deselect if you don't want this screen to be displayed every time that you open the management console.

Figure 2.1 Click Cancel to Avoid Scanning Anything at This Time

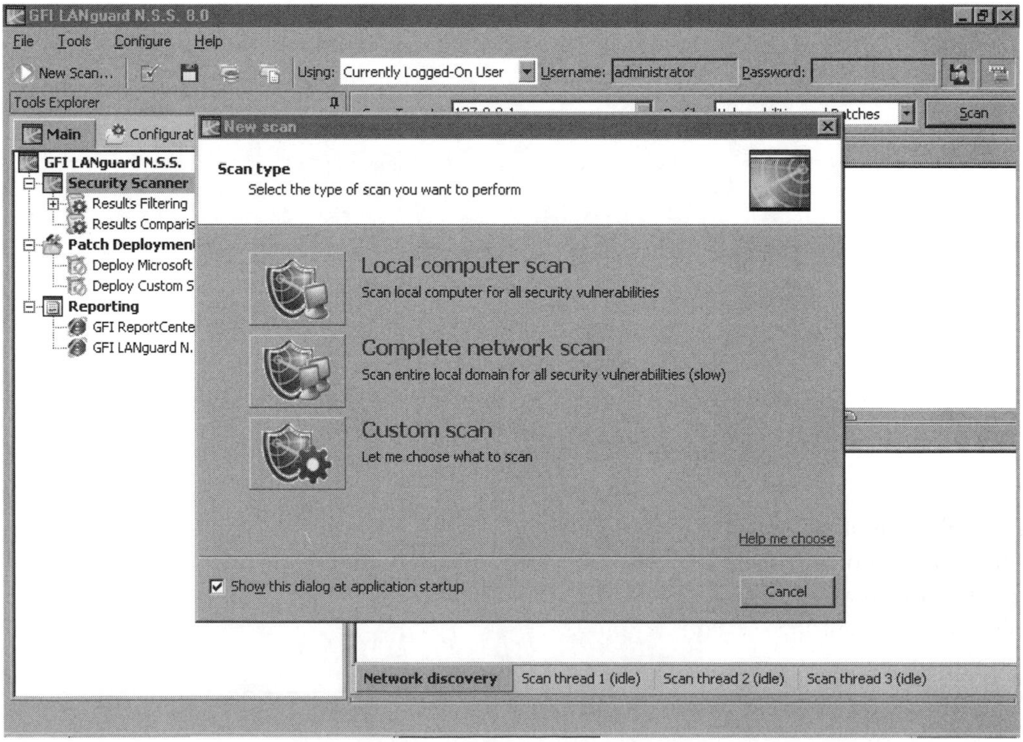

When you click **Cancel**, Windows will display the main management console screen. You can see what the console looks like in Figure 2.2.

Figure 2.2 The GFI LANguard Network Security Scanner Management Console Is the Product's Primary Administrative Interface

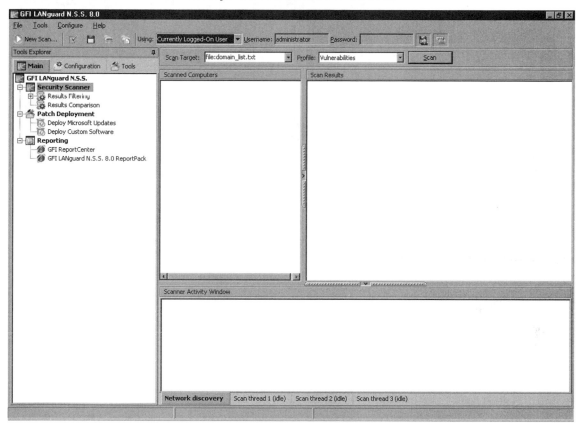

In the screen capture above, you can see that the console is divided into a few different sections, or panes. The pane on the left is a navigation pane. This is the pane that you will use to move around in the console. Functions such as initiating a scan, filtering the scan results, and deploying patches are all invoked from this pane.

The right side of the console is currently split into three separate panes, although in some situations only two of the panes are used. The upper middle pane is the Scanned Computers pane. When you perform a security scan, the computers that have been scanned will be listed in this pane. Typically, this pane will show each machine's Internet Protocol (IP) address, Network Basic Input/ Output System (NetBIOS) name, operating system, and service pack level.

Just to the right of the Scanned Computers pane is the Scan Results pane. When you first complete a security scan, this pane will show you a brief summary of the scan's outcome. If you click on an individual computer in the Scanned Computers pane, the information in the Scan Results pane will change to display information related specifically to the currently selected machine.

The pane in the lower right portion of the management console is the Scanner Activity pane. This pane isn't always used, but when it is used, it will show you how the current scan is progressing.

The management console offers a lot of other functions, but it has been my experience that 99 percent of the time when you are working with the management console, you will be using the four panes that I have just described.

Tools & Traps...

Screen Resolution

Most servers aren't exactly known for using high-end video cards, or even offering anything beyond minimal screen resolution. However, in the case of using the management console, screen resolution is relatively important. Once you begin scanning the computers on your network and analyzing the results, you will see that the management console attempts to display a lot of information. At lower resolution levels, a lot of this information will not fit on the screen. Your server console (or remote server session) will need to be running a display resolution of at least 1024 x 768, but higher resolutions work even better.

The Configuration Screen

If you look just above the navigation pane, you will notice three links; Main, Configuration, and Tools. If you click the Configuration link, it puts the console into configuration mode, as shown in Figure 2.3.

Figure 2.3 Configuration Mode Allows You to Customize GFI LANguard
Network Security Scanner's Configuration Settings

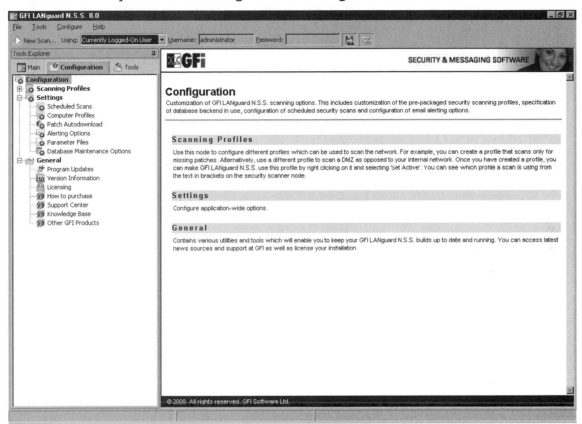

At the beginning of the book I made a promise not to waste your time by going on and on about a bunch of obscure features that you will never use in real life. Most of the settings found in the Configuration pane are things that you will probably never use. There are a few settings that are useful, but I will talk about those settings in later chapters, as we fine-tune the scanning process. That being the case, I'm just going to give you a quick overview of this section, without going into too much detail. The way I see it, it is important for you to know that you can customize the various settings, and for you to know where to look if you ever do need to do a customization, but you can get the specifics from the instruction manual.

Scanning Profiles

If you look at the navigation pane, you will see that the first section listed is the Scanning Profiles section. The Scanning Profiles section is actually pretty simple. If you expand the Scanning Profiles container, you will see a list of all of the different types of scans that the software supports, as shown in Figure 2.4. If you click on an individual scanning profile, the pane on the right will display the various elements that make up the scan. As you can see in the figure, you can select or deselect the various check boxes to control which elements are scanned as a part of the profile.

Figure 2.4 You Can Enable or Disable the Individual Components of a Scanning Profile

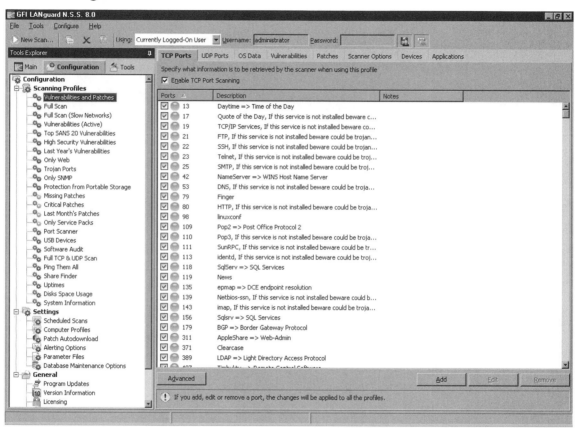

TIP

It's easy to miss, but there are several tabs listed above the individual elements of the scanning profile. Each of these tabs contains more elements that you can enable or disable.

WARNING

At the bottom of the scanning profile are buttons labeled Add, Edit, and Remove. You can use these buttons to customize individual profile elements, or to create your own elements, or delete existing elements. It is important to understand, however, that any changes you make using these three buttons are global, and will affect all of the other scanning profiles that use the element that has been modified, created, or deleted.

The Settings Section

The Settings section is located beneath the Scanning Profiles section, as shown in Figure 2.5. This section allows you to schedule automated scans or control the way that patches are downloaded. I will be talking a lot more about these options later on.

Figure 2.5 The Settings Section Allows You to Control GFI LANguard Network Security Scanner's Basic Settings

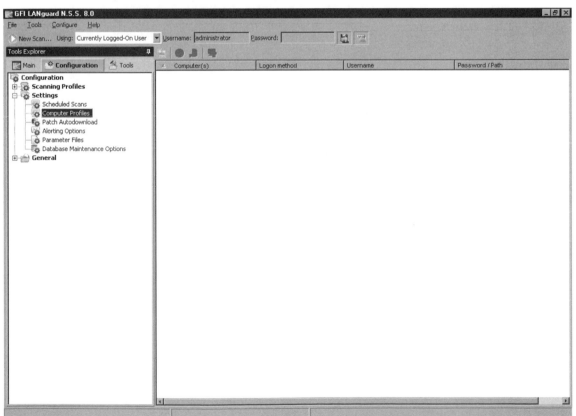

This section also allows you to change some of the things that you configured during the initial setup process, such as the various alerting and database options.

Computer Profiles

One other feature that I want to mention is the Computer Profiles option. Normally, when you perform a network scan, GFI LANguard Network Security Scanner will have no trouble detecting and scanning the computers on your network. However, in some cases, you may have a computer that uses a non-standard administrative password, or that is running a non-Windows operating system such as Linux. If you have trouble scanning such a machine, you can create a computer profile for the machine. Creating a computer profile basically just involves specifying the target computer's identity, and the authentication credentials that should be used to connect to that computer. To create a computer profile, follow these steps:

1. Right-click on the **Computer Profile** container, and choose the **New | Computer Profile(s)** options from the resulting shortcut menus.

2. When the Computer Profile properties sheet opens, enter the name or IP address of the target computer into the space provided.

3. Select the properties sheet's **Logon Credentials** tab.

4. Specify the authentication credentials for the target computer, as shown in Figure 2.6.

5. Click **OK**.

Figure 2.6 A Computer Profile Allows You to Specify the Credentials That Should Be Used for Connecting to a Specific Machine

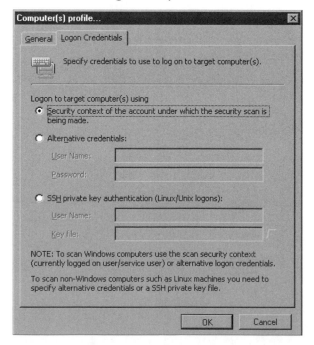

The General Section

The General section of the Configuration screen, shown in Figure 2.7, is primarily designed to give you information about the product. As you can see in the figure, this section contains links to various purchase- and support-related Web pages. There are also some containers that you can click on to see what updates have been applied, which version of the software you are running, or even to update your license key.

Figure 2.7 The General Section Is Where You Go to Get Information about the Software Version, or about Your Support and Licensing Options

The Tools Screen

The Tools screen, shown in Figure 2.8, provides you with several common diagnostic tools. Before you get too excited, however, let me point out that these tools are all available in other forms. In fact, many of them are included with Windows.

Figure 2.8 The Tools Container Provides You with a Variety of Diagnostic Tools

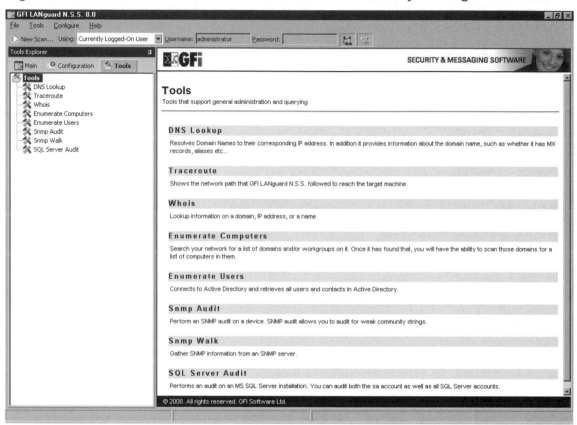

So why did GFI decide to include these tools in LANguard Network Security Scanner? Well, I haven't actually asked any of the product developers, but there are at least two different reasons that seem logical.

First, it's handy to have a collection of diagnostic tools all in one place. Besides that, if you look at which tools are included, you will notice that although most of these tools were originally designed for diagnostic purposes, many of them can be used to help test your network's security.

Another reason why I think that GFI included these tools in the management console is to make the tools easier to use. A lot of the tools are typically used from the command line, but GFI has provided us with a nice GUI interface to each tool. For example, the first tool on the list is Domain Name System (DNS) lookup. You can perform a DNS lookup from within Windows by using the NSLOOKUP command. However, if you don't know how the command works, or if you have a chronic case of command-line aversion, then using NSLOOKUP may not be an option.

If you look at Figure 2.9, you can see what NSLOOKUP looks like when run from a command prompt. Figure 2.10 shows the exact same host name resolution when run through the GFI management console. As you can see, both resolutions returned the same results. The only difference is that the management console displayed the results within the GUI.

Figure 2.9 This Is What the NSLOOKUP Command Looks Like

Figure 2.10 Here Is the Same Hostname Resolution When Performed
Through the GFI Management Console

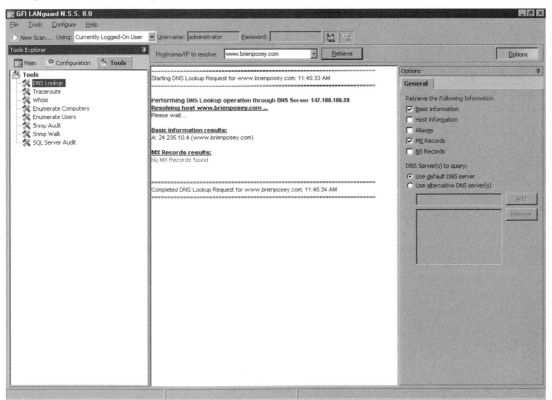

You might have noticed in the figure above, that there are a number of check boxes that you can use to gain more detailed information about the name resolution being performed. You can perform these same kinds of tasks from the command line using various switches and in some cases, some alternate commands. The management console doesn't really give you any new functionality, it just makes resolving hostnames easier.

Notes from the Underground...

Hackers Have Tools Too

Most of the tools that are listed on the Tools screen are very common, and are not proprietary to GFI LANguard Network Security Scanner. For example, DNS Lookup is a part of Windows (although the Windows version is called NSLOOKUP). Likewise, Traceroute is a Transmission Control Protocol (TCP)/IP function that can be invoked from a command line using the TRACERT command. The point is that the bad guys have the same tools that you have. Some of the tools aren't quite as effective when a hacker uses them from outside of your perimeter firewall, but that's beside the point.

The reason why I am telling you this is that you need to learn about the types of information that these tools provide, and think about how a hacker could exploit that information. Only then can you truly begin to harden your network.

Summary

In this chapter, I have explained the various components that make up the management console. You are going to be using the management console for almost every task that you will perform with GFI LANguard Network Security Scanner, so understanding how the management console is laid out is critical to being able to use the product in an efficient and effective manner.

Solutions Fast Track

The Main Console Screen

☑ The main console screen is used to invoke most of the product's functions.

☑ Computers that have been scanned are displayed in the Scanned Computers section.

☑ The Scan Results pane shows you the outcome of the scan.

The Configuration Screen

☑ You will never have to touch the majority of the settings on the Configuration screen.

☑ The Scanning Profiles section allows you to make changes to the information that is collected during a scan.

☑ The Settings section allows you to reconfigure the scanner's basic settings

☑ The General section is used to access version, licensing, and support information.

The Tools Screen

☑ All of the tools provided are mainstream tools that exist outside of the management console.

☑ The management console provides a GUI interface to tools that have traditionally been command line only.

☑ You can use the tools to help assess your network's security.

Frequently Asked Questions

Q: How can I find the Windows equivalent to the various tools?

A: Not all of the tools are a part of Windows, but some are. I suggest doing a Google search on the tool's function.

Q: Is it possible to use the console's General section to download software updates?

A: Yes, right-click on the Program Updates container, and select the Check for Updates command from the resulting menu.

Q: Why does the General section contain an option to use a different license key?

A: If you are using an evaluation version and decide to purchase the product later on, you can enter your product key without having to reinstall the product.

Chapter 3

Performing a Security Scan

Solutions in this chapter:

- **Performing Your First Security Scan**
- **A Shortcut to Scanning**
- **Performing a Full Network Security Scan**

☑ **Summary**

☑ **Solutions Fast Track**

☑ **Frequently Asked Questions**

Introduction

By now you should be somewhat familiar with the management console, but don't worry too much if you still don't completely understand what all of the features do. When I first started using GFI LANguard Network Security Scanner, I didn't understand what all of the options were, even after I had read the manual. I ended up throwing caution to the wind, and started experimenting with the console. As I began to work with the console, I realized that it was fairly intuitive, and not nearly as complicated as it had seemed when I had initially read the description of the console in the user manual.

Performing Your First Security Scan

In the previous chapter, I showed you the splash screen that is displayed the first time that you open the management console, as shown in Figure 3.1. This screen gives you the choice of performing a local computer scan, a complete network scan, or a custom scan.

Figure 3.1 The Initial Splash Screen Gives You a Choice of Performing Three Different Types of Scans

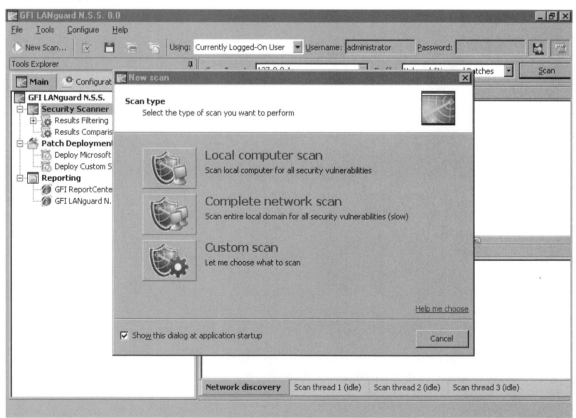

TIP

The New Scan dialog box opens automatically when you open the management console. You can use this dialog box as a shortcut to launching a new scan.

For your initial scan, I think that it is important to perform a local computer scan. As the name implies, a local computer scan checks the computer that GFI LANguard Network Security Scanner is running on for any missing patches or known vulnerabilities. The reason why I think that it is important to start out with this type of scan, is because you will be depending on this server to give you accurate information about the other servers on your network. If the server that's running GFI LANguard Network Security Scanner is missing security patches or has other known vulnerabilities, then there is a chance that the server could be compromised by a hacker, Trojan, or by some other means. That being the case, I would advise you to make sure that the server that's running GFI LANguard Network Security Scanner is secure before you even think about trying to use GFI LANguard Network Security Scanner to secure the rest of your network.

Since this is our first scan, and you are probably still trying to get used to the administrative interface, let's perform a scan using the default settings. This will give you a good starting point, and I will walk you through the process of performing more advanced scans later on. For right now though, let's get started by scanning the local server.

1. Begin the process by clicking the **New Scan** button. You can find this button located in the upper left portion of the management console.

2. GFI LANguard Network Security Scanner will now launch the New Scan wizard, as shown in Figure 3.2.

Figure 3.2 The New Scan Wizard Asks You What Type of Scan Job You Want to Perform

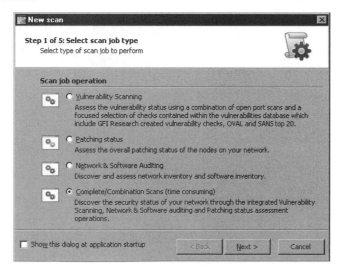

As you can see in the figure, there are four different types of scans that you can perform:

■ **Vulnerability Scanning** A Vulnerability scan will report any vulnerabilities that are detected on the target server, and will also report any missing patches.

■ **Patching Status** A Patching Status scan will only display a list of missing patches. It will not test the target computers for any other types of vulnerabilities.

■ **Network and Software Auditing** A Network and Software Auditing scan collects inventory information about the target computers, but does not test the target machines for any vulnerabilities.

■ **Complete/Combination Scan** A Complete/Combination scan is the most comprehensive type of scan. It checks for any known vulnerabilities or missing patches. During the scanning process, network and software auditing information is also collected.

3. Since our goal is to verify the integrity of the local server, choose the **Complete/ Combination Scans** option, and click **Next**. Keep in mind, however, that this type of scan will be more time consuming than the less thorough scanning methods.

You will now see a screen asking you to choose the scan profile that will be used for the scan job that you are about to perform. As you can see in Figure 3.3, this screen presents you with three different scanning options:

Figure 3.3 You Must Choose the Scan Profile That You Want to Use for the Scan

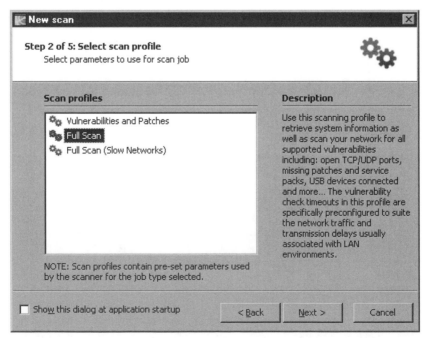

- **Vulnerabilities and Patches** A Vulnerability and Patch scan checks the selected server or servers for any known vulnerabilities, and checks to see if any patches are missing. However, this option does not check for vulnerabilities related to applications or to Universal Serial Bus (USB) devices.

- **Full Scan** A Full scan is similar to a Vulnerability and Patch scan in that it checks for known vulnerabilities and missing patches. At the same time, however, this type of scan is more thorough than a vulnerability and patches scan, in that it also checks for issues related to any USB devices that are connected and to any applications that may be installed.

- **Full Scan (Slow Networks)** This option works the same as the Full Scan option, except that the time out thresholds have been adjusted to account for the latency that typically exists as a result of slow WAN links.

4. Since we are performing a local scan, and because we want to be as thorough as possible, choose the **Full Scan** option, and click **Next**.

5. At this point, the wizard asks you to specify which network segment you want to scan, as shown in Figure 3.4. As you can see in the figure, you are given the option of scanning a single computer, a range of computers (or more correctly, a range of Internet Protocol [IP] addresses), a list of computers, or an entire domain or workgroup. Since we are going to be scanning the local server, choose the **Scan a Single Computer** option, and click **Next**.

Figure 3.4 Choose the Scan a Single Computer Option, and Click Next

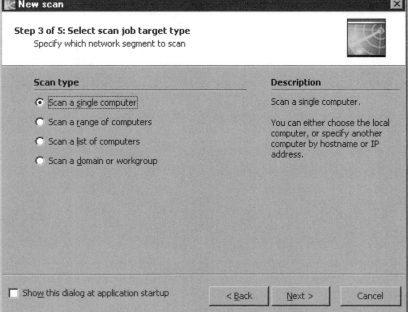

6. The wizard will now display a screen asking you if you want to scan the local server, or another computer. Choose the **Scan this Computer** option, and click **Next**.

In order for the scan to be run, you need to provide GFI LANguard Network Security Scanner with some credentials that it can use to gain access to the computer in question, as shown in Figure 3.5. As you can see in the figure, you have the option of using the credentials of the user who is currently logged on, another user's credentials, a null session, or even a Secure Shell (SSH) private key.

Figure 3.5 You Must Specify the Credentials That Will Be Used by the Scanning Process

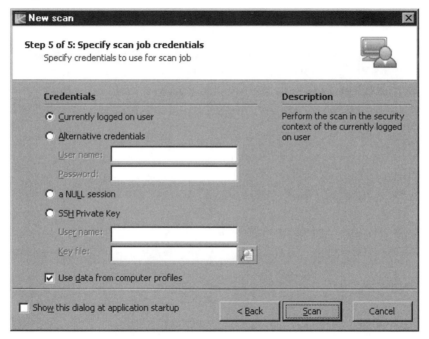

7. Since we are scanning the local server, I recommend using administrative credentials for the scan. If you are logged in using an account with local administrative permissions, then use the **Currently logged on user** option. Otherwise, choose the **Alternative credentials** option, and specify an appropriate set of credentials.

Using an administrative account for a local scan is a good idea, because the administrative credentials will help to ensure that the scanner has full access to the system. However, later on when we scan other servers, keep in mind that using administrative credentials isn't always your best option. Sure, administrative credentials will give GFI LANguard Network Security Scanner the most comprehensive access to the target systems, but I recommend starting out performing remote scans using a null session.

My reason for this is that if a hacker is attacking your network, they will typically start out using a null session unless they have somehow gained access to a user account. I consider vulnerabilities uncovered while scanning using a null session to be the most serious, since hackers can often detect these vulnerabilities, and they are therefore likely to be one of the first things targeted in an attempt to break into your network.

I will talk a lot more about remote scans later on. For right now, though, just make sure that you specify an account that has administrative credentials.

Click the **Scan** button. When you do, GFI LANguard Network Security Scanner will initialize the network scanning engine, detect your local server (yes, that sounds strange, but it really does detect itself), and begin the scanning process, as shown in Figure 3.6.

Figure 3.6 GFI LANguard Network Security Scanner Initializes the Scanning Engine and Begins the Scan

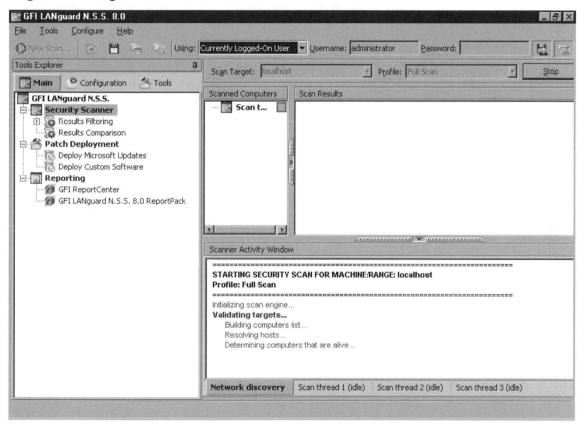

When the scan completes, you will see a summary screen similar to the one that is shown in Figure 3.7. As you can see in the figure, this screen tells you how long the scan took to complete, and the average vulnerability level. The lower portion of the screen gives you some statistics on how many vulnerabilities and missing patches were detected, and how many of those issues were critical. The summary also lists the number of installed applications, and the number of open ports.

Figure 3.7 When the Vulnerability Scan Completes, This Screen Provides You With a Summary of the Scan's Results

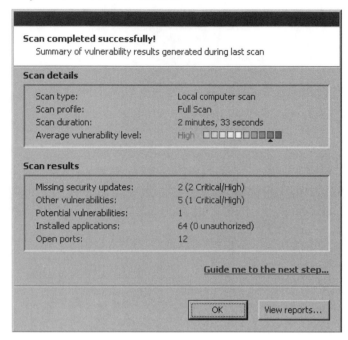

Obviously, this is just a summary screen, and you can get a lot more detailed information through the management console. In the next chapter, I'm going to show you how to analyze the scan results, so feel free to skip ahead if you want to. I'm going to use the remainder of this chapter to show you some shortcuts to the scanning process.

A Shortcut to Scanning

As you saw in the previous section, the management console allows you to initiate a scan by clicking the New Scan button. Once you do, however, GFI LANguard Network Security Scanner launches a wizard with five screens full of questions that you have to answer before the scan can even begin. Now I'll admit that most of the wizard's questions are pretty simple, and it doesn't take that long to answer them, but there is an even easier way of initiating a scan.

Figure 3.8 You Can Use the Management Console's Drop Down Lists as a Shortcut Instead of Going Through the Wizard Every Time You Want to Run a Scan

If you look at Figure 3.8, you will notice a series of drop down lists. These are located in the upper right corner of the management console. These drop down lists allow you to answer the wizard's questions without actually having to use the wizard. If you want to quickly initiate a scan, follow these steps:

1. Choose the credentials that you want to use for the scan from the Using drop down list.

2. If necessary, enter a username and password into the Username and Password fields, respectively.

3. Either choose the **localhost** option from the Scan Target drop down list, or enter the IP address of the server that you want to scan.

4. Select the profile for the scan from the Profile drop down list.

5. Click the **Scan** button.

While I'm on the subject of the Profile drop down list, I should point out that it provides you with a lot more scanning profile options than the wizard does. For example, some of the additional profiles that you can access through the drop down list include the top SANS 20 vulnerabilities, high security vulnerabilities, last year's vulnerabilities, and the list goes on and on. Although it's impossible to display the full list of profiles in a single screen capture, you can see a partial list in Figure 3.9.

Figure 3.9 The Profile Drop Down List Provides You with Many Additional Scanning Profiles That are not Available Through the Wizard

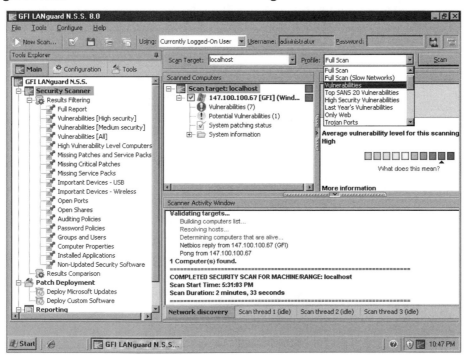

Performing a Full Network Security Scan

In the previous section, I showed you how to perform a security scan of the local server, and you are probably anxious to see the scan results and correct the security problems that were found. I will talk you through the process of working through the scan results in the next chapter. For right now though, I want to walk you through one more scan.

This time, we are going to run a vulnerability scan of the entire network. This will give us something interesting to look at in the next chapter. The procedure that you will use for scanning the network for vulnerabilities is really similar to the procedure that you used to scan the local server, but with one big exception; it takes a really long time to complete. In my lab, it took about six hours to scan 16 machines. To perform a vulnerability scan of your network, follow these steps:

WARNING

This type of scan is extremely time consuming!

1. Open the management console.
2. Right click on the **Security Scanner container**, and choose the **New Scan** command from the resulting shortcut menu.
3. The management console will now launch the New Scan wizard, which will prompt you as to the type of scan that you want to perform. Choose the **Vulnerability Scanning** option, as shown in Figure 3.10.

Figure 3.10 Choose the Vulnerability Scanning Option, and Click Next

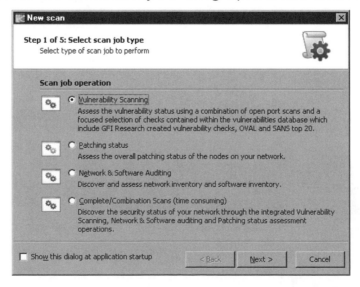

4. Click **Next.**

5. The wizard will now prompt you to select a scan profile. Choose the **Vulnerabilities** profile, and click **Next.**

6. At this point, you will see a screen asking you to select the scan job target type. You have the option of scanning a single computer, a range of computers, a list of computers, or a domain or workgroup. Any of these options will work (other than the option to scan a single computer). For this exercise, choose the **Scan a Domain or Workgroup** option. We'll use this option so that you can see how it works, and I will show you how to use some of the other scanning options in other chapters.

7. Click **Next**.

8. You will now see a list of the domains on your network. You can select the domain that you want to scan, but you also have the option of expanding the domain and selecting or deselecting individual computers within the domain, as shown in Figure 3.11. Make your selection, and click **Next**.

Figure 3.11 You Have the Option of Selecting or Deselecting Individual Computers Within the Domain

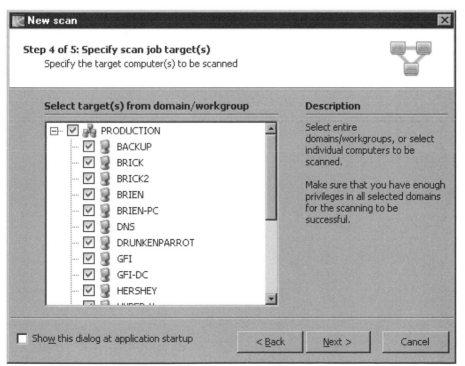

9. Choose the credentials that you want to use for the scan job, and click the **Scan** button.

10. When the scan completes, click **OK** to see the scan's results. You can see what the results look like in Figure 3.12.

Figure 3.12 This Is What Your Scan Results Will Typically Look Like

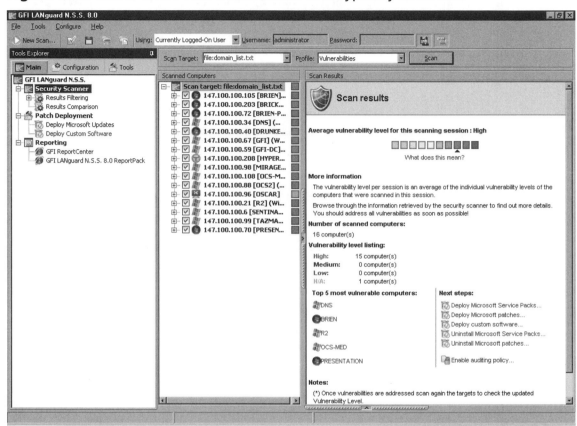

Aborting a Scan

Depending on the size of your network, the complexity of the scan that you are performing, and your hardware's capabilities, some scans may take a really long time to complete. If you decide that you need to abort a scan, you can easily do so by right-clicking on the **Security Scanner** container, and choosing the **Stop Scan** command from the resulting shortcut menu, as shown in Figure 3.13.

Figure 3.13 Right-Click on the Security Scanner Container, and Choose the Stop Scan Command to Abort a Scan

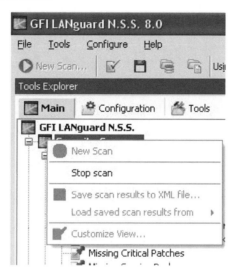

Summary

As you can see, the management console is capable of performing quite a few different types of scans. However, no matter what type of scan you are using, the basic steps are always the same. Later on, you will see how this holds true as I show you how to perform some other types of scans in later chapters.

Solutions Fast Track

Performing Your First Security Scan

- ☑ Click the **New Scan** button.
- ☑ Choose the **Complete/Combination Scan** option.
- ☑ Choose the **Full Scan** option.
- ☑ Select the **Scan a Single Computer** option.
- ☑ Select the **Scan this Computer** option.
- ☑ Enter your credentials
- ☑ Click the **Scan** button.

A Shortcut to Scanning

- ☑ Enter the IP address of the target computer into the Scan Target field.
- ☑ Choose your scanning profile from the Profile drop down list.
- ☑ Enter your administrative credentials.
- ☑ Click the **Scan** button.

Performing a Full Network Security Scan

- ☑ Click the **New Scan** button.
- ☑ Choose the **Vulnerability Scanning** option.
- ☑ Select the **Vulnerabilities** option
- ☑ Choose the **Scan a Domain or Workgroup** option.
- ☑ Select your domain.
- ☑ Enter your credentials.
- ☑ Click the **Scan** button.

Frequently Asked Questions

Q: Is performing an initial scan of the server that's running GFI LANguard Network Security Scanner an absolute requirement?

A: No, but it is a really good idea.

Q: Are there other types of scans that you can perform?

A: The software includes a lot of different scanning profiles, and I would encourage you to spend some time experimenting with them. I will also be talking about some other types of scans in later chapters.

Q: Can you use a shortcut scan to scan the entire network?

A: Yes, but you will need to create a text file with the names or IP addresses of the computers that you want to scan. You would enter the path and filename for this text file into the Scan Target field.

Chapter 4

Analyzing the Scan Results

Solutions in this chapter:

- **Viewing the Scan Results**

- **Viewing the Vulnerabilities That Were Detected**

- **Saving the Scan Results**

- **Printing the Scan Results**

- **Getting More Information**

- **Querying Open Ports**

- **Filtering the Scan Results**

- ☑ **Summary**

- ☑ **Solutions Fast Track**

- ☑ **Frequently Asked Questions**

Introduction

In the previous chapter, I showed you how to perform a basic security scan against your GFI LANguard Network Security Scanner server, and how to perform a vulnerability scan on your network. Scanning is nice, but the scan itself is meaningless unless you take the time to analyze the results, and to correct any issues that are discovered. The analysis consists of determining which of the reported security issues are relevant to your organization, and making a plan to remedy those issues.

Viewing the Scan Results

When a scan completes, GFI LANguard Network Security Scanner displays a summary screen similar to the one that's shown in Figure 4.1. If you look at the bottom of this screen, you will see that it contains an OK button and a View Reports button. It may seem as though clicking the View Reports button would be the obvious choice, but before you can use this option, you will have to install the GFI LANguard Network Security Scanner ReportPack.

Figure 4.1 For Right Now, Ignore the View Reports Button and Click OK

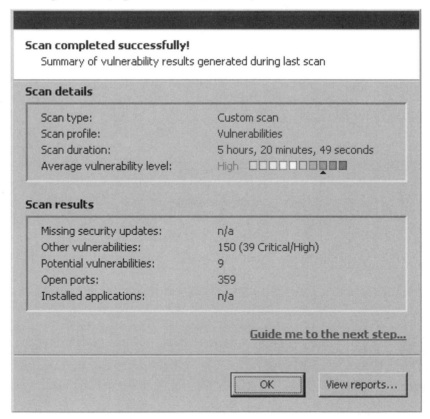

The ReportPack gives you the ability to generate all sorts of different types of reports based on the data that was collected through the scan. Even so, there are things that you can find through the

management console that may not be displayed in the various reports. Therefore, I want to spend this
chapter talking about how to analyze your scan results without the aid of the ReportPack. In the next
chapter, I will discuss the ReportPack in depth.

Upon clicking **OK**, Windows will return you to the main management console screen. As you
can see in Figure 4.2, the management console has been populated with the scan results.

Figure 4.2 The Management Console Now Displays the Scan Results

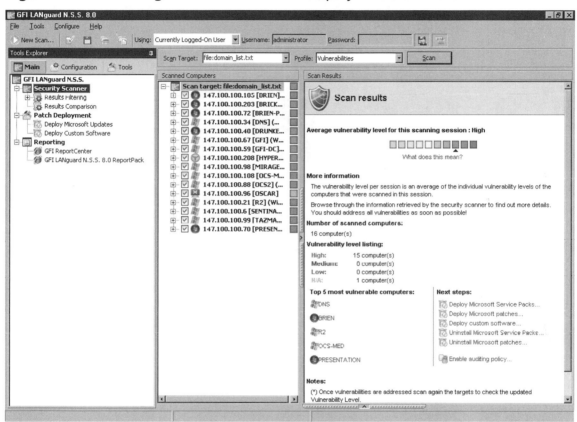

As you look at the figure above, you can see that the console's middle pane lists all of the computers that were scanned. You can tell at a glance which computers are most at risk, because the block just
to the right of each listing is color-coded. It might be hard to tell in the screen shot, however, because
the book is printed in black and white, and each computer that I scanned produced a vulnerability
level of orange. Orange means that the vulnerabilities that were detected on the computers were nearly
at the critical level. Had the computers contained fewer vulnerabilities, the vulnerability levels would
have been displayed as yellow or green. If the detected vulnerabilities had been critical, they would
have been displayed in red.

With this in mind, take a look at the Scan Results pane in the figure above. This pane displays a
color-coded summary of the scan, which represents the average vulnerability level of the machines that
were scanned. Not surprisingly, the average vulnerability level in this case is orange.

Just beneath the color-coded scan summary, you can see the number of detected vulnerabilities ranked from high, to medium, to low. In this case, 15 computers had high-priority vulnerabilities.

The bottom section of this pane lists the five most vulnerable computers on the network, and also offers a section called "Next Steps" with links that you can use to correct various security problems. It is important to understand that these are generic links that don't necessarily have anything to do with the vulnerabilities that actually exist. For example, the first item on the list is Deploy Microsoft Service Packs. At the time that this chapter was written, all of the machines that were scanned had the most recent service packs installed.

Notes from the Underground…

Hackers Use Security Scanners Too

Obviously, GFI LANguard Network Security Scanner was designed as a tool that can help you to secure your network. It's important to remember, however, that hackers also use security scanners. They may not necessarily use GFI's product, but using security scanners is a common practice. Security scanners help hackers look for vulnerabilities on networks that they are intending to attack. The best defense against this type of technique is to make sure that your firewall is running as strong of a security configuration as is practical.

GFI LANguard Network Security Scanner uses several different methods to analyze the computers on a network. It detects computers using things like ping responses, Simple Network Management Protocol (SNMP), and Network Basic Input/Output System (NetBIOS) names. Solid firewall rules can block all of these methods.

Viewing the Vulnerabilities that Were Detected

Now that you have seen a summary of the vulnerabilities that were detected, let's take a look at the actual vulnerabilities that exist. The easiest way of doing this is to click on one of the computers that was scanned. When you do, the Scan Results pane will display the top five issues that were detected on that computer. For example, if you look at Figure 4.3, you can see the top five issues that were detected on a server named R2 on my network.

Figure 4.3 Clicking on a Computer Causes the Scan Results Pane to List the Top Five Issues That Were Detected on That Machine

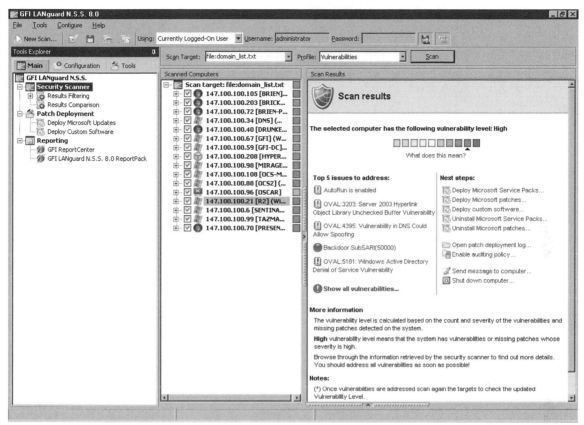

Now that you see the summary of the issues that were detected, hopefully you have a better understanding of why the machine's vulnerability level was listed as orange. The information in the screen capture above really helps us to see why the machine is at risk, but there are a couple of problems with it. First, we are only seeing the top five issues that were detected on that machine. Second, the management console hasn't told us what to do to correct these issues.

One of the things that you might have noticed in the previous figure is that there is a plus sign to the left of each computer that was listed, indicating that the listing is actually an expandable container. If you expand this container, you will see that it contains sub containers for Vulnerabilities, Potential Vulnerabilities, and System Information. The System Information container contains sub-containers for Open TCP Ports, Open UDP Ports, NETBIOS Names, and some basic information about the computer.

Since it's the vulnerabilities that we are most interested in right now, click on the **Vulnerabilities** container. As you can see in Figure 4.4, there were a total of 11 confirmed vulnerabilities found on this server. These vulnerabilities are all listed in the Scan Results pane, and are organized from high, to medium, to low priority. Most of the vulnerabilities listed include additional text that explains how to correct the vulnerability.

Figure 4.4 The Scan Results Pane Lists the Vulnerabilities That Were Detected, and Their Solutions

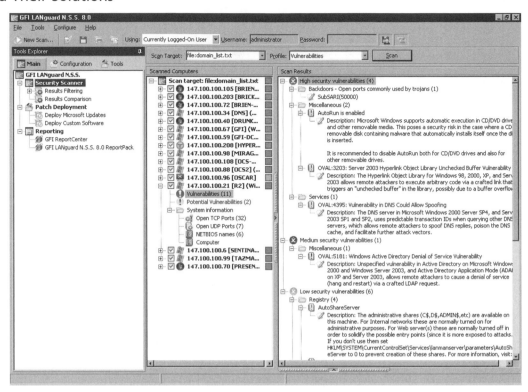

Tools & Traps…

The Vulnerability List is Only a Guide

As you can probably see, GFI LANguard Network Security Scanner can make the task of securing your network a whole lot easier. Even so, it is important that you use the tool only as a guide, and not treat the scan results as gospel. Having a security scanner is no substitute for implementing good security policies and sticking to them. To give you an example of why this is so important, I intentionally configured the password on the server shown in Figure 4.4, to use a four-character password, and set the group policy not to even require a password. These are definite vulnerabilities, and yet they were not reported during the scan. Therefore, you should use the list of vulnerabilities that were detected to help improve your network's security, but don't assume that a vulnerability doesn't exist just because it didn't show up during the scan.

Potential Vulnerabilities

If you looked at the last screen capture, you might have noticed that two potential vulnerabilities were detected. So what on earth are potential vulnerabilities? Well, potential vulnerabilities are things that could possibly be a risk, but may be required for the server to function normally. For example, if you look at Figure 4.5, you can see that the potential vulnerabilities that were detected simply involve a modem being installed in the server. In this case, however, there is no way that the modem could possibly be a real vulnerability, because it isn't even connected to a phone line.

Figure 4.5 GFI LANguard Network Security Scanner Sees Modems as a Potential Vulnerability

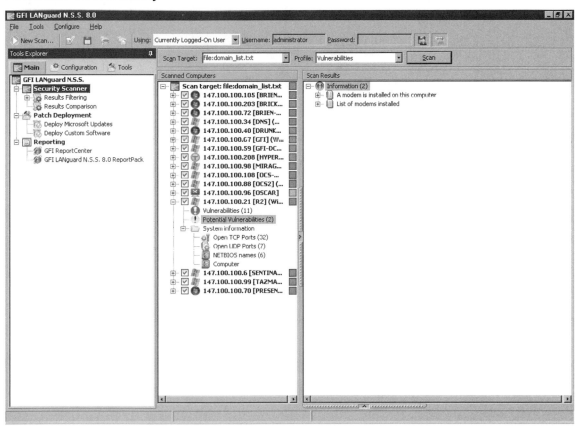

> **TIP**
>
> Don't make the mistake of immediately dismissing a potential vulnerability. A modem can potentially be a very real security threat if an intruder can use it to gain access to the server.

Saving the Scan Results

Right about now, it's probably tempting to jump in with both feet and start fixing the vulnerabilities that have been detected. Before you do, however, you need to save the scan results. You can do this by selecting the Save Scan Results command from the console's File menu.

There are a couple of reasons why it is important to save your results. First, there are some actions that you can perform through the console that have the potential to clear the scan results. It takes a long time to scan a network for vulnerabilities, and you don't want all that time spent scanning to be undone by a few careless mouse clicks.

Another reason why it is important to save your scan is because doing so creates an audit trail. Saving a scan makes it possible to go back in time and find out when a vulnerability was first detected. The console also offers a function that allows you to compare a current scan against a past scan, to find out how well you have done in cleaning up the issues that have been reported. I will show you how to compare scans against each other in Chapter 7.

Printing the Scan Results

Unfortunately, the management console lacks the ability to automatically correct most types of vulnerabilities. Therefore, you are going to need to compile the information that has been collected, and then come up with a game plan for fixing the various vulnerabilities.

I strongly recommend using the ReportPack, which I will discuss in the next chapter, to help you produce reports detailing the various vulnerabilities. However, if you decide to tackle the issues on your own, there are some things that you can do to make life easier.

Surprisingly, the management console does not allow you to print the scan results, or at least not in the usual way. You can, however, select the scan results and then right-click on them and choose the **Copy to Clipboard** command from the resulting shortcut menu. You can then paste the scan results into a Microsoft Word document.

> **NOTE**
>
> Reports produced by the ReportPack are usually easier to read than documents created by pasting data directly from the management console.

Getting More Information

The management console displays quite a bit of information about most of the vulnerabilities that are detected. In some cases, however, the information that is presented may be a bit cryptic, and you may need more help in addressing the vulnerability. In most cases, if you need more help, you can right-click on a vulnerability and choose the **More Detail** command from the resulting shortcut menu. When you do, the console will display the More Detail dialog box, shown in Figure 4.6.

Figure 4.6 The Edit Vulnerability Properties Sheet Gives You Additional Information About the Vulnerability

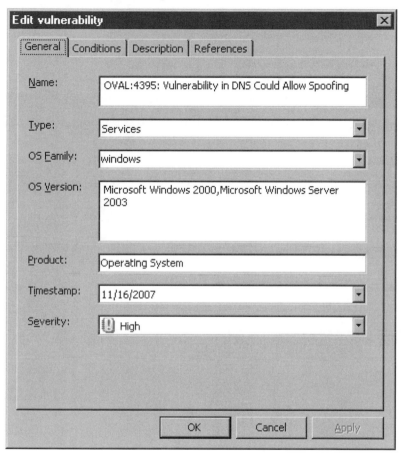

OK, I'll admit that the figure above doesn't really give you much information that would help you to figure out what you need to do to address the vulnerability. The Description tab isn't much better either. It just displays the same description that was already displayed through the management console. Check out the References tab shown in Figure 4.7, as it tells you where you can go to get more information about the problem.

Figure 4.7 The References Tab Tells You Where to Go to Get More Information on the Issue

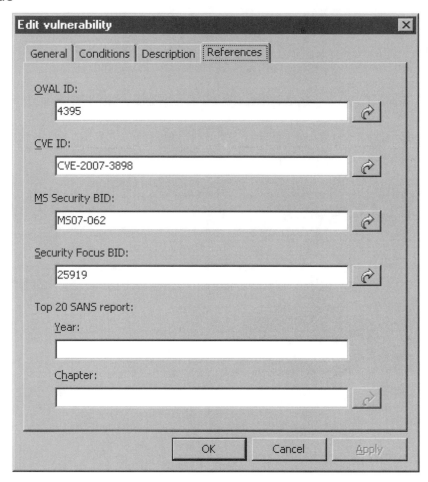

As you can see in the figure, the References tab lists the issue number that Microsoft, Security Focus, and some others use to report on the issue. There is also a link next to each issue number that you can use to go to a Web site that describes the issue more fully. For example, if I click the link next to the MS Security BID section, I am taken to the Web page shown in Figure 4.8.

Figure 4.8 You Can Find More Detailed Information about the Various Issues Online

Tools & Traps...

Researching Vulnerabilities

Occasionally you may run into a vulnerability that is reported, but you're not quite sure why. In these rare situations, I recommend taking a look at the Edit Vulnerability properties sheet's Conditions tab, shown below. The Conditions tab shows you exactly which conditions existed that caused the vulnerability to be reported. You still won't get a straight answer as to why the vulnerability exists, but this tab may offer you some clues.

Continued

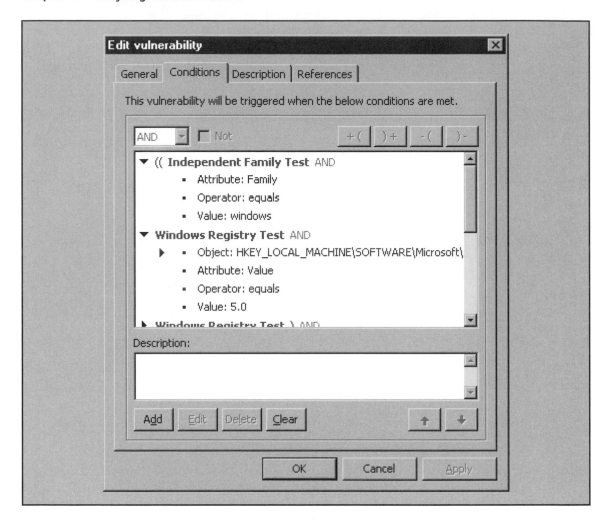

Querying Open Ports

You might have noticed in some of the earlier screen captures that some of the issues that are reported for each machine involve open Transmission Control Protocol (TCP) or User Datagram Protocol (UDP) ports. Often, this isn't really an issue, because the computer may be running applications that depend on the given port being open. In any case, it's a good idea to check up on each open port to see what is revealed if a hacker attempts to connect through the port. To do so, follow these steps:

1. Select the **Open TCP Ports** container found beneath the listing for the computer that you are testing. When you do, the Scan Results pane will display a list of the open ports, as shown in Figure 4.9.

2. Right-click on a port, and choose the **Query Port** command from the resulting shortcut menu.

Windows will now open either Telnet or Internet Explorer and attempt to connect to the machine through the open port. For example, if you look at Figure 4.10, you can see that the reason why port 25 is open on the target machine is because the server is acting as an SMTP server.

Figure 4.9 Right-Click on an Open Port, and Choose the Query Port Command From the Resulting Shortcut Menu

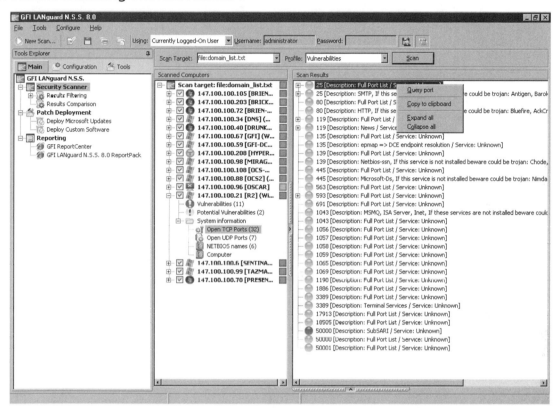

Are You Owned?

Malicious Ports

You might have noticed in the scan results that one of the vulnerabilities that was reported was listed as:

Backdoors – Open Ports Commonly Used By Trojans

Continued

> This is listed as a high-security vulnerability, but it isn't always cause for alarm. The vulnerability was listed because TCP port number 5000 is open on that server, and that just happens to be the same port number that is used by a Trojan named SubSARI.
>
> The important thing to remember is that there is no such thing as a malicious port, only malicious uses of ports. Therefore, if you see a message like this one listed in your scan results, it does not necessarily mean that your computer is infected. It only means that it shows one symptom (a specific port being open) of being infected. In my case, the open port is being used by a legitimate application.

Figure 4.10 Telnet Attempts to Attach to the Target Computer Through the Open Port

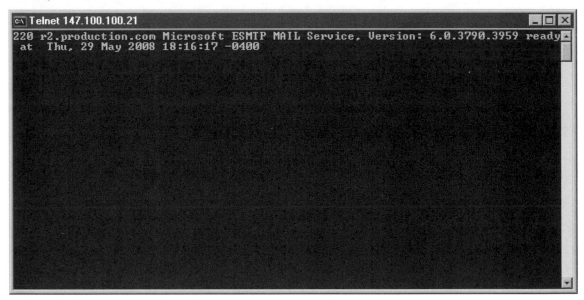

WARNING

Sometimes if you attempt to Telnet to a port on a target machine, the Telnet window will be blank. This doesn't mean that no applications are using the port. It only means that the application does not respond to Telnet. I recommend checking the documentation for your applications to find out which ports they require to be open prior to closing any ports.

Filtering the Scan Results

If you have a lot of computers on your network, then addressing the various vulnerabilities that have been detected can be an overwhelming task. Fortunately, you can apply some filters to the results so that you are viewing only the results that you are the most interested in.

The easiest way of filtering the results is to follow these steps:

1. Navigate through the console tree to **Security Scanner | Results Filtering**.

2. Expand the **Results Filtering** container.

3. Click on the filter of your choice.

For example, if you look at Figure 4.11, you can see what it looks like when I apply a filter that shows only computers with a high level of vulnerability.

Figure 4.11 Filters Can Help You Locate the Most Important Issues so That You Can Address Those Issues First

Although the built-in filters are nice, sometimes they may not meet your needs perfectly. Fortunately, it's easy to create a custom filter. For example, let's pretend that I wanted to create a filter that would show me only machines that are running Windows Server 2003. To do so, I would perform the following steps:

1. Navigate through the management console to **Security Scanner | Results Filtering**.

2. Right click on the **Results Filtering** container, and choose the **New | Filter** commands from the resulting shortcut menus.

3. When the Advanced Properties sheet appears, enter a name for the filter that you are creating. I'll call this filter **Win2K3 High**.

4. Click the **Add** button.

5. Choose the **Operating System** option, as shown in Figure 4.12, and click **Next**.

Figure 4.12 Choose the Operating System Option

6. Make sure that the Condition field is set to **Equal to**.

7. Enter **Windows Server 2003** into the Value field, as shown in Figure 4.13.

Figure 4.13 Enter Windows Server 2003 Into the Value Field

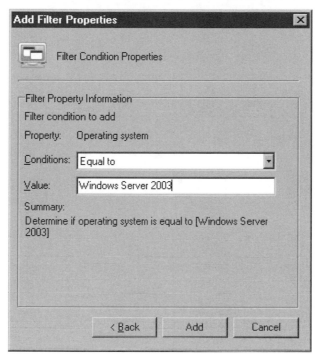

8. Click the **Add** button.

9. Verify that the Advanced Properties sheet shows the condition that you have established, as shown in Figure 4.14.

Figure 4.14 The Condition That You Have Established Should Have Been Added to the Advanced Properties Sheet

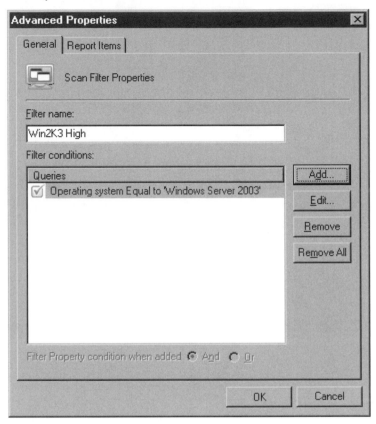

10.   Go to the **Reported Items** tab.
11.   Select the **Vulnerability Level** check box, as shown in Figure 4.15.

Figure 4.15 Select the Vulnerability Level Check Box

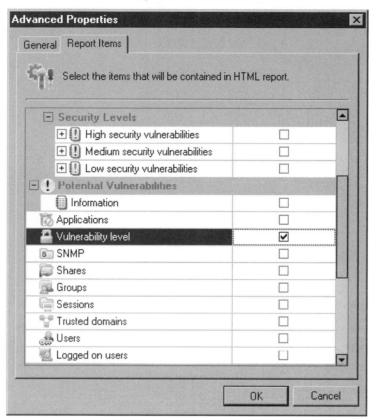

12.   Click **OK**.

When you are done, the filter that you have created will automatically be added to the list of filters. As you can see in Figure 4.16, when you select this new filter, the console shows you the vulnerability level of every computer that is running Windows Server 2003. Of course this is just a demonstration. You can actually create some really powerful custom filters.

Figure 4.16 You Can Access Your Custom Filter Through the Results Filtering List

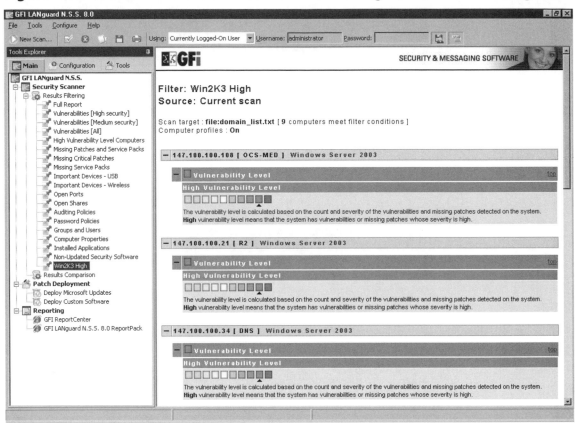

Summary

Understanding how to analyze the data that has been collected is absolutely critical to securing your network. In this chapter, I have shown you several different ways of examining the data that the console collects. In the next chapter, I will show you how to use the ReportPack to make the process of analyzing the data a little bit easier.

Solutions Fast Track

Viewing the Scan Results

☑ When a scan completes, the results are displayed within the management console.

☑ Although the management console can display the scan results, the results are often easier to digest in report form.

Viewing the Vulnerabilities that were Detected

☑ Click on a computer in the Scanned Computers list.

☑ The Scan Results pane lists that computer's vulnerabilities.

Saving the Scan Results

☑ Right-click on the **Security Scanner** container.

☑ Choose the **Save Scan Results to XML File** command from the shortcut menu.

Printing the Scan Results

☑ You cannot print the scan results directly.

☑ You can copy and paste the scan results into a Microsoft Office document and then print them.

☑ A better option is to use the ReportPack to print the scan results.

Getting More Information

☑ You can usually get more information about a vulnerability by right clicking on it and choosing the More Detail command from the shortcut menu.

☑ The Edit Vulnerability properties sheet's References tab provides you with knowledgebase article numbers that you can reference for more information about the vulnerability.

☑ The Edit Vulnerability properties sheet's Conditions tab can sometimes yield cliues as to why a particular vulnerability was reported.

Querying Open Ports

- ☑ Go to the **Scanned Computers** pane and expand the listing for the computer that you want to examine.

- ☑ Expand the computer's **System Information** container.

- ☑ Select the **Open TCP Ports** container.

- ☑ Right-click on the port that you want to test, and choose the **Query Port** command from the shortcut menu.

Filtering the Scan Results

- ☑ Expand the **Results Filtering** container.

- ☑ Click on the filter that you want to use.

Frequently Asked Questions

Q: Is there any way of seeing the scan results for all of the computers at once?

A: Yes, use the ReportPack to generate a comprehensive report.

Q: Why does the NetBIOS Names container beneath a computer on the Scanned Computers pane list multiple results?

A: For Windows machines there will be a NetBIOS name assigned to the machine assigned to the computer's Workstation service, Server service, and there will be a NetBIOS name for the machine's domain.

Q: What types of information are found in a machine's Computer container?

A: It varies depending on the machine's operating system, but generally you will find information about the operating system version, the machine's domain membership, and its MAC address.

Chapter 5

Using the ReportPack

Solutions in this chapter:

- **Installing the ReportPack**
- **Creating a Report**
- **Favorite Reports**
- **Custom Reports**
- **Scheduled Reports**

- ☑ **Summary**
- ☑ **Solutions Fast Track**
- ☑ **Frequently Asked Questions**

Introduction

In the previous chapter, I briefly mentioned that GFI offered a reporting package that you could use to create comprehensive security reports in a printer-friendly format. In this chapter, I will show you how to install, configure, and use the ReportPack feature.

Installing the ReportPack

You can download the ReportPack from the GFI Web site at: www.gfi.com/downloads/downloads. aspx?pid=lanss&lid=EN

The download consists of an executable file that is just under 12 MB in size. Once you have downloaded the file, follow these steps to install the ReportPack.

1. Download the file to a temporary folder, and then double-click on it to begin the installation process.

2. Depending on the version of Windows that you are using, you may receive a Windows security warning, asking you if you are sure that you want to run the file. If you receive this warning message, click the **Run** button.

3. Windows will now launch the GFI LANguard Network Security Scanner 8 ReportPack Setup wizard. Click **Next** to bypass the wizard's welcome screen.

4. You will now see a screen telling you that GFI Report Center framework version 3.5 is required for installation, as shown in Figure 5.1. Choose the option to download and install the GFI Report Center framework version 3.5, and click **Next**.

Figure 5.1 Select the Download and Install the GFI Report Center Framework Version 3.5 Option and Click Next

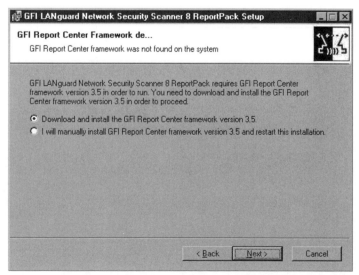

Windows will now download the Report Center framework. In case you are wondering, version 3.5 of the framework is 19.6 MB in size. When the download completes, the setup wizard will automatically install the framework without you having to do anything.

5. At this point, the setup wizard will offer you the chance to check for a new version of the ReportPack on the GFI Web site. Go ahead and choose the option to check for a new version, and click **Next**. Since you have just downloaded the ReportPack, there shouldn't be a new version, but it is always a good idea to check just in case.

6. The next screen that you will encounter displays the End User License Agreement (EULA), as it has become to be known. Choose the option to accept the license agreement, and click **OK**.

7. You will now see the screen shown in Figure 5.2, asking you to enter your full name, your company name, and your license key. As you can see in the figure, you can enter the word Evaluation in place of a license key if you have not yet purchased a license key, and want to take the ReportPack for a test drive. Using the evaluation version will allow you to use the ReportPack and all of its features for ten days. I should point out, however, that although the ReportPack is a separate download, a ReportPack license is included when you buy a license for GFI LANguard Network Security Scanner. If you've already bought a GFI LANguard Network Security Scanner license, then you can use the same license key for the ReportPack that you used for the main product.

Figure 5.2 Enter Your License Key into the Space Provided

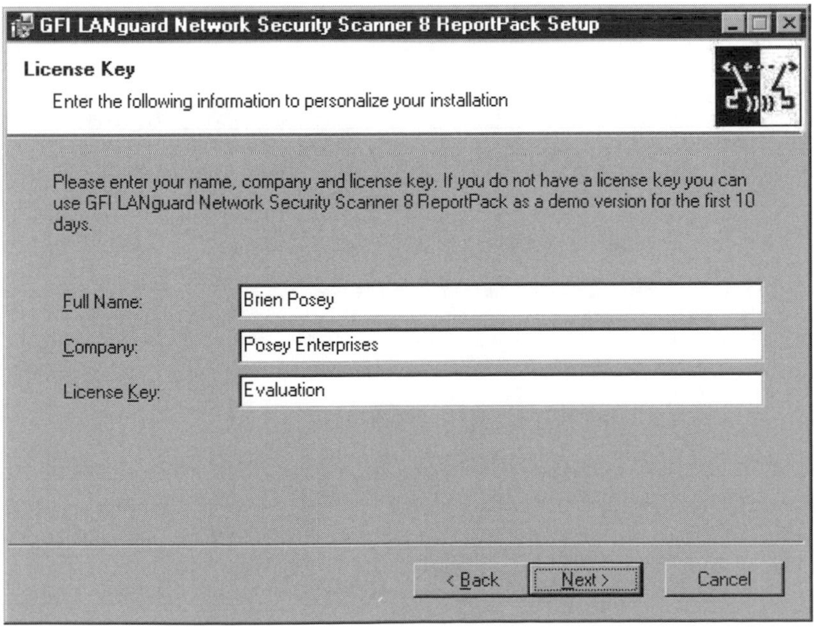

8. Click **Next**.

9. Setup will now display a screen similar to the one shown in Figure 5.3, asking you which type of database you want to use. As you can see in the figure, you have the option of using a test database, a Microsoft Access database, or a Structured Query Language (SQL) Server or MSDE database. In case you are not familiar with MSDE, or Microsoft Database Engine, is Microsoft's free version of SQL Server. It has the same basic capabilities as SQL Server, but is a bit lacking in the areas of performance and management. It is worth noting that Microsoft no longer refers to this database as MSDE, but rather as Microsoft SQL Server 2005 Express Edition.

    Unless you truly are evaluating the ReportPack, you should select the same database that you used when installing LANguard Network Security Scanner. Since I used a SQL Server database when I walked you through the LANguard Network Security Scanner installation process, I will be using the SQL Server database option on this screen as well. If you are performing an evaluation installation, then using a test database will be your only option.

Figure 5.3 You Should Choose the Database Option that Matches the Database Used by GFI LANguard Network Security Scanner

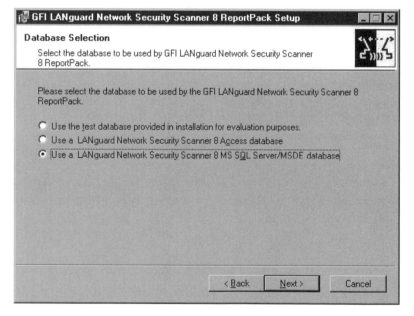

> **NOTE**
>
> You must use the same database for both GFI LANguard Network Security Scanner and the ReportPack.

10. You should now see a screen that's similar to the one shown in Figure 5.4. Notice that the drop down lists every SQL Server that I detected on your network. You should make sure to select the SQL Server that is currently hosting your GFI LANguard Network Security Scanner database.

Figure 5.4 Choose the SQL Serve That Is Hosting Your GFI LANguard Network Security Scanner Database

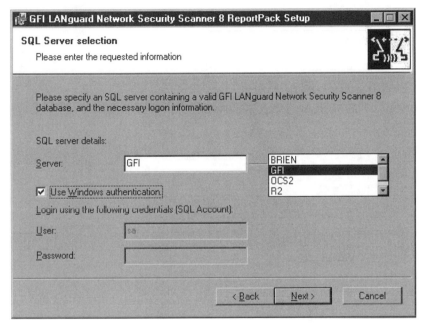

11. If the database is running on your local server, then selecting it alone is not enough. You must enter the server's name, followed by a slash and the database instance name into the server field. For example, both my server and my database instance are named GF, so I entered **GFI\GFI**. As an alternative, I could have also entered **[local]\GFI**.

12. Either enter the authentication credentials for your SQL Server, or select the Use Windows Authentication check box if you have allowed Windows authentication.

13. Click **Next**. Setup will now perform a check to make sure that it is able to attach to the SQL Server.

14. When the connection check is complete, you will see a screen like the one shown in Figure 5.5.

As you can see in the figure, this screen asks you to configure the mail settings for the ReportPack. I spent a lot of time covering the mail settings in Chapter 1, so I don't want to waste your time by covering it all again. You can use exactly the same mail settings for the ReportPack as you did for the main product. If you need any help setting up the mail settings, you can refer back to Chapter 1.

Figure 5.5 Fill Out the Mail Settings Screen in Exactly the Same Way as You Did When You First Configured GFI LANguard Network Security Scanner

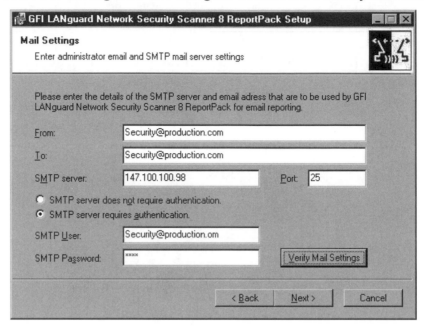

15.   Click **Next**, and you will be taken to a screen that asks you to confirm the installation path. Unless you've got a compelling reason to change the installation path, just go with the defaults, and click **Next**.

16.   You should now see a screen that tells you that Setup is ready to install the ReportPack. Click **Next** and the installation process will begin.

17.   When the installation process completes, click **Finish**.

Creating a Report

Now that we have installed the ReportPack, you are probably anxious to see what it can do. That being the case, let's get started by running a full scan against the local server. When the scan completes, you should see a scan summary, as shown in Figure 5.6.

Figure 5.6 When the Scan Completes, GFI LANguard Network Security Scanner Will Display a Summary Screen Similar to This One

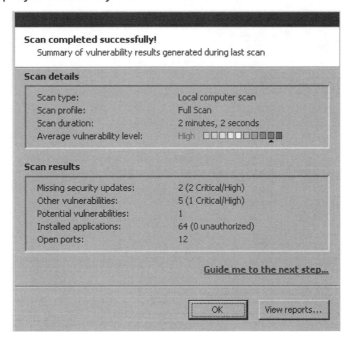

WARNING

Some of the reports that the ReportCenter produces are huge. You may want to look at the page count for a report before you try to print it.

To generate a report from the scan results, follow these steps:

1. Click the **View Reports** button.

2. After a brief delay, the GFI ReportCenter console will open and display the screen that's shown in Figure 5.7.

Figure 5.7 This Is the Main ReportCenter Console

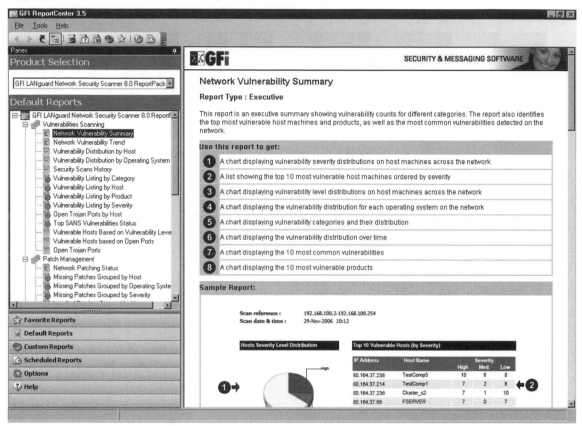

At first glance, the ReportCenter probably appears to be displaying a report, but it actually isn't. If you look at the console's left pane, you will see a list of all of the built-in reports. The pane on the right provides you with a description of the report that is currently selected. For example, if you look at the figure above, you will notice that the pane on the right starts out by listing eight different things that the currently selected report will tell you. You can click through the list of Default Reports until you find a report that gives you the information that you want.

Not every report will display eight different things; some will include more, and some will include less. If you read the description of what the report includes, and you are still not sure whether or not the report is really what you are looking for, then try scrolling through the pane on the right. As you can partially see in the figure above, the ReportCenter provides you with a sample of what the report will look like.

As you look at the figure above, notice that the sample report shows a number 1 and a number 2 with arrows pointing to different sections of the report. These numbers refer to the list at the top of the pane that tells you what the report will include. For example, the figure shows a number 1 pointing to a pie chart. If we look at the top of the pane, we can see that number 1 refers to a chart displaying vulnerability and severity distributions on host machines across the network.

Since we have only scanned the local server, the currently selected Network Vulnerability Summary report may not be the report that really gives us the most relevant information about the state of the host. However, since that is the report that is selected by default, I'm going to go ahead and use it, just to show you how the report generation process works. If you wanted to produce a different report, the steps that I am about to show you would still apply, you would simply select a different report first.

Continue the report generation process by following these steps:

3. Right-click on the report that you want to run, and then choose the **Run | For Last Scan** options from the resulting menus, as shown in Figure 5.8.

Figure 5.8 Run the Report for the Most Recent Scan

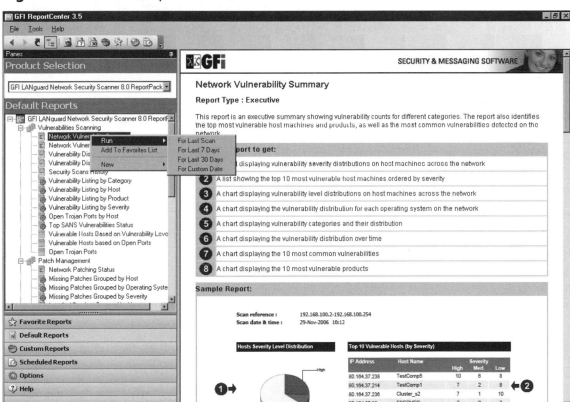

When the report completes, the ReportCenter displays the report within the console. Unfortunately, it is impossible for me to capture enough of the report in a screen capture to show you what it really looks like. However, there are a series of icons that appear just above the report. These icons allow you to navigate through the report's various pages, or to print or e-mail the report. One of these icons allows you to create a PDF version of the report, which is a lot easier to capture.

Notes from the Underground…

Watch out for Stolen Reports

The information in a security report is sensitive, and may actually be of even more value to a hacker than it is to you. I have seen various studies over the years that have indicated that the majority of security breaches are inside jobs. I don't really know if those statistics are true or not, since most security breaches probably go unreported, but I digress. At any rate, you should treat security reports as sensitive documents, and avoid storing them in places where they could be easily stolen by a disgruntled employee.

Favorite Reports

When you looked at the screen captures in the previous section, you probably noticed that the ReportCenter contains a whole lot of reports. In addition to the built in reports, you can even create your own custom reports, which I will show you how to do in the next section.

Another thing that I hope that you picked up on the previous section was that I demonstrated the Network Vulnerability Summary report, even though it was not necessarily the best fit for the type of scan that I had performed. The reason why I did that was to prove a point. The point is that while it's nice to have access to lots and lots of reports, odds are that only a hand full of those reports are actually going to be of interest to your organization. Furthermore, with so many available reports, it's easy for the reports that you do need to get lost in the clutter caused by the reports that you don't need.

This is where the Favorite Reports feature comes into play. The Favorite Reports section is used to maintain a list of the reports that you do find useful in your organization. You can store both built-in and custom reports in your favorites list.

Adding a report to the Favorite Reports list is simple. To do so, simply right-click on the report that you are interested in. The resulting shortcut menu contains an option to add the report to your favorite list, as shown in Figure 5.9. When you want to access your favorite reports later on, click the Favorite Reports box found in the lower-left portion of the console. When you do, the console will display a list of your favorite reports, as shown in Figure 5.10.

Figure 5.9 Right-clicking on a Report Gives You the Option of Adding the Report to Your Favorites List

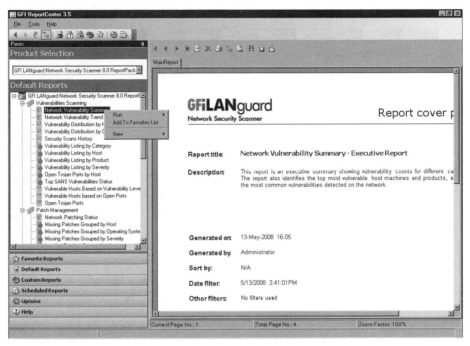

Figure 5.10 The Favorite Reports Section Displays Your Favorites List

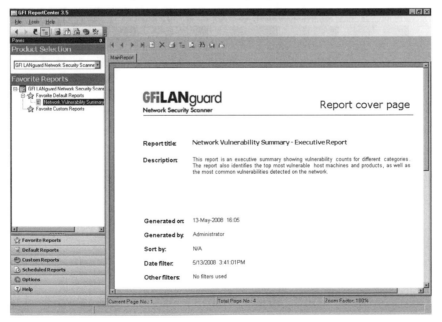

There are two things that are worth paying attention to in the figure above. First, notice how the reports on the favorites list are organized. The reports are separated into sublists of default reports and custom reports.

The other thing that is worth noticing is that when you click on one of these reports, you do not see a sample report, but rather the report that was most recently generated (assuming that a report has been run). Actually, this is also true of the main Default Reports list and the Custom Reports List, but on those lists you will probably have a much bigger mix of real reports and sample reports, because there will probably be quite a few reports that you never actually run. The reason why I am telling you this, is to help you realize that the Favorite Reports section is a great place to go if you want to skim all of the latest and most relevant reports that have been generated.

Custom Reports

As nice as all of the default reports are, the odds are pretty good that they are not going to meet your organization's needs perfectly. After all, every company is different, ergo every company has slightly different needs. Fortunately, the ReportCenter console makes it simple to create custom reports that are specifically tailored to your needs.

The nice thing about the Custom Reports feature is that you don't have to start completely from scratch when building your custom reports. Instead, go to the Default Reports section, and look for a report that is somewhat similar to the report that you want to create. Once you have found such a report, follow these steps:

1. Right-click on the report, and then choose the **New | Custom Report** options from the resulting shortcut menus, as shown in Figure 5.11.

Figure 5.11 Right-click on the Report That You Want to Use as a Template, and Choose the New | Custom Report Commands from the Shortcut Menus

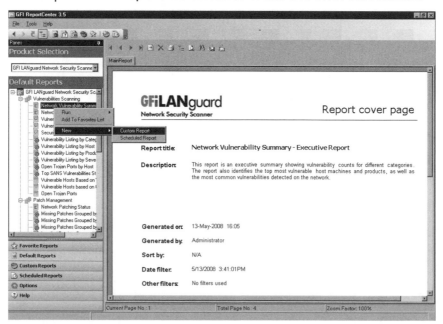

2. At this point, the Report Center will launch the Custom Report Wizard. Click **Next** to bypass the wizard's Welcome screen.

3. The wizard will now display a screen asking you which scans you would like to include in the report. You have the option of including the most recent scan, a particular scan, or all of the scans that have taken place within a specific date and time range. Make your selection, and click **Next**.

4. The next screen that you will see asks you if you want to apply any data filters to the report. Filters allow you to analyze a particular subset of the data. There aren't any filters that are initially in place, so you will have to click the **Add** button to create one. When you do, the wizard will display the Add Filter Property dialog box, as shown in Figure 5.12.

Figure 5.12 The Add Filter Property Dialog Box Helps You to Create a Filter

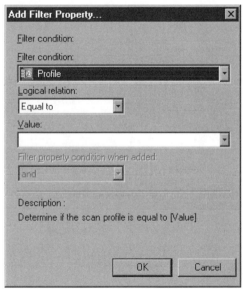

Creating Data Filters

Even though this dialog box looks fairly simple, I want to stop for a moment and spend some time talking about it in more detail, because understanding how this dialog box works is crucial to being able to create the custom reports that you want.

As I mentioned earlier, filters allow you to control the information that is processed when a report is run. This dialog box allows you to select a filter condition, a logical relation, and a value. For example, suppose that for some reason we wanted to structure the report so that it only displayed information about servers that were running Windows Server 2003. To accomplish this, we would choose the Operating System option from the Filter Condition drop-down list.

We would then set the logical relation to Equal To. Finally, we would enter Windows Server 2003 into the value field. You can see an example of this in Figure 5.13. If you want to create a report based on a different operating system, you can usually get away with just typing the operating system's name. If you need to find out exactly how the operating system's name should be entered, right-click on the Computer option on the system's Start menu, and select the Properties command from the shortcut menu. When you do, Windows will display the System Properties sheet, which lists the operating system name.

Figure 5.13 You Can Easily Filter Servers by Operating System

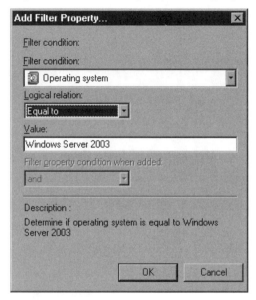

When you have filled in the various fields to your satisfaction, click **OK**, and you will be returned to the Data Filters screen. From this screen, you can either click the Add button to set up additional filters, or you can click the Next button to continue working through the wizard.

Before I move on, you might have noticed in the figure above that there is a field called "Filter Property Condition When Added," that is grayed out. This field only becomes active when you create multiple filters. Once you create multiple filters, you can set conditions such as And or Or. For example, if you look at Figure 5.14, you can see that I have created two different filters. However, the And condition means that the filter will only go into effect when the operating system is equal to Windows Server 2003, and the server's domain is equal to Production.

Figure 5.14 The Wizard's Data Filters Screen Allows You to Create Multiconditional Filters

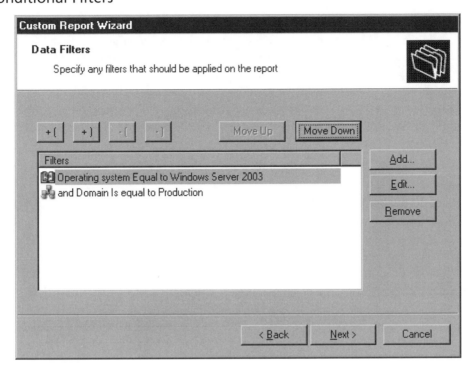

The filter that I have set up is relatively simple, but in the real world you can end up creating filters that have a lot more than two conditions. Once you get to the point where a filter contains three or more conditions, structuring the various elements that make up the filter becomes critical. Suppose, for example, that you needed to create a filter with four different conditions. In the interest of keeping them simple, let's call these conditions A, B, C, and D, rather than using actual conditions.

If you need all four of the conditions to be true, then the filter's structure isn't really an issue. You could just create a filter that looks something like this:

```
Condition A and Condition B and Condition C and Condition D
```

Things get a little bit more tricky when you start working in Or and other logical operators. Suppose, for instance, you needed to create a filter where either A and C could be true, or B and D could be true. In this type of situation, listing the conditions in A, B, C, and D order no longer makes sense. If you look back at Figure 5.15, however, you will notice that the screen offers a Move Up and a Move Down button. These buttons allow you to rearrange the filter's conditions so that you can create the desired logical structure.

Okay, so let's pretend that we have rearranged conditions A, B, C, and D, and now we try to create our filter. As it stands now, the filter would look like this:

```
Condition A and Condition C or Condition B and Condition D
```

Anybody else see a problem with this structure? Depending on whether the application gives higher priority to the And or to the Or operator, the results of the filter could end up being completely different. To see how you can solve these types of situations, look back at Figure 5.15 one more time. Notice the four icons just above the filter list. These icons allow you to group conditions into parenthesis. Groups of conditions within parenthesis are processed first, thus giving the parenthesis higher priority. Therefore, we could take the ambiguity out of the set of conditions above by putting the parenthesis to work and creating a set of conditions that looks like this:

```
(Condition A and Condition C) or (Condition B and Condition D)
```

If you need a more concrete example, check out Figure 5.15. In this figure, I have set up a bunch of random conditions and grouped them into parenthesis using the And and the Or operators, as a way of showing you what a more complex filter might look like.

Figure 5.15 The Custom Report Wizard Can Create More Complex Filters

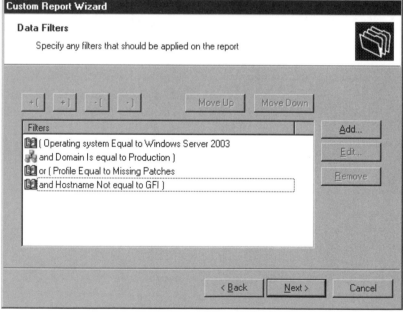

Creating a Custom Report

In the previous section, I showed you all kinds of crazy ways that you could create filters with multiple conditions. However, at the same time, my purpose in writing this chapter is to teach you how the ReportCenter works, not to confuse you. As such, I want to move forward with creating a custom report, but at the same time, I want to keep things simple. That being the case, I am going to remove all of the filters from the Data Filters list, except for the Domain is Equal to Production filter, as shown in Figure 5.16. This is the point at which I will be continuing the process of creating a custom report.

Figure 5.16 Verify That Your List of Data Filters Looks the Way That You Want It to Before Continuing

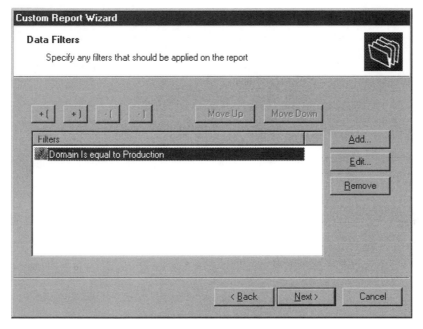

You can continue the report creation process by following these steps:

5. Click **Next**.
6. Enter a report name, a report title, and a report description into the fields provided, and click **Next**.
7. Click **Finish** to close the wizard.

At this point, your custom report will be displayed in the Custom Reports section, as shown in Figure 5.17. Notice in the figure that if you right-click on the report, you have the option of editing it, deleting it, or of running the report.

Figure 5.17 This Is What Your Custom Report Initially Looks Like

At first glance, the custom report looks exactly like the default report that you created it from. However, check out what happens when you run it. If you look at Figure 5.18, you can see that the report title and description that you provided to the wizard are listed on the report's cover page. The cover page also lists the filters that you have specified to be included in the custom report.

Figure 5.18 The Custom Report is Based on the Filters That You Have Specified

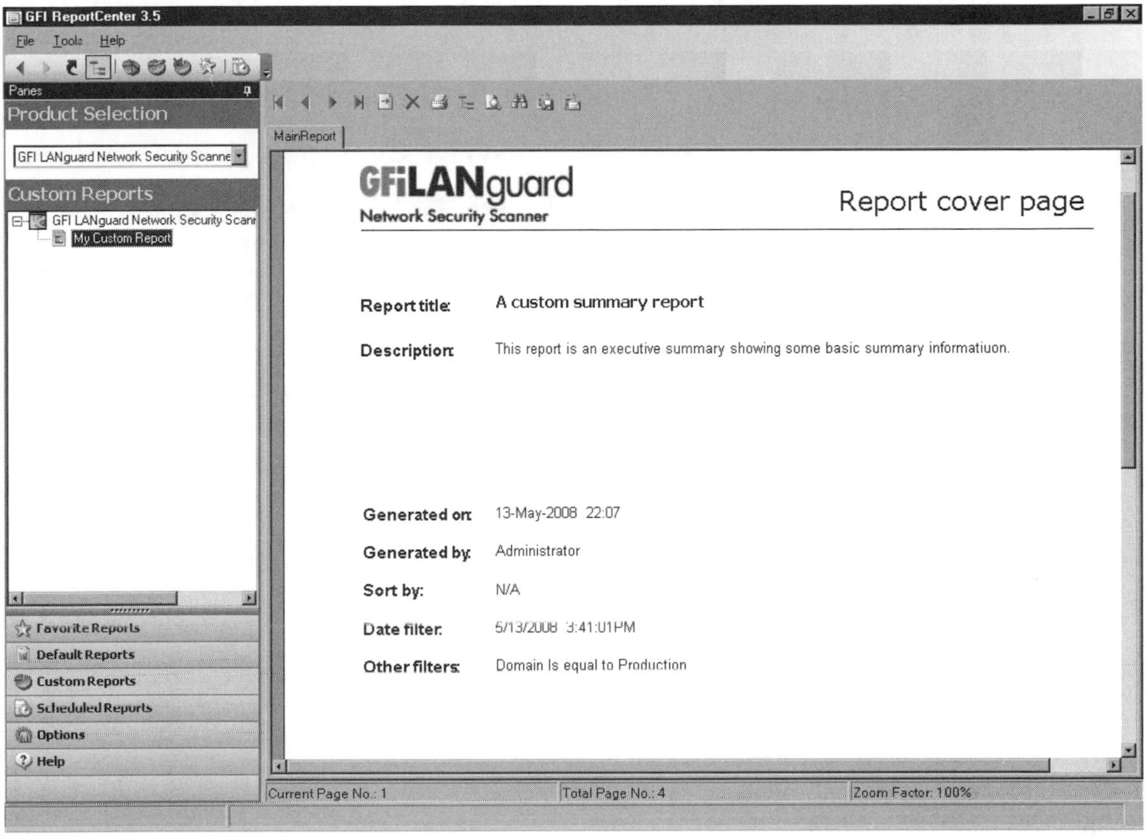

Scheduled Reports

A scheduled report is a lot like a default report or a custom report, except that you schedule the report to run at a specific time. Scheduled reports can be a one-time occurrence, or you can schedule them to run on a periodic basis. The resulting reports can be written to a document file, sent by e-mail, or both.

To create a custom report, follow these steps:

1. Right-click on a report that you want to schedule, and choose the **New | Scheduled Report** commands from the resulting shortcut menus.

2. The ReportCenter will now launch the Schedule Report Wizard. Click **Next** to bypass the wizard's Welcome screen.

3. At this point, the Schedule Report Wizard will ask you to specify a date and time range on which to base the report. You can choose to use the most recent scan, a specific scan, or all of the scans that have occurred within a specific date and time range. Make your selection, and click **Next**.

4. You will now see a screen that gives you the opportunity to choose when the report will be generated. As you can see in Figure 5.19, you have the option of either generating the report once, at a specific date and time, or you can generate the report on an ongoing basis at specific intervals.

Figure 5.19 You Must Decide When You Would Like the Report to Run

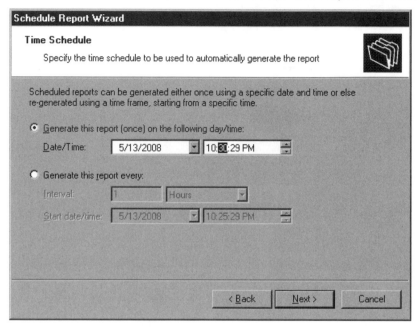

5. Make your selection, and click **Next**.

6. You must now decide how you want the report to be delivered. As you can see in Figure 5.20, the report can either be written to a document file, transmitted by e-mail, or both. In any case, you will have to click the Settings button to provide specific information about the destination and the report format. Regardless of which option you choose, you can create the report in Adobe Acrobat (.pdf), Microsoft Excel (.xls), Microsoft Word (.doc), or Rich Text (.rtf) format.

Figure 5.20 You Can Write a Scheduled Report to a Document File, Transmit the Report by E-mail, or Both

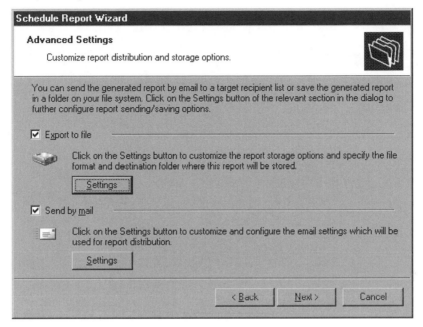

7. After making your selection, click **Next**.
8. You are now given the chance to modify the report's name, title, and description. This is an optional step.
9. Click **Next**.
10. Click **Finish**.

Now that you have created your scheduled report, go to the console's Scheduled Reports section. If you look at the left pane in Figure 5.21, you can see that the Scheduled Reports section is divided into two parts: the Scheduled Reports List and the Scheduled Reports Activity log.

Figure 5.21 The Scheduled Reports List Shows You Any Reports That Are Scheduled to Be Run

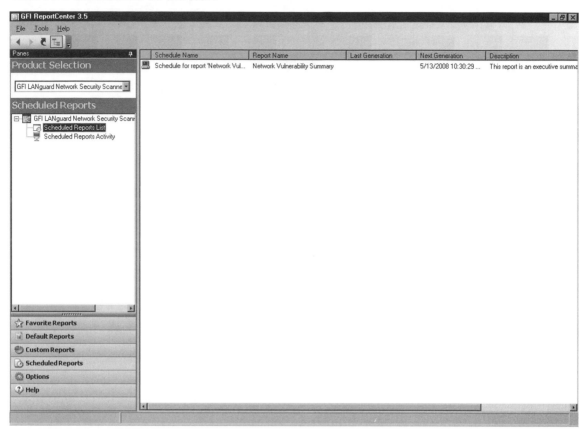

As you might expect, the Scheduled Reports List shows you all of the reports that are scheduled to run. You can right-click on a report and choose the Properties command from the shortcut menu to access a properties sheet that allows you to modify the report, delete it, or to force the report to be generated now.

The Scheduled Reports Activity list is a log of all of the scheduled reports that have been run.

Other Options

The Options section, shown in Figure 5.22 offers you a few different options for changing the way that the ReportPack is configured. As you can see in the figure, there are four different configuration options, and you can alter any one of them by simply right-clicking on the option that you want to adjust, and choosing the appropriate command from the resulting shortcut menu.

Figure 5.22 The Options Section Allows You to Set Some of the ReportPack's Basic Configuration Options

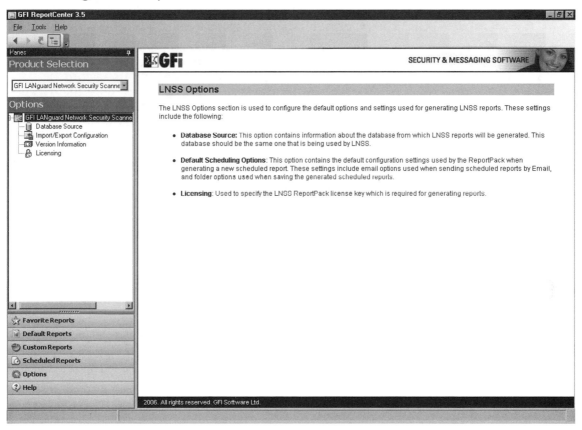

Normally, you shouldn't even have to worry about changing any of these options, so I don't want to waste a lot of space by talking about them in great detail. However, I did want to at least mention the capabilities that are available to you, so Table 5.1 contains a brief description of each option and what it is used for:

Table 5.1 These Are the Configuration Options That Are Available to You

Option	Function
Database Source	The Database Source option allows you to change the database instance that the ReportPack is configured to use.
Import/Export Configuration	The Import/Export Configuration allows you to make a backup of things like scheduled reports and custom reports. Although it is nice to be able to perform a backup in this way, I recommend performing full backups of your server and the backend database instead.
Version Information	The Version Information option displays the current version of the ReportPack software, and allows you to check for newer builds.
Licensing	The Licensing option allows you to retrieve your license key, or to enter a new license key.

Summary

GFI LANguard Network Security Scanner can produce a mountain of data during a scan. The key to benefiting from the scan results is to be able to sort through the data and get the information that you need. In most cases, the ReportPack will provide you with your best options for doing so. As we continue to use the ReportPack in future chapters, I hope that you will continue to see the benefits that it provides.

Solutions Fast Track

Installing the ReportPack

- ☑ The ReportPack is included in a separate download than the core LANguard Network Security Scanner product.
- ☑ A setup wizard guides you through the installation process.
- ☑ The ReportPack must be configured to use the same database or database instance as LANguard Network Security Scanner is using.

Creating a Report

- ☑ Locate the report of choice on the Default Reports list.
- ☑ Right-click on the report, and choose the **Run | For Last Scan** options from the shortcut menu.

Favorite Reports

- ☑ Right-click on a default or on a custom report.
- ☑ Choose the Add to Favorites List command from the resulting menu.

Custom Reports

- ☑ Right-click on a default report.
- ☑ Choose the **New | Custom Reports** commands from the shortcut menus.

Scheduled Reports

- ☑ Right-click on a default report.
- ☑ Choose the **New | Scheduled Report** options from the resulting shortcut menus.

Frequently Asked Questions

Q: Is there a way to create a custom report completely from scratch?

A: Sadly, the software does not provide this capability directly. The reports are based on Hypertext Markup language (HTML) templates though, so you could likely study those templates and use them as a basis for creating your own reports.

Q: Why doesn't the ReportPack install automatically as a part of GFI LANguard Network Security Scanner?

A: I don't know why GFI requires a separate installation for the ReportPack. I suspect that maybe the ReportPack used to be an entirely separate product, but I don't really know for sure.

Q: Where do I get a license key for the ReportPack?

A: You can use the same license key as you used to install GFI LANguard Network Security Scanner.

Q: What formats can reports be exported in?

A: Adobe Acrobat (.pdf), Microsoft Excel (.xls), Microsoft Word (.doc), or Rich Text (.rtf) format.

Chapter 6

Inventories and Auditing

Solutions in this chapter:

- **Performing a Hardware Inventory**
- **Compiling a Software Inventory**
- **Analyzing the Results**
- **Blacklisting and Whitelisting Applications**
- **Network Documentation**

☑ **Summary**

☑ **Solutions Fast Track**

☑ **Frequently Asked Questions**

Introduction

As a network administrator, one of your biggest responsibilities is to know what's on your network. You need to know what devices are attached to the network, and what software is installed on those devices. After all, if you don't even know what is connected to your network, or how those devices are set up, then how in the world can you possibly consider your network to be secure?

Fortunately, GFI LANguard Network Security Scanner can help with this problem. Some of the product's scanning capabilities are designed to help you compile hardware and software inventories, and even to help you document your network. In this chapter, I'll show you how it works.

Performing a Hardware Inventory

One thing that you have to keep in mind is that GFI LANguard Network Security Scanner is not specifically designed for compiling hardware inventories, so the inventory information that you get is not going to be as comprehensive as it would be with a dedicated network documentation product. The hardware inventories primarily consist of information about disks, network connections, and Universal Serial Bus (USB) devices. At the same time, however, the product does offer the benefit of not requiring an agent to be installed on workstations. Most of the applications that can compile a more comprehensive hardware inventory require agents.

To perform a hardware inventory, follow these steps:

NOTE

GFI LANguard Network Security Scanner is not capable of producing a full blown hardware inventory report. It primarily collects information about storage devices and network interfaces.

1. Open the management console, and click the **New Scan** button.

2. When the New Scan wizard begins, select the **Network and Software Auditing** option, as shown in Figure 6.1.

Figure 6.1 Select the Software Auditing Option

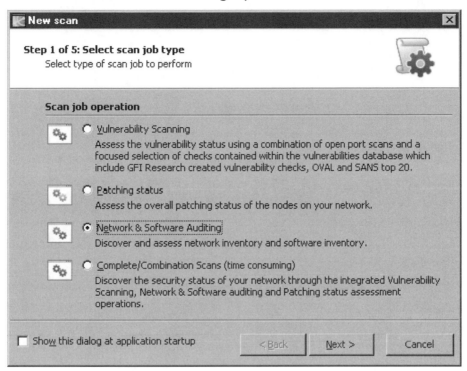

3. The wizard's next screen asks you to choose a scanning profile to use. Choose the **System Information** profile, and click **Next**.

4. At this point, the wizard will ask you what type of scan you want to perform. You have the option of scanning a single computer, a range of computers, a list of computers, or an entire domain or workgroup. For demonstration purposes, choose the **Scan a Range of Computers** option, and click **Next**.

5. The wizard will now prompt you to enter the IP address range that you want to scan, as shown in Figure 6.2. Notice in the figure that I have specified an entire subnet. For the record, I don't actually own this address range; it is just a random address range that I chose to use on my private network.

Figure 6.2 Enter the IP Address Range That You Want to Scan

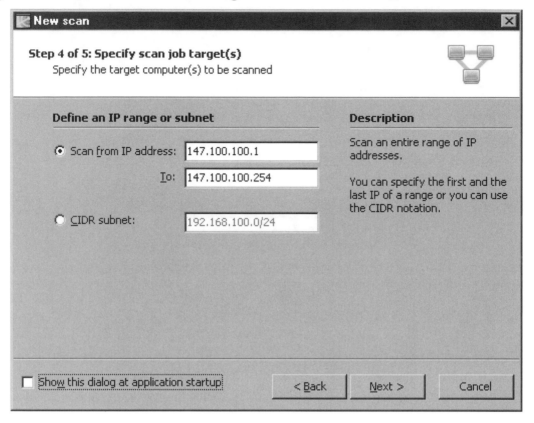

6. Click **Next** and you will be prompted as to which credentials you want to use during the scan. If you are logged on as a domain administrator, go ahead and use the **Currently Logged On User** option. Otherwise, you will have to specify an alternate set of credentials.

7. Click the **Scan** button, and GFI LANguard Network Security Scanner will initialize the scanning engine, and begin hunting for any computers within the specified address range, as shown in Figure 6.3. Keep in mind that the computers must be powered on in order to be detected.

Figure 6.3 Click the Scan Button to Initialize the Scan

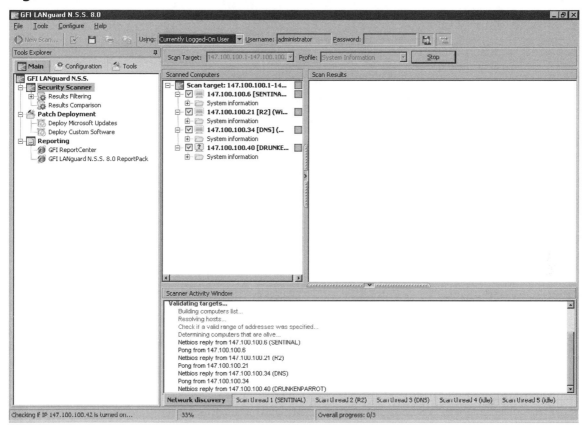

8. When the scan completes, you will see a screen similar to the one that's shown in Figure 6.4. This screen gives you some information about what has been detected, but it doesn't provide you with comprehensive information about the scan results. To get more detailed information, click the **View Reports** button.

Figure 6.4 The Scan Completed Screen Gives You a Minimal Amount of Detail About the Scan Results

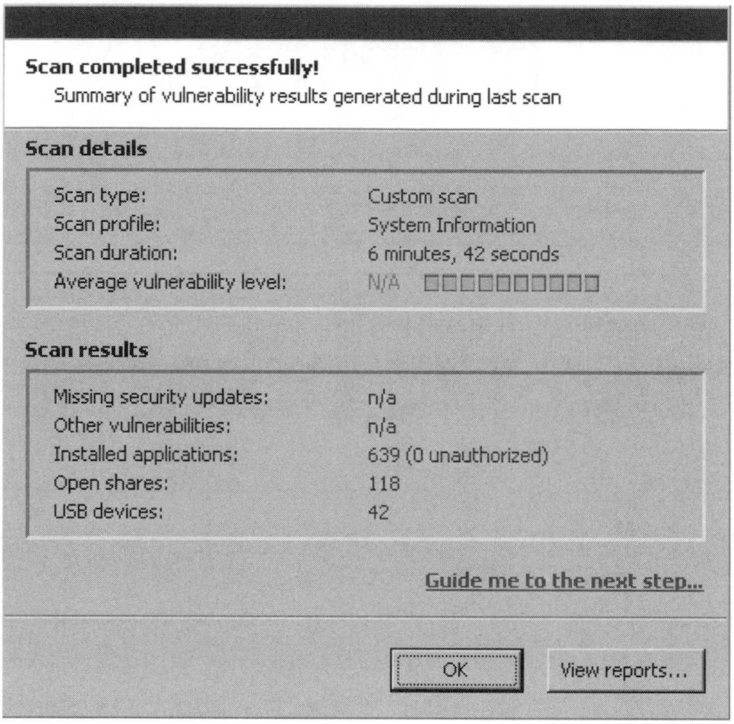

WARNING

This type of report can produce an extremely long document. Check the document length before you attempt to print it.

9. Windows will now launch the ReportCenter console. If you scroll through the list of available reports, you will notice that there is an entire section called "System Information." There are a wide variety of reports found in this section, but the System Information report (which is found inside the System Information container) provides you with the most detailed information. Go ahead and right-click on the **System Information** report, and choose the **Run | For Last Scan** commands from the resulting shortcut menus.

Depending on the number of nodes that are detected on your network, this can end up being a really long report. I have provided an excerpt from this report below, just so that you can see what types of information the report gives you. Keep in mind that this excerpt only shows the details for a single server, even though the complete report provides this type of information for every single computer that was detected. In fact, I only have a couple dozen computers on my network, but the full report was over 300 pages long. Here is an excerpt from the report:

Report title:	**System Information**
Description:	This report lists detailed technical information for each host machine, including services, installed applications, policies and devices.

Generated on:	18-May-2008 22:39
Generated by:	Administrator
Sort by:	IP - Ascending
Date filter:	5/18/2008 10:04:50PM
Other filters:	No filters used

Scan reference :   147.100.100.1-147.100.100.254
Scan date & time :   5/18/2008 10:04:50PM

147.100.100.6 - SENTINAL

Operating System
Windows Server 2003

Service Pack
1

Computer Properties

MAC Address:	00-11-95-FD-CB-B8 (D-Link Corporation)
Time to live:	128 (128)
Network role:	Member Server
Domain:	PRODUCTION
LAN manager:	Windows Server 2003 5.2

Uptimes

Time of Day	Up Time
18 May 2008, 22:05:21	2 days, 35 hours, 42 minutes, 18 seconds

Disk Utilization

Name	Total Space	Free Space	File System Type
A:	N/A	N/A	N/A
C:	75.00 GB	37.85 GB	NTFS
D:	N/A	N/A	N/A
E:	N/A	N/A	N/A
F:	204.47 GB	48.57 GB	NTFS
G:	279.47 GB	19.87 GB	NTFS

Groups and Users

Groups

Name	Description
Administrators	Administrators have complete and unrestricted access to the computer/domain
Members: SENTINAL\Administrator, PRODUCTION\Domain Admins	
Backup Operators	Backup Operators can override security restrictions for the sole purpose of backing up or restoring files
Distributed COM Users	Members are allowed to launch, activate and use Distributed COM objects on this machine.
Guests	Guests have the same access as members of the Users group by default, except for the Guest account which is further restricted
Members: SENTINAL\Guest, SENTINAL\IUSR_SENTINAL	
Network Configuration Operators	Members in this group can have some administrative privileges to manage configuration of networking features
Performance Log Users	Members of this group have remote access to schedule logging of performance counters on this computer
Members: NT AUTHORITY\NETWORK SERVICE	
Performance Monitor Users	Members of this group have remote access to monitor this computer
Members: NT AUTHORITY\SYSTEM	
Power Users	Power Users possess most administrative powers with some restrictions. Thus, Power Users can run legacy applications in addition to certified applications
Print Operators	Members can administer domain printers
Remote Desktop Users	Members in this group are granted the right to logon remotely

Replicator	Supports file replication in a domain
Users	Users are prevented from making accidental or intentional system-wide changes. Thus, Users can run certified applications, but not most legacy applications
Members: NT AUTHORITY\INTERACTIVE, NT AUTHORITY\Authenticated Users, PRODUCTION\Domain Users, SENTINAL\ASPNET	
HelpServicesGroup	Group for the Help and Support Center
Members: SENTINAL\SUPPORT_388945a0	
IIS_WPG	IIS Worker Process Group
Members: NT AUTHORITY\SYSTEM, NT AUTHORITY\SERVICE, NT AUTHORITY\NETWORK SERVICE, SENTINAL\IWAM_SENTINAL	
SQLServer2005DTSUser$SENTINAL	Members in the group have the required access and privileges to be assigned as the log on account for the associated instance of SQL Server Integration Services in SQL Server 2005.
Members: NT AUTHORITY\NETWORK SERVICE	
SQLServer2005MSFTEUser$SENTINAL$MI	
SQLServer2005MSFTEUser$SENTINAL$MS	Members in the group have the required access and privileges to be assigned as the log on account for the associated instance of SQL Server and SQL Server FullText Search in SQL Server 2005.
Members: NT AUTHORITY\SYSTEM	
SQLServer2005MSOLAPUser$SENTINAL$M	Members in the group have the required access and privileges to be assigned as the log on account for the associated instance of SQL Server Analysis Services in SQL Server 2005.
Members: NT AUTHORITY\SYSTEM	
SQLServer2005MSSQLServerADHelperUser	Members in the group have the required access and privileges to be assigned as the log on account for the associated instance of SQL Server Active Directory Helper in SQL Server 2005.
Members: NT AUTHORITY\NETWORK SERVICE	
SQLServer2005MSSQLUser$SENTINAL$MI	Members in the group have the required access and privileges to be assigned as the log on account for the associated instance of SQL Server 2005 Embedded Edition.
Members: NT AUTHORITY\NETWORK SERVICE	
SQLServer2005MSSQLUser$SENTINAL$MS	Members in the group have the required access and privileges to be assigned as the log on account for the associated instance of SQL Server and SQL Server FullText Search in SQL Server 2005.
Members: NT AUTHORITY\SYSTEM	
SQLServer2005NotificationServicesUser$S	Members in the group have the required access and privileges to be assigned as the log on account for the associated instance of SQL Server Notification Services in SQL Server 2005.
SQLServer2005SQLAgentUser$SENTINAL$	Members in the group have the required access and privileges to be assigned as the log on account for the associated instance of SQL Server Agent in SQL Server 2005.
Members: NT AUTHORITY\SYSTEM	
SQLServer2005SQLBrowserUser$SENTINA	Members in the group have the required access and privileges to be assigned as the log on account for the associated instance of SQL Server Browser in SQL Server 2005.
Members: NT AUTHORITY\SYSTEM	
TelnetClients	Members of this group have access to Telnet Server on this system.
WSUS Administrators	WSUS Administrators can administer the Windows Server Update Services server.
WSUS Reporters	WSUS Administrators who can only run reports on the Windows Server Update Services server.

Users

Administrator()
  Privilege : Administrator (*)
  Flags : SCRIPT,NORMAL_ACCOUNT
  Comment : Built-in account for administering the computer/domain
  LastLogon : 20 Apr 2008, 11:06:36

PasswordAge : 979 days, 3 hours, 39 minutes, 50 seconds
Logons : 17

ASPNET(ASP.NET Machine Account)
  Full Name : ASP.NET Machine Account
  Privilege : User
  Flags : SCRIPT,PASSWORD_NOT_REQUIRED,PASSWORD_CANNOT_BE_CHANGED,NORMAL_ACCOUN
    T
  Comment : Account used for running the ASP.NET worker process (aspnet_wp.exe)
  User Comment : Account used for running the ASP.NET worker process (aspnet_wp.exe)
  LastLogon : 18 Feb 2007, 00:26:13
  PasswordAge : 455 days, 21 hours, 39 minutes, 2 seconds
  # Logons : 6

Guest()
  Privilege : Guest
  Flags : ACCOUNT_DISABLED,PASSWORD_NOT_REQUIRED,PASSWORD_CANNOT_BE_CHANGED,NOR
    MAL_ACCOUNT
  Comment : Built-in account for guest access to the computer/domain
  LastLogon : Never
  PasswordAge : 787 days, 10 hours, 45 minutes, 19 seconds

IUSR_SENTINAL(Internet Guest Account)
  Full Name : Internet Guest Account
  Privilege : Guest
  Flags : SCRIPT,PASSWORD_NOT_REQUIRED,PASSWORD_CANNOT_BE_CHANGED,NORMAL_ACCOUN
    T
  Comment : Built-in account for anonymous access to Internet Information Services
  User Comment : Built-in account for anonymous access to Internet Information Services
  LastLogon : 18 May 2008, 06:09:42
  PasswordAge : 856 days, 21 hours, 52 minutes, 38 seconds
  # Logons : 5,134

IWAM_SENTINAL(Launch IIS Process Account)
  Full Name : Launch IIS Process Account
  Privilege : Guest
  Flags : SCRIPT,PASSWORD_NOT_REQUIRED,PASSWORD_CANNOT_BE_CHANGED,NORMAL_ACCOUN
    T
  Comment : Built-in account for Internet Information Services to start out of process applications
  User Comment : Built-in account for Internet Information Services to start out of process applications
  LastLogon : 22 May 2006, 21:36:10
  PasswordAge : 856 days, 21 hours, 52 minutes, 38 seconds

SUPPORT_388945a0(CN=Microsoft Corporation,L=Redmond,S=Washington,C=US)
  Full Name : CN=Microsoft Corporation,L=Redmond,S=Washington,C=US
  Privilege : Guest
  Flags : ACCOUNT_DISABLED,PASSWORD_CANNOT_BE_CHANGED,NORMAL_ACCOUNT
  Comment : This is a vendor's account for the Help and Support Service
  LastLogon : Never
  PasswordAge : 978 days, 23 hours, 31 minutes, 45 seconds

SNMP Information

No SNMP Information found.

Services

Services

AeLookupSvc

Service Name	Status	Startup Type	Account Name
Application Experience Lookup Service	Running	Automatic	LocalSystem

Alerter

Service Name	Status	Startup Type	Account Name
Alerter	Stopped	Disabled	NT AUTHORITY\LocalService

ALG

Service Name	Status	Startup Type	Account Name
Application Layer Gateway Service	Stopped	Manual	NT AUTHORITY\LocalService

AppMgmt

Service Name	Status	Startup Type	Account Name
Application Management	Stopped	Manual	LocalSystem

aspnet_state

Service Name	Status	Startup Type	Account Name
ASP.NET State Service	Stopped	Manual	NT AUTHORITY\NetworkService

AudioSrv

Service Name	Status	Startup Type	Account Name
Windows Audio	Running	Automatic	LocalSystem

BITS

Service Name	Status	Startup Type	Account Name
Background Intelligent Transfer Service	Running	Manual	LocalSystem

Browser

Service Name	Status	Startup Type	Account Name
Computer Browser	Running	Automatic	LocalSystem

CiSvc

Service Name	Status	Startup Type	Account Name
Indexing Service	Stopped	Disabled	LocalSystem

ClipSrv

Service Name	Status	Startup Type	Account Name
ClipBook	Stopped	Disabled	LocalSystem

clr_optimization_v2.0.50727_32

Service Name	Status	Startup Type	Account Name
.NET Runtime Optimization Service	Stopped	Manual	LocalSystem

COMSysApp

Service Name	Status	Startup Type	Account Name
COM+ System Application	Stopped	Manual	LocalSystem

CryptSvc

Service Name	Status	Startup Type	Account Name
Cryptographic Services	Running	Automatic	LocalSystem

DcomLaunch

Service Name	Status	Startup Type	Account Name
DCOM Server Process Launcher	Running	Automatic	LocalSystem

Dfs

Service Name	Status	Startup Type	Account Name
Distributed File System	Running	Automatic	LocalSystem

Dhcp

Service Name	Status	Startup Type	Account Name
DHCP Client	Running	Automatic	NT AUTHORITY\NetworkService

dmadmin

Service Name	Status	Startup Type	Account Name
Logical Disk Manager Administrative Service	Stopped	Manual	LocalSystem

dmserver

Service Name	Status	Startup Type	Account Name
Logical Disk Manager	Running	Automatic	LocalSystem

DNS

Service Name	Status	Startup Type	Account Name
DNS Server	Running	Automatic	LocalSystem

Dnscache

Service Name	Status	Startup Type	Account Name
DNS Client	Running	Automatic	NT AUTHORITY\NetworkService

ERSvc

Service Name	Status	Startup Type	Account Name
Error Reporting Service	Running	Automatic	LocalSystem

Eventlog

Service Name	Status	Startup Type	Account Name
Event Log	Running	Automatic	LocalSystem

EventSystem

Service Name	Status	Startup Type	Account Name
COM+ Event System	Running	Automatic	LocalSystem

FontCache3.0.0.0

Service Name	Status	Startup Type	Account Name
Windows Presentation Foundation Font Cache	Stopped	Manual	NT AUTHORITY\LocalService

helpsvc

Service Name	Status	Startup Type	Account Name
Help and Support	Running	Automatic	LocalSystem

HidServ

Service Name	Status	Startup Type	Account Name
Human Interface Device Access	Stopped	Disabled	LocalSystem

HTTPFilter

Service Name	Status	Startup Type	Account Name
HTTP SSL	Running	Manual	LocalSystem

idsvc

Service Name	Status	Startup Type	Account Name
Windows CardSpace	Stopped	Manual	LocalSystem

IISADMIN

Service Name	Status	Startup Type	Account Name
IIS Admin Service	Running	Automatic	LocalSystem

ImapiService

Service Name	Status	Startup Type	Account Name
IMAPI CD-Burning COM Service	Stopped	Disabled	LocalSystem

IsmServ

Service Name	Status	Startup Type	Account Name
Intersite Messaging	Stopped	Disabled	LocalSystem

kdc

Service Name	Status	Startup Type	Account Name
Kerberos Key Distribution Center	Stopped	Disabled	LocalSystem

lanmanserver

Service Name	Status	Startup Type	Account Name
Server	Running	Automatic	LocalSystem

lanmanworkstation

Service Name	Status	Startup Type	Account Name
Workstation	Running	Automatic	LocalSystem

LicenseService

Service Name	Status	Startup Type	Account Name
License Logging	Stopped	Disabled	NT AUTHORITY\NetworkService

LmHosts

Service Name	Status	Startup Type	Account Name
TCP/IP NetBIOS Helper	Running	Automatic	NT AUTHORITY\LocalService

Messenger

Service Name	Status	Startup Type	Account Name
Messenger	Stopped	Disabled	LocalSystem

mnmsrvc

Service Name	Status	Startup Type	Account Name
NetMeeting Remote Desktop Sharing	Stopped	Disabled	LocalSystem

MSDTC

Service Name	Status	Startup Type	Account Name
Distributed Transaction Coordinator	Running	Automatic	NT AUTHORITY\NetworkService

MsDtsServer

Service Name	Status	Startup Type	Account Name
SQL Server Integration Services	Running	Automatic	NT AUTHORITY\NetworkService

MSExchangeMGMT

Service Name	Status	Startup Type	Account Name
Microsoft Exchange Management	Running	Automatic	LocalSystem

msftesql

Service Name	Status	Startup Type	Account Name
SQL Server FullText Search	Running	Automatic	LocalSystem

MSIServer

Service Name	Status	Startup Type	Account Name
Windows Installer	Stopped	Manual	LocalSystem

MSSQL$MICROSOFT##SSEE

Service Name	Status	Startup Type	Account Name
SQL Server 2005 Embedded Edition	Running	Automatic	NT AUTHORITY\NetworkService

MSSQLSERVER

Service Name	Status	Startup Type	Account Name
SQL Server (MSSQLSERVER)	Running	Automatic	LocalSystem

MSSQLServerADHelper

Service Name	Status	Startup Type	Account Name
SQL Server Active Directory Helper	Stopped	Disabled	NT AUTHORITY\NetworkService

MSSQLServerOLAPService

Service Name	Status	Startup Type	Account Name
SQL Server Analysis Services	Running	Automatic	LocalSystem

msvsmon80

Service Name	Status	Startup Type	Account Name
Visual Studio 2005 Remote Debugger	Stopped	Disabled	LocalSystem

NetDDE

Service Name	Status	Startup Type	Account Name
Network DDE	Stopped	Disabled	LocalSystem

NetDDEdsdm

Service Name	Status	Startup Type	Account Name
Network DDE DSDM	Stopped	Disabled	LocalSystem

Netlogon

Service Name	Status	Startup Type	Account Name
Net Logon	Running	Automatic	LocalSystem

Netman

Service Name	Status	Startup Type	Account Name
Network Connections	Running	Manual	LocalSystem

NetTcpPortSharing

Service Name	Status	Startup Type	Account Name
Net.Tcp Port Sharing Service	Stopped	Disabled	NT AUTHORITY\LocalService

Nla

Service Name	Status	Startup Type	Account Name
Network Location Awareness (NLA)	Running	Manual	LocalSystem

NtFrs

Service Name	Status	Startup Type	Account Name
File Replication	Running	Automatic	LocalSystem

NtLmSsp

Service Name	Status	Startup Type	Account Name
NT LM Security Support Provider	Stopped	Manual	LocalSystem

NtmsSvc

Service Name	Status	Startup Type	Account Name
Removable Storage	Stopped	Manual	LocalSystem

ose

Service Name	Status	Startup Type	Account Name
Office Source Engine	Stopped	Manual	LocalSystem

PlugPlay

Service Name	Status	Startup Type	Account Name
Plug and Play	Running	Automatic	LocalSystem

PolicyAgent

Service Name	Status	Startup Type	Account Name
IPSEC Services	Running	Automatic	LocalSystem

ProtectedStorage

Service Name	Status	Startup Type	Account Name
Protected Storage	Running	Automatic	LocalSystem

RasAuto

Service Name	Status	Startup Type	Account Name
Remote Access Auto Connection Manager	Stopped	Manual	LocalSystem

RasMan

Service Name	Status	Startup Type	Account Name
Remote Access Connection Manager	Running	Manual	LocalSystem

RDSessMgr

Service Name	Status	Startup Type	Account Name
Remote Desktop Help Session Manager	Stopped	Manual	LocalSystem

RemoteAccess

Service Name	Status	Startup Type	Account Name
Routing and Remote Access	Stopped	Disabled	LocalSystem

RemoteRegistry

Service Name	Status	Startup Type	Account Name
Remote Registry	Running	Automatic	NT AUTHORITY\LocalService

RpcLocator

Service Name	Status	Startup Type	Account Name
Remote Procedure Call (RPC) Locator	Running	Automatic	NT AUTHORITY\NetworkService

RpcSs

Service Name	Status	Startup Type	Account Name
Remote Procedure Call (RPC)	Running	Automatic	NT Authority\NetworkService

RSoPProv

Service Name	Status	Startup Type	Account Name
Resultant Set of Policy Provider	Stopped	Manual	LocalSystem

sacsvr

Service Name	Status	Startup Type	Account Name
Special Administration Console Helper	Stopped	Manual	LocalSystem

SamSs

Service Name	Status	Startup Type	Account Name
Security Accounts Manager	Running	Automatic	LocalSystem

SATARaid5 Config Service

Service Name	Status	Startup Type	Account Name
SATARaid5 Configuration Service	Running	Automatic	LocalSystem

SCardSvr

Service Name	Status	Startup Type	Account Name
Smart Card	Stopped	Manual	NT AUTHORITY\LocalService

Schedule

Service Name	Status	Startup Type	Account Name
Task Scheduler	Running	Automatic	LocalSystem

seclogon

Service Name	Status	Startup Type	Account Name
Secondary Logon	Running	Automatic	LocalSystem

SENS

Service Name	Status	Startup Type	Account Name
System Event Notification	Running	Automatic	LocalSystem

SharedAccess

Service Name	Status	Startup Type	Account Name
Windows Firewall/Internet Connection Sharing	Stopped	Disabled	LocalSystem

ShellHWDetection

Service Name	Status	Startup Type	Account Name
Shell Hardware Detection	Running	Automatic	LocalSystem

SiteClientService

Service Name	Status	Startup Type	Account Name
SiteClient Service for VMS	Running	Automatic	LocalSystem

Spooler

Service Name	Status	Startup Type	Account Name
Print Spooler	Running	Automatic	LocalSystem

SQLBrowser

Service Name	Status	Startup Type	Account Name
SQL Server Browser	Running	Automatic	LocalSystem

SQLSERVERAGENT

Service Name	Status	Startup Type	Account Name
SQL Server Agent (MSSQLSERVER)	Running	Automatic	LocalSystem

SQLWriter

Service Name	Status	Startup Type	Account Name
SQL Server VSS Writer	Running	Automatic	LocalSystem

stisvc

Service Name	Status	Startup Type	Account Name
Windows Image Acquisition (WIA)	Stopped	Disabled	NT AUTHORITY\LocalService

swprv

Service Name	Status	Startup Type	Account Name
Microsoft Software Shadow Copy Provider	Stopped	Manual	LocalSystem

SysmonLog

Service Name	Status	Startup Type	Account Name
Performance Logs and Alerts	Stopped	Manual	NT Authority\NetworkService

TapiSrv

Service Name	Status	Startup Type	Account Name
Telephony	Running	Manual	LocalSystem

TermService

Service Name	Status	Startup Type	Account Name
Terminal Services	Running	Manual	LocalSystem

Themes

Service Name	Status	Startup Type	Account Name
Themes	Stopped	Disabled	LocalSystem

TlntSvr

Service Name	Status	Startup Type	Account Name
Telnet	Stopped	Disabled	NT AUTHORITY\LocalService

TrkSvr

Service Name	Status	Startup Type	Account Name
Distributed Link Tracking Server	Stopped	Disabled	LocalSystem

TrkWks

Service Name	Status	Startup Type	Account Name
Distributed Link Tracking Client	Running	Automatic	LocalSystem

Tssdis

Service Name	Status	Startup Type	Account Name
Terminal Services Session Directory	Stopped	Disabled	LocalSystem

UMWdf

Service Name	Status	Startup Type	Account Name
Windows User Mode Driver Framework	Stopped	Manual	NT AUTHORITY\LocalService

uploadmgr

Service Name	Status	Startup Type	Account Name
Upload Manager	Stopped	Manual	LocalSystem

UPS

Service Name	Status	Startup Type	Account Name
Uninterruptible Power Supply	Stopped	Manual	NT AUTHORITY\LocalService

vds

Service Name	Status	Startup Type	Account Name
Virtual Disk Service	Stopped	Manual	LocalSystem

Virtual Server

Service Name	Status	Startup Type	Account Name
Virtual Server	Stopped	Automatic	NT AUTHORITY\NetworkService

vrmonsvc

Service Name	Status	Startup Type	Account Name
ViRobot for WinNT(tm) Monitoring	Stopped	Automatic	LocalSystem

vrupsvr

Service Name	Status	Startup Type	Account Name
ViRobot for WinNT(tm) Update	Running	Automatic	LocalSystem

VSS

Service Name	Status	Startup Type	Account Name
Volume Shadow Copy	Stopped	Manual	LocalSystem

W32Time

Service Name	Status	Startup Type	Account Name
Windows Time	Running	Automatic	NT AUTHORITY\LocalService

W3SVC

Service Name	Status	Startup Type	Account Name
World Wide Web Publishing Service	Running	Automatic	LocalSystem

WebClient

Service Name	Status	Startup Type	Account Name
WebClient	Stopped	Disabled	NT AUTHORITY\LocalService

WinHttpAutoProxySvc

Service Name	Status	Startup Type	Account Name
WinHTTP Web Proxy Auto-Discovery Service	Stopped	Manual	NT AUTHORITY\LocalService

winmgmt

Service Name	Status	Startup Type	Account Name
Windows Management Instrumentation	Running	Automatic	LocalSystem

WmdmPmSN

Service Name	Status	Startup Type	Account Name
Portable Media Serial Number Service	Stopped	Manual	LocalSystem

Wmi

Service Name	Status	Startup Type	Account Name
Windows Management Instrumentation Driver	Stopped	Manual	LocalSystem

WmiApSrv

Service Name	Status	Startup Type	Account Name
WMI Performance Adapter	Stopped	Manual	LocalSystem

WSusCertServer

Service Name	Status	Startup Type	Account Name
WSusCertServer	Stopped	Manual	LocalSystem

WsusService

Service Name	Status	Startup Type	Account Name
Update Services	Running	Automatic	NT AUTHORITY\NetworkService

wuauserv

Service Name	Status	Startup Type	Account Name
Automatic Updates	Running	Automatic	LocalSystem

WZCSVC

Service Name	Status	Startup Type	Account Name
Wireless Configuration	Running	Automatic	LocalSystem

xmlprov

Service Name	Status	Startup Type	Account Name
Network Provisioning Service	Stopped	Manual	LocalSystem

Processes

CliSvc.exe

PID : 724
PPID : 884
User Name : SYSTEM
Path : C:\SiteClient\clisvc.exe
Domain : NT AUTHORITY
Command Line : C:\SiteClient\clisvc.exe
Handle Count : 80
Thread Count : 5
Priority : 8

csrss.exe

PID : 632
PPID : 332
User Name : SYSTEM
Path : C:\WINDOWS\system32\csrss.exe
Domain : NT AUTHORITY
Command Line : C:\WINDOWS\system32\csrss.exe ObjectDirectory=\Windows SharedSection=1024,3072,512
Windows=On SubSystemType=Windows ServerDll=basesrv,1 ServerDll=winsrv:UserServerDllInitialization,3
ServerDll=winsrv:ConServerDllInitialization,2 ProfileControl=Off MaxRequ

Handle Count : 121
Thread Count : 10
Priority : 13

csrss.exe

PID : 776
PPID : 332
User Name : SYSTEM
Path : C:\WINDOWS\system32\csrss.exe
Domain : NT AUTHORITY
Command Line : C:\WINDOWS\system32\csrss.exe ObjectDirectory=\Windows SharedSection=1024,3072,512
Windows=On SubSystemType=Windows ServerDll=basesrv,1 ServerDll=winsrv:UserServerDllInitialization,3
ServerDll=winsrv:ConServerDllInitialization,2 ProfileControl=Off MaxRequ

Handle Count : 762
Thread Count : 16
Priority : 13

ctfmon.exe

PID : 428
PPID : 1944
User Name : Administrator
Path : C:\WINDOWS\system32\ctfmon.exe
Domain : PRODUCTION

Command Line : "C:\WINDOWS\system32\ctfmon.exe"
Handle Count : 68
Thread Count : 1
Priority : 8

ctfmon.exe

PID : 12812
PPID : 11884
User Name : Administrator
Path : C:\WINDOWS\system32\ctfmon.exe
Domain : PRODUCTION
Command Line : "C:\WINDOWS\system32\ctfmon.exe"
Handle Count : 68
Thread Count : 1
Priority : 8

dfssvc.exe

PID : 2344
PPID : 884
User Name : SYSTEM
Path : C:\WINDOWS\system32\Dfssvc.exe
Domain : NT AUTHORITY
Command Line : C:\WINDOWS\system32\Dfssvc.exe
Handle Count : 76
Thread Count : 9
Priority : 8

dns.exe

PID : 560
PPID : 884
User Name : SYSTEM
Path : C:\WINDOWS\System32\dns.exe
Domain : NT AUTHORITY
Command Line : C:\WINDOWS\System32\dns.exe
Handle Count : 166
Thread Count : 13
Priority : 8

exmgmt.exe

PID : 2424
PPID : 884
User Name : SYSTEM
Path : C:\Program Files\Exchsrvr\bin\exmgmt.exe
Domain : NT AUTHORITY
Command Line : "C:\Program Files\Exchsrvr\bin\exmgmt.exe"
Handle Count : 97
Thread Count : 6
Priority : 8

explorer.exe

PID : 1944
PPID : 3732
User Name : Administrator
Path : C:\WINDOWS\Explorer.EXE
Domain : PRODUCTION
Command Line : C:\WINDOWS\Explorer.EXE
Handle Count : 353
Thread Count : 8
Priority : 8

explorer.exe

PID : 11884

PPID : 13884
User Name : Administrator
Path : C:\WINDOWS\Explorer.EXE
Domain : PRODUCTION
Command Line : C:\WINDOWS\Explorer.EXE
Handle Count : 371
Thread Count : 9
Priority : 8

inetinfo.exe

PID : 920
PPID : 884
User Name : SYSTEM
Path : C:\WINDOWS\system32\inetsrv\inetinfo.exe
Domain : NT AUTHORITY
Command Line : C:\WINDOWS\system32\inetsrv\inetinfo.exe
Handle Count : 187
Thread Count : 9
Priority : 8

jucheck.exe

PID : 1828
PPID : 2112
User Name : Administrator
Path : C:\Program Files\Java\j2re1.4.2_05\bin\jucheck.exe
Domain : PRODUCTION
Command Line : -auto
Handle Count : 187
Thread Count : 4
Priority : 8

jucheck.exe

PID : 12872
PPID : 12592
User Name : Administrator
Path : C:\Program Files\Java\j2re1.4.2_05\bin\jucheck.exe
Domain : PRODUCTION
Command Line : -auto
Handle Count : 190
Thread Count : 4
Priority : 8

jusched.exe

PID : 2112
PPID : 1944
User Name : Administrator
Path : C:\Program Files\Java\j2re1.4.2_05\bin\jusched.exe
Domain : PRODUCTION
Command Line : "C:\Program Files\Java\j2re1.4.2_05\bin\jusched.exe"
Handle Count : 37
Thread Count : 1
Priority : 8

jusched.exe

PID : 12592
PPID : 11884
User Name : Administrator
Path : C:\Program Files\Java\j2re1.4.2_05\bin\jusched.exe
Domain : PRODUCTION
Command Line : "C:\Program Files\Java\j2re1.4.2_05\bin\jusched.exe"
Handle Count : 34
Thread Count : 1

Priority : 8

locator.exe

PID : 508
PPID : 884
User Name : NETWORK SERVICE
Path : C:\WINDOWS\system32\locator.exe
Domain : NT AUTHORITY
Command Line : C:\WINDOWS\system32\locator.exe
Handle Count : 42
Thread Count : 3
Priority : 8

lsass.exe

PID : 908
PPID : 832
User Name : SYSTEM
Path : C:\WINDOWS\system32\lsass.exe
Domain : NT AUTHORITY
Command Line : C:\WINDOWS\system32\lsass.exe
Handle Count : 727
Thread Count : 37
Priority : 9

msdtc.exe

PID : 492
PPID : 884
User Name : NETWORK SERVICE
Path : C:\WINDOWS\system32\msdtc.exe
Domain : NT AUTHORITY
Command Line : C:\WINDOWS\system32\msdtc.exe
Handle Count : 168
Thread Count : 20
Priority : 8

MsDtsSrvr.exe

PID : 1104
PPID : 884
User Name : NETWORK SERVICE
Path : C:\Program Files\Microsoft SQL Server\90\DTS\Binn\MsDtsSrvr.exe
Domain : NT AUTHORITY
Command Line : "C:\Program Files\Microsoft SQL Server\90\DTS\Binn\MsDtsSrvr.exe"
Handle Count : 234
Thread Count : 6
Priority : 8

msftesql.exe

PID : 1472
PPID : 884
User Name : SYSTEM
Path : C:\Program Files\Microsoft SQL Server\MSSQL.1\MSSQL\Binn\msftesql.exe
Domain : NT AUTHORITY
Command Line : "C:\Program Files\Microsoft SQL Server\MSSQL.1\MSSQL\Binn\msftesql.exe" -s:MSSQL.1 -
f:MSSQLSERVER
Handle Count : 391
Thread Count : 6
Priority : 8

msmdsrv.exe

PID : 1836
PPID : 884
User Name : SYSTEM

Path : C:\Program Files\Microsoft SQL Server\MSSQL.2\OLAP\bin\msmdsrv.exe
Domain : NT AUTHORITY
Command Line : "C:\Program Files\Microsoft SQL Server\MSSQL.2\OLAP\bin\msmdsrv.exe" -s "C:\Program Files\Microsoft SQL Server\MSSQL.2\OLAP\Config"
Handle Count : 692
Thread Count : 17
Priority : 8

ntfrs.exe

PID : 356
PPID : 884
User Name : SYSTEM
Path : C:\WINDOWS\system32\ntfrs.exe
Domain : NT AUTHORITY
Command Line : C:\WINDOWS\system32\ntfrs.exe
Handle Count : 257
Thread Count : 17
Priority : 8

rdpclip.exe

PID : 2728
PPID : 996
User Name : Administrator
Path : C:\WINDOWS\system32\rdpclip.exe
Domain : PRODUCTION
Command Line : rdpclip
Handle Count : 67
Thread Count : 3
Priority : 8

SATARaid5ConfigService.exe

PID : 660
PPID : 884
User Name : SYSTEM
Path : C:\Program Files\Silicon Image\3124-W-I32-R SATARAID5\SATARaid5ConfigService.exe
Domain : NT AUTHORITY
Command Line : "C:\Program Files\Silicon Image\3124-W-I32-R SATARAID5\SATARaid5ConfigService.exe"
Handle Count : 51
Thread Count : 2
Priority : 8

services.exe

PID : 884
PPID : 832
User Name : SYSTEM
Path : C:\WINDOWS\system32\services.exe
Domain : NT AUTHORITY
Command Line : C:\WINDOWS\system32\services.exe
Handle Count : 541
Thread Count : 16
Priority : 9

SiteCli.exe

PID : 944
PPID : 724
User Name : SYSTEM
Path : C:\SiteClient\SiteCli.exe
Domain : NT AUTHORITY
Command Line : "C:\SiteClient\SiteCli.exe"
Handle Count : 50
Thread Count : 2
Priority : 8

smss.exe
PID : 332
PPID : 4
User Name : SYSTEM
Domain : NT AUTHORITY
Command Line : \SystemRoot\System32\smss.exe
Handle Count : 25
Thread Count : 2
Priority : 11

spoolsv.exe
PID : 448
PPID : 884
User Name : SYSTEM
Path : C:\WINDOWS\system32\spoolsv.exe
Domain : NT AUTHORITY
Command Line : C:\WINDOWS\system32\spoolsv.exe
Handle Count : 173
Thread Count : 14
Priority : 8

SQLAGENT90.EXE
PID : 2700
PPID : 884
User Name : SYSTEM
Path : C:\Program Files\Microsoft SQL Server\MSSQL.1\MSSQL\Binn\SQLAGENT90.EXE
Domain : NT AUTHORITY
Command Line : "C:\Program Files\Microsoft SQL Server\MSSQL.1\MSSQL\Binn\SQLAGENT90.EXE" -i
MSSQLSERVER
Handle Count : 418
Thread Count : 12
Priority : 8

sqlbrowser.exe
PID : 1328
PPID : 884
User Name : SYSTEM
Path : C:\Program Files\Microsoft SQL Server\90\Shared\sqlbrowser.exe
Domain : NT AUTHORITY
Command Line : "C:\Program Files\Microsoft SQL Server\90\Shared\sqlbrowser.exe"
Handle Count : 390
Thread Count : 12
Priority : 8

sqlservr.exe
PID : 1508
PPID : 884
User Name : NETWORK SERVICE
Path : C:\WINDOWS\SYSMSI\SSEE\MSSQL.2005\MSSQL\Binn\sqlservr.exe
Domain : NT AUTHORITY
Command Line : C:\WINDOWS\SYSMSI\SSEE\MSSQL.2005\MSSQL\Binn\sqlservr.exe -sMICROSOFT##SSEE

Handle Count : 550
Thread Count : 31
Priority : 8

sqlservr.exe
PID : 1620
PPID : 884
User Name : SYSTEM
Path : C:\Program Files\Microsoft SQL Server\MSSQL.1\MSSQL\Binn\sqlservr.exe

Domain : NT AUTHORITY
Command Line : "C:\Program Files\Microsoft SQL Server\MSSQL.1\MSSQL\Binn\sqlservr.exe" -sMSSQLSERVER

Handle Count : 478
Thread Count : 34
Priority : 8

sqlwriter.exe

PID : 1572
PPID : 884
User Name : SYSTEM
Path : C:\Program Files\Microsoft SQL Server\90\Shared\sqlwriter.exe
Domain : NT AUTHORITY
Command Line : "C:\Program Files\Microsoft SQL Server\90\Shared\sqlwriter.exe"
Handle Count : 71
Thread Count : 3
Priority : 8

svchost.exe

PID : 444
PPID : 884
User Name : LOCAL SERVICE
Path : C:\WINDOWS\system32\svchost.exe
Domain : NT AUTHORITY
Command Line : C:\WINDOWS\system32\svchost.exe -k regsvc
Handle Count : 58
Thread Count : 3
Priority : 8

svchost.exe

PID : 752
PPID : 884
User Name : SYSTEM
Path : C:\WINDOWS\System32\svchost.exe
Domain : NT AUTHORITY
Command Line : C:\WINDOWS\System32\svchost.exe -k WinErr
Handle Count : 54
Thread Count : 2
Priority : 8

svchost.exe

PID : 1132
PPID : 884
User Name : SYSTEM
Path : C:\WINDOWS\system32\svchost.exe
Domain : NT AUTHORITY
Command Line : C:\WINDOWS\system32\svchost.exe -k DcomLaunch
Handle Count : 83
Thread Count : 6
Priority : 8

svchost.exe

PID : 1456
PPID : 884
User Name : SYSTEM
Path : C:\WINDOWS\System32\svchost.exe
Domain : NT AUTHORITY
Command Line : C:\WINDOWS\System32\svchost.exe -k tapisrv
Handle Count : 216
Thread Count : 14
Priority : 8

svchost.exe

PID : 1744
PPID : 884
User Name : NETWORK SERVICE
Path : C:\WINDOWS\system32\svchost.exe
Domain : NT AUTHORITY
Command Line : C:\WINDOWS\system32\svchost.exe -k rpcss
Handle Count : 342
Thread Count : 12
Priority : 8

svchost.exe

PID : 1812
PPID : 884
User Name : NETWORK SERVICE
Path : C:\WINDOWS\system32\svchost.exe
Domain : NT AUTHORITY
Command Line : C:\WINDOWS\system32\svchost.exe -k NetworkService
Handle Count : 155
Thread Count : 10
Priority : 8

svchost.exe

PID : 1856
PPID : 884
User Name : LOCAL SERVICE
Path : C:\WINDOWS\system32\svchost.exe
Domain : NT AUTHORITY
Command Line : C:\WINDOWS\system32\svchost.exe -k LocalService
Handle Count : 169
Thread Count : 12
Priority : 8

svchost.exe

PID : 1904
PPID : 884
User Name : SYSTEM
Path : C:\WINDOWS\System32\svchost.exe
Domain : NT AUTHORITY
Command Line : C:\WINDOWS\System32\svchost.exe -k netsvcs
Handle Count : 10,479
Thread Count : 86
Priority : 8

svchost.exe

PID : 2788
PPID : 884
User Name : SYSTEM
Path : C:\WINDOWS\System32\svchost.exe
Domain : NT AUTHORITY
Command Line : C:\WINDOWS\System32\svchost.exe -k iissvcs
Handle Count : 155
Thread Count : 16
Priority : 8

svchost.exe

PID : 3316
PPID : 884
User Name : SYSTEM
Path : C:\WINDOWS\System32\svchost.exe
Domain : NT AUTHORITY

Command Line : C:\WINDOWS\System32\svchost.exe -k termsvcs
Handle Count : 187
Thread Count : 23
Priority : 8

System

PID : 4
User Name : SYSTEM
Domain : NT AUTHORITY
Handle Count : 988
Thread Count : 64
Priority : 8

System Idle Process

Thread Count : 1

VrUpSvr.exe

PID : 2192
PPID : 884
User Name : SYSTEM
Path : C:\Program Files\ViRobot NT\vrupsvr.exe
Domain : NT AUTHORITY
Command Line : "C:\Program Files\ViRobot NT\vrupsvr.exe"
Handle Count : 26
Thread Count : 2
Priority : 8

w3wp.exe

PID : 17712
PPID : 2788
User Name : NETWORK SERVICE
Path : c:\windows\system32\inetsrv\w3wp.exe
Domain : NT AUTHORITY
Command Line : c:\windows\system32\inetsrv\w3wp.exe -a \\.\pipe\iisipmeb3ba131-945b-4b0d-b462-87a83035a550 -t 20 -ap "WsusPool"
Handle Count : 787
Thread Count : 34
Priority : 8

w3wp.exe

PID : 18128
PPID : 2788
User Name : NETWORK SERVICE
Path : c:\windows\system32\inetsrv\w3wp.exe
Domain : NT AUTHORITY
Command Line : c:\windows\system32\inetsrv\w3wp.exe -a \\.\pipe\iisipm40958b73-ecd2-4afe-a75f-1fd8c1dc6f23 -t 20 -ap "DefaultAppPool"
Handle Count : 129
Thread Count : 11
Priority : 8

winlogon.exe

PID : 832
PPID : 332
User Name : SYSTEM
Path : C:\WINDOWS\system32\winlogon.exe
Domain : NT AUTHORITY
Command Line : winlogon.exe
Handle Count : 639
Thread Count : 21
Priority : 13

winlogon.exe

PID : 996
PPID : 332
User Name : SYSTEM
Path : C:\WINDOWS\system32\winlogon.exe
Domain : NT AUTHORITY
Command Line : winlogon.exe
Handle Count : 344
Thread Count : 14
Priority : 13

wmiprvse.exe

PID : 1500
PPID : 1132
User Name : SYSTEM
Path : C:\WINDOWS\system32\wbem\wmiprvse.exe
Domain : NT AUTHORITY
Command Line : C:\WINDOWS\system32\wbem\wmiprvse.exe
Handle Count : 160
Thread Count : 4
Priority : 8

wmiprvse.exe

PID : 17480
PPID : 1132
User Name : NETWORK SERVICE
Path : C:\WINDOWS\system32\wbem\wmiprvse.exe
Domain : NT AUTHORITY
Command Line : C:\WINDOWS\system32\wbem\wmiprvse.exe
Handle Count : 209
Thread Count : 11
Priority : 8

wsusservice.exe

PID : 2252
PPID : 884
User Name : NETWORK SERVICE
Path : C:\Program Files\Update Services\Service\bin\WsusService.exe
Domain : NT AUTHORITY
Command Line : "C:\Program Files\Update Services\Service\bin\WsusService.exe"
Handle Count : 603
Thread Count : 17
Priority : 8

Devices

USB Devices

USB Root Hub

Description:	USB Root Hub
Manufacturer:	(Standard USB Host Controller)

USB Root Hub

Description:	USB Root Hub
Manufacturer:	(Standard USB Host Controller)

Generic USB Hub

Description:	Generic USB Hub
Manufacturer:	(Generic USB Hub)

No blacklisted USB Devices detected.

Network Devices

Phisical Device

Intel(R) PRO/100 VE Network Connection
DHCP Set:	True
Status:	Unplugged

1394 Net Adapter
MAC Address:	62:D1:8B:C0:A3:4B
DHCP Set:	True
Status:	Unplugged

D-Link DGE-530T Gigabit Ethernet Adapter
MAC Address:	00:11:95:FD:CB:B8
IP Address(es):	147.100.100.6
Hostname:	sentinal
DHCP Set:	False
DNS Server(s):	147.100.100.34, 147.100.100.6
Gateway(s):	147.100.100.100
Status:	Plugged in

Virtual Devices

WAN Miniport (L2TP)
DHCP Set:	False
Status:	Unplugged

WAN Miniport (PPTP)
MAC Address:	50:50:54:50:30:30
DHCP Set:	False
Status:	Unplugged

WAN Miniport (PPPOE)
MAC Address:	33:50:6F:45:30:30
DHCP Set:	False
Status:	Unplugged

Direct Parallel
DHCP Set:	False
Status:	Unplugged

WAN Miniport (IP)
DHCP Set:	False
Status:	Unplugged

Software Enumerated Devices

RAS Async Adapter
DHCP Set:	False
Status:	Unplugged

No blacklisted devices detected.

Shares

Name	Remark
ADMIN$	Remote Admin
C$	Default share
data	N/A
F	N/A
F$	Default share
G	Server Backups
G$	Default share
IPC$	Remote IPC
UpdateServicesPackages	A network share to be used by client systems for collecting all
WsusContent	A network share to be used by Local Publishing to place
WSUSTemp	A network share used by Local Publishing from a Remote

Open Ports

No Open Ports found.

Installed Applications

Installed Applications

Application Name	Publisher	Version
3124-W-I32-R SATARAID5	Silicon Image	0.0.1
Active Directory Management Pack Helper Object	Microsoft Corporation	1.0.3
DGE-530T	D-Link	1.00.000
GDR 3054 for SQL Server Analysis Services 2005 ENU (KB934458)	Microsoft Corporation	9.2.3054
GDR 3054 for SQL Server Database Services 2005 ENU (KB934458)	Microsoft Corporation	9.2.3054
GDR 3054 for SQL Server Integration Services 2005 ENU (KB934458)	Microsoft Corporation	9.2.3054
GDR 3054 for SQL Server Notification Services 2005 ENU (KB934458)	Microsoft Corporation	9.2.3054
GDR 3054 for SQL Server Tools and Workstation Components 2005 ENU (KB934458)	Microsoft Corporation	9.2.3054
Hotfix for Windows Server 2003 (KB928388)	Microsoft Corporation	1
Hotfix for Windows Server 2003 (KB929120)	Microsoft Corporation	1
Java 2 Runtime Environment, SE v1.4.2_05	Sun Microsystems, Inc.	1.4.2_05
LANsurveyor	Neon Software	9.6.1
MGI PhotoSuite		
Microsoft .NET Framework 2.0	Microsoft Corporation	
Microsoft .NET Framework 3.0	Microsoft Corporation	
Microsoft Exchange	Microsoft Corporation	
Microsoft Office 2003 Web Components	Microsoft Corporation	11.0.6558.0
Microsoft SQL Server 2005	Microsoft Corporation	
Microsoft SQL Server 2005 Backward compatibility	Microsoft Corporation	8.05.2004
Microsoft SQL Server 2005 Books Online (English)	Microsoft Corporation	9.00.1399.06
Microsoft SQL Server Native Client	Microsoft Corporation	9.00.3042.00
Microsoft SQL Server Setup Support Files (English)	Microsoft Corporation	9.00.3042.00
Microsoft SQL Server VSS Writer	Microsoft Corporation	9.00.3042.00
Microsoft Visual Studio 2005 Premier Partner Edition - ENU	Microsoft Corporation	8.0.50728
Microsoft Windows Server Update Services 3.0	Microsoft Corporation	3.0.6000.318
MSXML 6.0 Parser	Microsoft Corporation	6.10.1129.0
Security Update for Exchange Server 2003 (KB894549)	Microsoft Corporation	1
Security Update for Microsoft .NET Framework 2.0 (KB917283)	Microsoft Corporation	1
Security Update for Microsoft .NET Framework 2.0 (KB922770)	Microsoft Corporation	1
Security Update for Windows Media Player (KB911564)	Microsoft Corporation	
Security Update for Windows Media Player 6.4 (KB925398)	Microsoft Corporation	
Security Update for Windows Server 2003 (KB890046)	Microsoft Corporation	1
Security Update for Windows Server 2003 (KB893756)	Microsoft Corporation	1
Security Update for Windows Server 2003 (KB896358)	Microsoft Corporation	20050421.234609
Security Update for Windows Server 2003 (KB896422)	Microsoft Corporation	1
Security Update for Windows Server 2003 (KB896424)	Microsoft Corporation	1
Security Update for Windows Server 2003 (KB896428)	Microsoft Corporation	1
Security Update for Windows Server 2003 (KB899587)	Microsoft Corporation	1
Security Update for Windows Server 2003 (KB899588)	Microsoft Corporation	1
Security Update for Windows Server 2003 (KB899589)	Microsoft Corporation	1
Security Update for Windows Server 2003 (KB899591)	Microsoft Corporation	1
Security Update for Windows Server 2003 (KB901017)	Microsoft Corporation	1
Security Update for Windows Server 2003 (KB901214)	Microsoft Corporation	1
Security Update for Windows Server 2003 (KB902400)	Microsoft Corporation	1
Security Update for Windows Server 2003 (KB904706)	Microsoft Corporation	1
Security Update for Windows Server 2003 (KB905414)	Microsoft Corporation	1
Security Update for Windows Server 2003 (KB908519)	Microsoft Corporation	1

Security Update for Windows Server 2003 (KB908531)	Microsoft Corporation	1
Security Update for Windows Server 2003 (KB911280)	Microsoft Corporation	1
Security Update for Windows Server 2003 (KB911562)	Microsoft Corporation	1
Security Update for Windows Server 2003 (KB911567)	Microsoft Corporation	1
Security Update for Windows Server 2003 (KB911927)	Microsoft Corporation	1
Security Update for Windows Server 2003 (KB912919)	Microsoft Corporation	1
Security Update for Windows Server 2003 (KB913446)	Microsoft Corporation	1
Security Update for Windows Server 2003 (KB914388)	Microsoft Corporation	1
Security Update for Windows Server 2003 (KB914389)	Microsoft Corporation	1
Security Update for Windows Server 2003 (KB917159)	Microsoft Corporation	1
Security Update for Windows Server 2003 (KB917422)	Microsoft Corporation	1
Security Update for Windows Server 2003 (KB917537)	Microsoft Corporation	1
Security Update for Windows Server 2003 (KB917734)	Microsoft Corporation	1
Security Update for Windows Server 2003 (KB917953)	Microsoft Corporation	1
Security Update for Windows Server 2003 (KB918439)	Microsoft Corporation	1
Security Update for Windows Server 2003 (KB920213)	Microsoft Corporation	1
Security Update for Windows Server 2003 (KB920214)	Microsoft Corporation	1
Security Update for Windows Server 2003 (KB920670)	Microsoft Corporation	1
Security Update for Windows Server 2003 (KB920683)	Microsoft Corporation	1
Security Update for Windows Server 2003 (KB920685)	Microsoft Corporation	1
Security Update for Windows Server 2003 (KB921398)	Microsoft Corporation	1
Security Update for Windows Server 2003 (KB921883)	Microsoft Corporation	1
Security Update for Windows Server 2003 (KB922616)	Microsoft Corporation	1
Security Update for Windows Server 2003 (KB922819)	Microsoft Corporation	1
Security Update for Windows Server 2003 (KB923191)	Microsoft Corporation	1
Security Update for Windows Server 2003 (KB923414)	Microsoft Corporation	1
Security Update for Windows Server 2003 (KB923689)	Microsoft Corporation	1
Security Update for Windows Server 2003 (KB923694)	Microsoft Corporation	1
Security Update for Windows Server 2003 (KB923980)	Microsoft Corporation	1
Security Update for Windows Server 2003 (KB924191)	Microsoft Corporation	1
Security Update for Windows Server 2003 (KB925902)	Microsoft Corporation	1
Security Update for Windows Server 2003 (KB930178)	Microsoft Corporation	1
Security Update for Windows Server 2003 (KB931784)	Microsoft Corporation	1
Security Update for Windows Server 2003 (KB932168)	Microsoft Corporation	1
Service Pack 1 for SQL Server Database Services 2005 ENU (KB913090)	Microsoft Corporation	9.1.2047
Service Pack 2 for SQL Server Analysis Services 2005 ENU (KB921896)	Microsoft Corporation	9.2.3042
Service Pack 2 for SQL Server Database Services 2005 ENU (KB921896)	Microsoft Corporation	9.2.3042
Service Pack 2 for SQL Server Integration Services 2005 ENU (KB921896)	Microsoft Corporation	9.2.3042
Service Pack 2 for SQL Server Notification Services 2005 ENU (KB921896)	Microsoft Corporation	9.2.3042
Service Pack 2 for SQL Server Tools and Workstation Components 2005 ENU (KB921896)	Microsoft Corporation	9.2.3042
SQLXML4	Microsoft Corporation	9.00.3042.00
Update for Windows Server 2003 (KB898715)	Microsoft Corporation	20050502.084329
Update for Windows Server 2003 (KB904942)	Microsoft Corporation	1
Update for Windows Server 2003 (KB907265)	Microsoft Corporation	1
Update for Windows Server 2003 (KB908521)	Microsoft Corporation	1
Update for Windows Server 2003 (KB910437)	Microsoft Corporation	1
Update for Windows Server 2003 (KB911897)	Microsoft Corporation	2
Update for Windows Server 2003 (KB916846)	Microsoft Corporation	1
Update for Windows Server 2003 (KB922582)	Microsoft Corporation	1
Update for Windows Server 2003 (KB925720)	Microsoft Corporation	1
Update for Windows Server 2003 (KB925876)	Microsoft Corporation	1
ViRobot 2000 Advanced Server		
VMS SiteClient 2.0		
Windows Imaging Component	Microsoft Corporation	3.0.0.0
Windows Internet Explorer 7	Microsoft Corporation	20061107.210142

No Unauthorized Applications Found.

Policies

Password Policy

Minimum Password Length	Maximum Password Age	Minimum Password Age	Force Logoff	Password History
0 chars	42 days, 22 hours, 47 minutes, 31 seconds	no delay	never force	no history

Security Audit Policy

Auditing Policy	Success	Failure
Audit account logon events	True	False
Audit account management	False	False
Audit directory service access	False	False
Audit logon events	True	False
Audit object access	False	False
Audit policy change	False	False
Audit privilege use	False	False
Audit process tracking	False	False
Audit system events	False	False

Registry Information

Node Name	Registry Entry
	~MHz : 1594
	CSDVersion : Service Pack 1
	CurrentBuildNumber : 3790
	CurrentType : Uniprocessor Free
	CurrentVersion : 5.2
	Default : 0409
	DriverDesc : NVIDIA RIVA TNT2 Model 64/Model 64 Pro (Microsoft Corporation)
	Identifier : x86 Family 15 Model 1 Stepping 2
	InstallLanguage : 0409
	PathName : C:\WINDOWS
	ProductId : 69712-347-5727824-42248
	ProductName : Microsoft Windows Server 2003
	RegisteredOrganization : Posey Enterprises
	RegisteredOwner : Brien Posey
	SoftwareType : SYSTEM
	SourcePath : E:\ENGLISH\WIN2003\STANDARD\I386
	SystemRoot : C:\WINDOWS
	VendorIdentifier : GenuineIntel
Run	InitClient : C:\SiteClient\InitCli.exe
Run	SiteClient : C:\SiteClient\SiteCli.exe
Run	SunJavaUpdateSched : C:\Program Files\Java\j2re1.4.2_05\bin\jusched.exe
Run	VrBootScan : C:\Program Files\ViRobot NT\VRBScan.exe

Notes from the Underground…

Component Theft

It probably seems weird talking about compiling a hardware inventory in a book about network security, but it does have its place. Many years ago, I was working for an organization that had a network with over 25,000 nodes locally, and no telling how many nodes internationally. At any rate, one of the members of the help desk staff decided to supplement his income by stealing memory and other components out of workstations.

When it came to components such as hard drives and video cards, he would just report the component as being faulty, replace the component, and then keep and resell the original component, which was still good. When it came to memory though, he would simply steal one of the memory modules out of each workstation that he worked on, with the assumption that none of the end users would ever notice.

Unfortunately, this practice went on for quite some time before the individual was caught. Had the organization performed regular hardware inventories, he would have been caught much sooner.

In case you are wondering how the technician was eventually caught, a computer savvy user called his boss to complain that his computer wasn't performing as well since memory had been removed. The boss called the helpdesk to find out why the memory had been removed, and of course the help desk didn't know anything about it. The boss had kept purchase receipts for all of the computers in the department and did his own department wide hardware audit and discovered that many of the machines were missing memory. After becoming suspicious, the boss ordered everyone in the department to tell him any time someone from the help desk worked on their computer, and to give him the technician's name. It wasn't long before a clear pattern developed, and the thief was caught. He would have been caught a lot sooner, however if a product like GFI LANguard Network Security Scanner had existed back then.

Dealing With Information Overload

I have to admit that when I wrote the previous section, I was reluctant to include the excerpt report. One reason for this is that if you look through the report, you can see that the server listed (which I picked at random) is basically a mockery of good security practices. Another reason why I was so hesitant to include the sample report is because it includes information about my network that I would rather not publish in a book. In the end, though, I decided to go ahead and include the report so that I could make two points.

- The Systems Information report provides you with all kinds of fantastic information about your network.

■   If you are gathering information on more than a handful of machines, the Systems Information report probably gives you too much information.

So what do you do if you need to gather specific information from such a massive report? Well, you've actually got a few different options. One option is to export the report to a Microsoft Office document, and then use the Microsoft Office search feature to find the information that you are looking for.

A better option may be to generate an additional report. The nice thing about the way that GFI LANguard Network Security Scanner works is that you don't have to rescan your network every time you want to create a report. You can create as many reports as you want off of the most recent scan.

The reason why this is so handy is because if you look at the report excerpt that I showed you in the previous section, you can see that the report is divided into several different sections. The ReportCenter console offers a separate report for each individual section. For example, if you were primarily interested in the information found in the Devices section, you could run the Devices report on the most recent scan to create a separate report that contains only device-related information.

Another option is to close the ReportCenter. When you do, you will be taken back to the dialog box shown in Figure 6.4. This time, instead of clicking the View Reports button, click the OK button. When you do, the console will display a screen similar to what you see in Figure 6.5.

Figure 6.5 The Management Console Shows Detailed Information About Each Network Device That has Been Scanned

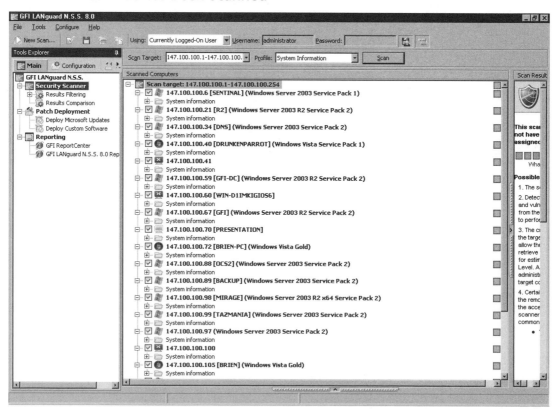

If you look at the figure, you can see that the console displays a hierarchical view of the computers that have been detected. For each detected machine, the console lists the machine's Internet Protocol (IP) address, Network Basic Input/Output System (NetBIOS) name, operating system, and service pack level.

If you look more closely at the figure, you will notice that there are some computers for which only an IP address is listed. The reason for this is because not every device within the IP address range that I scanned is a PC. For example, 147.100.100.100 is a router. Another example of a machine with no system information listed is 147.100.100.41, which is running Red Hat Linux. You can get a minimal amount of information off of non-Windows devices, but this particular scan is really designed to collect information from Windows machines.

With that in mind, let's take a look at the server that I showed you in the report excerpt. As you may recall, the server's name was Sentinal, which I have to admit I misspelled when I originally set the server up. In case you are wondering about the server's rather strange name, it is a reference to a Judas Priest song that was playing at the time that I was setting the server up, but I digress.

Each detected machine contains a folder named System Information. If you expand this folder, you will see sub-folders that correspond to the individual parts of the report. If you select one of these sub-folders, the pane on the right will display the information related to the specified folder, as shown in Figure 6.6.

Figure 6.6 You Can Drill Down to Locate the Specific Information That You Are Looking For

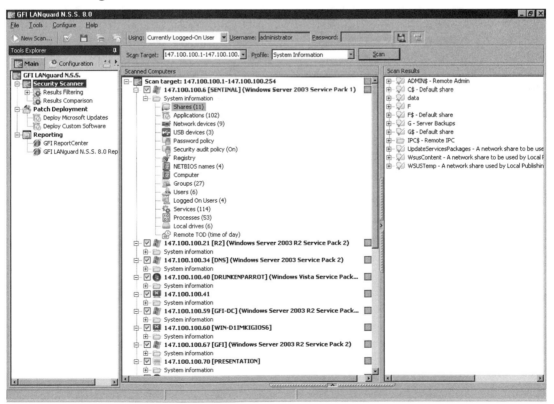

As you can see, the console makes it simple to drill down through the tree and locate specific information about a specific computer.

Compiling a Software Inventory

In the previous section, I showed you how to use a scan as a way of compiling information about the hardware that is in use on your network. However, GFI LANguard Network Security Scanner is much more effective at performing software audits. If you want to see what software is in use on your network, follow these steps:

1. Open the management console, and click the **New Scan** button.

2. When prompted to select the type of scan that you want to perform, choose the Network and Software Auditing option, and click **Next**.

3. The following screen will ask you to choose a scanning profile. Select the **Software Audit** option, as shown in Figure 6.7, and click **Next**.

Figure 6.7 Select the Software Audit Profile

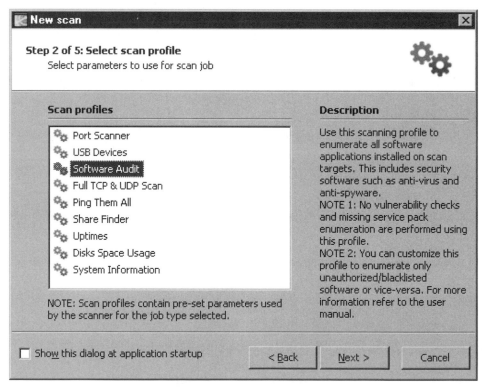

4. The next screen that you encounter will ask you to choose which computers you want to scan. Choose the **Scan a Range of Computers** option, and click **Next**.

5. When prompted, enter the range of IP addresses that you want to scan, and click **Next**.

6. At this point, you will be prompted to enter the credentials that will be used for the scan. Remember that you must specify a user who has administrative permissions for the machines in the IP address range that you specified.

7. Click the **Scan** button to launch the scan.

Are You Owned?

The Problem With Unauthorized Software

When a lot of network administrators go on a hunt for unauthorized software, they are looking for things like video games, malware, or peer-sharing applications. However, any unauthorized software can be a serious issue.

For starters, the software is installed on a computer owned by the company. That makes the company responsible for owning a license for the unauthorized software. If you've got unauthorized software on your workstations, a software audit could end up costing you a bundle.

Another problem with unauthorized software is that it increase support costs. The unauthorized software can potentially cause Windows or other applications to behave abnormally. If the help desk staff members do not even know that the unauthorized software is installed (much less causing the undesirable behavior), then the troubleshooting process will likely take longer than if the computer were in the state that the help desk staff assumes it to be in.

Analyzing the Results

The best way of analyzing the results of the scan, depends on what it is that you want to accomplish. If you want a simple software inventory, I would recommend clicking the **View Reports** button, and running the **Installed Application** report (found under the "System Information" section). This type of report will show you all of the applications that are installed on each machine that was scanned, and what version of each application is installed. You can see a partial view of such a report in Figure 6.8.

Figure 6.8 The Installed Applications Report Lists the Applications That Are Installed on Each Machine

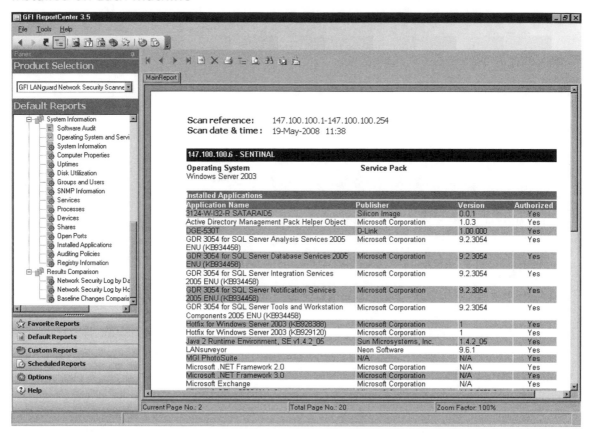

Another way that you can view the scan results, is to go to the management console, and then click on the Applications folder, found beneath the System Information folder for a particular computer. When you do, the applications that have been detected on that machine will be displayed in the column on the right, as shown in Figure 6.9.

Figure 6.9 You Can View the Detected Applications on a PC-By-PC Basis
Through the Management Console

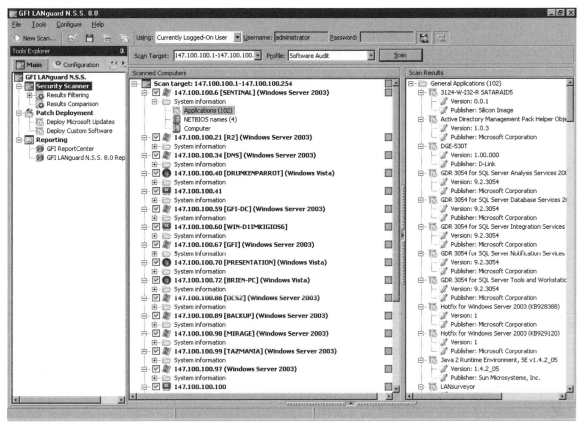

Unfortunately, the management console seems to always take a computer-centric approach to displaying data. This means that while it is easy to look at the security or inventory information for a specific PC, there is no built-in way to look at the data on an application-by-application basis. For example, the console does not allow you to see how many copies of Microsoft Office 2007 are installed, and on which computers.

If you are trying to get a license count for some of your applications, you may be able to get it through the ReportCenter. The ReportCenter offers a report called Software Audit. This report is primarily designed to tell you which machines contain unauthorized applications (which I will talk more about in a moment). However, the report also lists the 20 most commonly installed applications. For each of those applications, the report will tell you how many machines the application is installed on, along with the host name, IP address, and operating system used by each of those machines.

Before you get too excited, I should warn you that the results may not be what you would expect. If you look at Figure 6.10, you can see that the two most commonly installed applications on my network are Microsoft Silverlight, and the Windows Imaging Component, neither of which I am concerned about a license count for.

Figure 6.10 The Software Audit Report Contains a List of the 20 Most Commonly Installed Applications on Your Network

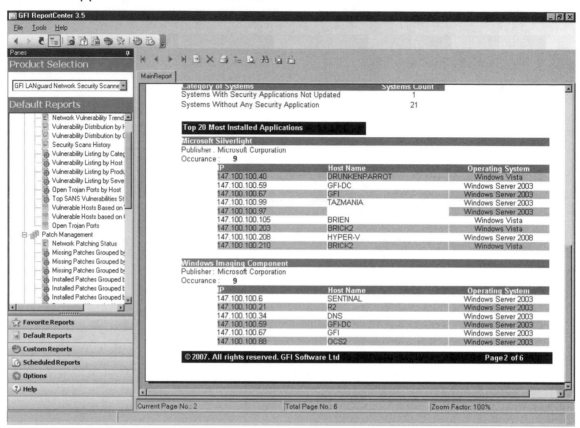

I don't want to waste your time and kill a bunch of trees by reprinting the entire report, but I do feel like you need to be aware of the types of applications that the report tends to give you information on. That being the case, I want to show you a list of the "applications" that were reported as being the most common on my network. You can see the list in Table 6.1.

Table 6.1 These Are the 20 Most Commonly Installed Applications on My Network, as Reported by GFI LANGuard Network Security Scanner

Application Name	Number of Occurrences
Microsoft Silverlight	9
Windows Imaging Component	9
Microsoft .NET Framework 3.0	8
Security Update for Windows Server 2003 (KB925902)	8

Continued

Table 6.1 Continued. These Are the 20 Most Commonly Installed Applications on My Network, as Reported by GFI LANGuard Network Security Scanner

Application Name	Number of Occurrences
Security Update for Windows Server 2003 (KB930178)	8
Security Update for Windows Server 2003 (KB931784)	8
Security Update for Windows Server 2003 (KB932168)	8
Update for Windows Server 2003 (KB925876)	8
Internet Explorer 7	8
MSXML 4.0 SP2 (KB927978)	7
Windows Server 2003 Service Pack 2	7
Microsoft .NET Framework 2.0	6
Microsoft Visual C++ Redistributable	6
Security Update for Windows Media Player 6.4 (KB925398)	6
Adobe Flash Player 9 ActiveX	5
MSXML 4.0 SP2 (KB936181)	5
Update for Windows Server 2003 (KB931836)	5
Update for Windows Server 2003 (KB943729)	5
Microsoft .NET Framework 2.0 Service Pack 1	4
Microsoft Exchange	4

If you look at the list above, you can see why I don't particularly care for this report. Of the twenty items listed, I really only consider two of them to be "real" applications (Internet Explorer 7 and Microsoft Exchange).

Another problem is that all of my Exchange Servers were lumped together. I actually have one Exchange 2003 Server and three Exchange 2007 Servers, but the report just reported four Exchange Servers, which isn't good if I were trying to get a license count.

I also have to question why Microsoft Office 2007 wasn't displayed on the list, since it is installed on at least seven workstations.

Unfortunately, I think that GFI LANguard Network Security Scanner really needs some help in the software inventory department. The good news is that all of the inventory information is stored in a SQL Server database, and it should be simple to write an application that extracts the data and creates a report that better meets your needs. Another option is to use a workaround that I will show you in the next section. You can also improve the report's results by using blacklisting and whitelisting.

Blacklisting and Whitelisting Applications

When I talked about the Software Audit report in the previous section, I mentioned that the report is primarily designed to show you the use of unauthorized applications in your organization. That being the case, you are probably wondering where the list of unauthorized applications comes from.

The first time that I heard about this feature, I assumed that the list of unauthorized applications was pulled from software restriction policies (which is a part of the group policies that are built into Windows). Actually though, the GFI LANguard Network Security Scanner management console allows you to compile a simple list of blacklisted (unauthorized) applications.

To access this list, follow these steps:

1. Open the management console, and click the **Configuration** button.

2. Navigate through the console tree to **Configuration** | **Scanning Profiles** | **System Information**.

3. Select the **All Applications Except the Ones Which Name Contains** option, as shown in Figure 6.11.

Figure 6.11 Choose the "All Applications Except the Ones Which Name Contains" Option

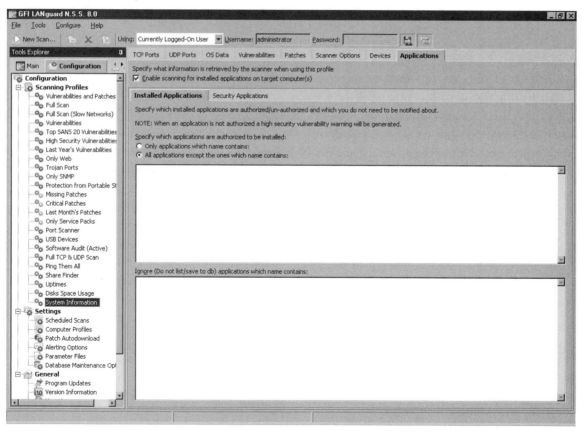

4. Begin populating the list with the names of the applications that you want to blacklist.

If you look back at Figure 6.11, you will notice that the lower section of the screen contains a text box labeled "Ignore." This text box is used for whitelisting applications. The basic idea is that there are some applications that are installed on computers on your network that are supposed to be installed. Since these applications are authorized by you, there is no reason for the Software Audit report to report them to you. Therefore, you can enter the names of these applications into the Ignore list, and the report will not include those applications in its list of most commonly installed applications.

For example, if I know that every server in my organization contains Windows Server 2003 Service Pack 2, I could add the service pack to the list to keep the report from wasting my time telling me about it. You can do this for security updates as well.

Keep in mind that any time you whitelist an application, you are only preventing information about the application from being written to the database during future scans. Any reports that are based on previous scans will still contain information about the whitelisted application.

NOTE

GFI LANguard Network Security Scanner sometimes makes it difficult to know exactly how to type an application name. Generally, the name should be entered in the same way as it appears within the various reports. However, you may have to experiment with entering application names in order to get the results that you are expecting.

Network Documentation

As a network administrator, it is important for you to document your network, and to keep that network documentation up-to-date. After all, you never know when you could be hit by a bus and someone else has to step in and manage the network. Even if you aren't worried about that, I would still recommend that you document your network for a variety of reasons.

Perhaps the most important of these reasons is that good documentation provides evidence of competence. I once knew a guy who was at risk of being fired because some of his network management practices were being called into question. Fortunately, he had documented everything, and the documentation that he had compiled proved that his management techniques adhered to industry best practices.

Another good reason for keeping your network documentation up-to-date is that sometimes the network documentation can help you solve problems. I remember once in the mid 90s, the company that I worked for had a bunch of machines scattered throughout the building that would intermittently lose connectivity. For several weeks nobody could figure out why the problem was happening. Eventually, someone got the idea to check the network documentation and see what all of these machines had in common, and how they differed from the machines that were functioning correctly. It turned out that the machines all had a model of network card that had proven to be defective. Although we had tried swapping network cards on several of the machines, we were using the same model of card for the replacement. The point is that the network documentation helped us to figure out the answer to a rather difficult problem.

Hopefully as you have seen the various reports that GFI LANguard Network Security Scanner makes available, you have realized that this product is not just a security tool, but also rather a product that can also help you with your network documentation. Unfortunately though, GFI LANguard Network Security Scanner was not designed specifically to act as a network documentation product, so there are some areas for which you may need to go outside of the product to complete your documentation. One such area involves creating network diagrams.

Network Diagrams

Although this book is supposed to be about GFI products, I wanted to go ahead and discuss the topic of diagramming your network, because I believe that network diagrams are essential to good network documentation. Since GFI LANguard Network Security Scanner comes so close to being able to thoroughly document a network, I just wanted to show you some extra steps that you can take to augment the documentation that the product is capable of producing.

If you have Windows Vista or Windows Server 2008 machines in your organization, diagramming your network is fairly easy. If you open the Windows Vista Control Panel and then click on the Network and Internet link, followed by the Network and Sharing Center link, you will see a screen similar to the one that's shown in Figure 6.12.

Figure 6.12 Windows Vista and Windows Server 2008 Have Network Mapping Capabilities Built In

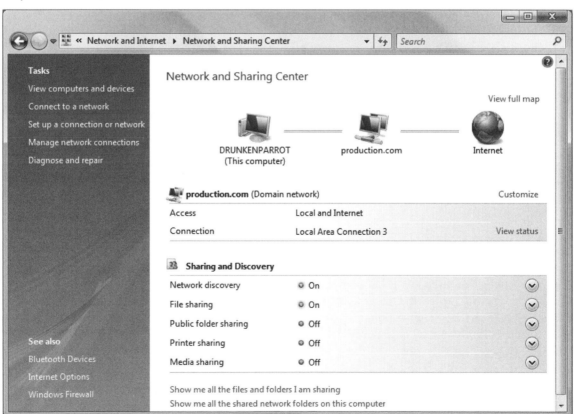

As you can see in the figure, Windows Vista shows you how your computer is connected to the Internet. There is also a link that you can click to display a full network map. Unfortunately, however, Microsoft chose to disable network mapping for any computer that is a domain member. If you want to enable network mapping for Vista you can do so by making some modifications to two group policy objects.

Before I show you how to modify these group policy settings, there is something that you need to understand. The group policy settings that control network mapping were first introduced in Windows Vista. This means that you won't be able to implement these group policy settings at the Site, Domain, or OU levels of your Active Directory, unless you have a domain controller that is running Windows Server 2008. If you do not have a Windows Server 2008 domain controller on your network, you can still enable network mapping by modifying the local security policy on your workstations. To do so, follow these steps:

1. Open the **Group Policy Object Editor** for the policy that you want to modify.

2. Navigate through the console tree to **Computer Configuration | Administrative Templates | Network | Link Layer Topology Discovery**.

3. As you can see in Figure 6.13, there are two group policy settings found in the Link Layer Topology Discovery container. Both of these settings must be enabled.

Figure 6.13 You Must Enable the Link Layer Topology Discovery Through Group Policy Settings

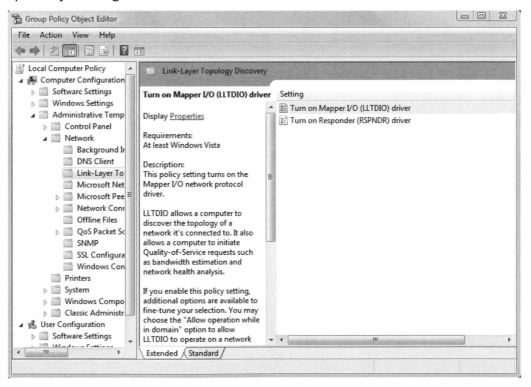

4. When you enable the group policy settings, you must select the **Allow Operation While in Domain** check box for both of the policy settings, as shown in Figure 6.14.

Figure 6.14 You Must Choose the Allow Option While in Domain Mode Option

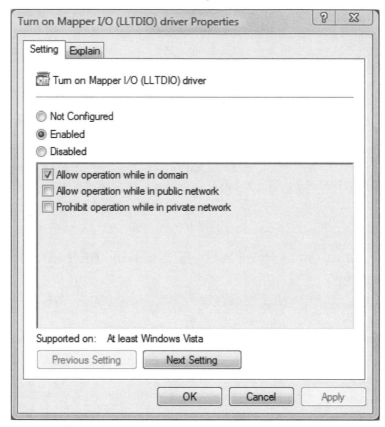

5. Make sure that no other check boxes are selected.

After you enable this setting on a couple of PCs, you can go back to the Network and Sharing Center, and click on the **View Full Map** link. When you do, you will see the PCs for which the group policy settings have been enabled displayed on the map, as shown in Figure 6.15.

Figure 6.15 This is What Vista's Network Map Looks Like

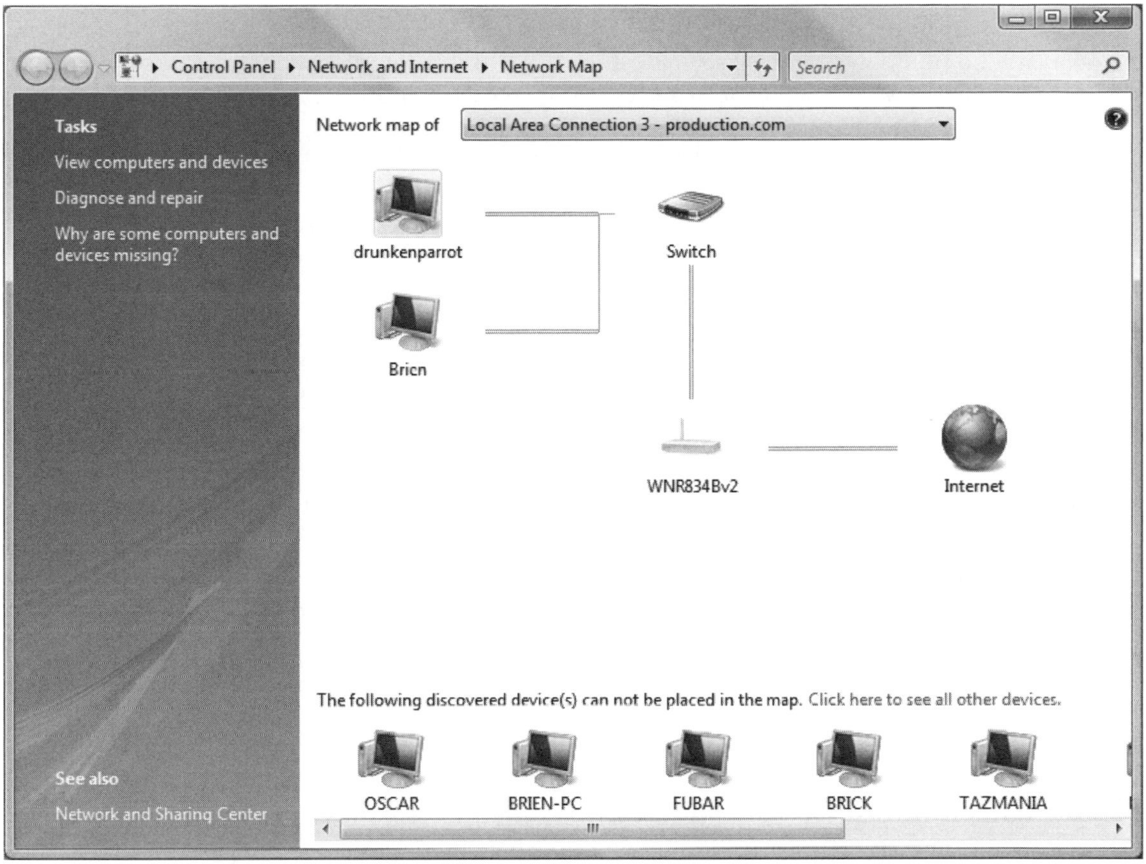

If you look closely at the figure above, you will notice that there are a lot of computers that have not yet been placed on the map. Some of these machines are running Windows Vista or Windows Server 2008, and I just haven't enabled network mapping yet. Others are running Windows Server 2003 or Windows XP, neither of which natively support network mapping. Like most things in life, however, there is a workaround.

Network Mapping for Windows XP

Network mapping is based on the Link Layer Topology Discovery protocol. Neither Windows XP nor Windows Server 2003 natively support this protocol. Microsoft does offer a package that adds Link Layer Topology Discovery support to Windows XP though. You can download the package from: http://support.microsoft.com/kb/922120 Simply install this package onto a computer that is running Windows XP, and the Windows XP computer will appear on all future network maps.

Network Mapping for Windows Server 2003

Microsoft doesn't offer a Link Layer Topology Discovery module for Windows Server 2003, but there is a workaround (but only for 32-bit servers). Keep in mind that this workaround is not supported by Microsoft. To get network mapping to work with Windows Server 2003, follow these steps:

1. Go to http://support.microsoft.com/kb/922120 and download the Windows XP version of the network-mapping patch.

2. When prompted to either run or save the file, choose the **Run** option.

3. Windows will unpack the file, and then display a message telling you that the version of Windows you have installed does not match the update that you are trying to install. *DO NOT CLICK OK.*

4. Open **My Computer**, and then double-click on the **C:** drive.

5. Look for a folder with a long hexadecimal name. On my test server the folder was named **C:\5898e8a8b6b585f5f2**.

6. Open this folder and copy all of the files in it except for the $shtdwn$.req file to a temporary folder.

7. Click **OK** to close the Setup error message. This will cause the original folder containing the Setup files to be automatically deleted.

8. Go to the folder where you copied the files, and then double-click on a subfolder named **Update**.

9. Right-click on the file named **Update.exe** and choose the **Properties** command from the resulting shortcut menu.

10. When the file's properties sheet appears, select the **Compatibility** tab.

11. Select the **Run this Program in Compatibility Mode for** check box.

12. Choose **Windows XP** from the drop-down list, as shown in Figure 6.16.

Figure 6.16 Choose the Windows XP Option From the Drop-down List

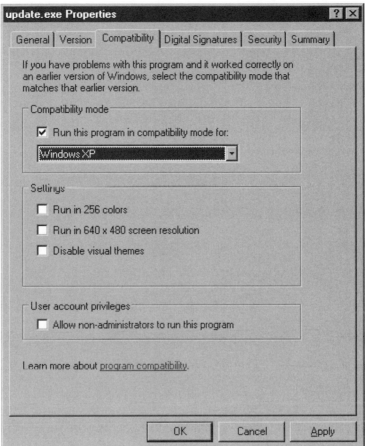

13. Click **OK.**

14. Double click on the **Update.exe** file to install the patch.

It has been my experience that the patch works like a charm on Windows Server 2003, but since it is unsupported, you should use it at your own risk.

Figure 6.17 shows you what a more comprehensive network map looks like. I haven't enabled network mapping for all of my machines, but I did enough for you to get the idea of how network mapping works. Notice in the diagram how Vista differentiates between wireless and wired connections.

Figure 6.17 This is What a More Detailed Network Map Looks Like

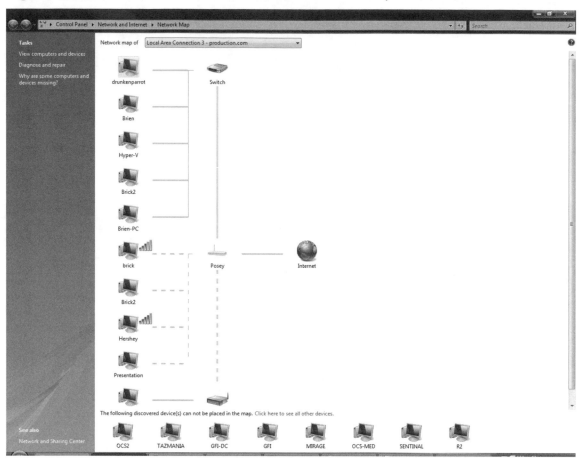

Unfortunately, Windows Vista does have its limits when it comes to mapping. The maps are domain- and network segment-specific. If you need more detailed maps, I would recommend using Microsoft Office Visio 2007. It won't make the maps for you, but it does give you everything that you need to create really detailed network diagrams.

What Else is Missing?

I don't want to get too far off topic, but I do want to at least mention that there are other things that should also be included in your network documentation. Specifically, your documentation should include contact information for the administrative staff, a full description of the policies and procedures used by your organization, and a log of any changes made to network servers.

If you Google the phrase Network Documentation Checklist, you can find various checklists that can help you to complete the documentation process. Here is a link to a checklist that I recently developed: http://searchnetworkingchannel.techtarget.com/generic/0,295582,sid100_gci1308066,00.html

Summary

Hardware and software audits, and network documentation are an important part of keeping a network secure. Only when you know which applications are installed on a computer can you properly maintain those applications. I will talk about how GFI LANguard Network Security Scanner can help you with application maintenance in the next chapter.

Solutions Fast Track

Performing a Hardware Inventory

- ☑ Click the **New Scan** button.
- ☑ Choose the **Network and Software Auditing** button.
- ☑ Choose the **System Information** option.
- ☑ Select the **Scan a Range of Computers** option.
- ☑ Enter the IP addresses that you want to scan.
- ☑ Enter your authentication credentials.
- ☑ Click the **Scan** button.

Compiling a Software Inventory

- ☑ Click the **New Scan** button.
- ☑ Choose the **Network and Software Auditing** button.
- ☑ Choose the **Software Audit** option.
- ☑ Select the **Scan a Range of Computers** option.
- ☑ Enter the IP addresses that you want to scan.
- ☑ Enter your authentication credentials.
- ☑ Click the **Scan** button.

Analyzing the Results

- ☑ The Installed Application Report is often the best report for collecting software auditing information.
- ☑ The System Information Report gives you the most comprehensive hardware information, but may also give you a lot of information that you are not interested in.
- ☑ You may want to use filtering or run a smaller report to get the information that you are really interested in.

Blacklisting and Whitelisting Applications

☑ The report of applications that are installed often contains applications and patches that are irrelevant to what you are trying to discover.

☑ You can use whitelisting to keep the ReportCenter from reporting on applications that you already know about.

Network Documentation

☑ Although GFI LANguard Network Security Scanner is primarily intended as a security tool, it can also be used for network documentation purposes.

☑ Windows Vista's network mapping capabilities can help to augment your network documentation.

Frequently Asked Questions

Q: Is there a way of making the ReportCenter report hardware information such as the type of CPU or the amount of memory that a system has installed?

A: Unfortunately not. Let's hope that GFI adds this capability in the next version.

Q: How long does a software audit scan or a system information scan take?

A: It depends on how many machines you are scanning and on the speed of your network. On my network, the scan took about 20 minutes to complete. System information and software audit scans take a lot less time than vulnerability scans.

Q: How is blacklisting useful if blacklisted applications are not automatically removed?

A: Once you remove the applications that you have blacklisted, you can periodically run a report to see if anyone has those particular applications installed.

Chapter 7

Patch Management

Solutions in this chapter:

- **Downloading Microsoft Patches**
- **Scanning for Missing Updates**
- **Applying Microsoft Service Packs**
- **Deploying Microsoft Patches**
- **Double Check the Patch Management Status**
- **Deploying a Specific Patch**
- **Performing a Scan Comparison**
- **Uninstalling a Patch**
- **Deploying Custom Software**

- ☑ Summary
- ☑ Solutions Fast Track
- ☑ Frequently Asked Questions

Introduction

One of the main functions that GFI LANguard Network Security Scanner provides is that of patch management. As I'm sure you know, patch management is crucial to keeping your network secure. New vulnerabilities are discovered all the time, and it doesn't take hackers long to develop exploits that take advantage of those vulnerabilities. Applying security patches in a timely manner is the only sure way of making sure that hackers do not use a well-known exploit as an entry point into your system.

Downloading Microsoft Patches

Out of the box, GFI LANguard Network Security Scanner is aware of all of the latest Microsoft patches and service packs, but it doesn't download any of them until you tell it to. Later on when I walk you through the process of applying patches, I will show you how to manually download a patch, just so that you can see how it's done. In the real world though, you are going to want to configure GFI LANguard Network Security Scanner to download patches automatically.

Configuring GFI LANguard Network Security Scanner to automatically download Microsoft patches is pretty simple. To do so, follow these steps:

1. Open the management console, and click the **Configuration** button.

2. Navigate through the console tree to **Configuration** | **Settings** | **Patch Autodownload**.

3. Right-click on the **Patch Autodownload** container, and choose the **Properties** command from the resulting shortcut menu.

4. When the Patch Autodownload Properties sheet opens, go to the **Patch Repository** tab, shown in Figure 7.1.

Figure 7.1 The Patch Repository Screen Allows You to Set the Patch
Download Path

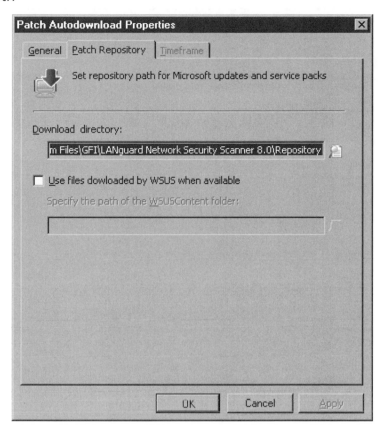

5. As you can see in the figure, the Patch Repository tab allows you to set the download
    directory. Normally, it's Okay to use the default download directory, but you will want to
    make sure that the volume containing this directory has plenty of free space. If you have
    a Microsoft Windows Server Update Service (WSUS) server on your network, you have
    the option of using the files that WSUS has already downloaded. You must simply provide
    the path to your WSUS server's WSUSContent folder.

6. Go to the properties sheet's General tab and click the **Enable Patch Autodownload**
    check box, as shown in Figure 7.2.

Are You Owned?

IP Address Redirection

Both GFI LANguard Network Security Scanner and WSUS are designed to download patches from a central repository owned by Microsoft. However, it is important that you verify the integrity of your network before downloading patches. There have been reports of hackers using DNS poisoning, or making modifications to the HOSTS file or the registry in order to redirect those attempting to download patches to a malicious Web site.

Figure 7.2 Select the Enable Patch Autodownload Check Box

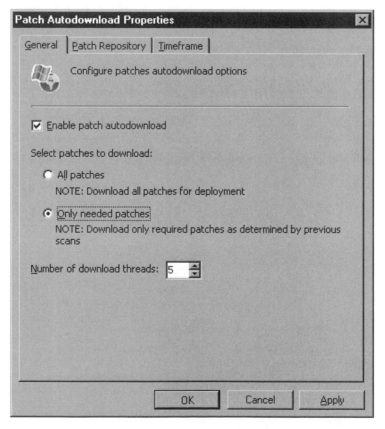

7. If your server is short on disk space, or if you are in a hurry to get the patches applied, then select the **Only Needed Patches** button.

8. Click **OK**.

Tools & Traps…

GFI LANguard Network Security Scanner vs. WSUS

If you've already got a WSUS server in place, you might be wondering what the advantage is of using GFI LANguard Network Security Scanner for patch management. The primary advantage is that GFI LANguard Network Security Scanner makes it easy to push patches to workstations. Most of the WSUS deployments that I have seen are ultimately dependant on a user to click the Automatic Update icon to begin the patching process. If a user does not click this icon, the machine may never be patched.

Scanning for Missing Updates

Before you can apply any Microsoft updates, you will have to perform a scan to find out which updates are missing from which computers. It is worth mentioning that this is not a one-time process. Each time that you plan on deploying updates, you will have to perform a new scan. This is one of the main reasons why GFI LANguard Network Security Scanner supports the use of scheduled scans. You can easily schedule an automated scan that will scan the network for missing patches on a periodic basis. That way, when you want to apply patches, the scan is already done.

Generally speaking, scans should be scheduled to run late at night so that they are not disruptive to the end users. Keep in mind, however, that this will only work if the users leave their computers turned on at night. The users do not have to stay logged in order for the scans to be completed successfully.

For the purpose of this chapter, I will walk you through a manual scan. If you want to turn this into a scheduled scan, then check out the section on scheduled scans earlier in this book.

To scan for missing patches, follow these steps:

1. Open the management console and click on the Main button.

2. Right-click on the **Security Scanner** container, and choose the **New Scan** option from the resulting shortcut menu.

3. When the New Scan wizard opens, choose the **Patching Status** option, and click **Next**.

4. The next screen that you will see gives you several different options for what types of missing patches you want to scan for, as shown in Figure 7.3. For our purposes, go ahead and choose the **Missing Patches** option, and click **Next**.

Figure 7.3 Choose the Missing Patches Option and Click Next

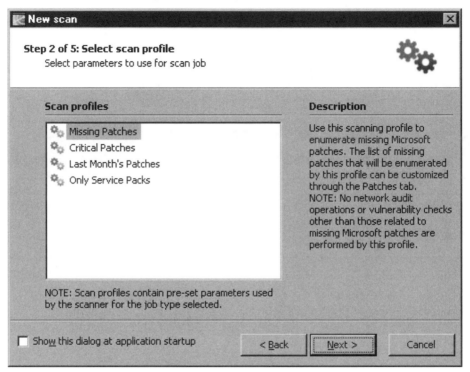

5. You will now see a screen asking you which computers you want to scan. Choose the **Scan a Range of Computers** option, and click **Next**.

6. Enter the IP address range that you want to scan, and click **Next**.

7. Enter the credentials that you want to use for the scan job.

8. Click the **Scan** button.

Viewing the Report

I tend to think that it is usually easier to view the patch management information that has been collected by going through the management console. Even so, the ReportCenter can give you some valuable information on the state of the machines on your network, so I want to at least show you what types of information are available. To create a report, follow these steps:

1. Click the **View Reports** button.

2. When the ReportCenter opens, scroll through the Default Reports to the Patch Management section.

The Patch Management section contains a number of different reports that allow you to view either the missing patches, or the installed patches, and these reports can be grouped by host, operating system, or severity. You can also view the patch deployment history, grouped by host, date, or patch.

It may seem that the report of choice should be the Network Patching Status report. However, this report is just a summary report that tells you the top ten missing patches, and the 20 most vulnerable computers on your network. This information can definitely be useful, but if you are trying to figure out which patches need to be installed, you need a report that is a bit more comprehensive. For that I recommend running the Missing Patches Grouped By Host report.

3. Right-click on the **Missing Patches Grouped by Host** report, and choose the **Run | For Last Scan** commands from the resulting shortcut menus.

You can see an excerpt from the resulting report below:

Report cover page

Report title: **Missing Patches Grouped by Host**

Description: This report lists missing patches grouped by host machine, including URL links providing
further information on each missing patch.

Generated on: 26-May-2008 17:26

Generated by: Administrator

Sort by: IP - Ascending, Patch Date Posted - Descending

Date filter: 5/26/2008 3:23:45PM

Other filters: No filters used

Reviewed by: _____   **Reviewed date:** _____   **Signature:** _____

Scan reference :   147.100.100.1-147.100.100.254
Scan date & time :   26-May-2008 15:23

147.100.100.6 - SENTINAL

Operating System	Service Pack	Patch Count
Windows Server 2003	1	40

Bulletin ID	Description	Posted Date	Severity
Not Available	Windows Malicious Software Removal Tool - May 2008 (KB890830)	2008-05-13	Critical
MS08-028	Security Update for Windows Server 2003 (KB950749)	2008-05-13	Critical
MS08-024	Cumulative Security Update for Internet Explorer 7 for Windows Server 2003 (KB947864)	2008-05-13	Critical
MS07-040	Security Update for Microsoft .NET Framework, Version 2.0 (KB928365)	2008-04-22	Critical
MS08-023	Security Update for ActiveX Killbits for Windows Server 2003 (KB948881)	2008-04-08	Moderate
MS08-021	Security Update for Windows Server 2003 (KB948590)	2008-04-08	Critical
MS08-020	Security Update for Windows Server 2003 (KB945553)	2008-04-08	Important
MS08-025	Security Update for Windows Server 2003 (KB941693)	2008-04-08	Important
MS08-008	Security Update for Windows Server 2003 (KB943055)	2008-02-12	Moderate
MS08-007	Security Update for Windows Server 2003 (KB946026)	2008-02-12	Important
MS08-005	Security Update for Windows Server 2003 (KB942831)	2008-02-12	Important
MS08-006	Security Update for Windows Server 2003 (KB942830)	2008-02-12	Important
Not Available	Microsoft .NET Framework 2.0 Service Pack 1 (KB110806)	2008-01-22	Critical
Not Available	Microsoft .NET Framework 3.0 Service Pack 1 (KB929300)	2008-01-22	Critical
MS08-002	Security Update for Windows Server 2003 (KB943485)	2008-01-08	Important
MS08-001	Security Update for Windows Server 2003 (KB941644)	2008-01-08	Important
Not Available	Windows Server 2003 Service Pack 2 (32-bit x86)	2008-01-08	Critical
MS07-068	Security Update for Windows Server 2003 (KB941569)	2007-12-11	Critical
MS07-067	Security Update for Windows Server 2003 (KB944653)	2007-12-11	Important
MS07-064	Security Update for Windows Server 2003 (KB941568)	2007-12-11	Critical
Not Available	Update for Windows Server 2003 (KB942763)	2007-12-11	Critical
MS07-061	Security Update for Windows Server 2003 (KB943460)	2007-11-13	Critical
MS07-062	Security Update for Windows Server 2003 (KB941672)	2007-11-13	Important
Not Available	Office 2003 Service Pack 3 (SP3)	2007-10-09	Critical
MS07-056	Security Update for Outlook Express for Windows Server 2003 (KB941202)	2007-10-09	Critical
MS07-058	Security Update for Windows Server 2003 (KB933729)	2007-10-09	Important
MS07-040	Security Update for Microsoft .NET Framework, Version 1.1 Service Pack 1 (KB933854)	2007-09-11	Critical
MS07-042	Security Update for Windows Server 2003 (KB936021)	2007-09-11	Moderate
MS07-042	Security Update for Microsoft XML Core Services 6.0 and Microsoft XML Core Services 6.0 Service Pack 1 (KB933579)	2007-08-14	Critical
MS07-050	Security Update for Internet Explorer 7 for Windows Server 2003 (KB938127)	2007-08-14	Critical
MS07-047	Security Update for Windows Server 2003 (KB936782)	2007-08-14	Important
MS07-039	Security Update for Windows Server 2003 (KB926122)	2007-07-10	Important
MS07-035	Security Update for Windows Server 2003 (KB935839)	2007-06-12	Critical
MS07-031	Security Update for Windows Server 2003 (KB935840)	2007-06-12	Important
MS07-034	Cumulative Security Update for Outlook Express for Windows Server 2003 (KB929123)	2007-06-12	Low
MS07-012	Security Update for Windows Server 2003 (KB924667)	2007-06-12	Important
MS07-008	Security Update for Windows Server 2003 (KB928843)	2007-02-13	Moderate
MS07-011	Security Update for Windows Server 2003 (KB926436)	2007-02-13	Important
MS07-013	Security Update for Windows Server 2003 (KB918118)	2007-02-13	Important
MS07-006	Security Update for Windows Server 2003 (KB928255)	2007-02-13	Important

MS08-013	Security Update for Office 2003 (KB945185)	2008-02-12	Important
MS08-008	Security Update for Windows Vista (KB943055)	2008-02-12	Critical
MS07-063	Security Update for Windows Vista (KB942624)	2007-12-11	Important
MS07-068	Security Update for Windows Vista (KB941569)	2007-12-11	Critical
MS07-064	Security Update for Windows Vista (KB941568)	2007-12-11	Critical
MS07-066	Security Update for Windows Vista (KB943078)	2007-12-11	Important
Not Available	Update for Windows Vista (KB942763)	2007-12-11	Critical
MS07-038	Security Update for Windows Vista (KB935807)	2007-12-11	Moderate
Not Available	Word Viewer 2003 Service Pack 3 (SP3)	2007-10-09	Critical
MS07-056	Security Update for Windows Mail for Windows Vista (KB941202)	2007-10-09	Important
MS07-058	Security Update for Windows Vista (KB933729)	2007-10-09	Important
MS07-053	Security Update for Windows Vista (KB939778)	2007-09-25	Important
MS07-052	Security Update for Microsoft Visual Studio 2005 Service Pack 1 (KB937061)	2007-09-13	Important
MS07-042	Security Update for Windows Vista (KB936021)	2007-09-11	Critical
MS07-050	Security Update for Windows Vista (KB938127)	2007-08-14	Critical
MS07-042	Security Update for Windows Vista (KB933579)	2007-08-14	Critical
MS07-042	Security Update for Microsoft XML Core Services 4.0 Service Pack 2 (KB936181)	2007-08-14	Critical
MS07-047	Security Update for Windows Vista (KB936782)	2007-08-14	Important
MS07-048	Security Update for Windows Vista (KB938123)	2007-08-14	Important

The report that I just showed you an excerpt from works great if you want to know exactly which patches are missing from which machines, but it does take a machine-centric view of the data. Sometimes you may want to look at the data on a patch-by-patch basis. For example, you may want to see a list of every server that is missing Windows Server 2003 SP2.

As odd as it may sound, if you want to get information on a specific patch through the ReportCenter, then the best bet is to run the Missing Patches Grouped by Operating System report. This report will be broken down by operating system, but it will also be broken down by individual patches for each specific operating system. You can see an excerpt from this report below:

Report cover page

Report title: **Missing Patches Grouped by Operating System**

Description: This report lists missing patches grouped by operating system, including the host machine names for each missing patch.

Generated on: 26-May-2008 22:41

Generated by: Administrator

Sort by: Operating System - Ascending, Patch Date Posted - Descending

Date filter: 5/26/2008 3:23:45PM

Other filters: No filters used

Reviewed by: _____   Reviewed date: _____   Signature: _____

Windows Server 2003

Patch : 890830   **Bulletin ID :** Not Available   **Posted Date :** 2008-05-13   **Severity :** Critical
Description: Windows Malicious Software Removal Tool - May 2008 (KB890830)

Host IP	Host Name	Service Pack
147.100.100.34	DNS	2
147.100.100.108	OCS-MED	2

Patch : 944338   **Bulletin ID :** MS08-022   **Posted Date :** 2008-05-13   **Severity :** Critical
Description: Security Update for Windows Server 2003 (KB944338)

Host IP	Host Name	Service Pack
147.100.100.108	OCS-MED	2

Patch : 890830   **Bulletin ID :** Not Available   **Posted Date :** 2008-05-13   **Severity :** Critical
Description: Windows Malicious Software Removal Tool - May 2008 (KB890830)

Host IP	Host Name	Service Pack
147.100.100.6	SENTINAL	1

Patch : 950749   **Bulletin ID :** MS08-028   **Posted Date :** 2008-05-13   **Severity :** Critical
Description: Security Update for Windows Server 2003 (KB950749)

Host IP	Host Name	Service Pack
147.100.100.6	SENTINAL	1

Patch : 947864   **Bulletin ID :** MS08-024   **Posted Date :** 2008-05-13   **Severity :** Critical
Description: Cumulative Security Update for Internet Explorer 7 for Windows Server 2003 (KB947864)

Host IP	Host Name	Service Pack
147.100.100.6	SENTINAL	1

Patch : 890830   **Bulletin ID :** Not Available   **Posted Date :** 2008-05-13   **Severity :** Critical
Description: Windows Malicious Software Removal Tool - May 2008 (KB890830)

Host IP	Host Name	Service Pack
147.100.100.88	OCS2	2

Patch : 947864   **Bulletin ID :** MS08-024   **Posted Date :** 2008-05-13   **Severity :** Critical
Description: Cumulative Security Update for Internet Explorer 7 for Windows Server 2003 (KB947864)

Host IP	Host Name	Service Pack
147.100.100.88	OCS2	2

Patch : 890830   **Bulletin ID :** Not Available   **Posted Date :** 2008-05-13   **Severity :** Critical
Description: Windows Malicious Software Removal Tool - May 2008 (KB890830)

Host IP	Host Name	Service Pack
147.100.100.89	BACKUP	2

Viewing Missing Patch Information Through the Management Console

The management console has kind of an odd way of displaying patching information. If you look at Figure 7.4, you will notice that there is a System Patching Status container located beneath the listing for each computer in the console's center pane. Notice though, that when you click on this container, the pane on the right will only show you the service packs and patches that are actually installed. Missing patches and service packs are listed beneath the Vulnerabilities container, as shown in Figure 7.5.

Figure 7.4 The System Patching Status Container Only Shows the Patches and Service Packs That Are Actually Installed on Each Computer

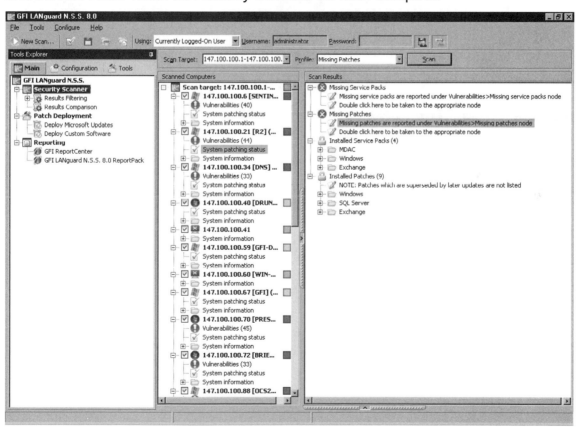

Figure 7.5 Missing Patches and Service Packs Are Listed Beneath Each Computer's Vulnerability Container

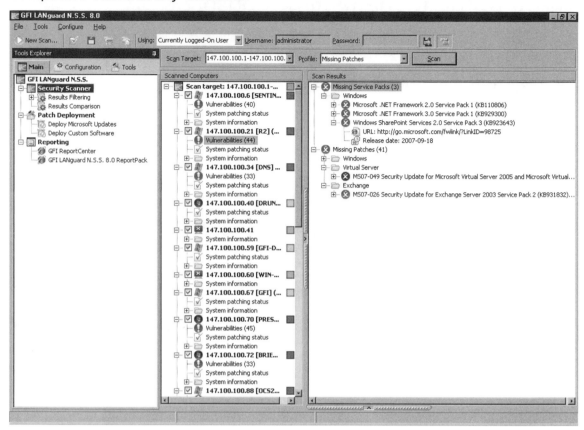

Notice in the figure above how all of the missing patches and service packs for each computer are grouped by product. This helps you to be able to tell how vulnerable the operating system is, or how vulnerable a particular application is on a given computer.

Applying Microsoft Service Packs

Now that we have scanned for missing patches and service packs, it is time to deploy the missing service packs. We'll do this first, and deploy the missing patches later on. If you look at Figure 7.6, you can see the management console as it appears after a missing patch scan completes. Notice in the figure that there is a colored block next to each machine on the network. The colored block gives you an indication of how vulnerable the machine is (at least in terms of missing patches). Green blocks indicate an up-to-date machine, while red blocks indicate a machine that is missing important security patches.

Figure 7.6 The Colored Blocks in the Center Pane Tell You the Patch Management Status of Each Machine

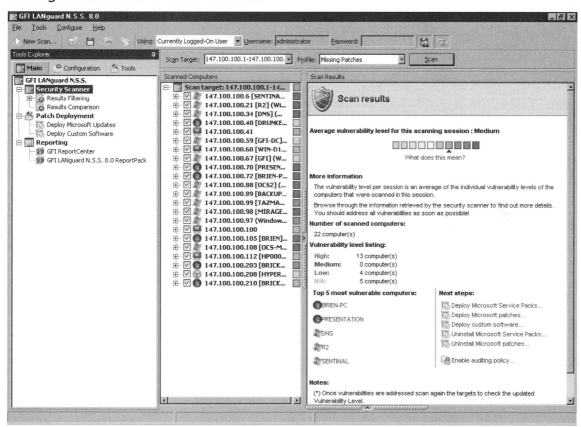

As you look at the figure above, take a quick look at the pane on the right. At the top of this pane, you can see a summary of the average vulnerability level for the machines on your network. This pane also shows you a list of the five most vulnerable machines on your network.

Obviously, the machines on my network are missing quite a few patches. To be completely honest though, I knew that I was going to be writing this book, and I wanted to be able to give you a good demonstration of the patching process, so it's been quite a while since I have applied any patches to the machines on my network. I think that it's time I bring my network up-to-date, though.

To apply the missing patches and service packs, follow these steps:

1. Right-click on the Scan Targets node at the top of the middle pane, and then choose the **Deploy Microsoft Updates | Patches On | Service Packs On | All Computers** options from the resulting shortcut menus.

At this point, you will see the screen that's shown in Figure 7.7. This is a very important screen, so I want to take a moment and explain all of the particulars of this screen before I continue with the step-by-step instructions.

Figure 7.7 This is the Most Important Screen That You Will Encounter During the Patch Deployment Process

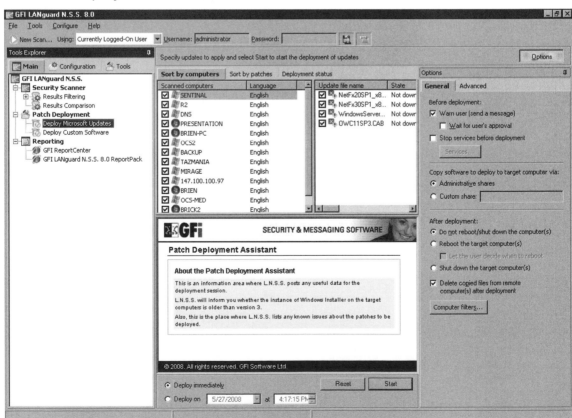

As you look at the figure above, one of the first things that you will probably notice is that the console's middle pane has been split into three separate panes. The lower portion of the middle pane really isn't important, but the upper portions are definitely worth paying attention to.

The left portion of the middle pane lists all of the computers that you are about to apply service packs to. The right portion of the pane lists the service packs that are going to be applied to the currently selected computer. In this figure, for instance, there are four different service packs that are going to be applied to the server Sentinal.

Now take a look at the Status column found in the right portion of the center pane. As you can see (or partially see) in the figure, the status of each service pack is set to Not Downloaded. As you may recall, earlier I showed you how to configure GFI LANguard Network Security Scanner to automatically download the necessary patches, but I also said that I would show you how to download the patches manually if necessary. Since you can't apply patches or service packs that haven't been downloaded, let's go ahead and download the service packs by following these steps:

2. Right-click on any of the patch files that are listed, and select the **Download All Checked Files** command from the resulting shortcut menu. When you do, all of the necessary patch files will be queued for download. You can observe the download status directly through the management console, as shown in Figure 7.8.

Figure 7.8 You Can Observe Each Service Pack's Download Status Directly Through the Management Console

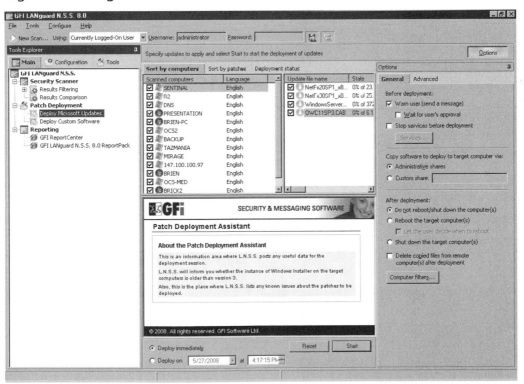

Once the service packs have been downloaded, there are a few more things that you need to check before you actually deploy them. Look directly beneath the center console in the figure above. Notice that the management console gives you the option of deploying the service packs immediately, or deploying them at a specific date and time.

Now take a look at the console's right pane. The first section on this pane allows you to choose whether or not you want to warn users of an imminent reboot after the service packs have been installed, by displaying a text message. If you do choose to give the users a warning, the warning message that the users will receive looks like the message shown in Figure 7.9.

Figure 7.9 You Have the Option of Warning the Users of an Upcoming Reboot

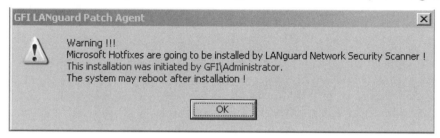

If you do choose to give the users a warning, then you also have the option of waiting for a user's approval before the reboot actually happens. This keeps the reboot from taking the users by surprise while they are in the middle of working on something (which happened to me a couple of times while I was writing this chapter). If you put the user in charge of rebooting the machine, then the user will see a message similar to the one shown in Figure 7.10 when it's time to reboot.

Figure 7.10 If You Choose to Allow the Users to Approve the Reboot, They Will See a Screen Like This One When It's Time to Reboot Their Machines

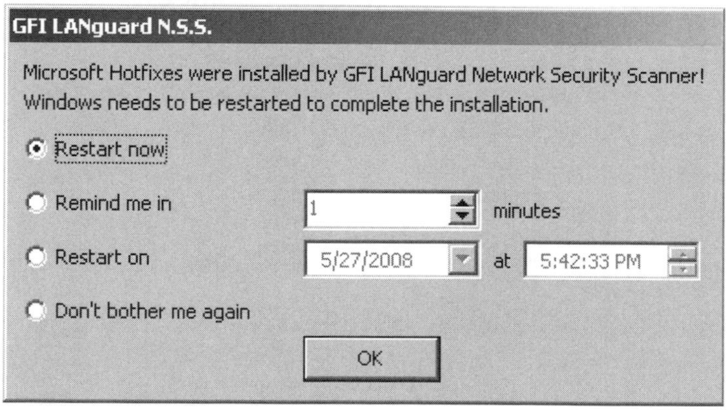

Another option found in this section allows you to stop services prior to deploying the service packs. You won't normally have to worry about doing this, but if there are some services that you need to stop, you can select the **Stop Services Before Deployment** check box, click the **Services** button, and then specify the services that you want to stop.

The next option that you will encounter allows you to choose the point on the target computers to which the service packs will be copied prior to deployment. By default, service packs are copied to the target computer's administrative share. You shouldn't typically have to change this option, but you can if you need to for some reason.

The lower section allows you to control whether the target computer is rebooted, shut down, or if it is allowed to continue to run without being rebooted. In experimenting with the various options while writing this book, I have found that in a lot of cases patches and service packs are not acknowledged as being installed until the target machine is rebooted. Furthermore, it can sometimes be impossible to install future patches until after the target machine has been rebooted, because the agent on the target computer still reports an update as being in process.

The second to the last option on this pane is the option to delete copied files from the remote machines after installation. It's usually a good idea to leave this option enabled. Some of the service packs can be pretty large, and there is no reason to waste all that disk space if the service pack has been installed.

At the bottom of the console's right pane, you will find the Computer Filters button. Before I explain what this button does, take a look back at the middle column. Notice that there is a check box next to each computer. You can control which computers will be patched by selecting or deselecting the corresponding check boxes. Likewise, you can choose to apply or not apply individual service packs by selecting or deselecting their corresponding check boxes.

This method works great in a small organization like mine, but in a larger organization it's impractical to individually select and deselect individual computers. This is where the Computer Filters button comes into play. If you click it, you will see a dialog box similar to the one that's shown in Figure 7.11. As you can see in the figure, this dialog box allows you to select the machines that you want to patch based on the operating system that they are running.

Figure 7.11 You Can Choose the Target Computers Based on the Operating System That They Are Running

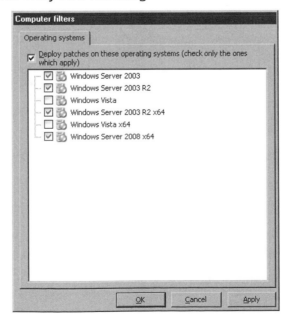

Now that I have explained the various options found on the console screen, let's go ahead and finish deploying the service packs. To do so, follow these steps:

3. Verify that you have selected the options that meet your individual needs.

4. Click the **Start** button.

The deployment process will now begin. The management console will show you the deployment process in real time. During the deployment process, the Start button is grayed out. The process is complete when the Start button once again becomes available. You can see what a completed deployment looks like in Figure 7.12.

Figure 7.12 This is What a Completed Deployment Looks Like

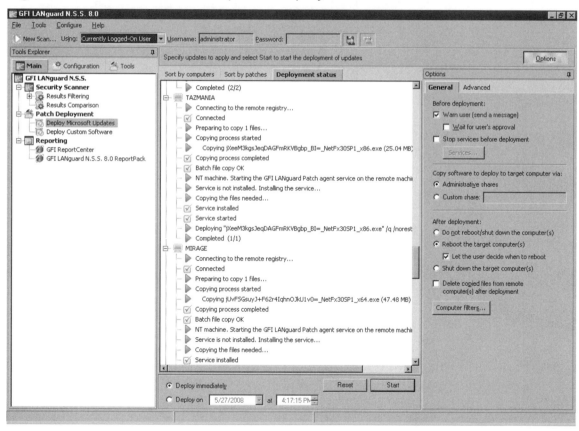

Notes from the Underground...

Malicious Patches

One of the nice things about a product like WSUS or GFI LANguard Network Security Scanner is that it automatically downloads patches from a reputable source. There is a lot of malware out there that is disguised to look like Microsoft patches, so it is important to know that your patches are coming from a reliable source. For example, check out this e-mail message that I got yesterday (see screen shot below).

Wasn't it nice of Microsoft to send me an e-mail alert? The problem is that this message wasn't really from Microsoft. In fact, Microsoft doesn't send out e-mail alerts about new patches. It's impossible to capture in a screen shot, but if I hover my mouse over the download link, Windows reveals a URL that most definitely does not belong to Microsoft.

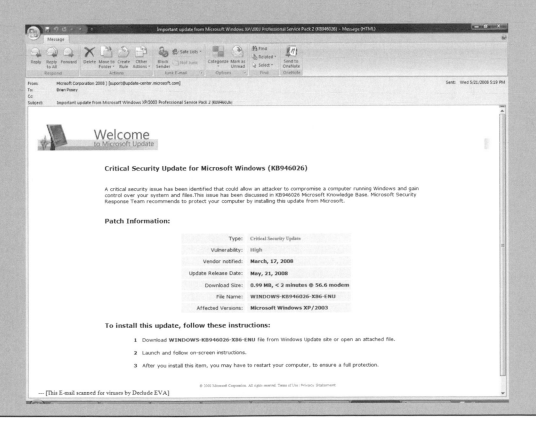

Deploying Microsoft Patches

Once you have deployed any necessary service packs, it's time to deploy Microsoft patches. The patch deployment process is very similar to the process of deploying service packs, so I will go through it rather quickly. To deploy Microsoft patches, follow these steps:

1. Right-click on the **Scan Target** container at the top of the middle pane, and choose the **Deploy Microsoft Updates | Patches On | All Computers** option from the resulting shortcut menus.

2. Verify that the correct target computers and patches are selected, and that you have chosen the reboot options that are appropriate for your individual situation.

3. Click the **Start** button.

Double Check the Patch Management Status

So far I have shown you how you can use GFI LANguard Network Security Scanner to deploy patches and service packs to machines on your network. I also showed you how the console displays the deployment status as those patches and service packs are installed. On a network as small as mine, it's easy to see which machines had problems during the deployment process. A simple glance through the management console's Deployment Status section will tell you everything that you need to know.

In larger organizations using the management console to do anything more than a quick spot check is impractical. The management console may display thousands of lines of text even if you are only installing a single patch.

The best way to find out how the patching process went is to perform a new scan. Granted, it can take a while to rescan your network, but that is by far the most effective way of figuring out which machines still need your attention.

It is important that you never assume that patches were applied successfully to all of the machines on the network. Even if you know that the process went perfectly, there may be machines on your network that were powered off during the previous scan, and therefore did not receive the patches. For example, while I was writing this chapter, my wife shut down her PC shortly after I initiated the patching process, because she had no idea that I was doing something to her machine. Consequently, it remained unpatched. This can happen in the real world too, because you never know when a user may choose to shut down their machine.

Another reason why it is so important to rescan your network is because if the machines on your network are missing a lot of patches like mine are, then you are probably going to have to perform the patching process several times. Some patches cannot be applied until other patches are in place. Therefore, you may have to patch the machine, and then "patch the patches" so to speak.

To show you what I mean, check out Figure 7.13. This figure shows a Missing Patch scan of my network after four rounds of patching. Notice that some of the machines on the list are still showing a vulnerability level of orange, because there are still patches or service packs that need to be applied, even after all of the patching that I have already done. Most of the machines are in the green now, however, and the network's overall vulnerability level is kind of on the border between yellow and green.

Figure 7.13 Even After Four Rounds of Patching, There are Still Additional Patches That Need to Be Applied

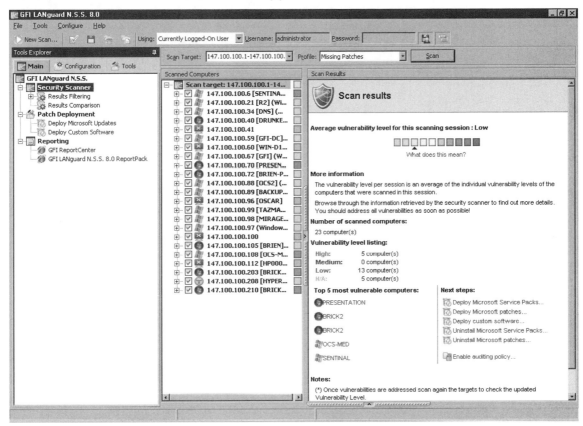

Deploying a Specific Patch

So far, I have been taking a mass deployment approach to the patching process. Sometimes, however, you may be more interested in deploying a specific patch than deploying every patch that has been released to date. This is particularly true if Microsoft releases a patch to correct a critical vulnerability, because you would want to apply that patch more quickly than less important patches. Fortunately, the management console makes it fairly easy to install a specific patch.

When I showed you my scan results in the previous section, you saw that there were still a few computers that were missing some patches and service packs. The reason why this is occurring is because the patches on my network were so out of date. Windows cannot apply some patches until after others are in place. Therefore, even though I had performed several rounds of patching, there are additional patches that still need to be applied.

Among the machines that are still missing patches, there were two computers that were missing Service Pack 1 for Windows Vista. That being the case, let's go ahead and deploy just that service pack, and nothing else. To do so, follow these steps:

1. Right-click in the results pane, and choose the **Deploy Microsoft Updates | Service Packs On | All Computers** options from the resulting shortcut menus.

2. The next screen that you encounter will show you all of the machines needing service packs, and the service packs that are available for installation. Click the **Sort By Patches** tab at the top of this console screen. You will now see the individual service packs that are available for deployment.

3. Deselect all of the service packs except for the one that is to be deployed, as shown in Figure 7.14.

4. Click the **Start** button.

Figure 7.14 Select Only the Patches That You Want to Deploy

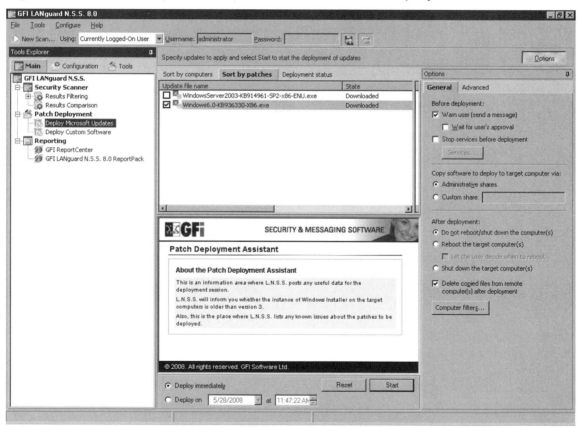

Performing a Scan Comparison

One of the cool things that the management console is able to do is to perform a comparison between two scans. In the previous section, I deployed service packs onto two machines, but how do I really know if my network is any more secure now than it was before?

Take a look at Figure 7.15. In this figure, the overall network vulnerability level has moved decidedly into the green, but the two machines that I patched (Brick2 and Presentation) are both still colored orange.

Figure 7.15 An Undated Scan Doesn't Look Much Different From a Previous Scan

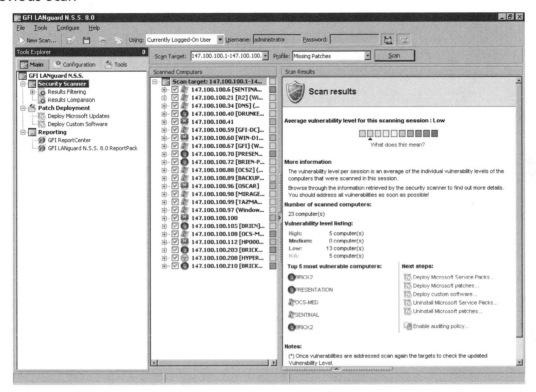

Looking at this screen, it would be easy to assume that this is because there are some other patches that still need to be applied to the two machines. Even so, we need to verify that the service packs were actually applied. Now in this particular situation, verifying the service packs is as simple as just moving the mouse pointer over the machines that we want to check. When you do, the management console will show you the operating system and service pack level for the machines.

That approach works in this particular situation, but it wouldn't work if I had been applying a service pack to an application rather than an operating system service pack. That being the case, it's good to learn an alternate method of finding out what has changed since the previous scan.

The management console actually allows you to compare two scans (assuming that you saved them). To compare two scans, follow these steps:

1. Perform your first scan.

2. When the scan completes, right-click on the console's **Security Scanner** container, and choose the **Save Scan Results to XML File** option from the resulting shortcut menu.

3. Now, do whatever it is that you need to do. For example, you may need to install additional patches or service packs.

4. Run your updated scan.

5. When the scan completes, right click on the console's **Security Scanner** container, and choose the **Save Scan Results to XML File** option from the resulting shortcut menu.

6. Navigate through the console tree to **GFI LANguard N.S.S | Security Scanner | Results Comparison**.

7. Just above the pane on the right are fields for Scan Result 1 and Scan Result 2. Click the **magnifying glass icon** next to Scan Result 1, and choose the **XML Source** option when prompted.

8. Select the older of the two scans, and click the **Open** button.

9. Click the **magnifying glass icon** next to Scan Result 2, and choose the **XML Source** option when prompted.

10. Select the more recent scan, and click the **Open** button.

11. Click the **Compare** button.

A comparison can take a little while to complete, but when it's done, you should see a screen similar to the one that's shown in Figure 7.16. As you can see in the figure, this screen will show you everything that has changed from one scan to the next.

Figure 7.16 The Results Comparison Report Tells You What Has Changed Since the Previous Scan

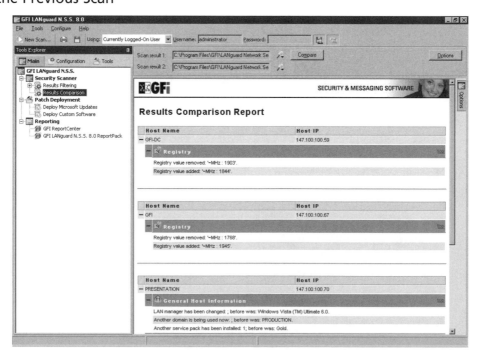

Uninstalling a Patch

Microsoft recommends that you always test patches before performing any kind of a large-scale deployment. Sometimes, however, issues come up later on that were not revealed during the initial testing, and it becomes necessary to uninstall a particular patch. If you find yourself needing to roll back a patch, you can do so by following these steps:

1. Perform a Missing Patch scan.

2. Right click on the list of computers that have been scanned, and choose the **Uninstall Microsoft Updates | Patches From | All Computers** options from the resulting shortcut menus. Of course you also have the option of uninstalling service packs or of removing patches from select computers.

3. At this point, you will see a screen similar to the one shown in Figure 7.17. As you can see in the figure, this screen lists patches on a machine-by-machine basis. If you are intending to remove a specific patch, click the **Sort by Patches** link found just above the list of computers.

4. Scroll through the list of patches, and select the patch that you want to remove, as shown in Figure 7.18.

5. Click the **Start** button.

Figure 7.17 This View Isn't Practical Unless You Are Removing a Patch From a Specific Computer

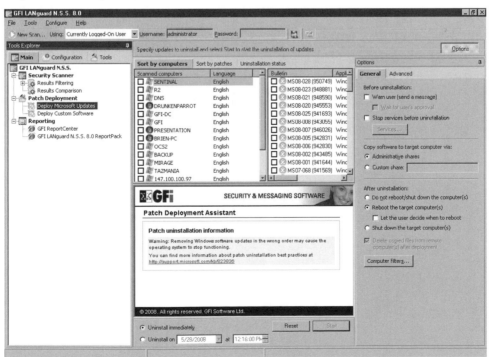

Figure 7.18 Choose the Patch That You Want to Remove, and Then Click Start

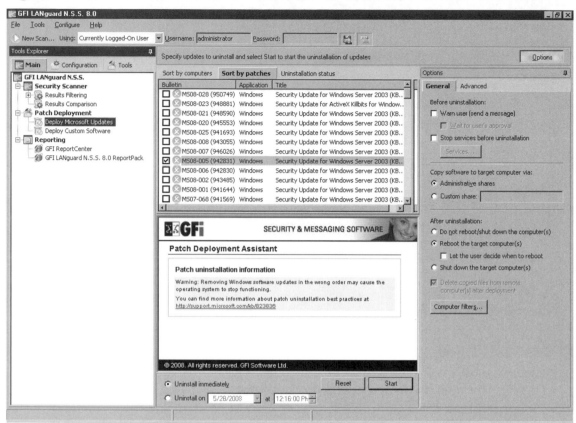

Deploying Custom Software

Although it's nice to be able to deploy Microsoft patches, third-party application vendors often offer patches too (although probably not quite as frequently as Microsoft does). You can use the management console to deploy these third-party patches or even to deploy applications if you want to.

Believe it or not, deploying third-party applications or patches is fairly easy. To do so, follow these steps:

1. Navigate through the console tree to **Patch Deployment | Deploy Custom Software**.

2. Click the **Add** button found in the "Software to deploy" section.

3. When the Add Custom Software dialog box appears, provide the path and filename to the executable file that you want to deploy, as shown in Figure 7.19.

Figure 7.19 Enter the Path and the Filename of the Executable File That You Want to Deploy

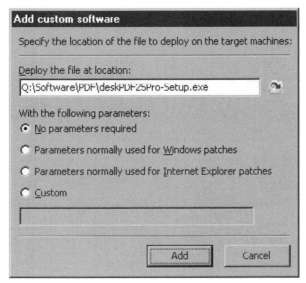

4. If necessary, provide any parameters required for deploying the application or patch.

5. Click the **Add** button.

6. Click the **Select** button next to the console's "Computers to Deploy Software On" section. You also have the option of manually specifying a computer by Network Basic Input/ Output System (NetBIOS) name or Internet Protocol (IP) address, or of importing a list of computers.

7. When you have made your selection, click **OK**. The console screen should now look similar to what you see in Figure 7.20.

Figure 7.20 This is What the Deploy Custom Software Screen Looks Like

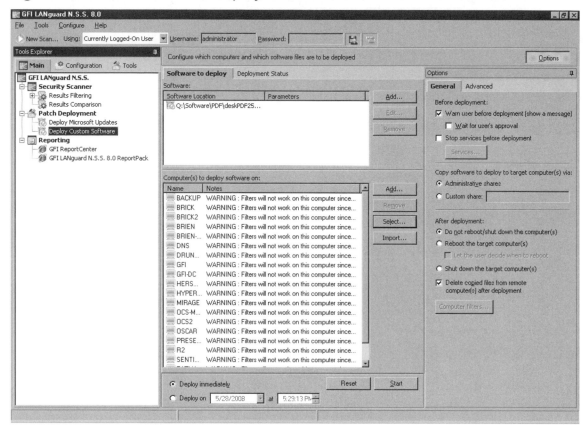

8. Verify that the various deployment options regarding rebooting the target computer are set appropriately for your organization.

9. Click the **Start** button.

Summary

Patch management is absolutely critical to the security of the computers on your network. Only by keeping your computers up-to-date can you keep hackers from using well-known vulnerabilities as an exploit against your network. Keep in mind, however, that patching is not a one-time process. You need to create a scheduled scan that will routinely check for missing patches, so that you can keep the computers on your network up-to-date.

Solutions Fast Track

Applying Microsoft Service Packs

- ☑ Right-click on the scan results.
- ☑ Select the **Deploy Microsoft Updates | Service Packs On | All Computers** commands.
- ☑ Select the computers that you want to deploy service packs to.
- ☑ Click the **Scan** button.

Deploying Microsoft Patches

- ☑ Right-click on the scan results.
- ☑ Select the **Deploy Microsoft Updates | Service Patches On | All Computers** commands.
- ☑ Select the computers that you want to deploy service packs to.
- ☑ Click the **Scan** button.

Double Check the Patch Management Status

- ☑ Patch information is not automatically refreshed.
- ☑ You must perform an additional scan to see updated patch management information.

Deploying a Specific Patch

- ☑ Right-click on the scan results.
- ☑ Select the **Deploy Microsoft Updates | Patches On | All Computers** commands.
- ☑ Select the **Sort By Patches** tab.
- ☑ Select the patch that you want to apply.
- ☑ Click the **Start** button.

Performing a Scan Comparison

☑ Select the **Results Comparison** container.

☑ Use the icons above the results pane to load the two scan files that you want to compare.

☑ Click the **Compare** button.

Uninstalling a Patch

☑ Right-click on the scan results.

☑ Select the **Uninstall Microsoft Updates | Patches From | All Computers** commands.

☑ Select the computers that you want to remove the patch from.

☑ Select the patch that you want to remove.

☑ Click **Start**.

Deploying Custom Software

☑ Click on the **Deploy Custom Software** container.

☑ Click the **Add** button.

☑ Provide the path and filename of the executable file that you want to deploy.

☑ Use the other **Add** button to provide a list of computers that the software should be deployed to.

☑ Click **Start**.

Frequently Asked Questions

Q: Does using GFI LANguard Network Security Scanner offer any advantage over using WSUS for patch management?

A: There are two primary advantages. First, the GFI product is able to push updates to clients, while WSUS is usually dependant on users to click an update button. Second, WSUS does not offer the capability of deploying third-party updates.

Q: Why does a system still appear as missing patches even after patches have been deployed?

A: The data displayed in the console does not automatically get refreshed after patches are deployed. Try running another scan. If the machine still appears to be missing patches, there might be additional patches that need to be applied, but that could not be applied until the previous patches were put in place. In some cases, you may find that workstations need to be rebooted before a patch is acknowledged.

Q: How can I schedule a missing patch scan?

A: Go to the management console's Configuration screen. Next, navigate through the console tree to **Configuration | Settings | Scheduled Scans**. Right-click on the Scheduled Scans container and choose the **New | Scheduled Scan** commands from the shortcut menu.

Chapter 8

Installing GFI EndPointSecurity

Solutions in this chapter:

- **Hardware and Software Requirements**

- **Installing GFI EndPointSecurity**

- **Performing the Initial Configuration**

- **Installing the ReportPack**

☑ **Summary**

☑ **Solutions Fast Track**

☑ **Frequently Asked Questions**

Introduction

For many years, I have believed that one of the biggest threats to the security of most networks is the end user's workstation. You just never know when a user is going to try to install unauthorized software, copy sensitive data onto removable media, or perform some other action to try to circumvent your network's security.

GFI EndPointSecurity can help with these types of problems by allowing you to lock down any hardware devices that are not specifically required for a user to do their job. For example, you can create a policy that forbids end users from using Universal Serial Bus (USB) ports. This would prevent a user from using a USB flash drive to bring in unauthorized software, or from using a flash drive to copy sensitive data. Over the next few chapters, I will show you how to use GFI EndPointSecurity to lock down the computers on your network.

Hardware and Software Requirements

GFI EndPointSecurity has two different sets of system requirements. One set of requirements is for the server that will actually be running GFI EndPointSecurity. The other set of requirements is for the computers that are being managed, and will therefore run the GFI EndPointSecurity Agent. Details on how to deploy the agent will be covered in the next chapter.

Requirements for the GFI EndPointSecurity Server

The server's hardware requirements are fairly modest. Your server will need at least:

- A processor with a 2 GHz or higher clock speed
- 512MB of RAM (a gigabyte or more is recommended)
- At least 100MB of available hard disk space.

The software requirements are as follows:

- Windows 2000 (with SP4 or higher), Windows XP, Windows Server 2003, Windows Vista, or Windows Server 2008 (both the 32-bit and the 64-bit versions of Windows Server 2008 are supported)
- Internet Explorer 5.5. or higher
- Version 2.0 of the Microsoft .NET Framework
- SQL Server 2000, 2005, or 2008 (SQL Server can be installed on a separate server).

Additionally, you must open Transmission Control Protocol (TCP) port 1116 on the server's firewall.

The GFI EndPointSecurityAgent's Requirements

GFI EndPointSecurity requires an agent to be run on computers that are being locked down. This agent is aware of the protection policies that you set, and it intercepts calls to unauthorized hardware devices. This agent's requirements are minimal, but you should still verify that the managed machines meet the necessary criteria.

The Agent's Hardware Requirements

The agent's hardware requirements are:

- A Central Processing Unit (CPU) with a clock speed of at least 1 GHz.
- A minimum of 256MB of RAM (512MB or more is recommended)
- 50MB or more of available hard disk space

The Agent's Software Requirements

The agent does not really have any software requirements beyond requiring specific versions of the Windows operating system. The supported versions of Windows are:

- Windows 2000 (with SP4 or higher)
- Windows XP
- Windows Server 2003
- Windows Vista
- Windows Server 2008 (X86 and X64 versions are both supported)

Installing GFI EndPointSecurity

Now that you have verified that your server meets the various hardware and software requirements, it is time to install GFI EndPointSecurity. To do so, follow these steps:

1. Log into the server with local administrative privileges.
2. Begin the process by downloading GFI EndPointSecurity from the GFI Website at: www. gfi.com/downloads/downloads.aspx?pid=esec&lid=EN TE. Once again, it can be risky to include outside links to Web pages that cannot be controlled. If the link changes, it makes the reference in the book obsolete. You can also download the installation manual and the product's user manual from the same location. The file that you will be downloading is a 10.6MB self-extracting executable named EndPointSecurity4.exe. Save this file to a temporary directory, and then double-click on it to start the installation process.
3. If Windows presents you with a security warning, click the **Run** button to move forward with the installation process.
4. You will now be prompted to select the language that you want to use for the installation. Choose the **English** option (or another language if you prefer), and click **OK**.
5. Windows will now launch the GFI EndPointSecurity Setup Wizard. Click **Next** to clear the wizard's Welcome screen.

6. At this point, you will be prompted to accept the End User License Agreement (EULA). After doing so, click the **Next** button.

7. The next screen that you will encounter explains that GFI EndPointSecurity uses agents to generate event information, and that you will need to use a service account to listen for these events. Because of the nature of the job, you will have to provide credentials for a domain administrator account. After doing so, click **Next** to continue.

8. You will now be prompted to enter your name, the name of your company, and your license key. If you are installing GFI EndPointSecurity in trial mode, then enter the word **EVALUATION** (all caps) into the License Key field, as shown in Figure 8.1. Using an evaluation key will give you full use of the product for ten days. After that time expires, you can purchase a license and add a license key to your existing installation without having to reinstall the software.

Figure 8.1 You Can Enter the Word EVALUATION in Place of a License Key

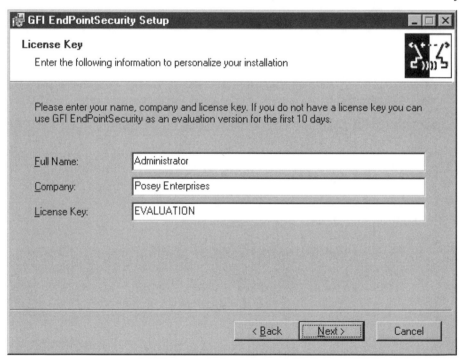

9. Click **Next**.

10. You will now be prompted to confirm the installation path to be used by the product. Unless you've got a compelling reason to use a different path, accept the defaults and click **Next**.

11. You will now see a message telling you that GFI EndPointSecurity is ready to be installed. Click **Next** to begin the installation process.

12. Setup will now begin copying all of the necessary files. When setup completes, click **Finish**.

Performing the Initial Configuration

Now that the initial installation is complete, go ahead and open the GFI EndPointSecurity console. The console should have opened automatically upon the completion of the installation process, but you can also open it manually by choosing the **GFI EndPointSecurity 4.0** command from the **Start | All Programs | GFI EndPointSecurity 4.0** menu. When the console opens, you will see the Component Configuration Quick Start screen, shown in Figure 8.2.

Figure 8.2 The Component Configuration Quick Start Screen Guides You Through the Initial Configuration Process

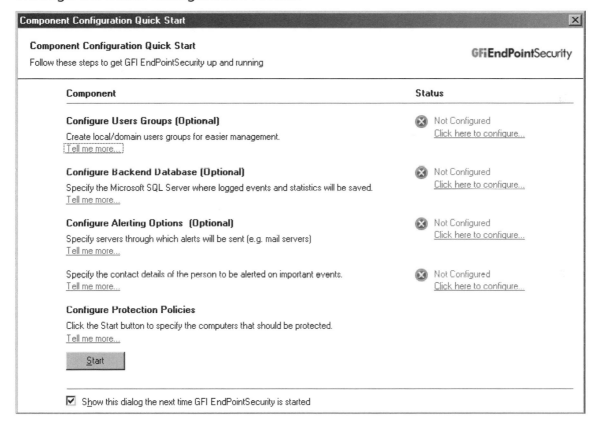

Configure User Groups

The first thing that you will want to configure is the user group. Personally, I think that the way that this section is labeled is a bit vague, and that it doesn't really give you a good idea of what this configuration task involves, or why you are performing it, so here's the deal. The Configure Users Groups configuration task gives you the chance to create various hardware groups that you can restrict later on. The reason why this is important is because you will want to lock down the hardware devices that pose a potential security threat, but you will probably need to leave some devices enabled for certain users so that they have the ability to access any hardware that they use for doing their jobs.

The actual way that you would configure the users groups in real life is going to vary depending on your company's needs. Let's pretend that most of the users in your organization are going to need access to the majority of the hardware devices on their computers, but that you want to deny access to the computer's USB and FireWire ports. We can't actually put this denial in place just yet, but we can create a group that allows us to manage USB and FireWire ports. To do so, follow these steps:

1. Click the **Click Here to Configure** link. When you do, you will see a list of all of the endpoint hardware devices that you can manage, as shown in Figure 8.3.

2. Deselect all of the hardware options except for USB and FireWire.

3. Click the **Create** button.

Figure 8.3 Deselect All of the Hardware Devices Except for the USB and FireWire Ports

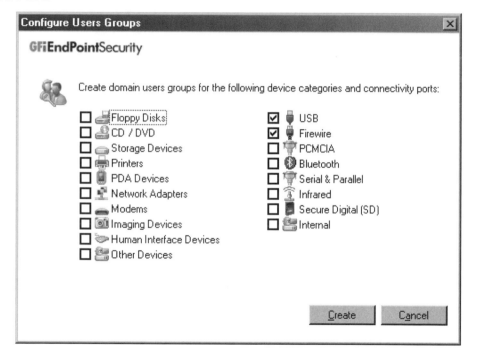

When you are done, you will see a message stating that Windows user groups were created successfully. Click **OK**, and you will be automatically returned to the Component Configuration Quick Start screen. Please be aware that because of a bug in the software, the Configure Users Groups option may still show a status of Not Configured.

You have the option of creating some additional groups, but rather than configure all of your groups at once, I want to stop here so that I can show you how to configure groups from within the console later on.

NOTE

When you click the OK button, the Component Configuration Quick Start screen may not acknowledge the Configure User Groups task as being complete. I have found that repeating the task seems to correct this issue.

Configure the Backend Database

The next step in the initial configuration process is to configure a backend database. Technically, configuring a backend database is optional (as are all of the initial configuration tasks), but it doesn't mean that using a database is optional. It only means that you do not have to configure a database right this minute if you don't want to. Since the database plays such an important role in GFI EndPointSecurity, I want to go ahead and set it up now. For demonstration purposes, I will be configuring GFI EndPointSecurity to use a Structured Query Language (SQL) Server 2005 database. Keep in mind that other versions of SQL Server are also supported, and that the SQL Server database does not have to reside locally.

To configure the SQL Server database, perform the following steps:

1. Click the **Click Here to Configure** link found in the Configure Backend Database section.

2. At this point, you will see a screen prompting you to enter the name of the server and database that you want to use. Enter either the name or the IP address of your database server, followed by a back slash and the name of the database instance. For example, I have a SQL Server instance named GFI installed onto my local server. Therefore, I am using [Local]\GFI as the server name. If your database is not installed locally, then just replace [local] with the Network Basic Input/Output System (NetBIOS) name or Internet Protocol (IP) address of your database server.

3. Enter **EndPointSecurity** into the Database field. Choose the **Windows Authentication** option, as shown in Figure 8.4.

4. Choose the **Use Windows Authentication** option.

5. Click **OK**.

6. GFI EndPointSecurity will now create the necessary database, as shown in Figure 8.5. When the process completes, click **OK**.

Figure 8.4 Enter the Server Name and the SQL Server Instance Name for the Database Server That You Want to Use

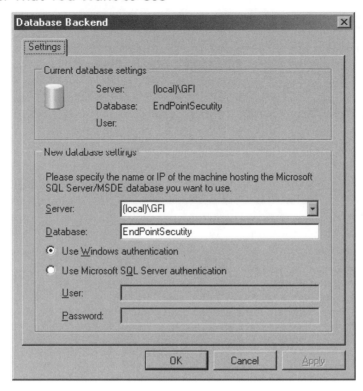

Figure 8.5 The Software Goes Through Several Different Steps to Create the Database

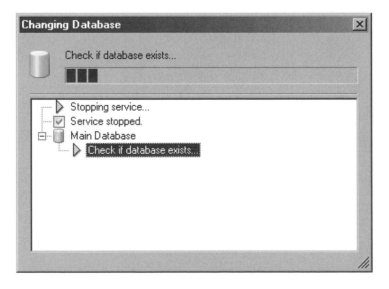

Configure Alerting Options

GFI EndPointSecurity has the ability to send e-mail alerts whenever certain events occur. Configuring the e-mail alerts can be a bit tricky, but in my opinion, it is well worth the effort. Since configuring e-mail alerts does tend to be a bit tricky, I'm going to show you two different ways of setting them up. The first method involves configuring Internet Information Server (IIS) to act as an Simple Mail Transfer Protocol (SMTP) server, and then using it to send e-mail alerts. The other method involves using a Microsoft Exchange Server. Both methods will work, but if you have an Exchange Server on your network, I recommend using it.

Configuring a Standalone SMTP Server

If you don't have access to an Exchange Server, you can configure your GFI EndPointSecurity server to act as a standalone SMTP server. Windows ships with everything that you need, but the SMTP components are not installed by default. The exact method of installing the SMTP components varies depending on the version of Windows that you are using. For the purposes of this book, I will be using Windows Server 2003.

1. Begin the process by having whoever is in charge of your organization's e-mail create a dedicated mailbox that you can use for receiving server notifications. For demonstration purposes, I am going to be using a mailbox with an address of Security@production.com. I do not actually own the production.com domain, it is just the name of an internal Active Directory domain that I use. You should use an e-mail address that reflects the mail domain that you use in real life.

2. Once the new mailbox has been created, open the server's Control Panel, and select the **Add or Remove Programs** option.

3. When Windows displays the Add or Remove Programs dialog box, click the **Add/ Remove Windows Components** icon.

4. After a brief delay, Windows will launch the Windows Component Wizard. Choose the **Application Server** option from the list of available components. Don't click on the check box, just click on the words **Application Server**.

5. Click the **Details** button, and you will see the various Application Server components.

6. Click on the **Internet Information Services (IIS)** component. Once again, you should click on the words, not the check box.

7. Click the **Details** button, and Windows will display a list of the various IIS components that are available.

8. Scroll toward the bottom of the list of components, and then select the **SMTP Service** option. This time you are actually going to select the check box rather than just clicking on the words, as shown in Figure 8.6.

Figure 8.6 You Must Select the SMTP Service Option

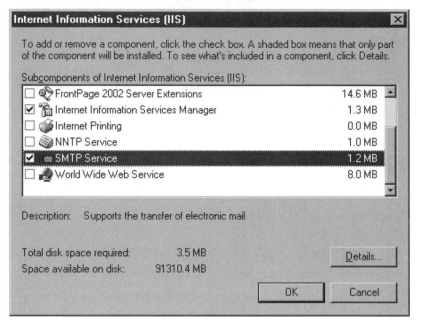

9.   Click **OK**.

10.   Click **OK**.

11.   Click **Next** and Windows will begin installing the necessary files. Depending on how your server is configured, you may be prompted to insert your Windows Server 2003 installation media.

12.   When the installation process completes, click the **Finish** button, and close the Control Panel.

13.   Now that the SMTP Service is installed, we need to configure it. Fortunately, the configuration process is pretty simple.

14.   Choose the **Internet Information Services (IIS)** option from the server's Administrative Tools menu.

15.   When the IIS Manager opens, navigate through the console tree to **Internet Information Services | your server | Default SMTP Virtual Server | Domains,** as shown in Figure 8.7.

Figure 8.7 Navigate Through the Console Tree to Internet Information Services | Your Server | Default SMTP Virtual Server | Domains

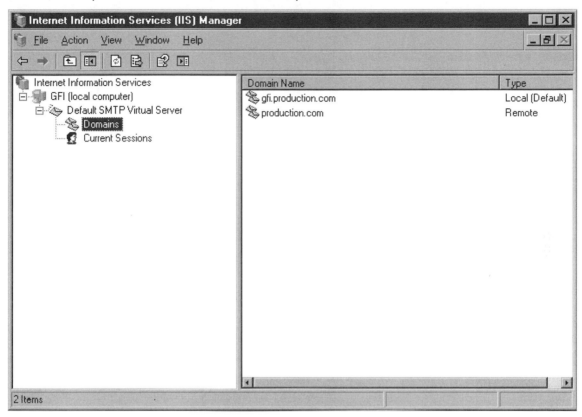

Notice in the screen capture above, that when I selected the Domains container, the pane on the right displayed two domain names. The top domain name, in this case gfi.production.com, was placed there by default. Gfi.production.com is actually the server's Fully Qualified Domain Name (FQDN), but the SMTP service treats it as though it were an independent domain.

As it stands right now, the SMTP service is only capable of sending e-mail to recipients in the gfi.production.com domain. Of course there aren't any mailboxes in this domain, because the server that we are configuring isn't a full blown mail server. The SMTP component only allows us to send mail, it does not allow for the storage of mailboxes on the server.

That being the case, we must make the SMTP Service aware of the domain that we want to send e-mail to. In this case, we will be sending messages to an e-mail address named Security@ production.com. Since this mailbox resides in the production.com domain (or at least in an internal domain named production.com), we need to make the SMTP Service aware of the domain's existence, which I did when I created the screen capture above. That's why you see the production. com domain listed in the console. Here's how it's done:

1. Right click on the **Domains** container, and choose the **New | Domain** options from the resulting shortcut menus.

2. Windows will now launch the New SMTP Domain Wizard. The wizard's initial screen asks you if you want to specify a remote domain or an alias. Choose the **Remote** option, and click **Next**.

3. Enter the name of the domain that you want to send mail to, into the space provided.

4. Click **Finish**, and the domain that you have specified will be added to the list of domains.

5. Right-click on the domain that you just added, and then select the **Properties** command from the resulting shortcut menu.

6. When the domain's properties sheet appears, select the **Allow Incoming Mail to be Relayed to this Domain** check box, as shown in Figure 8.8.

Figure 8.8 You Must Allow Incoming Mail to Be Relayed to the Domain That You Just Set Up

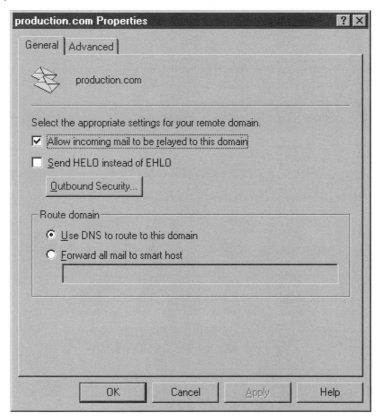

Now that we have configured Windows to act as an SMTP server, it's time to configure GFI EndPointSecurity to use the SMTP server to send mail. To do so, follow these steps:

1. Click the **Click Here to Configure** link found on the Component Configuration Quick Start screen's Configure Alerting Options section.

2. Windows will now display the Alerting Options properties sheet. Select the properties sheet's **Email** tab, and click the **Add** button.

3. Enter **127.0.0.1** into the Hostname/IP field. This is the server's local loopback address. By entering this address, you are telling the server to use itself as an SMTP server. Alternatively, you could also use the server's IP address in this field.

4. Verify that the Port field is set to **25**.

5. Make sure that the **This SMTP Server Requires Authentication** check box is not selected.

6. You can use any e-mail address in the From field, so long as the domain portion of the address reflects the server's FQDN. In this case, the server's FQDN is gfi.production.com.

7. Enter the destination e-mail address into the **To** field. Keep in mind that you can only send messages to recipients with mailboxes in domains that you have specified through the IIS Manager.

When you have finished filling in the Mailserver Properties sheet, it should look something like what you see in Figure 8.9.

Figure 8.9 This is How You Must Configure the Mailserver Properties Sheet

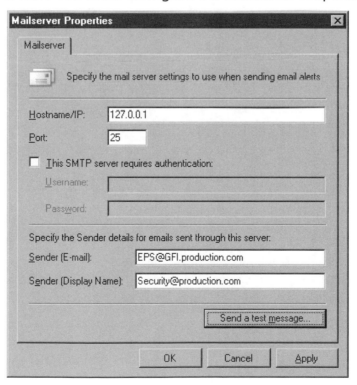

When you are done, click the **Send a Test Message** button. When you do, you should see a message telling you that the mail settings were successfully verified, and that a test message was sent. It is important to check the specified mailbox to make sure that the message has actually come through, because Setup has no way of knowing whether or not the test message was actually received.

Once you have confirmed that the test message was received, click **OK**, and you will be returned to the Alerting Options properties sheet. The address 127.0.0.1 should appear in the list of mail servers, as shown in Figure 8.10.

Figure 8.10 127.0.0.1 Now Appears in the List of Mail Servers

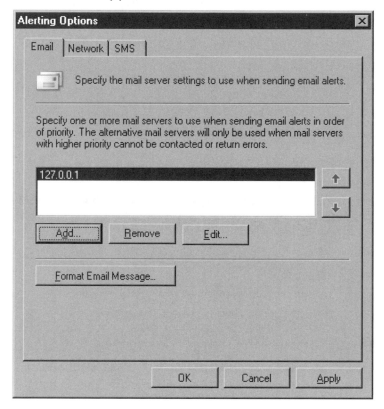

As you look at the figure, you will also notice a Format Email Message button. Clicking this button allows you to customize the messages that GFI EndPointSecurity sends out. Normally though, you should just stick with the default message format unless you have a compelling reason to change it.

One more thing that you might have noticed about the figure above is that the properties sheet also contains tabs labeled Network and SMS. These tabs contain other alerting options that I will talk about later in this chapter.

Notes from the Underground...

Mail Relay

You need to be careful about how you configure your SMTP server, and how it is used. As it is right now, your SMTP server can transmit mail without requiring authentication. Should this server become compromised, it could easily be turned into a "spam factory" and the resulting spam would be traced back to your IP address, which would likely get you blacklisted.

Configuring GFI EndPointSecurity for Use With Microsoft Exchange Server

Although I am writing this book on GFI security software, I am best known throughout the Information Technology (IT) community for my work with Microsoft Exchange Server. That being the case, I wanted to show you an alternate mail settings configuration that you can use if you have an Exchange Server organization in place.

As I mentioned earlier, my internal domain name is production.com. I therefore created an Exchange Server mailbox with an e-mail address of Security@production.com. Since I don't actually own the production.com domain name, this e-mail address is only accessible from within my perimeter network.

I'm not going to go through the steps of creating an Exchange Server mailbox, because these steps are performed in a very different manner from one version of Exchange Server to the next. Besides, if your company has an Exchange Server organization in place, I would think that it would be a safe assumption that somebody in the company knows how to create a mailbox. I will tell you that my Security@production.com mailbox resides on an Exchange 2007 server.

If your company has an Exchange Server organization in place, then the process of configuring the mail settings for GFI EndPointSecurity will be a lot simpler than what you saw in the previous section. That's because in the previous section, we had to build an SMTP server from scratch. Exchange Server is natively equipped to handle SMTP mail, so we don't have to bother with most of those configuration steps. In fact, all of the configuration takes place through the Alerting Options properties sheet. To configure GFI EndPointSecurity to use your Exchange Server to send e-mail alerts, follow these steps:

1. Click the **Click Here to Configure** link found in the Component Configuration Quick Start screen's Configure Alerting Options section.

2. Windows will now display the Alerting Options properties sheet. Verify that the properties sheet's **Email** tab is selected.

3. Click the **Add** button.

4. Enter your Exchange Server's IP address into the Hostname/IP field.

5. Verify that the port number is set to **25**.

6. Select the **This SMTP Server Requires Authentication** check box.

7. As you may recall, we created a mailbox called Security@production.com to receive e-mail alerts. We are going to use this mailbox as both the sender and the recipient. Of course you will want to substitute the e-mail address that you have configured for Security@production.com in the following steps. With that said, enter **Security@production.com** into the Username field. (Windows allows you to substitute an e-mail address for a username.)

8. Enter the mailbox password into the Password field.

9. Enter **Security@Production.com** into the Sender (e-mail) field.

10. Enter the words **GFI EndPointSecurity** into the Sender (Display Name) field. The Mailserver Properties dialog box should now look something like what you see in Figure 8.11.

11. Click the **Send a Test Message** button.

12. When prompted, enter the recipient's e-mail address. In this case, I am using Security@production.com as the recipient e-mail address.

13. Click **OK** to acknowledge that the message was sent.

14. Open Outlook or Outlook Web Access (OWA) to confirm that the test message has been received. You can see what the test message looks like in Figure 8.12.

15. Click **OK** to close the Mailserver properties sheet.

Figure 8.11 This is What the Mailserver Properties Dialog Box Should Look Like When Fully Populated

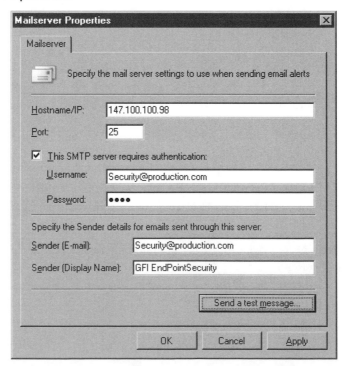

Figure 8.12 You Should Receive a Test Message From Setup

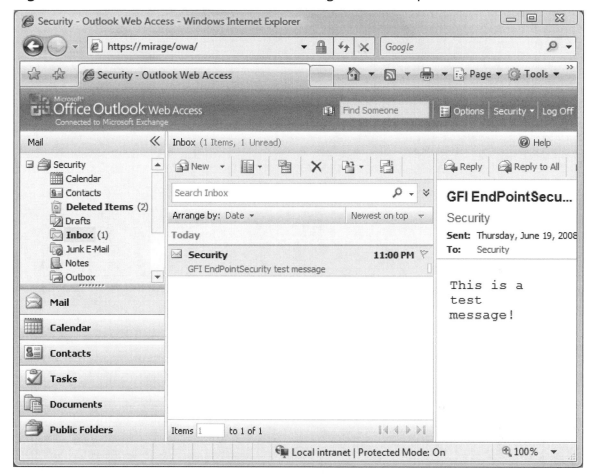

> **NOTE**
>
> It is important to verify that you have actually received the test message. GFI EndPointSecurity is only able to acknowledge that it has attempted to send a message. The software checks for common SMTP error codes, but ultimately it is up to you to make sure that message delivery has occurred.

If you are using Exchange Server 2007, there may be one more thing that you need to do before you will be able to receive the test message. Exchange 2007 is designed so that the hub transport only allows secure, authenticated connections. This means that if you simply specify the IP address of a hub transport server, the Exchange Server is going to reject the test message.

There are two ways of getting around this problem. The best option is to use the IP address of an edge transport server as the SMTP server address. If you don't have an edge transport server, then you will need to allow anonymous connections to the transport pipeline. You can do this by opening the Exchange Management Shell and entering the following command:

```
set-ReceiveConnector "Default <Servername>" -permissiongroups:"ExchangeUsers,
ExchangeServers,ExchangeLegacyServers,AnonymousUsers"
```

As you can see in Figure 8.13, the command doesn't really appear to do anything when executed, but it should allow you to send messages from your GFI EndPointSecurity server to a mailbox on the Exchange 2007 mailbox server.

Figure 8.13 The Set-ReceiveConnector Command Doesn't Appear to Do Anything When it is Executed

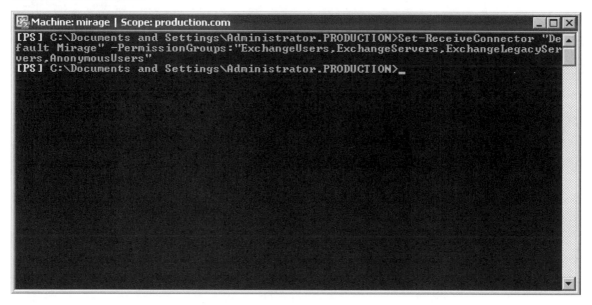

Formatting Your E-Mail Message

Regardless of whether you choose to use an Exchange Server or an SMTP Server, you have the option of customizing the e-mail message that is sent when an alert is triggered. To do so, click the **Format E-mail Message** button found on the Alerting Options properties sheet's Email tab. GFI provides you with a rather nice default e-mail message, but if you want to make modifications to this message, it is easy to do so. Clicking the **Format Email Message** button opens a text editor that you can use to compose your message. You can even insert EndPointSecurity specific tags and rich text.

Network Alerts

Although GFI EndPointSecurity's primary alert mechanism is e-mail, it also uses network messages and Systems Management Server (SMS) text messages as other mechanisms for sending alerts. If you look at Figure 8.14, you will see the Alerting Options properties sheet's Network tab. As you can see in the figure, there really isn't a lot that you can do on this tab, other than formatting the network message.

It may seem odd, but GFI does not provide you with a default network alert message. It is up to you to create a message that contains the information that you want to convey to your security staff. Fortunately, GFI does provide you with some tools to make this process easy.

If you click the Format Network Message button, windows will display the Format Message dialog box. This dialog box allows you to enter the text that you wish to display within the message. Usually though, a generic message isn't going to do your security staff a whole lot of good. Fortunately, the dialog box contains an Insert Tags option that you can use to insert specific information into the alert message. If you look at Figure 8.15, you can see the Insert Tag option overlayed above a simple message that I have begun creating. When you have finished creating your alert message, click the **Save** button.

Figure 8.14 You Can Compose a Network Message by Clicking the Format Network Message Button

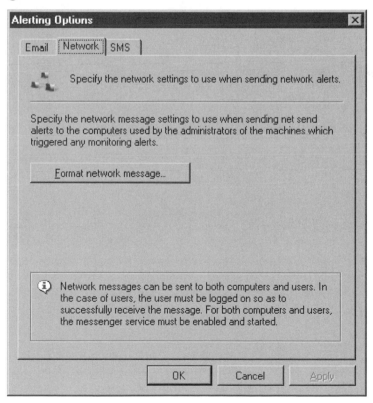

Figure 8.15 The Editor Allows You to Insert EndPointSecurity Specific Tags

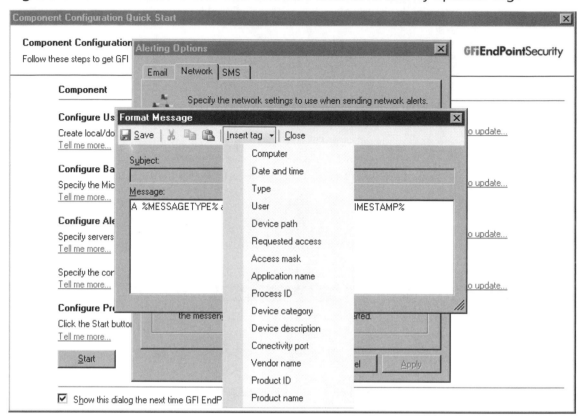

SMS Alerts

As I mentioned earlier, GFI EndPointSecurity also gives you the option of sending SMS text messages to mobile phones. SMS text messages are configured through the properties sheet's SMS tab, which is very similar to the Network tab. The only real difference is that the SMS tab provides the option of choosing the mechanism that you want to use for transmitting SMS messages. Normally, you shouldn't have to change the defaults. However, like your network alerts, you will need to compose the SMS message that you want to transmit.

NOTE

Many mobile phones only support very short SMS messages. Therefore, you probably won't be able to provide nearly as much detail in an SMS message as you would in an e-mail alert or in a network message.

Who Gets Alerted?

In case you haven't noticed, alerts are a major part of GFI EndPointSecurity. In the previous section, we set up some mechanisms for sending alerts via e-mail, Windows message, and SMS text message. You might have noticed, however, that we haven't told GFI EndPointSecurity which types of alerts to use and under what circumstances, or who to send the alerts to. If you look at Figure 8.16, you will notice that there is still a section that is labeled Not Configured on the Component Configuration Quick Start screen. Click the **Click Here to Configure** link to start the configuration process. When you do, Windows will display the EndPointSecurityAdministrator properties sheet, shown in Figure 8.17.

Figure 8.16 Click the Click Here to Configure Link

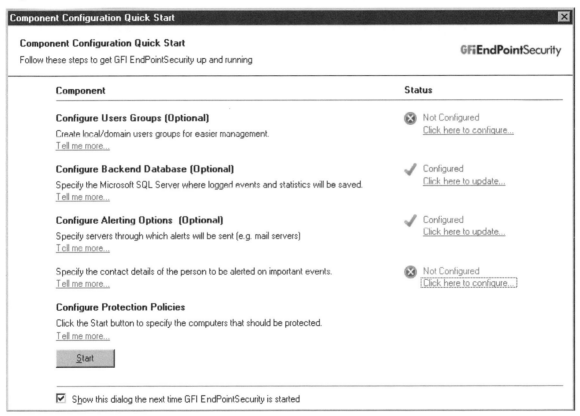

Figure 8.17 The EndPointSecurityAdministrator Properties Sheet Allows You to Control Which Administrators Receive the Alerts

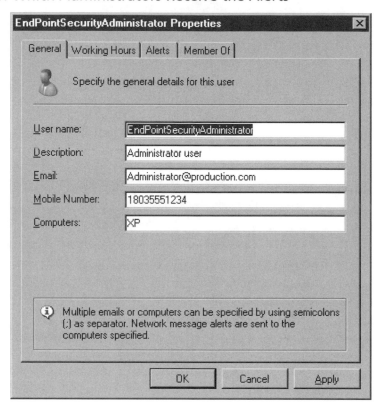

This property corresponds to a built-in security group called EndPointSecurityAdministrator. The basic idea is that you can add e-mail addresses, cell phone numbers, and computers to this group. When policies that you set later on mandate that alerts be sent to the EndPointSecurityAdministrator group, alerts will be sent using the information that you provide on this properties sheet.

As you can see in the figure above, the properties sheet's General tab is pretty simple. It allows you to enter any e-mail addresses, mobile numbers, or computers that you want to send alerts to. We have already told the Setup wizard that we want alerts to be sent to a specific mailbox (in my case it was Security@production.com), but now we need to tell GFI EndPointSecurity who the administrators are going to be, and how they should be alerted.

If you specify an e-mail address, the alert will arrive via e-mail. If you choose to provide any mobile numbers, then SMS-based text messages will be sent to those mobile devices. If you decide to list any computers, then Windows pop-up messages will be sent to those machines. Keep in mind that the Windows Messenger service must be running on any computer that you specify. If you need to enter multiple values for any of the fields, separate the values with a semicolon.

Once you have populated the alert list, go to the Working Hours tab, shown in Figure 8.18. As you can see in the figure, the Working Hours tab allows you to tell GFI EndPointSecurity what normal working hours are for your company.

After you finish telling GFI EndPointSecurity about your company's business hours, go to the properties sheet's Alerts tab. As you can see in the figure, you have the option of controlling which types of alerts will be sent to the group during business hours, and what types of alerts will be sent after hours. For example, if your IT security staff is glued to their computers all day long, then sending a network message alert might be a really good way to insure that the members of your security staff are alerted quickly when certain types of events occur. At night, however, those people have all gone home, so it wouldn't make sense to display a network message alert on their computer if they aren't there to see it. In such a situation, it would probably be better to send the alert to their cell phones, as shown in Figure 8.19.

Figure 8.18 You Can Tell GFI EndPoint Security What Your Company's Normal Office Hours Are

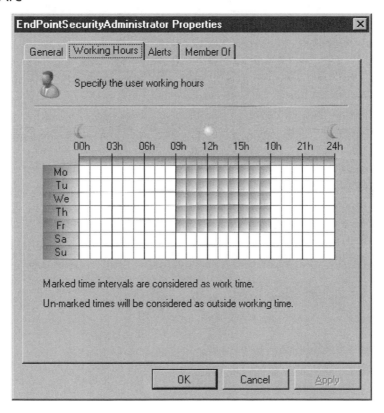

Figure 8.19 You May Need to Use a Different Alerting Mechanism After Hours

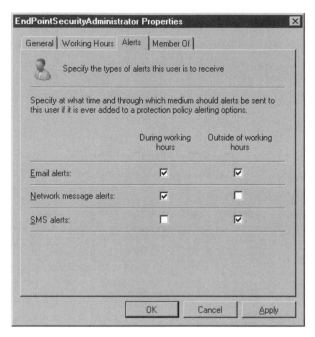

When you have finished deciding which alerting mechanisms should be used, click **OK**. The initial configuration process is now complete.

Installing the ReportPack

In the first section of this book, I showed you how to install the ReportPack that went with GFI LANguard Network Security Scanner. However, each of the GFI products that are ReportPack compatible uses its own version of the ReportPack, containing reports that are specifically designed for that product. Because of this, I want to walk you through the process of installing the GFI EndPointSecurity ReportPack.

1. Download the ReportPack software, and save it to a temporary directory. You can download the ReportPack at: www.gfi.com/downloads/downloads.aspx?pid=esec&lid=EN. The download consists of a 6MB self-extracting executable file named endpointsecurity4rp report pack.exe.

2. Double-click on the file that you've downloaded.

3. If you receive a Windows security warning, click the **Run** button.

4. Windows will now launch the GFI EndPointSecurity 4.0 ReportPack Setup Wizard. Click **Next** to bypass the wizard's Welcome screen.

5. You will now see a screen asking you if you want to check for a newer version of the ReportPack software. Choose the option to **check for a new version**, and click **Next**.

6. The next screen that you will encounter displays the EULA. Choose the option to accept the license agreement, and click **OK**.

7. You will now see a screen asking you to enter your full name, your company name, and your license key. If you have not yet purchased a GFI EndPointSecurity license, you can enter the word **Evaluation** in place of a license key. Using the evaluation version will allow you to use the ReportPack and all of its features for ten days. I should point out, however, that although the ReportPack is a separate download, a ReportPack license is included when you buy a license for GFI EndPointSecurity. If you've already bought a GFI EndPointSecurity, you can use the same license key for the ReportPack that you used for the main product.

8. Click **Next**.

9. Setup will now display a screen similar to the one shown in Figure 8.2, asking you which type of database you want to use. As you can see in the figure, you have the option of using a sample database or a Microsoft SQL Server database. Although the test database option allows you to play with the ReportPack and its features, you will have to use the same SQL Server database as GFI EndPoint Security is using if the ReportPack is to be of any value in a production environment. Therefore, select the **Use SQL Server Database** option.

10. Select the server that is hosting your SQL Server database.

11. Enter the name of the database server and the name of the SQL Server instance that GFI EndPointSecurity is using into the Database field. The server name and SQL instance name should be entered in SERVER\INSTANCE format, as shown in Figure 8.20.

12. Select the **Use Windows Authentication** check box.

13. Click **Next**.

14. You are now going to see a screen asking you to configure the mail settings for the ReportPack. Unfortunately, I can't tell you exactly what to type here, because it is going to be different for each organization. What I can tell you is that the settings that you use should be identical to the settings that you used earlier in this chapter when you configured the mail settings for GFI EndPointSecurity. You can see what the Mail Settings for my organization look like in Figure 8.21.

15. After entering your Mail Settings, click the **Verify Mail Settings** button. You should receive a message indicating that the test message was sent successfully. Keep in mind that it is possible that you will receive this message even if some of your mail settings are wrong. It is very important that you check to make sure that the message was actually delivered. You can see what the test message looks like in Figure 8.22.

16. Once you have confirmed that your mail settings are functioning properly, click **Next**.

17. You should now see a screen asking you to confirm the destination folder. Accept the default installation path, and click **Next**.

18. You should now see a message indicating that Setup is ready to install the application. Click **Next**, and the Setup wizard will begin copying the necessary files.

19. When the file copy process completes, click **Finish**.

Figure 8.20 This is How the Database Selection Screen Should Look

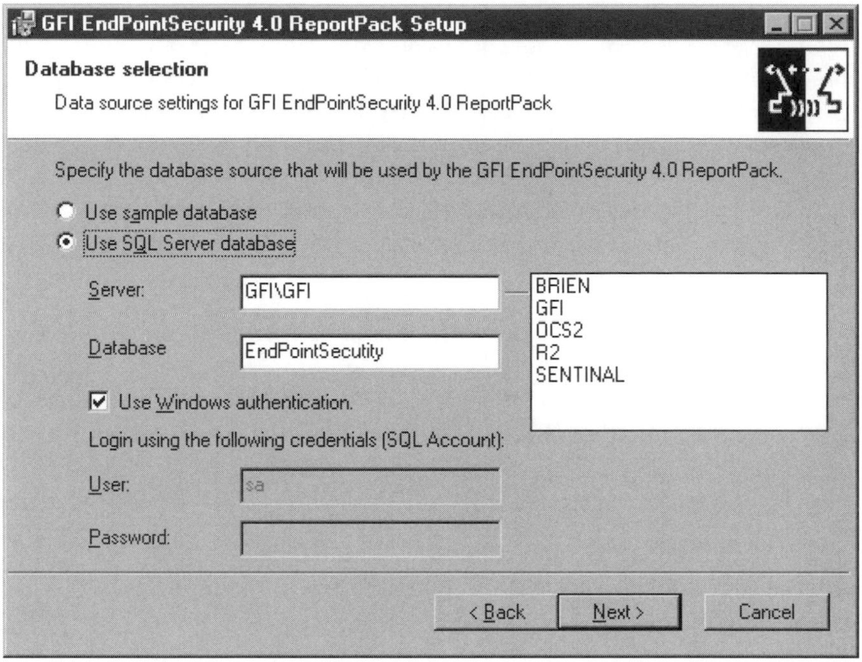

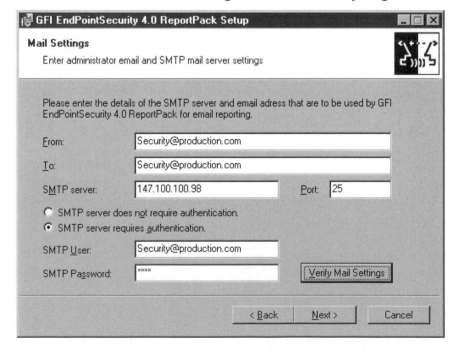

Figure 8.21 This is What the Mail Settings Look Like for My Organization

Figure 8.22 It is Very Important to Confirm That the Test Message Was Actually Delivered

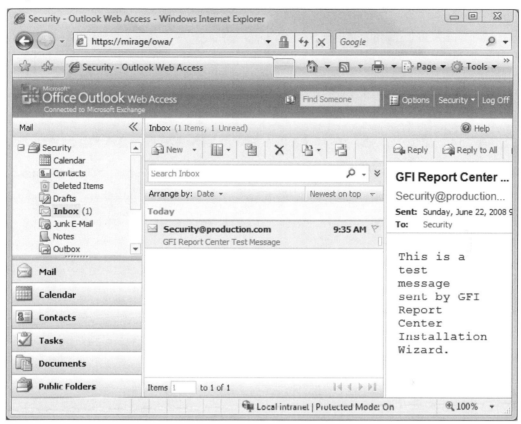

Summary

As you can see, the installation process and the initial configuration process for GFI EndPoint Security tend to be a bit tedious. Since so much work is involved, I recommend taking one last look at the Component Configuration Quick Start screen to make sure that everything has been configured, as shown in Figure 8.23. We will deal with configuring protection policies in the next chapter.

Figure 8.23 It's a Good Idea to Do One Last Check to Make Sure That Everything Has Been Configured

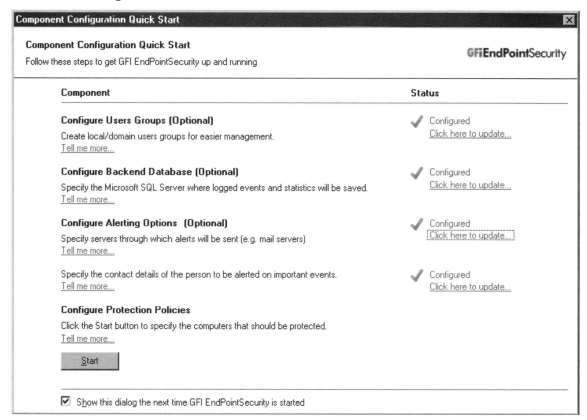

Solutions Fast Track

Hardware and Software Requirements

- ☑ A processor with a 2 GHz or higher clock speed
- ☑ 512MB of RAM (a gigabyte or more is recommended)
- ☑ At least 100MB of available hard disk space.

☑ Windows 2000 (with SP4 or higher), Windows XP, Windows Server 2003, Windows Vista, or Windows Server 2008 (both the 32-bit and the 64-bit versions of Windows Server 2008 are supported)

☑ Internet Explorer 5.5. or higher

☑ Version 2.0 of the Microsoft .NET Framework

☑ SQL Server 2000, 2005, or 2008 (Server can be installed on a separate server).

Installing GFI EndPointSecurity

☑ You can use either a SQL Server database or an Microsoft Database Engine (better known as MSDE or SQL Server 2005 Express Edition) database, but a SQL Server database is preferred in larger organizations.

☑ You can configure GFI EndPointSecurity to use either a Microsoft Exchange Server or a standalone SMTP server. If you have an Exchange Server in your organization, I recommend using it.

Performing the Initial Configuration

☑ Alerts can occur 24 hours a day, so it is important to configure alerts that happen after business hours in a way that administrators can receive them.

☑ The contact information that you provide during the initial configuration will be used for the delivery of alerts.

Installing the ReportPack

☑ Make sure that you configure the ReportPack to use the same database that GFI EndPointSecurity is using.

Frequently Asked Questions

Q: Can I use an MSDE database with GFI EndPointSecurity?

A: Sure, but I would only recommend doing so in smaller organizations, as MSDE does not scale well.

Q: Does GFI EndPointSecurity support the use of Microsoft Access databases?

A: No, some GFI products do allow Microsoft Access databases to be used, but this one doesn't.

Q: I don't have an Exchange Server, but I may want to use one later on. Is this possible?

A: Yes, the management console allows you to reconfigure your alerting options.

Q: How do I know if I need SQL Server?

A: Smaller organizations don't have to have SQL Server. However, if your organization has more than 100 PCs, I would recommend using SQL Server. Keep in mind that this is just my recommendation, not GFI's, and it certainly isn't a requirement.

Q: The installation process seems to be taking forever. Is this normal?

A: On my lab machines, the installation process was fairly quick. Keep in mind, however, that your server hardware has a lot to do with the speed of the installation.

Q: Can I piggyback GFI EndPointSecurity onto a server that is running other applications?

A: It is possible, but I would recommend using a dedicated server if possible for security and performance reasons.

Q: Can I install a SQL Server database onto the same server that is going to be running GFI EndPointSecurity?

A: Assuming that your server has the resources to run both, then yes.

Chapter 9

Defining Protection Policies

Solutions in this chapter:

- **Creating Protection Policies**
- **Deploying Agents**
- **Setting Device Permissions**

- ☑ **Summary**
- ☑ **Solutions Fast Track**
- ☑ **Frequently Asked Questions**

Introduction

In the previous chapter, we worked through the installation and initial configuration process for GFI EndPointSecurity. Now it's time to actually begin using the software. Throughout this chapter, and the remainder of the section on GFI EndPointSecurity, you will find that this is one of the more passive security tools. Using it involves setting up some policies, and then letting it do its thing.

Creating Protection Policies

Begin the process by launching GFI EndPointSecurity. You can access it by selecting the **All Programs | GFI EndPointSecurity 4.0 | GFI EndPointSecurity 4.0** commands from the server's Start menu. When the application starts, you will see the now familiar Component Configuration Quick Start screen, shown in Figure 9.1.

Figure 9.1 Click the Start Button to Begin Configuring the Server's Protection Policies

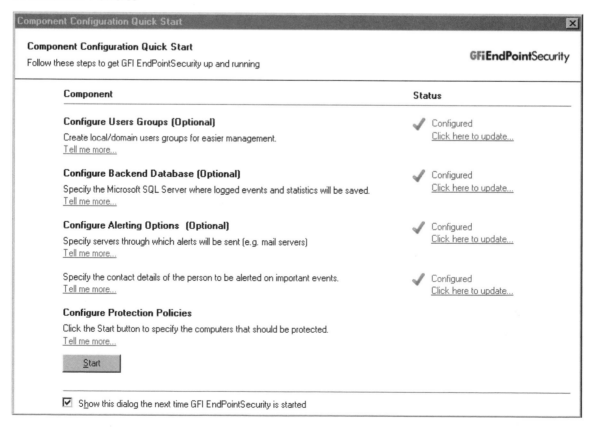

When you click the **Start** button, you will be taken to the screen shown in the Figure 9.2. If you look in the upper left portion of this figure, you can see that GFI EndPointSecurity allows you to create three different types of protection policies. By default, the Servers container is selected, so if you jump right into adding computers to the policy, you will actually be adding those computers to the Servers policy.

Figure 9.2 The Configuration Tab Allows You to Create Protection Policies

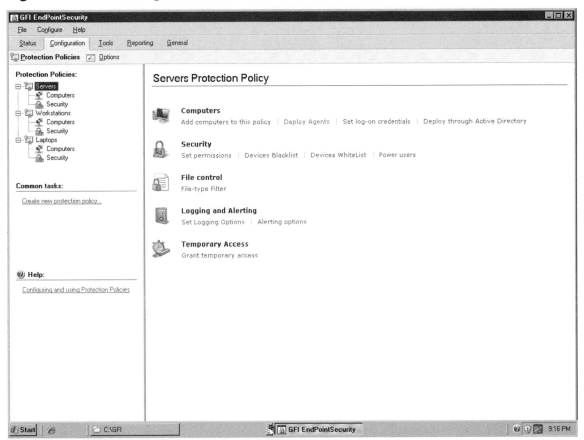

Obviously, every organization has its own unique security needs. My personal feelings are that unless you work in a regulated or high security environment, then setting endpoint policies on servers may be more trouble than it's worth. After all, if you control physical access to the server, and you limit who has the ability to log on directly to the server console so that only trusted administrators have the right to log on locally, then is there really any need to prevent the use of endpoint devices? In high-security or regulated organizations, the answer is probably yes. In other types of organizations, however, it may be common practice for administrators to use removable media for provisioning the server, and it would therefore be counterproductive to impose restrictions on removable media.

In my opinion, the real threats to security lie with workstations and laptops. Therefore, it is important to think long and hard about which types of devices your end users will need access to in order to do their jobs, in which devices you can safely disable. It has been my experience that you can often safely disable just about all of the devices on a desktop workstation. Road Warriors on the other hand, often need a little bit more flexibility. That's why there are separate protection policies for desktop workstations and for laptops.

The actual technique that you will use to create a protection policy is basically identical, whether you are defining a policy for servers, workstations, or laptops. That being the case, I think it would be too repetitive to walk you through each separate type of protection policy; however, I will walk you through the process of creating a workstation protection policy.

Creating a Workstation Protection Policy

Now that we have talked about the different types of protection policies, let's go ahead and create a workstation protection policy. There are a number of different tasks that you will have to perform in order to configure a comprehensive endpoint protection policy for your organization. If you take a moment and look at the figure above though, you will notice that all of the various configuration tasks that you must perform are organized in a logical manner.

Defining the Computers That You Want to Protect

The first step in setting up a workstation protection policy is to create a list of all of the computers that you want to protect. To do so, select the **Workstation** container from the Protection Policies tree, and then click the **Add Computers to This Polic**y link. When you do, you will be taken to a dialog box that allows you to enter the names of the computers that you want to add to the policy by either entering their Network Basic Input/Output System (NetBIOS) names or Internet Protocol (IP) addresses.

Although this method works, it isn't exactly practical, especially for large networks. If you look at Figure 9.3, however, you can see that there are a few other options for creating the list of computers. You have the option of selecting the computers that you want from a domain, searching a domain for computers to add to the list, or of importing a text file containing a list of computers that you want to add to the protection policy. In a large, enterprise class organization, importing a text file is probably going to be the most efficient way of adding computers to the protection policy. I've got a fairly small network, however, so for me it is easier to import computers directly from a domain.

Figure 9.3 You Have Several Different Options for Adding Computers to the Protection Policy

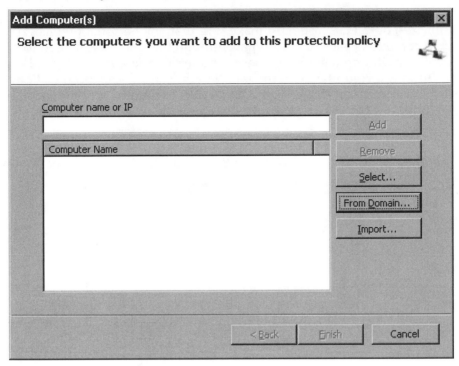

To import computers into the protection policy from a domain, follow these steps:

1. Click the **Select** button.
2. When the Select Computers dialog box appears, choose the appropriate domain from the drop down list.
3. Click the **Search** button.
4. The dialog box will now display all of the computers in the domain. Select the check box that corresponds to each computer that you want to add to the protection policy, as shown in Figure 9.4. It is worth noting that only computers that are powered on and connected to the network will appear on this list.
5. Click **OK**. The computers that you have selected should now appear on the Add Computers dialog box, as shown in Figure 9.5.
6. Click **Finish**.

WARNING

GFI EndPointSecurity communicates with its agents through Transmission Control Protocol (TCP) port 1116. You must make sure that any personal firewalls running on managed computers allow traffic to pass through this port. If you need to switch ports, you can click on the management console's **Configuration** tab, and then click on the **Options** link just beneath the tab. Now, select the **Advanced Options** container in the console tree, and then click the **Configure Advanced Options** link. The resulting properties sheet contains an option for changing the port number used by the agents.

Figure 9.4 Select the Machines That You Want to Add to the Protection Policy

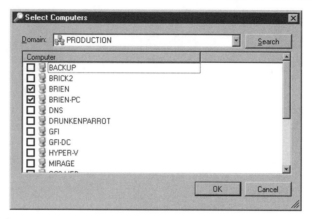

Figure 9.5 The Computers That You Have Selected Should Appear in the Add Computers Dialog Box

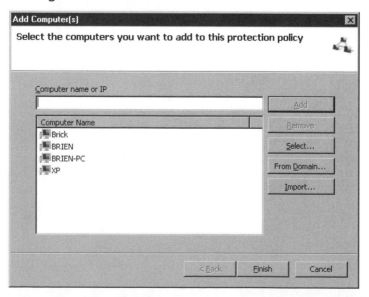

NOTE

GFI EndPointSecurity can't actually tell the difference between servers, workstations, and laptops. There is nothing stopping you from placing a device into the wrong protection policy, so you will need to be careful with your selections.

NOTE

The difference between the Select option and the Domain option is that the Select option allows you to select domain members that are currently powered on and connected to the network. The From Domain option allows you to search the Active Directory for specific computers.

Setting Log-on Credentials

Now that you have specified the computers that you want to include in the protection group, you must specify a set of authentication credentials for those machines. To do so, click the **Set Logon Credentials** link. When you do, Windows will display the Logon Credentials dialog box, shown in Figure 9.6. As you can see in the figure, you have the option of either using the same security context as GFI EndPointSecurity is currently running under, or you can specify a username and password that should be used for connecting to the computers in the protection group. In most cases, you will probably end up having to specify a set of logon credentials.

Figure 9.6 You Can Either Use the Security Context That GFI EndPointSecurity is Running Under, or You Can Provide a Set of Authentication Credentials to Be Used for the Computers in the Protection Group

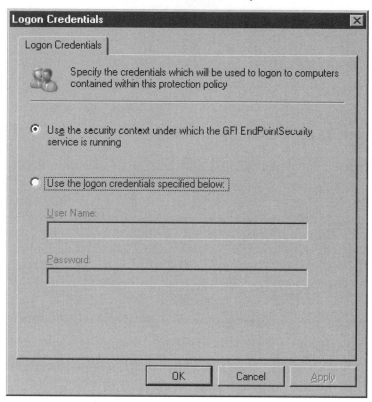

Are You Owned?

Using the Right Service Account

Although you have to use a service account that has domain administrative credentials, I recommend creating an account that can be used solely by GFI EndPointSecurity. Generally speaking, service accounts are some of the easiest accounts to compromise. Using a dedicated service account makes it easy to use Windows' auditing feature to look for any abnormal uses of the account.

Deploying Agents

The next step in the process is to deploy the necessary agents to the computers that are to be managed by the protection policy. It seems as though there is a bug in the GFI EndPointSecurity management console that causes the Deploy Agents link to be grayed out even after you have added computers to the policy and set your logon credentials. To get around this problem, select a different container from the Protection Policies tree, and then go back to the Workstations container. When you do, the Deploy Agents link should be available.

To deploy the agents to your target computers, follow these steps:

1. Click the **Deploy Agents** link.

2. You will now see a screen asking you to select the computers that you want to deploy the agents to. As you can see in Figure 9.7, only the computers that you have designated as members of the protection group are included on this list.

3. Click **OK**.

4. You will now be taken to the Deployment Status screen, shown in Figure 9.8. This screen allows you to monitor the agent deployment process. As you can see in the figure, an agent cannot be deployed to a computer that is offline. If a computer is offline, the deployment is scheduled for another time.

Figure 9.7 You Must Select the Computers That You Want to Deploy the Agents To

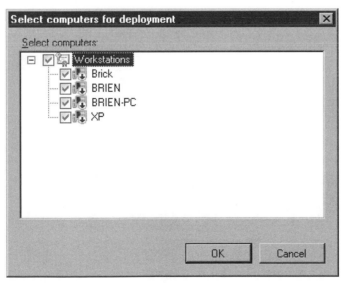

Figure 9.8 The Deployment Status Screen Allows You to Monitor the Agent Deployment Process

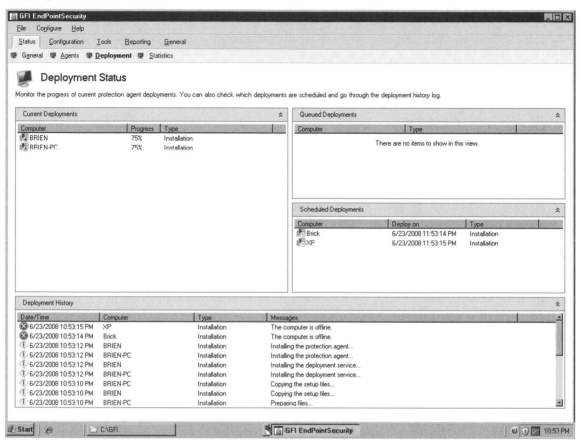

Tools & Traps...

Agent Inconsistencies

The agents tend to be very static in nature. Any time that you make a change to a protection policy, you will have to update the agents as well. Otherwise, the agents will be enforcing outdated policies. It is important to perform periodic checks to make sure that all of the agents are up to date. I will show you how in Chapter 12.

Active Directory Based Deployment

Even though GFI EndPointSecurity contains a built-in mechanism for deploying agents, you have the option of deploying agents through the Active Directory. If you look at Figure 9.9, you'll notice that there is a Deploy Through Active Directory option located in the Computers section. If you click on this link, you'll be taken to a screen that gives you the chance to save a copy of the agent to a location of your choice. In order for Active Directory based deployment to work correctly, you need to save this file to a central location that can be accessed by all of your domain controllers.

Figure 9.9 You Can Deploy an Agent Through the Active Directory

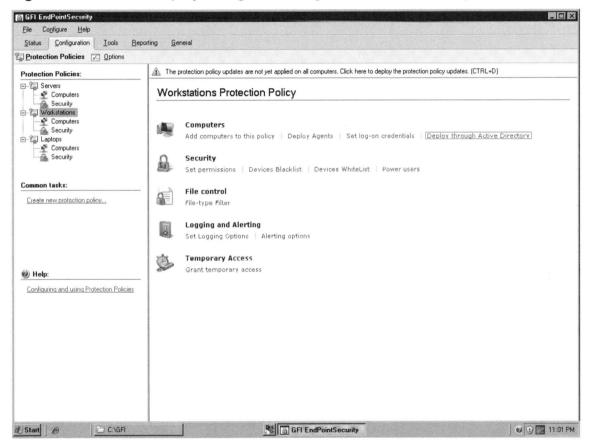

Once you have copied the file to an accessible location, it is time to configure the Active Directory to assign the agent to the target computers. Keep in mind that the Active Directory provides two different methods for deploying software. You can either assign applications, or you can publish them. In this case, it is better to assign the application, because assigning an application causes it to automatically be installed on the PC without any user intervention. In contrast,

publishing an application gives end users the option of installing or uninstalling the application
at will. If you would like to learn more about publishing and assigning applications, then check out
my article at: www.brienposey.com/kb/assigning_and_publishing_applications.asp.

The steps that you would use to assign the agent through a group policy setting vary depending
on which group policy you want to use. To assign the agent as a part of the domain policy, perform
the following steps on a domain controller:

1. Open the **Active Directory Users and Computers** console.

2. Right-click on the container representing your domain, and choose the **Properties**
    command from the resulting shortcut menu.

3. When the domain's properties sheet appears, select the **Group Policy** tab.

4. Select the **Default Domain Policy**, as shown in Figure 9.10, and click the **Edit** button.

Figure 9.10 Select the Default Domain Policy, and Click the Edit Button

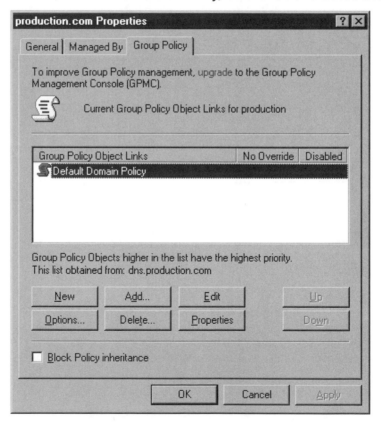

5. When the Group Policy Object Editor opens, navigate through the console tree to
    Computer Configuration | Software Settings | Software Installation.

6. Right-click on the Software Installation container, and select the **New** | **Package** commands from the resulting shortcut menus, as shown in Figure 9.11.

Figure 9.11 Right-Click on the Software Installation Container, and Select the New | Package Commands From the Resulting Shortcut Menus

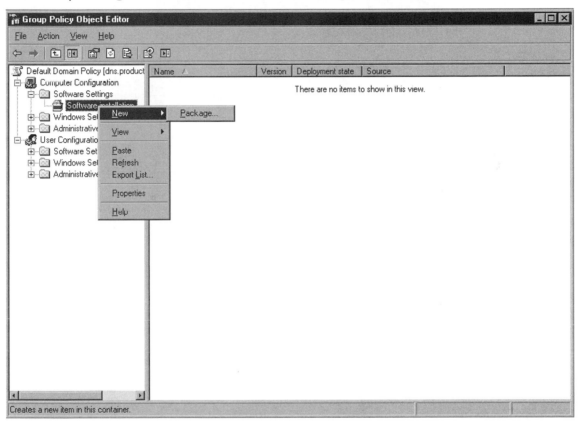

7. When prompted, select the agent installation package, and click **Open**.

8. If you see a message stating that Windows cannot verify that the path is a network location, make sure that you have accessed the installation package through a mapped drive or a Universal Naming Convention (UNC) share (not a local drive letter), and click **Yes** to use the path.

9. Choose the **Assigned** option from the Deploy Software dialog box, as shown in Figure 9.12.

10. Click **OK.**

Figure 9.12 Choose the Assigned Option and Click OK

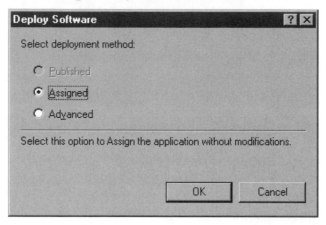

> **TIP**
>
> Active Directory deployment will only work if the managed machines are domain members and are subject to the Group Policy Object that you are using to assign the agent application.

Setting Device Permissions

Once the agents have been deployed to the computers in the protection group, it is time to set some security permissions that controls the level of access that computers falling under the protection policy have to the various devices. This is actually easier than it sounds. For most of the devices that GFI EndPointSecurity can manage, there are only two different security permissions that you can apply: Full Access or No Access. To set the security permissions for your various devices, follow these steps:

1.   Click on the **Set Permissions** link located in the Security section on the main Protection Policy screen. Windows will now display the Security node for the protection policy.

2. The security screen contains a tree view that displays all of the devices that you previously told GFI EndPointSecurity that you want to manage. If you expand this tree view, you can see the security settings that are currently applied to the devices, as shown in Figure 9.13.

3. As you can see in the figure, access to the devices is controlled by a single check box. Selecting the check box gives the computers within the protection policy full access to the device. Deselecting the check box denies access to the device, as shown in Figure 9.14.

Figure 9.13 Access to the Devices is Controlled By a Single Check Box

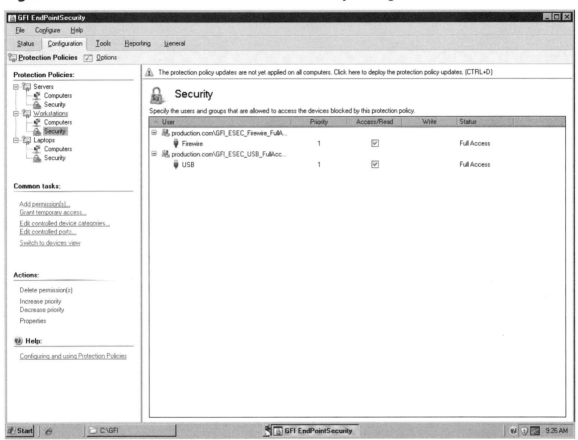

Figure 9.14 Deselecting the Check Box for a Device Blocks Access to the Device

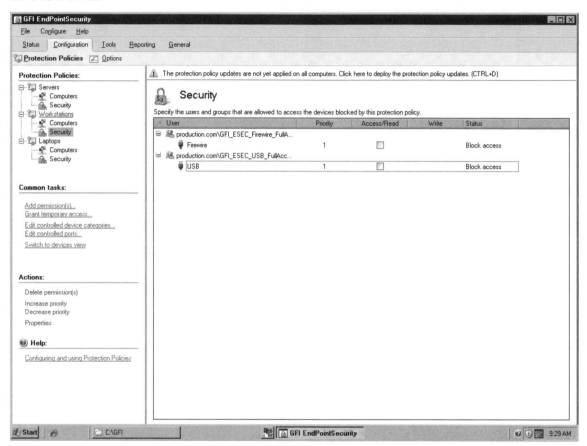

Admittedly, the tree view shown in Figure 9.13 can be a bit difficult to follow. That's because the descriptions of the devices can be a little cryptic. I don't think that following these descriptions is overly difficult, but at the same time you certainly can't glance at the screen and tell one device from another.

If you find a screen hard to read, try clicking the **Switch to Devices View** link, located in the Tasks section. Clicking this link will cause the screen to display devices by device type, as shown in Figure 9.15. If you want to switch back, click the **Switch to Users View** link.

Figure 9.15 The Devices View Tends to Be Easier to Read

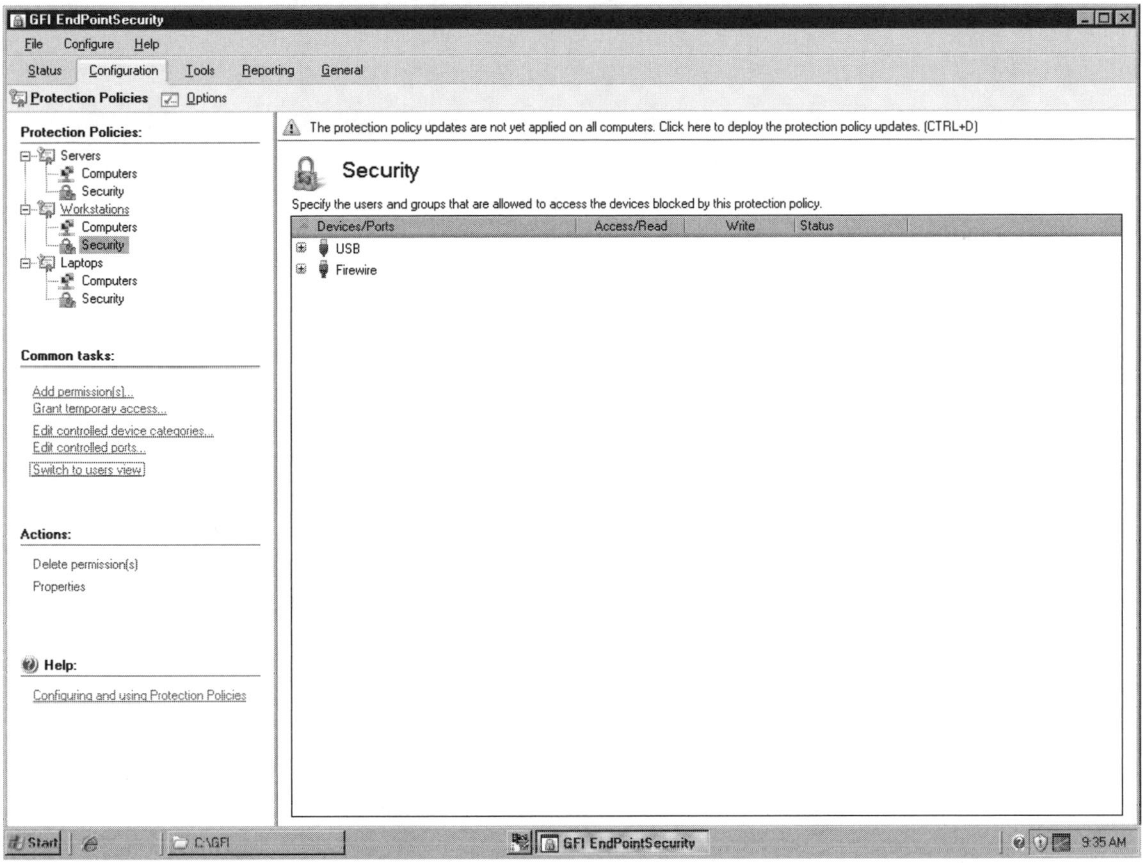

Adding Permissions

By now I'm sure that you have noticed that the only devices displayed on the Security screen in my screen shots are the USB and FireWire ports. The reason for this is that during the initial configuration process, I told GFI EndPointSecurity that these were the only devices that I wanted to manage. Of course, just because you are managing a device doesn't mean that you have to deny access to it.

Another thing that you have probably noticed is that so far we have taken an all or nothing approach to device security. What I mean by that is that the devices that we've looked at so far are either allowed or blocked; there really hasn't been anything in between. Furthermore, we have been applying the policy to all of the computers in the protection group with absolutely no regard for who's using the computers. That's a problem, because while you may want to block your end users from accessing certain devices, your technical support staff will most likely need full access to the hardware.

Fortunately, GFI EndPointSecurity gives you more granular control over device access than what it would initially appear to be available. To see how this works, let's do a simple exercise in which we tell GFI EndPointSecurity that we want to manage some additional devices, and then set some more granular security permissions for those devices. To do so, follow these steps:

1. Right-click on an empty area in the device window, and then choose the **Add Permissions** command from the resulting shortcut menu.

2. Windows will now display the Add Permissions dialog box, shown in Figure 9.16. As you can see in the figure, you have the option of adding permissions for device categories, connectivity ports, or for specific devices. Choose the **Device Categories** option, and click **Next**.

3. At this point, you'll see a screen similar to the one that as shown in Figure 9.17. Select the check boxes for all of the devices that you want to manage, and click **Next**.

Figure 9.16 You Have the Option of Adding Permissions for Device Categories, Connectivity Ports, or for Specific Devices

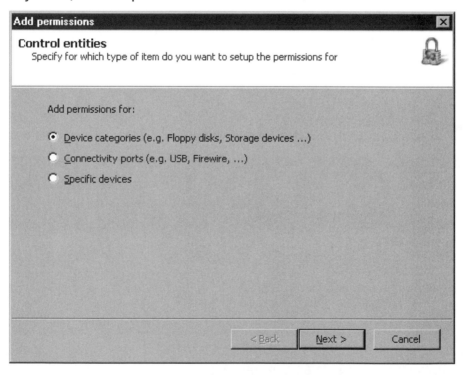

Figure 9.17 Select the Check Boxes for All of the Devices That You Want to Manage

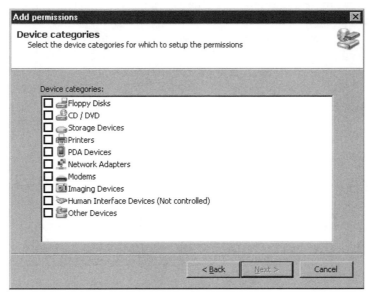

At this point, you will see the Add Permissions screen that is shown in Figure 9.18. As you can see in the figure, you have the ability to apply device security to the protection group, but to do so in a way that allows different security groups to have different levels of access to the devices.

Figure 9.18 The Add Permissions Dialog Box Allows You to Apply Per Security Group Permissions to the Protection Policy

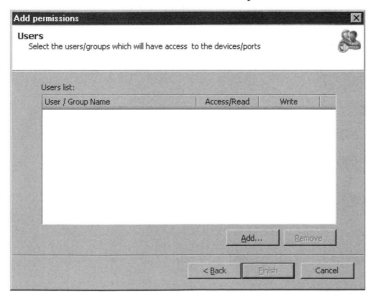

So far the only devices that you have seen in the console have been Universal Serial Bus (USB) ports and FireWire ports. Ports typically only allow you to enable or disable access, however, other types of devices support more granular access. One example of this is floppy disks. Nobody uses floppy disks anymore, but if they did, you could control whether users have read-only access to floppies, read-write access, or no access at all. You will find this same concept to be true of other types of devices as well.

In order to show you how device access control works, let's give everyone access to all of the devices except for USB and FireWire ports, which we will block access to. Since the Information Technology (IT) staff may occasionally need access to workstation hardware, let's give the administrators group full access to everything. To do so, let's continue the procedure that we started earlier by performing these steps:

4. Click the **Add** button.

5. When the Select Users or Groups dialog box appears, verify that your domain is listed in the From This Location field.

6. When prompted, enter the word **Everyone** into the Enter the Object Names to Select field.

7. Click the **Check Names** button, and make sure that Windows recognizes the Everyone group.

8. Click **OK**.

9. Click the **Add** button.

10. Enter the word **Administrators** into the Enter the Object Names to Select field.

11. Click the **Check Names** button to verify that Windows recognizes the Administrators group.

12. You should now be returned to the Add Permissions dialog box. Deselect the **Write** check box for the Everyone group, as shown in Figure 9.19.

13. Click **Finish**, and you will be returned to the main Security screen, as shown in Figure 9.20.

Figure 9.19 Do Not Allow the Everyone Group to Have Write Access

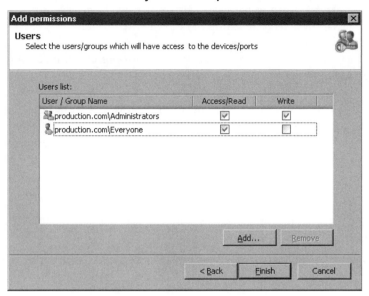

Figure 9.20 The Security Screen Displays the Revised Permissions

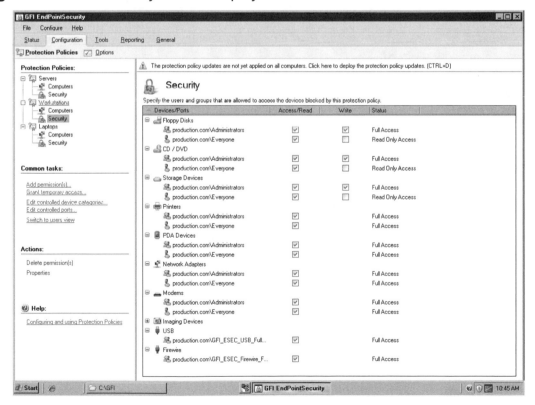

As you look at the figure above, there are a couple of different things that I want you to pay attention to. First, you can see that the hardware devices that we have selected have been added to the protection policy, and that the Everyone group has been denied write access for any devices that differentiate between read and write access.

Another thing that I want to point out is that the permissions check boxes on this screen are active. You can fine tune your security settings by selecting and deselecting check boxes for the various access levels.

One last thing that I want to point out about this screen is that we have not fully accomplished our objective. If you look at the bottom of the screen, you can see that the entire protection group has been granted full access to USB and FireWire ports. That's because when we worked through the Add Permissions wizard a moment ago, we only worked with the Device Categories option, not the Connectivity Ports option. You can remedy this situation by completing the following steps:

1. Right-click on an empty area of the Security screen, and choose the **Add Permissions** command from the resulting shortcut menu.

2. When the Add Permissions dialog box appears, select the **Connectivity Ports** option.

3. Click **Next**.

4. Select the **USB** and **Firewire** check boxes, and click **Next**.

5. Click the **Add** button.

6. Verify that your domain is displayed in the From this Location field.

7. Enter the word **Everyone** into the Enter Object Names to Select field.

8. Click the **Check Names** button to verify the spelling of the **Everyone** group.

9. Click **OK**.

10. Click the **Add** button.

11. Enter the word **Administrators** into the Enter the Object Names to Select field.

12. Click the **Check Names** button.

13. Click **OK**.

14. Deselect the check box next to the **Everyone** group, as shown in Figure 9.21.

15. Click **Finish**.

16. When Windows displays the Security screen, deselect the **USB** and **FireWire** check boxes that apply to the protection group as a whole. You can see an example of this in Figure 9.22.

Figure 9.21 Deselect the Checkbox Corresponding to the Everyone Group

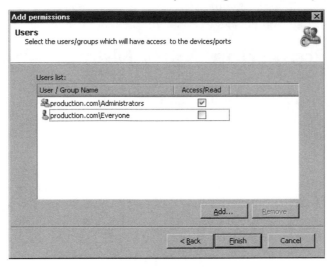

Figure 9.22 Deselect the USB and FireWire Checkboxes for the Protection Group

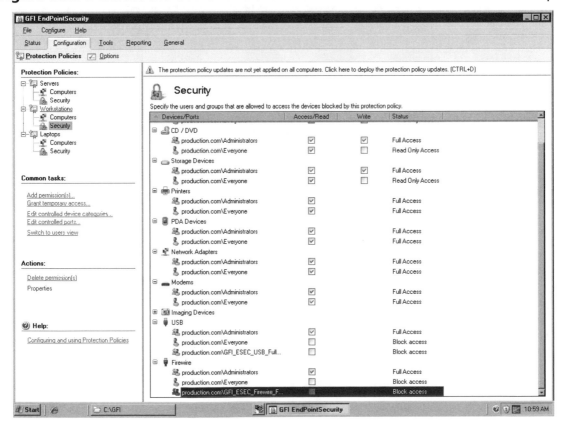

That's all there is to it. Keep in mind that you can modify your security settings at any time. You can access the screen shown in Figure 9.22 at any time by selecting the **Security** container located in the console's Protection Policies tree, beneath the protection policy that you want to modify.

Modifying Protection Policy Membership

So far in this chapter, I have talked a lot about security as it relates to users and groups, but it's important to remember that protection policies apply first, and foremost to computers. We created the list of computers within the protection policy early on, but you can modify the protection policy membership at any time.

To view the computers that are presently included in a protection policy, go to the console's Protection Policy tree, and select the **Computers** container that's located beneath the policy that you want to modify. If you right-click on a computer, you will have the option to remove it from the policy, or to move it to a different policy, as shown in Figure 9.23. As you can see in the figure, the shortcut menu also gives you the option to add additional computers to the protection policy, or to deploy an agent to the selected computer.

Figure 9.23 You Can Modify the Protection Policy's Membership Through the Protection Policy's Computers Container

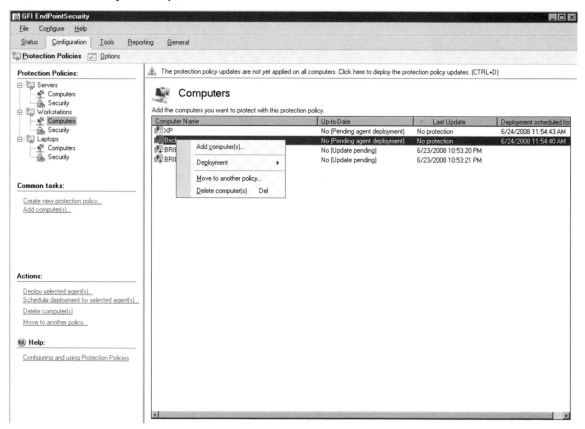

Summary

In this chapter, I have explained how to establish memberships and basic security for a protection policy. In Chapter 10, I will show you some of the more advanced security settings that you can apply to a protection policy.

Solutions Fast Track

Creating Protection Policies

- ☑ Protection policies control the level of device access that is allowed on a system.
- ☑ GFI EndPointSecurity allows you to create three separate protection policies: one for servers, one for workstations, and one for laptops.

Deploying Agents

- ☑ GFI EndPointSecurity communicates with agents through TCP port 1116, but this port can be changed.
- ☑ Agents residing on the computers that are being monitored are responsible for enforcing the protection policies.
- ☑ You can deploy the agents through the GFI EndPointSecurity management console, or through the Active Directory.
- ☑ If you want to install the agent manually, use the option to deploy the agent via Active Directory to create an agent installation file. After doing so, you can manually run the file that you have created on the target workstation.

Setting Device Permissions

- ☑ Protection policies allow you to apply device access permissions to individual domain security groups.
- ☑ The list of computers that a protection policy pertains to, or the individual permissions within a policy, can be modified at any time, but you will have to update the agents after you make a modification.

Frequently Asked Questions

Q: Can I mix and match computers in a protection group (e.g., placing laptops or servers in the Workstations protection group)?

A: Yes, the three different protection groups are only there to help you to stay organized, and to allow you to have up to three different protection policies. Which machines you actually place into a protection group is up to you.

Q: I'm having trouble deploying agents to some of my machines. What gives?

A: By default, the agents communicate with GFI EndPointSecurity through TCP port 1116. You should check to see if this port is open.

Q: Is it better to deploy the agents manually or by using Group Policy settings?

A: It really depends on how your network is configured. If you have a Group Policy Object in place that includes only the computers that need to be managed, then it is probably better to deploy the agents via group policy. Otherwise, you should probably deploy the agents through the management console.

Q: What happens if I add computers to my network later on?

A: You can add a computer to a protection policy at any time, but you will have to deploy an agent to the new computer.

Chapter 10

Advanced Security Configurations

Solutions in this chapter:

- **Regulating Specific Devices**
- **Blacklisting and Whitelisting Devices**
- **File Type Restrictions**

☑ **Summary**

☑ **Solutions Fast Track**

☑ **Frequently Asked Questions**

Introduction

In the previous chapter, I showed you how to set up some basic device permissions, but there is a whole lot more that you can do when it comes to security. In this chapter, I want to show you some of the more advanced security features that you can include in a protection policy.

Regulating Specific Devices

So far I have talked about how you regulate entire classes of devices, but sometimes this blanket approach to security isn't practical. For example, think about the needs of a magazine publisher. Like any other company, they probably want to prevent users from bringing in software on Universal Serial Bus (USB) flash drives, or copying sensitive data to USB flash drives, but it may not make sense to block all USB devices. After all, it is common for publishing companies to use USB-based cameras, scanners, and other imaging devices. Fortunately, GFI EndPointSecurity makes it possible to blacklist, whitelist, or set permissions for specific devices. In the case of a publisher who needs to block most USB devices but allow an USB-based scanner, it probably makes more sense to whitelist the scanner rather than to try to blacklist every other USB device that could potentially be used. Regardless of whether you want to allow or prevent certain types of devices, the first step is making GFI EndPointSecurity aware of the device that you want to regulate.

Locating a Device's Hardware ID

The first thing that you need to understand about regulating specific devices is that Windows assigns every device an individual hardware ID number. The exact method of acquiring the hardware ID for a device varies from one version of Windows to another, but the procedure is somewhat similar in most versions of Windows. In Windows Vista, you can determine a device's ID number by following the steps below. If you are using Windows XP, you can also use the Device Manager to look up a device ID number in a manner that's very similar to what I'm about to show you. There is also a shortcut that I will show you later on, which allows you to locate a device ID directly through the management console. To determine a device's ID number, follow these steps:

1. Open the Windows Control Panel.

2. Click on the **System and Maintenance** link.

3. Click on the **System** link.

4. When Windows displays the System Properties sheet, click the **Device Manager** link found in the Tasks list.

5. If you receive a User Access Control warning, click the **Continue** button.

6. When the Device Manager opens, locate the device that you want to get the hardware ID for, as shown in Figure 10.1.

7. Right-click on the selected device, and choose the **Properties** command from the resulting shortcut menu.

8. When the device's properties sheet appears, select the **Details** tab.

9. Choose the **Hardware IDs** option from the Property drop down list. When you do, Windows will display the device's hardware IDs, as shown in Figure 10.2.

Figure 10.1 Right-Click on the Device That You Want to Locate the Hardware ID For, and Choose the Properties Command From the Resulting Shortcut Menu

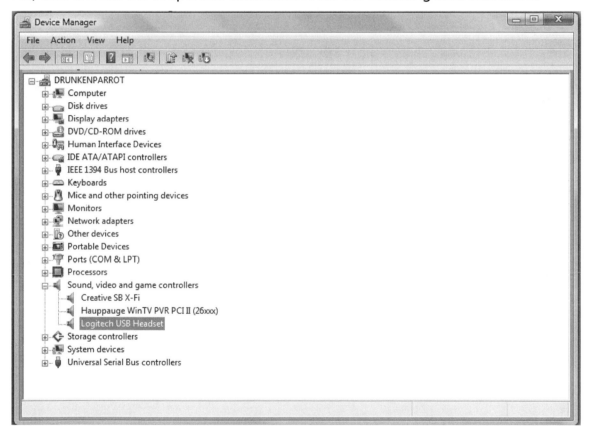

Figure 10.2 You Can Access the Device's Hardware IDs Through the Details Tab of the Device's Properties Sheet

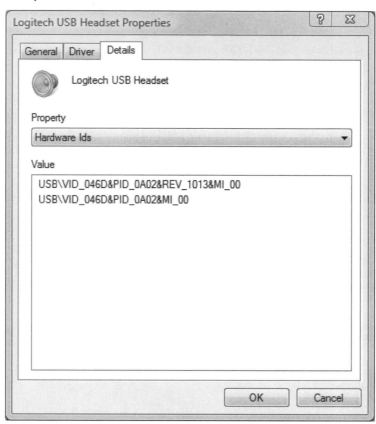

> **WARNING**
>
> Many devices have multiple hardware IDs. If a device makes use of multiple hardware IDs, you should make note of all of them.

Making GFI EndPointSecurity Aware of a Device

Now that you know how to get the hardware IDs for a device, let's work through the process of making GFI EndPointSecurity aware of that device's existence. To do so, follow these steps:

1. Open the GFI EndPointSecurity console, and go to the **Configuration** tab.

2. Select the protection policy that you want to add the device to.

3. Right-click on the policy's **Security** container, and select the **Add Permissions** command from the resulting shortcut menu.

4. Windows will now display the Add Permissions dialog box. Select the **Specific Devices** option, as shown in Figure 10.3.

Figure 10.3 Choose the Specific Devices Option, and Click Next

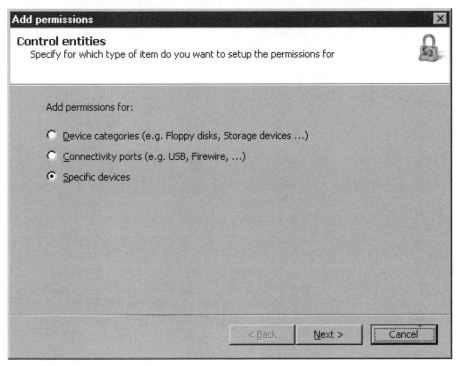

5. Click **Next**.

6. Windows will now display the Select Devices dialog box. Click the **Add New Devices** button.

7. When Windows displays the New Device dialog box, enter a description for the device that you plan to blacklist.

8. Now enter the first of the hardware IDs that you located earlier.

9. Choose the appropriate device category, as shown in Figure 10.4.

10. Click **OK**.

11. If there are any additional hardware IDs for the device that need to be added, click the **Add New Device** button, and repeat the process that you just completed. I will explain how you know whether or not you need to add an additional hardware ID in a moment.

Figure 10.4 This is What the New Device Dialog Box Should Look Like when Populated

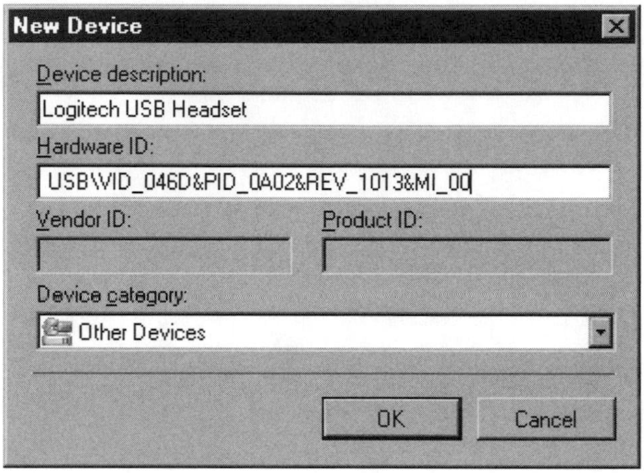

OK, so if you've got multiple hardware IDs, how do you know whether or not you need to add them all? The key is to understand how hardware IDs work. Although hardware IDs look pretty random, they can actually tell you quite a bit about the device.

If you look back at Figure 10.4, you can see that I entered Logitech USB Headset in the Device Description field. You can actually put anything that you want into this field. It's just a place where you can enter text that will help you to identify the device later on. Typically, you are going to want to enter something specific that includes the make and model of the device.

You might also have noticed that I entered a hardware ID, and that there are a couple of grayed out fields for Vendor ID and Product ID. The way that hardware IDs work is that they include the vendor ID and the product ID in the number. The hardware ID that I entered in the figure is:

```
USB\VID_046D&PID_0A02&REV1013&MI_00
```

The first part of the hardware ID tells Windows that this is a USB device. Next, there is a backslash and the following text:

```
VID_046D
```

The VID portion of the text tells Windows that this is the Vendor ID portion of the hardware ID. The Vendor ID is a four-digit hexadecimal number. In this case, the vendor is Logitech, so all of Logitech's products should have a vendor ID number of 046D.

The next part of the hardware ID is:

```
PID_0A02
```

This portion of the hardware ID identifies the individual product. This is known as the Product ID number. Like the Vendor ID number, the Product ID number is a four-digit hexadecimal number.

I mentioned earlier that some hardware devices include multiple hardware ID numbers. If a device does use multiple hardware IDs, then the Vendor ID and the product ID portions of the hardware ID should be identical for each of the device's hardware IDs. This is how Windows is able to tell that each of the hardware IDs corresponds to a common device.

The REV_1013 portion of the hardware ID is just a revision number. The MI_00 corresponds to the USB interface number. If you want Windows to load the device's driver for more than one USB interface, then Windows will need a separate hardware ID for each interface. For example, if we were to install this device in a different port, it might create a hardware ID that looks like this:

```
USB\VID_046D&PID_0A02&REV1013&MI_02
```

Now that I have explained how the hardware ID works, take a look at Figure 10.5. As you can see, when I select the All Devices option, you can see two separate instances of my Logitech USB Headset, because I have entered two different hardware IDs. Notice though that 046D is listed in the Vendors list. As I mentioned earlier, 046D identifies Logitech. If I were to select this vendor ID, then only one instance of the Logitech USB Headset appears, as shown in Figure 10.6, because Windows is smart enough to know that both hardware IDs go with the same device.

Figure 10.5 The Logitech USB Headset is Listed on the Select Devices Dialog Box

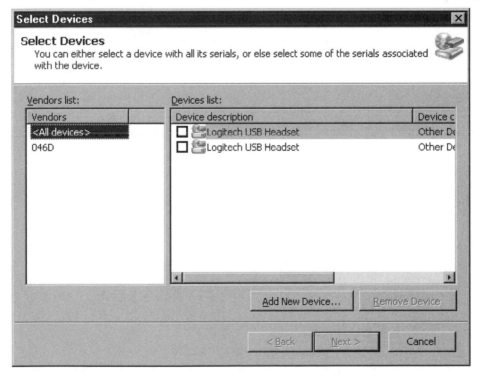

Figure 10.6 Selecting the Vendor ID Causes the Device Manufactured by that Vendor to be Displayed

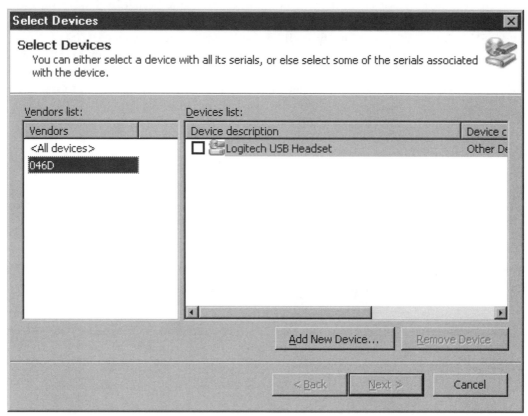

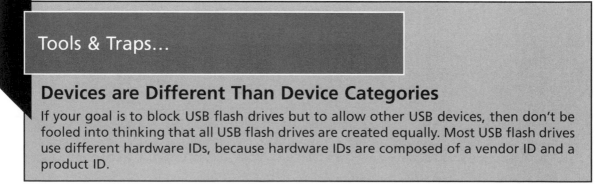

Tools & Traps…

Devices are Different Than Device Categories

If your goal is to block USB flash drives but to allow other USB devices, then don't be fooled into thinking that all USB flash drives are created equally. Most USB flash drives use different hardware IDs, because hardware IDs are composed of a vendor ID and a product ID.

How do you know whether or not you need to enter multiple hardware IDs? Well, if the hardware IDs are basically the same aside from the port number, then you are usually safe just entering the first hardware ID that Windows displays (the one without a port number). If the hardware IDs have a lot of other differences, however, then you are going to need to list multiple hardware IDs.

TIP

If you know for sure that a specific device has been installed onto a computer in your organization, then you can use a shortcut to making GFI EndPointSecurity aware of the device. To use the shortcut, follow these steps:

1. Select the console's **Tools** tab.
2. Enter the name of the computer containing the device into the **Scan Target** field.
3. Click the **Scan** button. When you do, the console will display a list of every device that the computer is aware of.
4. Select the device that you want to make GFI EndPointSecurity aware of.
5. Click the **Add Devices to Database** link.
6. Click **OK** to acknowledge that the device was added to the database.

Setting Permissions for a Specific Device

Now that I have talked about how GFI EndPointSecurity treats hardware IDs, it's time to actually regulate the device. The steps that you will perform next really depend on what you are trying to accomplish. If you want to blacklist or whitelist the device then you should click Cancel. You have already made GFI EndPointSecurity aware of the device's existence, but you will have to perform a separate procedure to blacklist or whitelist the device. If you want to set permissions on the device, follow these steps:

1. Select the check box corresponding to the device that you want to set the permissions for.
2. Click **Next**.
3. At this point, you will see the Add Permissions dialog box. Click the **Add** button.
4. Verify that the From this Location field is displaying the name of your domain.
5. Enter the name of the Windows security group that you want to apply the permissions to.
6. Click the **Check Names** button to verify the group's existence and its spelling.
7. Click **OK**.
8. You should now see the group that you entered displayed in the Add Permissions dialog box, as shown in Figure 10.7.

9. Select or deselect any permissions-related check boxes to establish the desired permission level.

10. If you need to add any additional permissions, click the **Add** button and repeat the process that you just performed.

11. When you are done, click the **Finish** button.

12. You should now see the device displayed on the Security screen for the protection policy, as shown in Figure 10.8.

Figure 10.7 You Should See the Group That You Have Specified Displayed in the Add Permissions Dialog Box

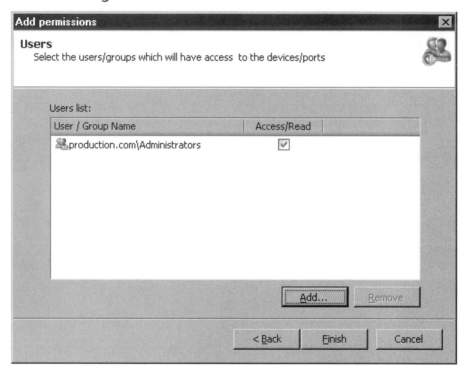

Figure 10.8 The Device and Its Permissions Should Be Added to the Protection Policy's Security Screen

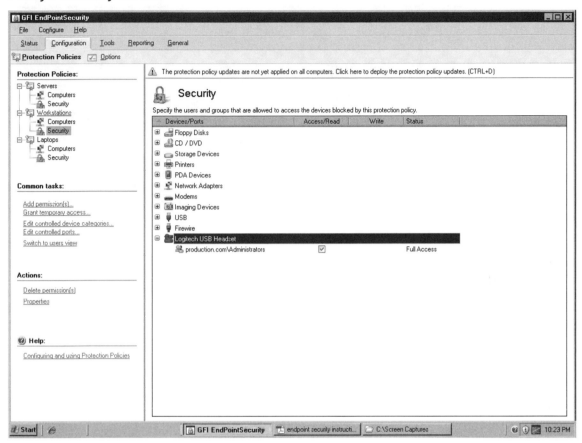

Blacklisting and Whitelisting Devices

So far I have shown you how to make GFI EndPointSecurity aware of individual devices, and how to apply permissions to a device within a protection policy. Sometimes, however, it's easier to just apply a blanket denial or a blanket approval to a device rather than creating individual permissions for a device. GFI EndPointSecurity allows you to incorporate such blanket denials or approvals through the use of blacklists and whitelists. In this section, I'll show you how it's done.

Are You Owned?

Device Boot Order

A system will only be protected against endpoint devices if the agent is running, and the agent can only run if Windows is running. One common technique for getting around a system's security is to install Windows PE onto a USB flash drive, and then boot the system from the flash drive. If you want to protect your systems from this type of exploit, configure the Basic Input Output System (BIOS) to prevent the system from being booted from a USB device, and then password-protect the BIOS.

Blacklisting a Specific Device

Now that I have shown you how to add a device to GFI EndPointSecurity and how to set permissions on the device, I want to show you how you can blacklist the device. The procedure for black listing a device is actually really simple. To do so, follow these steps:

1. Go to the GFI EndPointSecurity management console's **Configuration** tab, and then select the protection policy that you intend to add the blacklist to.

2. Click the **Devices Blacklist** link, shown in Figure 10.9.

3. At this point, Windows will display the Black List dialog box. Click the **Add** button.

4. Select the check box next to the device that you want to blacklist.

5. Click **Next**.

6. You will now see a screen asking if you want to blacklist all serials or only selected serials. Normally, you can just choose the **All Serials** option to blacklist all instances of the device. If the device supports serial numbers, and there are just specific instances of the device that you want to block, you can choose the **Only Selected Serials** option, and then choose the serial number that you want to block.

7. Click the **Finish** button, followed by the **OK** button.

Figure 10.9 Click the Devices Blacklist Link

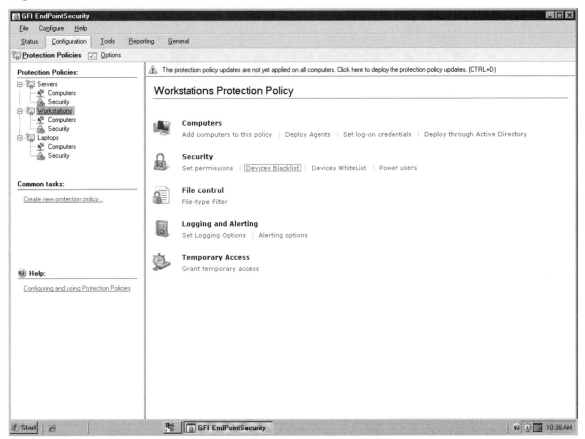

If you need to see which devices have been blacklisted, or make changes to the blacklist, you can do so by clicking the **Devices Blacklist** link on the main protection policy screen. Doing so will cause Windows to display the Black List dialog box, which gives you the opportunity to examine blacklisted devices, or to add a device to or remove a device from the blacklist. You can see an example of this dialog box in Figure 10.10.

Figure 10.10 The Black List Dialog Box Allows You to See Which Devices Have Been Blacklisted, Blacklist Additional Devices, or Remove a Device From the Blacklist

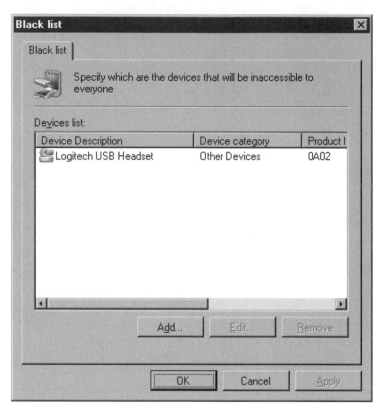

Whitelisting Devices

The procedure for whitelisting a device is almost identical to the procedure used for blacklisting a device. To whitelist a device, follow these steps:

1. Go to the GFI EndPointSecurity management console's **Configuration** tab, and then select the protection policy that you intend to add the whitelist to.

2. Click the **Devices Whitelist** link.

3. At this point, Windows will display the White List dialog box. Click the **Add** button.

4. Select the check box next to the device that you want to whitelist.

5. Click **Next**.

6. You will now see a screen asking if you want to whitelist all serials or only selected serials. Normally, you can just choose the **All Serials** option to whitelist all instances of the device. If the device supports serial numbers, and there are just specific instances of the device that you want to block, you can choose the Only Selected Serials option, and then

choose the serial number that you want to block. You can see what this dialog box looks like in **Figure 10.11**.

7.   Click the **Finish** button, followed by the **OK** button.

Figure 10.11 The Select Devices Dialog Box Allows You to Select All Serials or Selected Serials

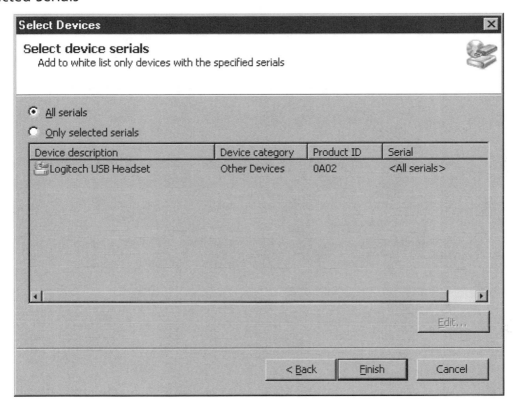

If you need to see which devices have been whitelisted, or make changes to the whitelist, you can do so by clicking the Devices Whitelist link on the main protection policy screen. Doing so will cause Windows to display the White List dialog box, which gives you the opportunity to examine whitelisted devices, or to whitelist additional devices, or remove a device from the whitelist.

Making Exceptions for Power Users

In the last chapter, I showed you how to assign some basic permissions to various Windows Security groups so that you could control device access within the protection policy by security group membership. The technique that I showed you works well enough, but it's kind of a pain in the butt to have to go in and grant the Administrators group (or other groups for that matter) access to devices that you are blocking everyone else from accessing.

The good news is that there is actually a much easier way of providing a security group with full access to otherwise restricted devices. All you have to do is to add the group to the Power Users list. Any users or groups that you add to the Power Users list will be granted full access to the devices that are managed by the protection policy.

> **NOTE**
>
> You cannot add a group to the Power Users list if you have already manually assigned permissions to the group. You can, however, remove any previously assigned permissions and then add the group to the Power Users list.

At a minimum, I recommend adding the domain Administrators group to the Power Users list. To do so, perform the following steps:

1. Select the management console's **Configuration** tab, and then select the protection policy that you want to manage.

2. Click the **Power Users** link, located in the Security section, as shown in Figure 10.12.

3. Windows will now display the Power Users dialog box. Click the **Add** button.

4. Verify that your domain is listed in the From This Location field.

5. Type the word **Administrators** into the Enter the Object Name to Select field.

6. Click the **Check Names** button.

7. Click **OK**.

8. You should now see the domain Administrators group listed on the Power Users list, as shown in Figure 10.13.

9. Click **OK**.

Figure 10.12 Click the Power Users Link to Access the Power Users List

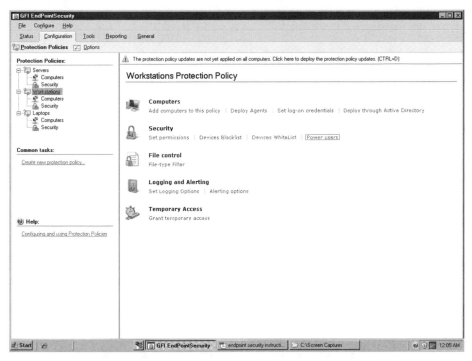

Figure 10.13 The Domain Administrators Group is Added to the Power Users List

If you ever need to make modifications to the Power Users list, click the Power Users link that's shown in Figure 10.12. As you can see in Figure 10.13, the resulting dialog box allows you to view, add, and remove list members.

Clearing Existing Permissions

In the previous section, I mentioned that you can't add a security group to the Power Users list if you have previously assigned permissions to the group. You can, however, get rid of the permissions that you assigned manually, and then add the group to the Power Users list.

To clear out permissions that you have manually assigned, follow these steps:

1. Select the **Security** container for the protection policy that you are working with. The Security container will show the existing permissions for each device, as shown in Figure 10.14.

2. Click the **Switch to Users View** link, located in the Common Tasks section.

3. The user's view will show each security group and the permissions that have been assigned to it, as shown in Figure 10.15. Right-click on the group that you want to remove, and select the **Delete Permissions** command from the resulting shortcut menu.

Figure 10.14 By Default, the Security Screen Displays Security Permissions Grouped by Device

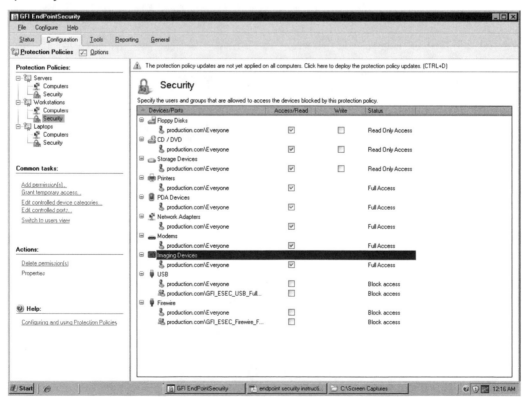

Figure 10.15 Users View Allows You to See the Existing Permissions, Sorted by Security Group

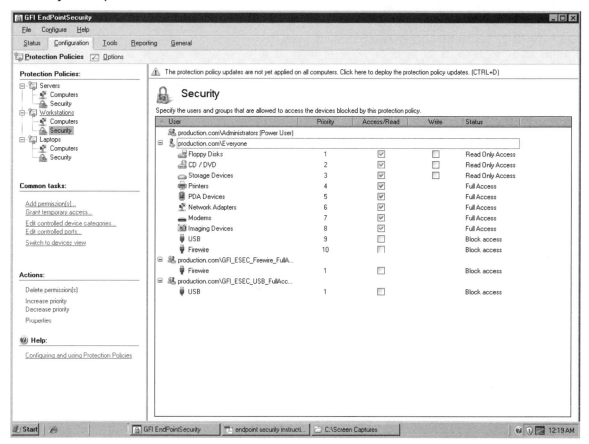

File Type Restrictions

One of the ideas that I have tried to stress in this chapter is that although security geeks love blanket denial policies, they are rarely suitable for the real world. A lot of times you can't completely deny access to devices, because the users have legitimate business needs that require them to use the devices that you probably wish that you could completely block.

If you find yourself in this kind of dilemma, you will be happy to know that one additional way that you can regulate device access is by controlling what types of files users can use with the devices.

For example, suppose that I need my users to be able to use USB flash drives for whatever reason. At the same time, however, I know that Troy Thompson (uber geek and Technical Editor for this book) is the lead guitarist for the heavy metal/gospel band Bride (www.bridepub.com), and that Bride is working on a new album. Troy would probably get a little bit upset if my users were bringing in bootleg copies of his new album on their USB flash drives, so it might be a good idea to block access to MP3 files now, to avoid any copyright issues later on when the new album is released.

If this situation were to occur in the real world, I could just set up a protection policy that says that my users have access to USB devices, but that they aren't allowed to have access to any .MP3 or .WMA files residing on USB media.

We can accomplish this configuration through a file type filter. To create a file type filter such as the one that I just described, perform the following steps:

WARNING

File type filters will only work if the specified users have access to the device. Otherwise, access is denied regardless of any file type filters that may exist.

Are You Owned?

Preventing Executable Files

Even if you aren't particularly concerned with limiting the types of files that a user can access through an end point device, it's a good idea to block access to executable files. This helps to prevent users from installing unauthorized applications, or from infecting the organization with malicious code.

1. Select the management console's **Configuration** tab, and then click on your protection policy.

2. Click on the **File Type Filter** link located in the console's File Control section.

3. Windows will now launch the File-Type Filter dialog box. Select the **Allow All Files But Block The Usage of the Following File Types** option, as shown in Figure 10.16.

4. Click the **Add** button.

5. Select the **.MP3** option from the File Type drop down list.

6. Click the **Add** button.

7. Verify that your domain is listed in the From This Location field.

8.   Enter the name of the security group that you want the file type ban to apply to.

9.   Click the **Check Names** button to verify the group name.

10. Click **OK**.

11. The File-Type Filter dialog box should now display the file type and the group that you want to restrict, as shown in Figure 10.17. If you need to add additional security groups to the list, click the **Add** button, and repeat the procedure that you have just performed.

12. Click **OK** to return to the main File-Type Filter screen. As you can see in Figure 10.18, you can use this screen to view any existing file filters for the protection group, or to create, edit, or remove file type filters.

13. When you are done, click **OK**.

Figure 10.16 Choose the Option to Allow All Files But Block the Usage of the Following File Types

Figure 10.17 The File-type Filter Dialog Box Should Display the Filter That You Have Just Created

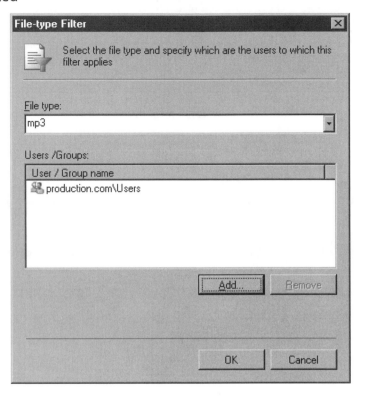

Figure 10.18 You Can Use the Main File-Type Filter Screen to Create Additional Filters, or to Edit or Remove Existing Filters

> **NOTE**
>
> The File –Type Filter dialog box also gives you the option of only allowing specific types of files, rather than allowing all files other than the types that you specify.

Summary

In the real world, applying blanket permissions to an entire device category usually isn't practical. In this chapter, I have shown you how to apply permissions that are much more granular than the ones that you learned about in Chapter 9. In the next Chapter, I will talk about how all of the permissions that you have set so far effect the end user experience.

Solutions Fast Track

Regulating Specific Devices

- ☑ Blocking entire device categories may not be practical in the real world.
- ☑ If you want to block a specific device, you will usually need to locate that device's hardware ID.
- ☑ You can use the Scan Target option on the management console's Tools tab to locate and make GFI EndPointSecurity aware of specific devices.

Blacklisting and Whitelisting

- ☑ Devices Blacklisting and whitelisting allows you to set blanket approvals or denials on devices.
- ☑ It is easier to make administrators members of the Power Users group than to create a separate set of permissions for the Administrators group.
- ☑ A user or a security group cannot be added to the Power Users group if other permissions apply to them.

File Type Restrictions

- ☑ File type permissions allow users to use endpoint devices, but restrict the types of files that they can use in conjunction with the devices.
- ☑ File type restrictions will only work if a user has access to a device. Otherwise, access to the device will simply be denied.
- ☑ Even if you want to allow users to use a particular device freely, it's a good idea to use file type restrictions to block the use of executable code.

Frequently Asked Questions

Q: What is the advantage of using the Power Users group?

A: The Power Users group keeps you from having to manually maintain administrative privileges throughout a protection policy. The Power Users group provides a blanket approval to all devices within a protection policy.

Q: Is it possible to make a user a power user in one protection policy and not another?

A: Yes. For example, this would allow a user to have full control over devices attached to their laptop, but to have a more limited set of device permissions for their desktop computer.

Q: Is it really practical to blacklist individual devices?

A: Unless there is device that you consider to be especially evil, blacklisting individual devices is usually more work than it is worth. It's usually more practical to whitelist the devices that you want to allow than to try to blacklist all the devices that you don't want to allow.

Q: Can I set file type restrictions on a device-by-device basis?

A: No, file type restrictions can only be set at the protection group level.

Q: What happens if I set contradictory permissions?

A: You can prioritize permissions by right-clicking on them and using the Increase Priority or the Decrease Priority commands found on the shortcut menu. Higher priority permissions take precedence over lower priority permissions.

Chapter 11

End Point Management

Solutions in this chapter:

- The End User Experience
- Removing the Agent Component
- Making Temporary Exceptions

☑ Summary

☑ Solutions Fast Track

☑ Frequently Asked Questions

Introduction

So far I've spent a lot of time talking about the various ways that you can regulate endpoint devices, so you are probably ready to move on and actually start locking things down. If you've been setting up protection policies, you have already begun the lock down process. Unlike some of the other products out there, you don't have to scan the computers on your network to see if anyone is using unauthorized devices. The agent component that resides on each computer in a protection group is designed to compare any attempted device use against the applicable protection policy, and take action if needed.

The End User Experience

In case you are wondering what the end user experience is like, check out Figure 11.1. I set up a protection policy blocking the use of Universal Serial Bus (USB) devices, and then I inserted a USB flash drive into one of my network workstations. As you can see in the figure, Windows displays a pop-up balloon telling the user that access to the device is forbidden.

Figure 11.1 This is What it Looks Like When a User Attempts to Access an Unauthorized Device

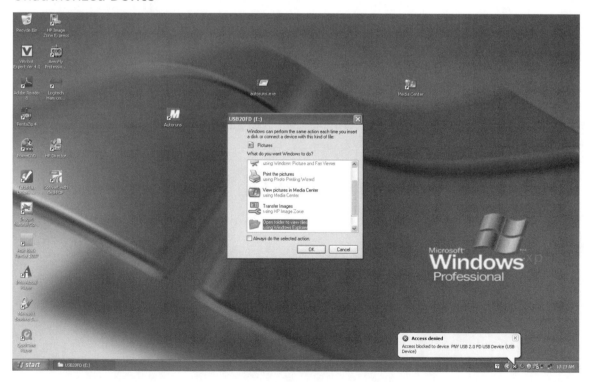

When you looked at the figure above, you probably also noticed that Windows has displayed the standard dialog box that it always displays when new media is inserted. This is a little bit disheartening

at first, but access to the USB flash drive really is blocked. If I click on the option to explore the media, Windows displays the error message that's shown in Figure 11.2.

Figure 11.2 Windows Generates an Access Denied Message When You Attempt to Access a USB Flash Drive

Removing the Agent Component

As you can see, the agent regulates control to endpoint devices on members of the protection group. However, this isn't always a good thing. Yesterday was one of those days when I had about a bazillion different projects going on at the same time. I needed to write the previous chapter in this book, but I also had some training videos that I was working on, so I needed to do some video editing. In an effort to make the best possible use of my time, I decided to deploy the agent to a few workstations on my network, and then start importing the video that I needed to edit while I was waiting for the agents to install (incidentally, the agent installation process ended up being very fast).

Although that sounded like a good idea at the time, I wasn't really thinking when I came up with it. One of the machines that I installed an agent onto was the same machine that I was using to edit my video. When I plugged my camcorder into the machine's FireWire port, I received an access denied message, and Windows prevented me from accessing my camcorder.

Rather than mess up the protection policies that I had worked hard to configure, I decided to temporarily remove the agent from that machine. Although removing the agent wasn't complicated or time consuming, the process is just a little bit tricky if you haven't done it before. Therefore, I want to go ahead and show you how to remove an agent.

To uninstall an agent, follow these steps:

1. Identify the name of the computer that you want to remove the agent from. The procedure for doing so varies from one version of Windows to the next. In Windows Vista, you can click on the workstation's **Start** button, and then right click on the **Computer** option on the Start menu, and choose the **Properties** command from the resulting menu. When you do, Windows will display the System Properties sheet, which lists the computer's name, as shown in Figure 11.3.

2. Open the **GFI EndPointSecurity console**, and select the **Configuration** tab.

3. Select the **Computer** container beneath the protection policy containing the computer that you want to remove the agent from.

4. Select the computer that you want to remove the agent from, as shown in Figure 11.4.

5. Press the **Delete** key.

6. When asked whether or not you want to delete the selected computer, click **Yes**.

7. At this point, the computer is removed from the protection group. Notice in Figure 11.5, that there is an uninstall pending for the computer. The tricky part is that uninstalling the agent does not happen automatically. Therefore, go to the console's **Status** tab, and click the **Agents** tab beneath it.

8. This screen lists the computer that you have removed from the protection group, and the Up-to-Date column lists the computer as having an uninstall pending. If you right-click on the computer, you will notice that there isn't an option for uninstalling the agent, as shown in Figure 11.6. As weird as it sounds, choose the **Deploy Selected Agents** option from the shortcut menu. When you do, GFI EndPointSecurity will begin removing the agent, as shown in Figure 11.7.

Figure 11.3 You Can Find a Computer's Name on Its System Properties Sheet

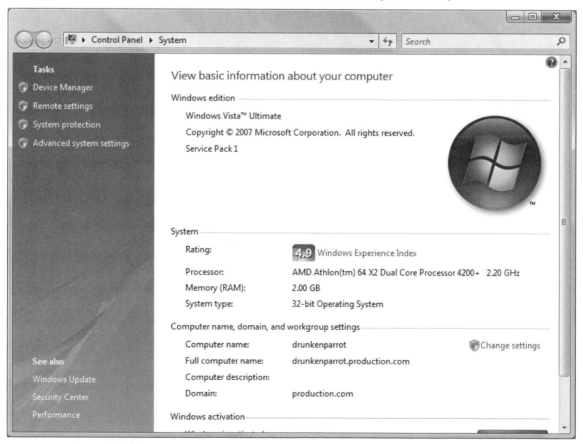

Figure 11.4 Select the Computer That You Want to Remove the Agent From

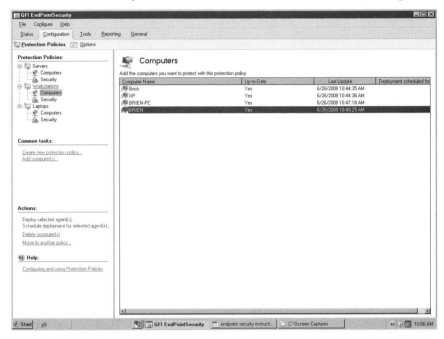

Figure 11.5 When a Computer is Removed From a Protection Group, the Console Lists an Uninstall as Pending

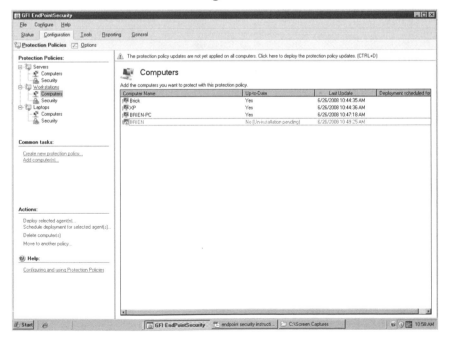

WARNING

Removing a computer from a protection group alone does not remove the agent. The computer remains locked down until the agent is removed.

Figure 11.6 There is No Menu Option for Removing an Agent

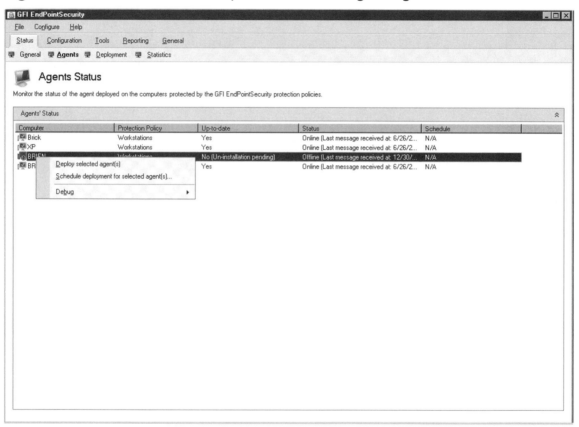

Figure 11.7 Choosing the Deploy Agent Option Shown in the Previous Figure, Causes the Agent to be Removed

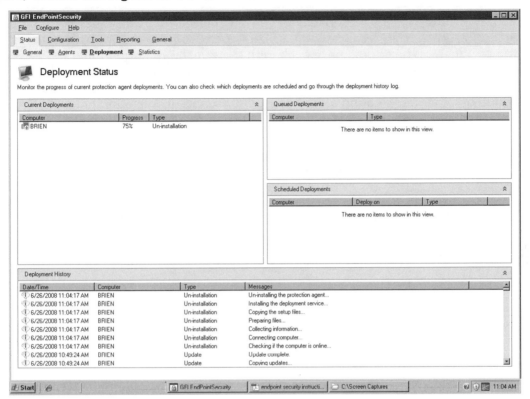

Making Temporary Exceptions

In the previous section, I talked about how I accidentally locked down a computer that I was going to need to use for video editing purposes. I solved the problem by removing the agent from the computer. That solution worked fine for me, because I had only installed the agent for demonstration purposes to begin with. In the real world, removing an agent just because a user needs access to some piece of hardware, really isn't a good solution. For one, the already busy and overworked administrator has to take time out and remove the agent. More importantly, once the agent has been removed, the user has full reign over the systems hardware. They not only have access to the device that they needed to use, but also to every other device on the system. Besides that, protection policies are typically applied to groups, not to individuals. If you start applying individual access permissions, your protection policies can become convoluted and difficult to manage.

A better solution to this problem is to have a user request temporary access to a device. The process is a little bit cumbersome, but it's still easier than modifying your protection policies. The process begins with the user accessing the Temporary Request applet. It's located on their workstation in the C:\Program Files\GFI\EndPointSecurity 4.0 Agent folder, as shown in Figure 11.8.

TIP

I tend to think that the reason why GFI put the mechanism for requesting temporary access in such an obscure location, is to keep users from making excessive requests for device access. Even so, I have dealt with some really computer illiterate users in my day, and as much as I hate to say it, a lot of them probably would not be able to figure out how to access the mechanism for requesting temporary access. As such, you might consider creating a desktop icon for requesting temporary access, if you find that your help desk staff is constantly having to walk users through the process.

Figure 11.8 There is a Temporary Access Mechanism Hidden in the Agent's Folder

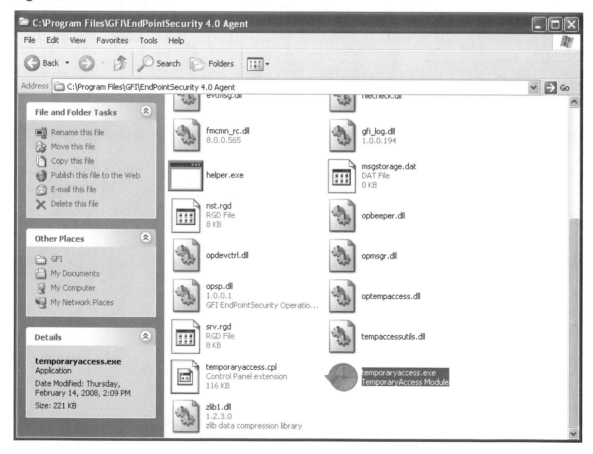

When the user opens the Temporary Access applet, it provides the user with a request code, as shown in Figure 11.9. Unfortunately, the Temporary Request applet does not contain a mechanism for automatically transmitting the request code to the administrator. Instead, the user has to e-mail

the request code. Technically, the user could even read the code over the phone, but I strongly recommend using e-mail, because the code is long and complicated to type. If you use e-mail, you can cut and paste the request code, greatly reducing the chances for errors.

Another reason why I recommend using e-mail is because the user needs to tell you how long they need the temporary access for, and when they need it. They will also have to tell you which devices or ports they need to access. You will see why this is so important later on.

Are You Owned?

Temporary Access, Long Term Effects

If a user requests temporary access to a device, I would recommend that you really scrutinize the request. After all, you have the ban in place for a reason, and temporarily granting access circumvents your policy. You need to be able to justify temporarily lifting this ban.

I would also recommend that you keep the temporary access period as short as possible. It doesn't take long for a user to use an endpoint device to make a copy of sensitive data or to use it to install unauthorized software. Always remember that the temporary access that you grant has the potential to have long-term effects.

Figure 11.9 User's Must E-mail the Request Code to the Administrator

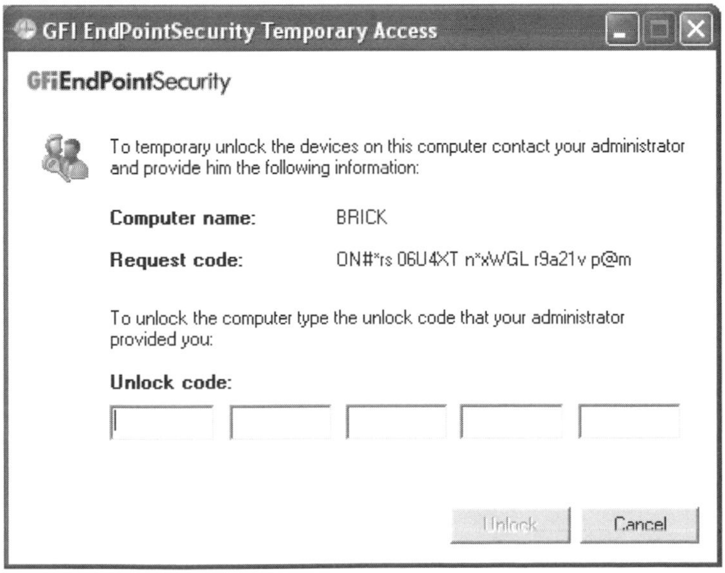

When you receive the e-mail message from the user containing the request code, you must complete the following steps to grant the requested access:

1. Open the **GFI EndPointSecurity management** console, click on the **Configuration** tab, and select the protection policy containing the user's computer.

2. Click on the **Grant Temporary Access** link, as shown in Figure 11.10.

Figure 11.10 Click the Grant Temporary Access Link

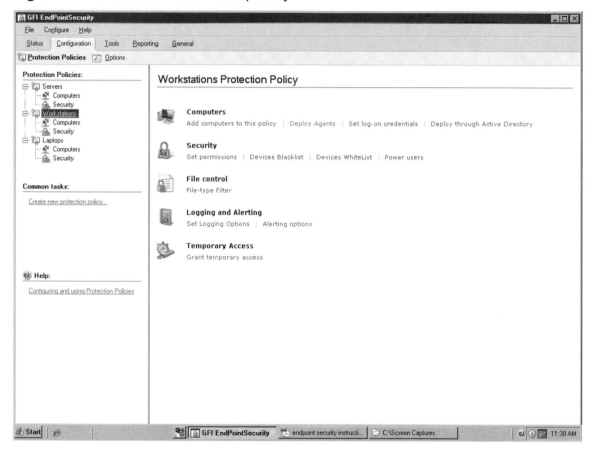

3. At this point, Windows will display the Grant Temporary Access dialog box, which will prompt you to enter the user's request code. Copy the request code from the user's e-mail message, and paste it into this dialog box. The dialog box will automatically identify the machine that made the request once the request code is entered, as shown in Figure 11.11.

4. Click **Next**.

Figure 11.11 GFI EndPointSecurity Automatically Identifies the Computer
That Made the Request

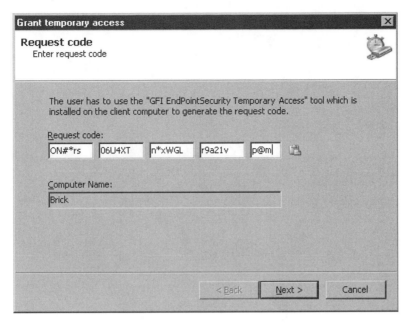

5.   Select the check boxes corresponding to the devices and ports that the user needs access to, as shown in Figure 11.12.

6.   Click **Next**.

Figure 11.12 Select the Device or Port That You Want to Grant
Temporary Access To

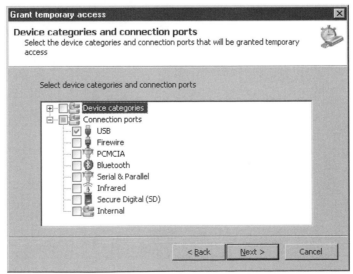

7. At this point, you will see the Time Restriction screen, as shown in Figure 11.13. As you can see in the figure, you must specify the duration of the temporary access that you are granting. You must also tell GFI EndPointSecurity when the unlock code can be used. The unlock code is only valid during the interval that you specify.

8. Click **Next**.

Figure 11.13 You Must Determine When the User Can Use Their Temporary Access and For How Long

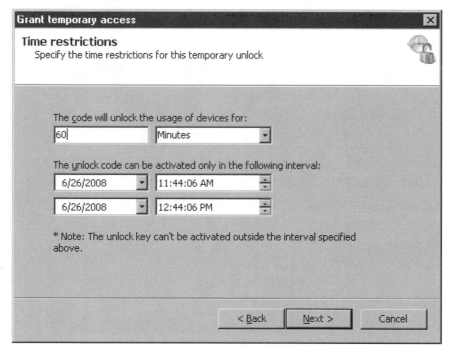

9. At this point, the Grant Temporary Access wizard will display an unlock code, as shown in Figure 11.14. You should e-mail this code to the user along with a description of any restrictions that you have imposed.

10. Click **Finish**.

Figure 11.14 The Grant Temporary Access Wizard Provides You With an Unlock Code That You Can Send to the User

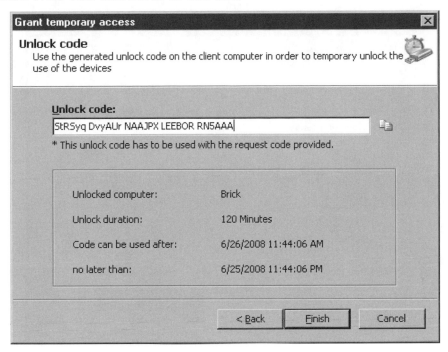

When the user receives your e-mail, all they have to do is to cut and paste the unlock code from your e-mail message into the Request Temporary Access dialog box, shown in Figure 11.15. When the user clicks the Unlock button, access will be granted.

TIP

It is important to note that the user who is requesting temporary access must keep the GFI EndPointSecurity Temporary Access dialog box open until they have entered the access code. You will need to train users on this. Otherwise, you could end up getting a lot of calls from users who are unable to get temporary access to devices because they have closed the dialog box prior to receiving the access code.

Figure 11.15 The User Must Enter the Unlock Code That You
Provide to Them

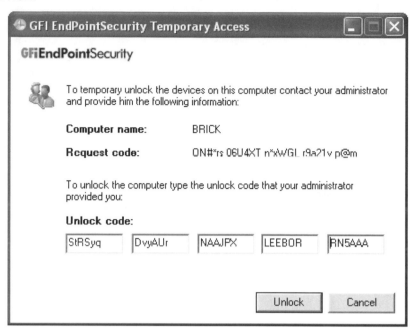

NOTE

The user will not be able to unlock their computer unless the current time is within
the time interval that you specified through the Grant Temporary Access wizard.

Summary

In this chapter, I have talked about what the end user experiences when access to a device has been blocked. I have also shown you how to lift a ban by either uninstalling an agent or by granting a user temporary access. In either case, this is something that you should do sparingly. Otherwise, what is the point of having the ban? In the next chapter, I will complete the section on GFI EndPointSecurity by showing you how the reporting and alerting options work.

Solutions Fast Track

The End User Experience

☑ When the user violates a protection policy, they receive a pop-up balloon telling them so.

☑ Windows may initially appear that it is going to allow the user access to a blocked device, but access is ultimately denied.

Removing the Agent Component

☑ Removing an agent is something that you should not normally have to do, but it is important to know how to remove an agent, just in case you ever have to.

☑ The removal process is less than intuitive. To remove an agent, remove the computer containing the agent from its protection group, and then use the Deploy Selected Agents option to remove the agent.

Making Temporary Exceptions

☑ It is usually better to make a temporary exception than to remove an agent.

☑ The process of entering request codes for temporary access is really tedious, so I recommend using e-mail so that you can copy and paste the codes rather than having to type them.

☑ Temporary access is only granted for a specific duration, and only within a time interval that you specify.

Frequently Asked Questions

Q: When a user inserts a forbidden USB flash drive, Windows displays the screen asking the user what action they want to take. What gives?

A: Although Windows gives the illusion that it is going to allow access to a device that has been blocked, the user is ultimately forbidden from taking any action.

Q: Why do you have to use the Deploy Selected Agents command to remove an agent?

A: I have no idea, but if I had to guess, I would say that GFI probably wanted to obscure the agent removal process to discourage you against removing agents.

Q: Is there any way to make the process of granting temporary access to a user any easier?

A: No, not that I know of.

Chapter 12

Monitoring Device Usage

Solutions in this chapter:

- **Setting Logging Options**

- **Setting Alerting Options**

- **Generating End Point Security Reports**

- **Keeping Tabs on Your Network**

☑ **Summary**

☑ **Solutions Fast Track**

☑ **Frequently Asked Questions**

Introduction

In the previous chapter, I showed you how GFI EndPointSecurity is able to lock down end point devices on network workstations. However, network security is not a "set it and forget it" proposition. You need a way of verifying that the policies that you have put into place are working. It would also be nice to know when someone is trying to violate the policies that you have established. That's where this chapter comes into play. In this chapter, I will show you how to keep tabs on GFI EndPointSecurity.

Setting Logging Options

The first thing that I want to talk about in this chapter is setting up some logging options. Before I do, however, it's time for a quick reality check. Any good book on network security covers some type of logging, right? And of course we all know that every good network administrator checks his or her security logs every single day, right? Well, I don't know about you, but I'm really busy. I know that I should review my security logs every day, but I don't have time. Since I'm being brutally honest here, I'll go ahead and admit that I haven't looked at my network's security logs in months. Hopefully, you are more diligent about checking your logs than I am. If not, then the last thing that you probably need is a function to create more log entries.

There is actually more to logging than meets the eye, and you may actually be interested in checking the logging function out, even if you aren't in the habit of checking your logs. GFI EndPointSecurity can generate some really interesting reports from the information that is contained in the logs. So, even if you aren't interested in reading through a bunch of boring log file entries, it is still a good idea to go ahead and enable the logging function so that you can generate reports if you should ever need them.

To access the logging function, follow these steps:

1. Open the GFI EndPointSecurity management console, and select the **Configuration** tab.

2. Select the protection policy that you want to establish logging for.

3. Click the **Set Logging Options** link found in the Logging and Alerting section. When you do, you will see the Logging Options dialog box, as shown in Figure 12.1.

Figure 12.1 You Can Write Log Entries to the Windows Event Logs, the GFI EndPointSecurity Database, or Both

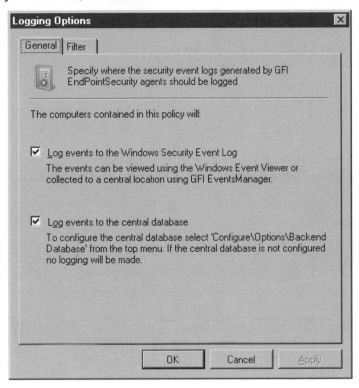

As you can see in the figure, you can write log entries to the Windows event logs, the GFI EndPointSecurity database, or both. There's really nothing out of the ordinary about writing data to the Windows event logs, but you're probably going to want to write events to the central database, even if you're not planning on looking at your event logs. The reason why I say this is that GFI EndPointSecurity contains a reporting mechanism that I will show you later on. This add-on allows you to generate all kinds of summary reports based on the data that has been collected in the database.

4. Select the properties sheet's **Filter** tab.

5. As you can see in Figure 12.2, the Filter tab allows you to control which types of events will be logged. If you are going to be using the Windows event logs, I recommend giving some serious thought as to which types of events you want to log. Otherwise, you may find that the application generates so many log entries that it becomes impossible to find the information that you're really interested in. If you are going to be writing events to the central database, however, then you're usually going to be okay leaving all of the check boxes selected.

WARNING

Log entries can take up a lot of space and could potentially fill up your server's hard drive. For the first few weeks that you are using GFI EventsManager, I recommend that you closely monitor the database size so that you can learn to predict its growth rate.

Figure 12.2 The Filter Tab Allows You to Select the Types of Events That You Want to Log

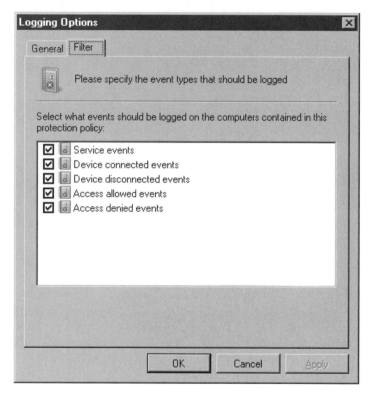

Setting Alerting Options

One of the nice things about the way that GFI EndPointSecurity is designed is that it allows you to send alerts when certain events occur. The process of configuring the alerting options is actually really similar to the process that you just used to set the various logging options. To configure the alerting options, follow these steps:

1. Open the GFI EndPointSecurity management console, and select the **Configuration** tab.

2. Select the protection policy that you want to configure the alerting options for.

3.   Click the **Alerting Options** link, found in the Logging and Alerting section. When you do, you will see the Alerting Options properties sheet, shown in Figure 12.3.

Figure 12.3 The Properties Sheet's General Tab Allows You to Select the Types of Alerts That You Want to Send

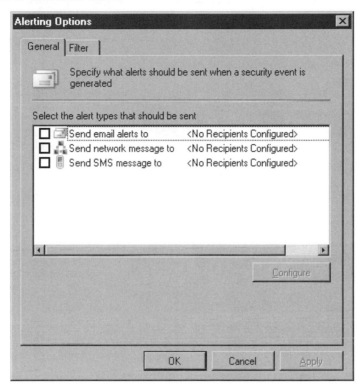

As you can see in the figure, the properties sheet's General tab allows you to choose the types of alerts that you want to send. You really don't have to do a lot of configuration work, because you performed most of the required configuration tasks during the initial installation process. For demonstration purposes, let's set up GFI EndPointSecurity to send e-mail and network message alerts. To do so, perform the following steps:

1.   Select the **Send E-mail Alerts** to check box.

2.   Click the **Configure** button.

3.   At this point you will see a dialog box that asks you to select the message recipients, as shown in Figure 12.4. Select the desired recipients, and click the **Add** button.

4.   Click **OK**.

5.   Select the **Send Network Messages** check box.

6. Once again, you'll see a dialog box similar to the one shown in Figure 12.4. Choose the users that you want to send messages to, and click the **Add** button.

7. Click **OK**.

Figure 12.4 Select the Options to Send E-mail Alerts and Network Messages to the EndPointSecurity Administrators Group

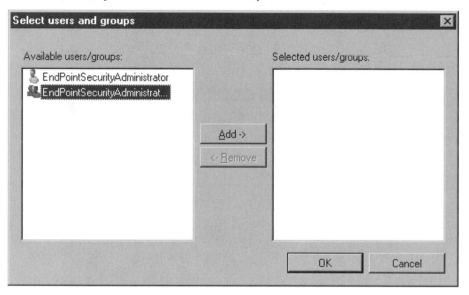

8. To complete the configuration process, we have to tell GFI EndPointSecurity which types of events should trigger alerts. You can do this by performing the following steps:

9. Select the **Filter** tab.

10. Now, select the check boxes corresponding to the types of events that you want to be alerted about. For demonstration purposes, let's clear all of the check boxes except for the **Access Denied Events** check box, as shown in Figure 12.5.

11. Click **OK** to complete the process.

Figure 12.5 Select the Access Deny Events Option

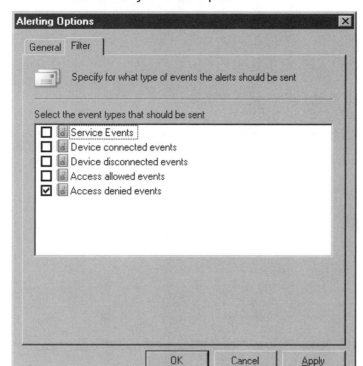

Configuring Alert Recipients

In the previous section, you saw that it was necessary to specify the recipient of the alerts that you're configuring. I need to point out though that the users and groups specified in the Select Users and Groups dialog box (shown in Figure 12.4) are not Active Directory users, nor are they local user accounts. The users and groups to which you assigned alerting options are actually internal to GFI EndPointSecurity.

I strongly recommend taking some time to check out the settings that have been assigned to these users and groups. To do so, follow these steps:

1.   Open the GFI EndPointSecurity management console, and go to the **Configuration** tab.

2.   Click the **Options** button found just beneath the Configuration tab.

3.   The users and groups can be managed within the Alerting Options portion of the console tree, as shown in Figure 12.6.

4.   You can check a user or group's configuration by right clicking on it and choosing the **Properties** command from the resulting shortcut menu. You can see what the resulting properties sheet looks like in Figure 12.7.

Figure 12.6 You Can Manage Users and Groups Through the Alerting Options
Portion of the Console Tree

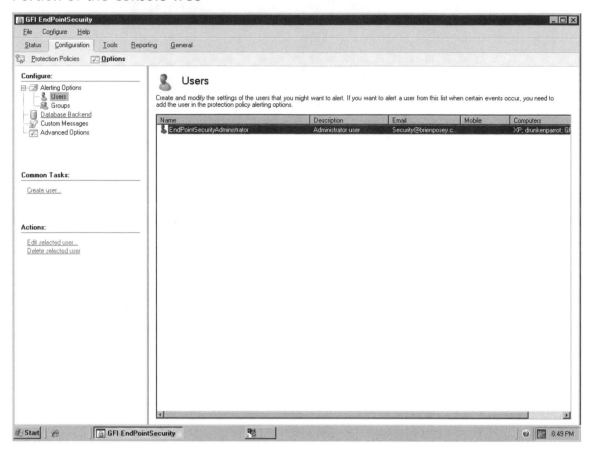

Figure 12.7 The User's Properties Sheet Allows You to Configure Alerting Options for the User

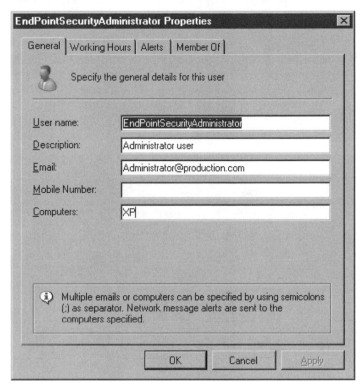

Generating End Point Security Reports

Earlier in this chapter, I mentioned that the information that gets logged to the central database can be used to create a variety of reports. In this section, I want to show you how to produce a report.

If you take a look at the GFI EndPointSecurity management console, you will notice that it contains a Reporting tab. If you click this tab, the console only displays an advertisement for GFI ReportCenter, as shown in Figure 12.8. Since some of the other GFI products actually make the ReportCenter accessible through the management console, this really threw me for a loop at first. I couldn't get the Reporting tab to do anything except for display advertisements, so I thought that maybe there was a problem with the ReportPack. I even uninstalled it and reinstalled it.

Figure 12.8 The Reporting Tab Just Displays Advertisements for GFI ReportCenter

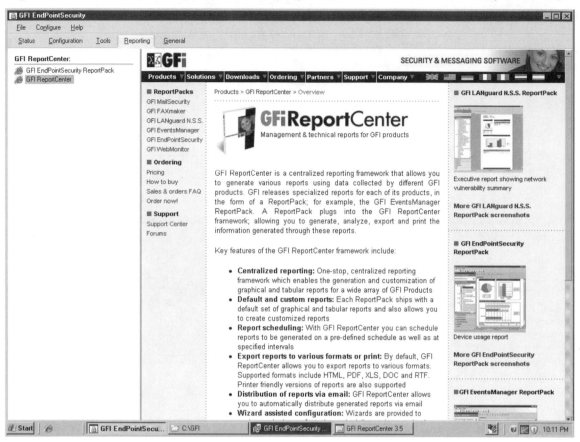

As it turns out, however, GFI EndPointSecurity uses a completely separate console for generating reports. You can access this console by clicking the **Start** button, and selecting the **All Programs | GFI ReportCenter | EndPointSecurity 4 ReportPack** commands from the Start menu. The main ReportCenter screen looks like the one that is shown in Figure 12.9.

Figure 12.9 This is What the GFI ReportCenter Console Looks Like

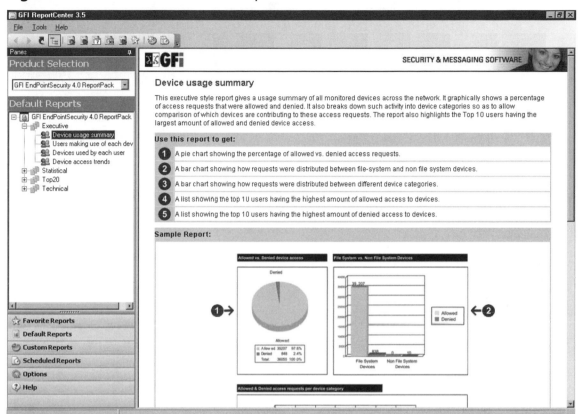

I'm not going to cover the ReportCenter in depth, because I have already done that in Chapter 5. However, I do want to show you how to create a report. If you would like to learn more about the ReportCenter and all of its capabilities, please read Chapter 5.

Creating a Report

If you look at Figure 12.9, you can see that the console contains a Default Reports tree. This tree contains about a dozen different types of reports that you can generate. If you select a report, the column on the right will display a sample report that shows you what types of information the report will contain. Once a report has been run for the first time, the column on the right will display the most recent version of the selected report, rather than a sample report.

Now, let's run a report. For demonstration purposes, I'm going to run the Device Usage Summary report, but this same procedure will work for running any of the other reports as well. To run the report, follow these steps:

1. Navigate through the Default Reports tree to **GFI EndPointSecurity 4.0 ReportPack | Executive | Device Usage Summary**.

2. Right-click on the **Device Usage Summary** container, and select the **Run |
For Last 30 Days** command from the resulting shortcut menus.

3. After a brief delay, the report will be displayed in the console screen, as shown in
Figure 12.10.

Figure 12.10 The Report is Displayed Within the ReportCenter Console

It is difficult to get a feel for the report by looking at the limited amount of information that can
be displayed within a screen capture. I am inserting a copy of this report so that you can see what it
looks like. As you look at this report, keep in mind that a real world report would typically reveal a
lot more information because you have real users interacting with the system. I am just running GFI
EndPointSecurity in a lab environment.

GFiEndPointSecurity

Report cover page

Report title: **Device usage summary**

Description: This executive style report gives a usage summary of all monitored devices across the network. It graphically shows a percentage of access requests that were allowed and denied. It also breaks down such activity into device categories so as to allow comparison of which devices are contributing to these access requests. The report also highlights the Top 10 users having the largest amount of allowed and denied device access.

Generated on: 01-Jul-2008 22:31

Generated by: Administrator

Date/Time filter: 02-Jun-2008 0:00 **to** 01-Jul-2008 23:59

Other filters: No filters used

Reviewed by: _____

Reviewed date: _____

Signature: _____

Allowed vs. Denied device access

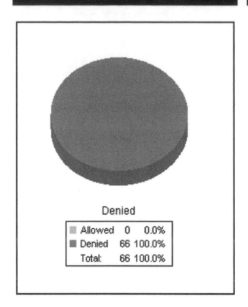

Denied

▨ Allowed	0	0.0%
■ Denied	66	100.0%
Total:	66	100.0%

File System vs. Non File System Devices

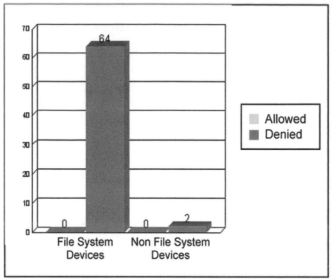

▨ Allowed
■ Denied

Allowed & Denied access requests per device category

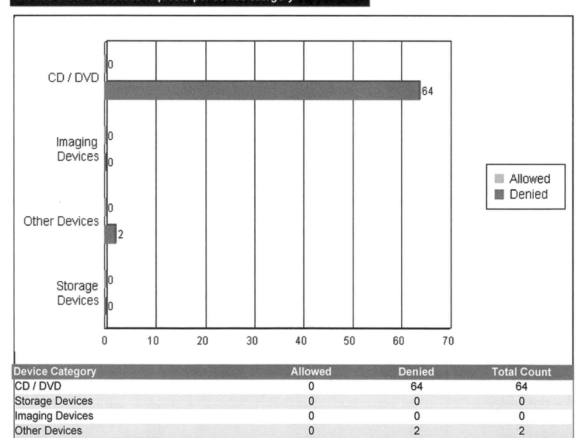

▨ Allowed
■ Denied

Device Category	Allowed	Denied	Total Count
CD / DVD	0	64	64
Storage Devices	0	0	0
Imaging Devices	0	0	0
Other Devices	0	2	2

Top 10 Users having allowed access

Username	Device Category	Count

Top 10 Users having denied access

Username	Device Category	Count
\\PRODUCTION\Administrator	CD / DVD	62
\\NT AUTHORITY\LOCAL SERVICE	Other Devices	2
\\PRODUCTION\Taz	CD / DVD	1
\\PRODUCTION\User3	CD / DVD	1

Keeping Tabs on Your Network

The reports that you can generate through the ReportCenter are nice, but sometimes it's handy to be able to check up on things at a glance, without having to run a report. Besides, the sample report that I showed you was only three pages including the cover sheet, but some of the reports can be pretty long.

If you want to get a quick feel for what's going on in your organization, open the EndPointSecurity management console, and click the **Status** tab, followed by the **General** link. When you do, you will see a screen similar to the one that is shown in Figure 12.11.

Figure 12.11 The General Status Screen Gives You a Quick Summary of What's Going On With GFI EndPointSecurity

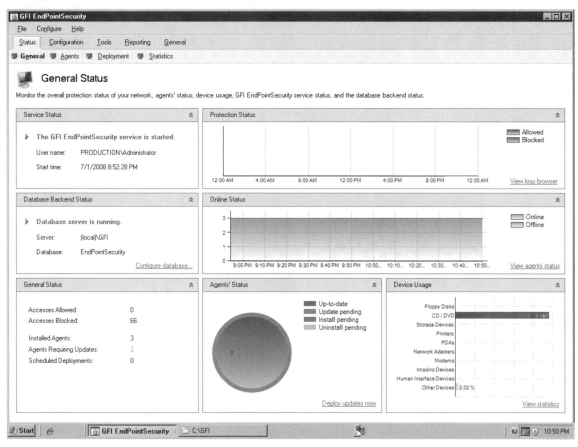

As you can see in the figure, the General Status screen is divided into seven different sections. The table below lists the sections and their functions:

Table 12.1 The General Status Screen's Features

Area	Function
Service Status	The Service Status section tells you when the GFI EndPointSecurity service was most recently started, whether or not the service is currently running, and what security context the service is running under.
Protection Status	Although the Protection Status section is empty in the diagram, it graphically displays the number of allowed and blocked requests for device access throughout the day.
Database Backend Status	The Database Backend Status section shows you which database is being used, and whether or not the database service is currently running.
Online Status	The Online Status section shows you how many of the deployed agents have remained online throughout the day, and how many have gone offline.
General Status	The General Status section tells you things like the number of allowed and blocked access attempts, and the number of agents that are installed.
Agents Status	The Agents Status section graphically displays the number of agents that are up-to-date, the number of agents that have updates pending, and the number of agents that have installs pending.
Device Usage	The Device Usage section is designed to show you which types of devices users attempt to access the most frequently.

Updating Agents

If you look back at Figure 12.11, you will notice that my agents require updates. The reason for this is that any time you make a change to a protection policy, your agents will need to be brought up-to-date so that they are aware of the change.

Updating your agents isn't difficult or time consuming, but it is important. Otherwise, your protection policies will not be enforced properly. To update your agents, follow these steps:

1. Select the GFI EndPointSecurity management console's **General status** tab, and then click the **Agents** link located just beneath the tab.

2. Check the Agents Status screen shown in Figure 12.12, to see whether or not your agents are up-to-date.

3. Select the agents that need to be updated.

4. Right-click on the selected agents, and then choose the **Deploy Selected Agent(s)** option from the shortcut menu.

5. The console will switch to the Deployment Status screen and perform the update. You can go back to the Agents Status screen to confirm that the updates were successful. The General Status screen should also reflect the updates, as shown in Figure 12.13.

Figure 12.12 The Agents Status Screen Tells You Whether or Not Your Agents are Up-to-Date

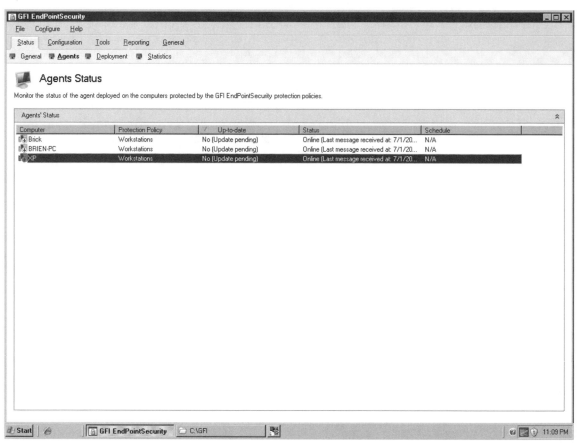

> **TIP**
>
> You can click on the Up-to-Date column header to sort your list of agents based on whether or not the agents are up-to-date. This makes it a lot easier to figure out which agents need updating.

Figure 12.13 The General Status Screen Should Show the Agents as Being Up-to-Date

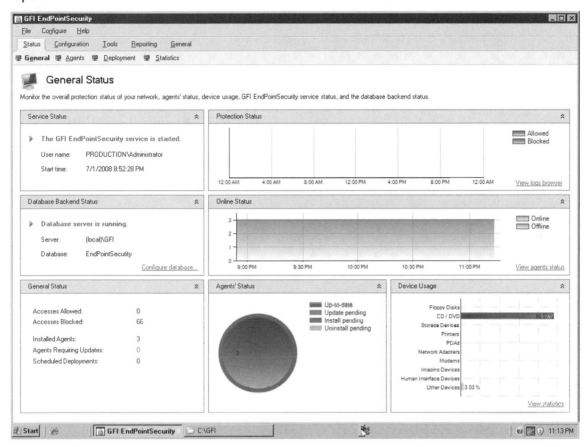

Are You Owned?

Updating Agents

Unless you keep your agents up-to-date, you are not enforcing the current protection policies.

Device Statistics

So far I have shown you several different ways that you can get information about the devices that users attempt to access. Although each of these methods have their own merits, I wanted to show you one last method of looking at device access information. If you click the management console's **Status** tab, and then click the **Statistics** link just beneath it, you will see the Statistics screen, shown in Figure 12.14.

Figure 12.14 The Statistics Screen Provides You With Granular Information About the Devices That Users are Trying to Access

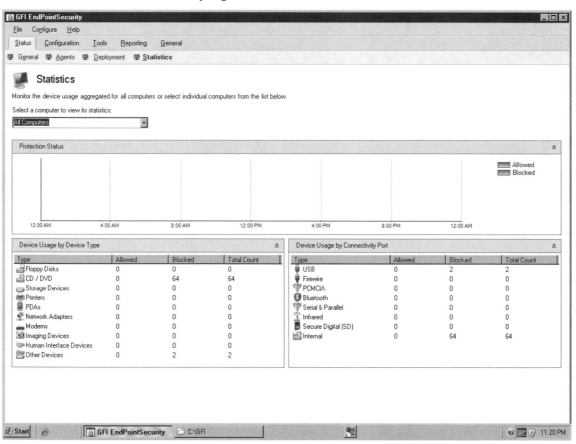

As you can see in the figure, the Statistics screen provides you with information about the number of allowed and blocked access attempts for each type of device. Although blank in this screen capture, the Protection Status section provides you with a time line view of the more recent access requests.

The nice thing about this screen is that it allows you to look at the device access requests on an individual computer basis. All you have to do is choose the computer that you want to examine from the drop-down list. For example, Figure 12.15 shows the access requests related to a computer named Brick.

Figure 12.15 You Can Select an Individual Computer From the Drop-Down List to See the Access Requests That It Has Generated

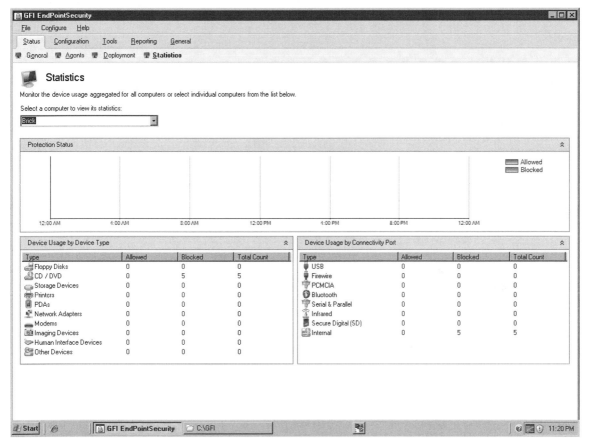

Summary

In this chapter, I have explained that although access protection begins when you set a protection policy and deploy the agents, it is a good idea to verify that the protection policy is doing its job. I then went on to show you several different methods for obtaining statistical information about device usage in your organization, and I showed you how you could generate an alert if certain situations occur.

Solutions Fast Track

Setting Logging Options

☑ Logging can be used as a way of writing information to GFI EndPointSecurity's internal database. This information can be used to generate reports later on.

☑ Logging information can also be written to the Windows event logs.

☑ If you do write information to the Windows event logs, I recommend keeping the logging options to a minimum to avoid information overload.

Setting Alerting Options

☑ Like log entries, alerts are triggered by specific types of events.

☑ You can send alerts by Windows network message, e-mail, or SMS message.

☑ You will have to take some time to configure the alert recipients.

Generating End Point Security Reports

☑ Reports are generated through the ReportCenter, which is installed along with the ReportPack.

☑ To generate a report, right-click on the report, choose the Run command, and then specify the time period for the data that is to be used in the report.

Keeping Tabs on Your Network

☑ The management console's Status tab gives you a nice overview of the network status.

☑ It is necessary to update the agents any time that you make a change to a protection policy.

☑ The Statistics screen (found on the management console's Status tab) allows you to view device request on a per computer basis.

Frequently Asked Questions

Q: GFI EndPointSecurity does not seem to be enforcing my protection policy. What happened?

A: Check to see if your agents need to be updated. Changes to the protection policy do not take effect until the agents are brought up-to-date.

Q: Why do you recommend that only a couple of types of events be written to the Windows event logs?

A: Logging an excessive number of events can cause the log files to grow to the point that it becomes impossible to track down the events that you are really interested in.

Q: I can't seem to receive network message alerts. What's going on?

A: Check to make sure that the computer that has been designated to receive the alerts is running the Alerter service and the Messenger service. You should also make sure that there are no firewall rules blocking the alerts. There is a Microsoft Knowledgebase article that addresses common issues at: http://support.microsoft.com/kb/330904

Q: Can I use the ReportCenter that came with GFI LANguard Network Security Scanner or some other GFI product to generate EndPointSecurity reports?

A: No, each copy of the ReportCenter contains reports geared toward specific products.

Chapter 13

Installing GFI EventsManager

Solutions in this chapter:

- **Installing GFI EventsManager**
- **Performing the Initial Configuration**
- **Installing the ReportPack**

☑ **Summary**

☑ **Solutions Fast Track**

☑ **Frequently Asked Questions**

Introduction

If you have ever tried to diagnose a problem with a computer that is running Windows, you know that the Windows Event Logs contain a wealth of information. Unfortunately though, the log files often contain so much information that nobody even bothers to look at them, because finding exactly what you need becomes next to impossible due to so many "noise" entries in the logs. The really sad part though is that oftentimes the log files contain clues to an impending security breach or system problem, but these clues typically go unnoticed. GFI EventsManager is designed to help you cut through the log file clutter. It organizes event log entries in a more meaningful way and alerts you when important events occur. GFI EventsManager acts as a networkwide events manager that lets administrators monitor and manage events through a single user console.

Hardware and Software Requirements

The hardware and software requirements vary depending on the machine where you plan to install the software. Table 13.1 lists the hardware requirements.

Table 13.1 GFI EventsManager Hardware Requirements

Installation on Windows 2000, XP, or Server 2003	Installation on Windows Vista
2GHz or faster processor	2.8GHz or faster processor
512MB of RAM	2GB of RAM
1.5GB of free hard disk space	1.5GB of free hard disk space

The software requirements for the machine onto which you are installing GFI EventsManager include:

- Windows 2000, XP, 2003, or Vista
- NET Framework 2.0
- Microsoft Data Access Components (MDAC) 2.8 or later
- MSDE or SQL Server

The machines being monitored also have some software requirements. These vary depending on the types of logs you will be monitoring. Table 13.2 lists these requirements.

Table 13.2 Software Requirements for Scanned Machines

Windows Event Log Scanning	■ The Remote Registry service3 must be enabled. ■ The Windows Audit Logs must be enabled. ■ Vista machines must be in the same domain as the GFI EventsManager Server, and have User Accounts Control disabled.
W3C Log Scanning	■ The source folders must be accessible through Windows UNC shares.
Syslog and SNMP Traps	■ The Sources/Senders must be configured to send information to the GFI EventsManager server.

Installing GFI EventsManager

The process of installing GFI EventsManager is very similar to the installation process used by so many other GFI products. To install GFI EventsManager, perform the following steps:

1. Download the latest version of GFI EventsManager. You can download the software from the GFI Web site at www.gfi.com/downloads/downloads.aspx?pid=esm&lid=EN.

2. Save the EVENTSMANAGER8.EXE file you downloaded to a temporary folder on your server's hard drive.

3. Double-click the file you just downloaded.

4. If Windows issues a security warning, click the **Run** button.

5. When the Setup Wizard starts, the first screen you will see is the one shown in Figure 13.1. As you can see in the figure, GFI EventsManager requires a SQL Server database. In order to make things easy on you, the Setup Wizard offers to install Microsoft SQL Server 2005 Express Edition (formerly known as MSDE or Microsoft Database Engine) for you. This will work fine in small to medium-sized organizations, but larger organizations will likely end up needing a full-blown SQL Server instance. For the sake of this book, I will use SQL Server 2005 Developers Edition, which I have already installed on the server. Therefore, I will make sure the check box is not selected prior to clicking **Next**.

Figure 13.1 GFI EventsManager Requires a SQL Server Database

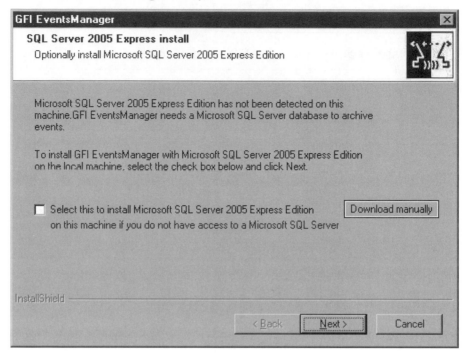

6. Windows will now display the wizard's Welcome screen. Click **Next** to continue.

7. The following screen prompts you to accept the End User License Agreement, or EULA as it has come to be known. Go ahead and accept the license agreement, and then click **Next**.

8. The screen shown in Figure 13.2 should appear, prompting you to enter a serial number. If you have purchased a license for GFI EventsManager, you should have been issued a serial number. You can enter that here. If you have not yet purchased a license, just enter the word **Evaluation** in place of a serial number. Doing so provides you with full access for an unlimited number of users for ten days.

Figure 13.2 Enter the Word EVALUATION in Place of a Serial Number

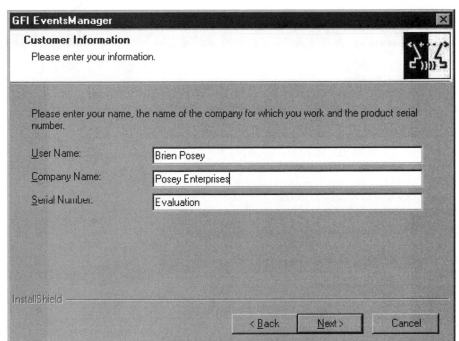

9. Click **Next**. You will be taken to a screen that asks you to provide a set of credentials to an account that GFI EventsManager can use as a service account. You can either use the domain administrator's account, or create a dedicated service account. Either way, the account must be a member of the Domain Admins group. Click **Next** to continue.

10. Setup will now ask you to choose an installation path for the EventsManager software. Go ahead and accept the default path by clicking **Next**.

11. You will now see a screen that tells you the installation process is about to begin. If you need to make any changes to the information you have entered prior to initiating the installation process, click the **Back** button. Otherwise, click the **Install** button.

12. When the installation process completes, click the **Finish** button.

Performing the Initial Configuration

When the installation process completes, the screen shown in Figure 13.3 will appear. As you can see in the figure, you must complete four primary configuration tasks (even though some are labeled optional) prior to using GFI EventsManager.

Figure 13.3 You Must Complete Four Configuration Tasks After Installing
GFI EventsManager

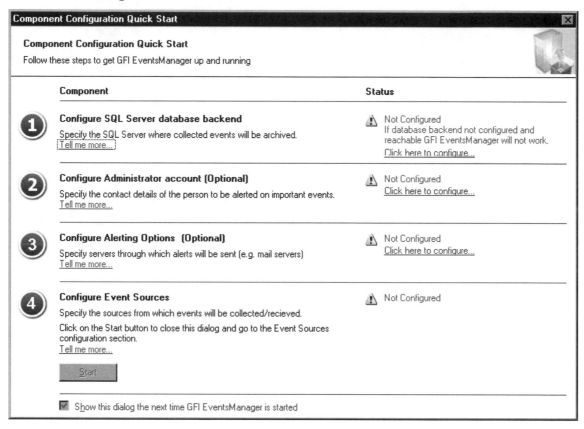

Configuring the Backend Database

The first step in the initial configuration process is to configure a backend SQL Server database.
As I mentioned before, I will be configuring GFI EventsManager to use a SQL Server 2005
Developers Edition database rather than a SQL 2005 Express Edition Database. Keep in mind though
that other versions of SQL Server are also supported, and that the SQL Server database does not have to
reside locally.

To configure the SQL Server database, perform the following steps:

1. Click the **Click Here To Configure** link, found in the **Configure SQL Server
   Database Backend** section.

2. Windows will now display the Database Backend properties sheet, which prompts you to
   enter the name of the server and database you want to use. Enter either the name or the
   IP address of your database server, followed by a backslash, and then the name of the
   database instance. For example, I have a SQL Server instance named GFI installed on my
   local server. Therefore, I am using GFI\GFI as the server name. If your database is not

installed locally, then just replace [local] with the NetBIOS name or IP address of your database server.

3.   Enter **EventsManager** into the **Database** field.

4.   Choose the **Windows Authentication** option, as shown in Figure 13.4.

Figure 13.4 Enter the Server Name and the SQL Server Instance Name for the Database Server You Want to Use

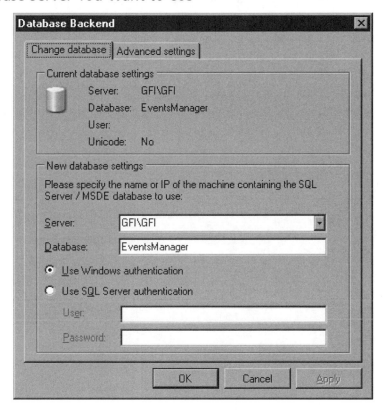

5.   Click **OK**.

6.   GFI EventsManager will now create the necessary database. When the process completes, click **OK**.

Configuring an Administrative Account

The second step in the configuration process involves configuring an administrative account. This is the account that will be alerted when important events occur. To create an administrative account, perform the following steps.

1.   Click the **Click Here To Configure** link found in the **Configure Administrator Account (Optional)** section.

2. You will now see the EventsManagerAdministrator Properties sheet shown in Figure 13.5.
    The basic idea behind the properties sheet's General tab is that you can add an e-mail
    address, cell phone number, and the name of the computer the administrator uses. If you
    want to specify the contact information for multiple administrators, you can separate each
    value with a semicolon.

Figure 13.5 This Is Where You Add Your Contact Information

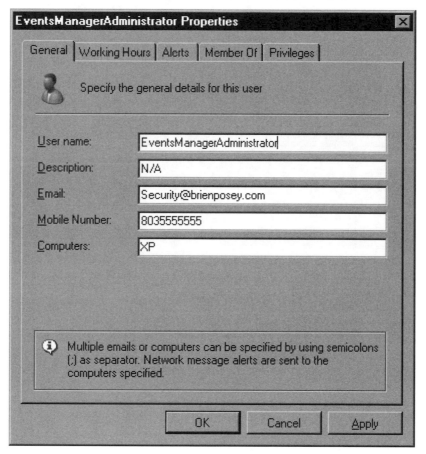

3. Once you have populated the General tab, go to the **Working Hours** tab, shown
    in Figure 13.6. As you can see in the figure, the Working Hours tab lets you tell GFI
    EventsManager what the normal working hours are for the administrator. That way,
    different types of alerts can be sent, depending on whether or not the event that
    triggered the alert occurred during business hours.

Figure 13.6 You Can Tell GFI EventsManager What Your Company's Normal Office Hours Are

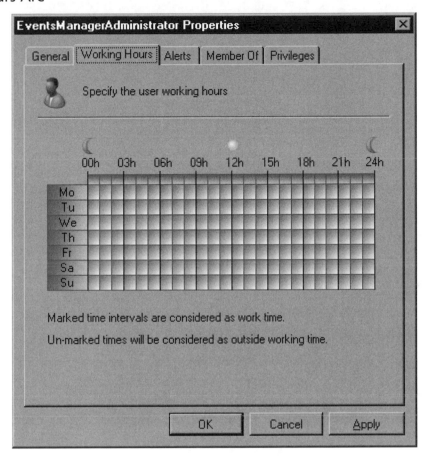

4. After you finish telling GFI EventsManager about your company's business hours, go to the **Properties** sheet's **Alerts** tab. As you can see in Figure 13.7, you have the option of controlling which types of alerts will be sent to the group during business hours, and which types of alerts will be sent after hours. For example, if your IT security staff is glued to their computers all day long, then sending a network message alert might be a really good way to insure that the members of your administrative staff are alerted quickly when certain types of events occur. At night though, those people have all gone home, so it wouldn't make sense to display a network message alert on their computer if they aren't even there to see it. In such a situation, it would probably be better to send the alert to their cell phones.

Figure 13.7 You May Need to Use a Different Alerting Mechanism After Hours

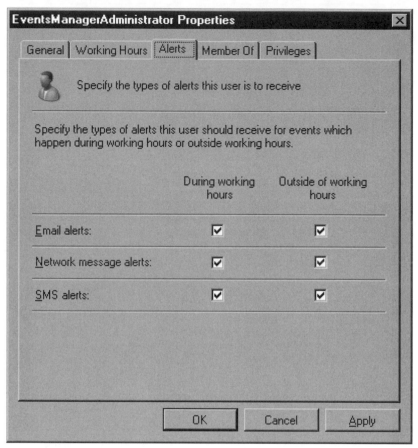

5.   Now, take a look at the **Properties** sheet's **Member Of** tab. Verify that the tab lists the **EventsManagerAdministrators** group.

6.   Go to the **Properties** sheet's **Privileges** tab and make sure the user has full privileges, as shown in Figure 13.8.

Figure 13.8 Make Sure the Administrator Has Full Privileges

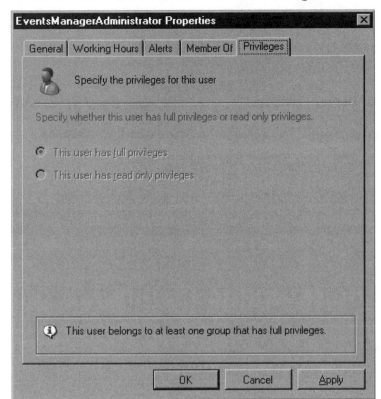

7.   Click **OK** to finish configuring the administrative account.

Configuring Alerting Options

GFI EventsManager has the ability to send e-mail alerts whenever certain events occur. Configuring the e-mail alerts can be a bit tricky, but in my opinion, it is well worth the effort. Since configuring e-mail alerts can be confusing, I'll show you two different ways to set them up. The first method involves configuring IIS to act as an SMTP server, and then using it to send e-mail alerts. The other method involves using a Microsoft Exchange Server. Both methods will work, but if you have an Exchange Server on your network, I recommend using it.

Configuring a Stand-Alone SMTP Server

If you don't have access to an Exchange Server, you can configure your GFI EventsManager server to act as a stand-alone SMTP server. Windows ships with everything you need, but the SMTP components are not installed by default. The exact method of installing the SMTP components varies depending on the version of Windows you are using. For the purposes of this book, I will be using Windows Server 2003.

1. Begin the process by having whoever is in charge of your organization's e-mail create a dedicated mailbox for you that you can use for receiving server notifications. For demonstration purposes, I'll use a mailbox with the address of Security@production.com. I do not actually own the production.com domain, it is just the name of an internal Active Directory domain I use. You should use an e-mail address that reflects the mail domain you use in real life.

2. Once the new mailbox has been created, open the server's **Control Panel** and select the **Add or Remove Programs** option.

3. When Windows displays the **Add or Remove Programs** dialog box, click the **Add/Remove Windows Components** icon.

4. After a brief delay, Windows will launch the **Windows Component Wizard**. Choose the **Application Server** option from the list of available components. Don't click the check box—just click the words **Application Server**.

5. Click the **Details** button to reveal the various Application Server components.

6. Click the **Internet Information Services (IIS)** component. Once again, you should click the words, not the check box.

7. Click the **Details** button. Windows will then display a list of the various IIS components available.

8. Scroll toward the bottom of the list of components, and then select the **SMTP Service** option. This time you are actually going to select the check box rather than just clicking the words, as shown in Figure 13.9.

Figure 13.9 You Must Select the SMTP Service Option

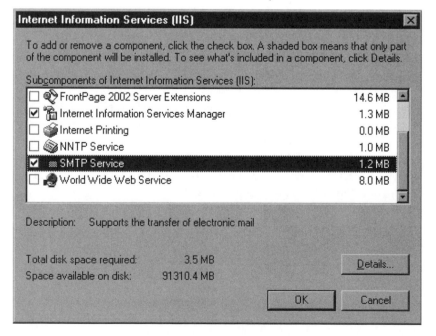

9. Click **OK**.

10. Click **OK** again.

11. Click **Next** and Windows will begin installing the necessary files. Depending on how your server is configured, you may be prompted to insert your Windows Server 2003 installation media.

12. When the installation process completes, click the **Finish** button, and then close the **Control Panel**.

Now that the SMTP Service is installed, we need to configure it. Fortunately, the configuration process is pretty simple.

1. Choose the **Internet Information Services (IIS)** option from the server's Administrative Tools menu.

2. When the IIS Manager opens, navigate through the console tree to **Internet Information Services | *your server* | Default SMTP Virtual Server | Domains**, as shown in Figure 13.10.

Figure 13.10 Navigate Through the Console Tree to Internet Information Services | *Your Server* | Default SMTP Virtual Server | Domains

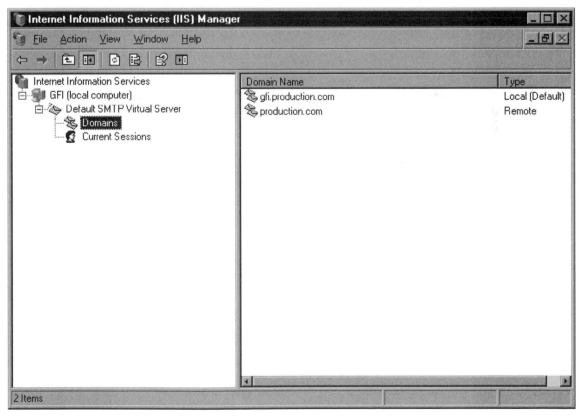

Notice in Figure 13.10 that when I selected the Domains container, the pane on the right displayed two domain names. The top domain name—in this case, gfi.production.com—was placed there by default. Gfi.production.com is actually the server's fully qualified domain name, but the SMTP service treats it as though it were an independent domain.

As it stands right now, the SMTP service is only capable of sending e-mail to recipients in the gfi.production.com domain. Of course, no mailboxes exist in this domain, because the server we are configuring isn't a full-blown mail server. The SMTP component only allows us to send mail, it doesn't let us store the mailboxes on the server.

That being the case, we must make the SMTP Service aware of the domain to which we want to send e-mail. In this case, we will be sending messages to an e-mail address named Security@ production.com. Since this mailbox resides in the production.com domain (or at least in an internal domain named production.com), we need to make the SMTP Service aware of the domain's existence. I had already done that when I created the screen capture for Figure 13.10. That's why you see the production.com domain listed in the console. Here's how it's done.

1. Right-click the **Domains** container and choose the **New | Domain** options from the resulting shortcut menus.

2. Windows will now launch the **New SMTP Domain Wizard**. The wizard's initial screen asks if you want to specify a remote domain or an alias. Choose the **Remote** option, and then click **Next**.

3. In the space provided, enter the name of the domain to which you want to send mail.

4. Click **Finish** and the domain you have specified will be added to the list of domains.

5. Right-click the domain you just added, and then select the **Properties** command from the resulting shortcut menu.

6. When the domain's **Properties** sheet appears, select the **Allow Incoming Mail To Be Relayed To This Domain** check box, as shown in Figure 13.11.

Figure 13.11 You Must Allow Incoming Mail to Be Relayed to the Domain
You Just Set Up

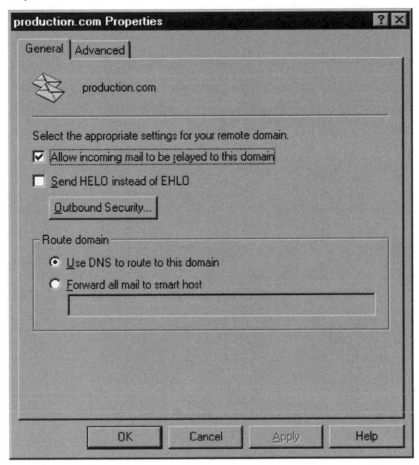

Now that we have configured Windows to act as an SMTP server, it's time to configure GFI
EventsManager to use the SMTP server to send mail. To do so, perform the following steps:

1. Click the **Click Here To Configure** link, found on the **Component Configuration
   Quick Start** screen's **Configure Alerting Options** section.

2. Windows will now display the **Alerting Options** properties sheet. Select the properties
   sheet's **Email** tab, and then click the **Add** button.

3. Enter **127.0.0.1** into the **Hostname/IP** field. This is the server's local loopback address.
   By entering this address, you are telling the server to use itself as an SMTP server.
   Alternatively, you could also use the server's IP address in this field.

4. Verify that the Port field is set to **25**.

5. Make sure the **This SMTP Server Requires Authentication** check box is not selected.

6. You can use any e-mail address in the Sender field, so long as the domain portion of the address reflects the server's fully qualified domain name. In this case, the server's fully qualified domain name is gfi.production.com.

7. Enter the sender's display name into the **Sender (Display Name)** field. When you have finished filling in the Mailserver Properties sheet, it should look something like that in Figure 13.12.

Figure 13.12 How the Mailserver Properties Sheet Must Be Configured

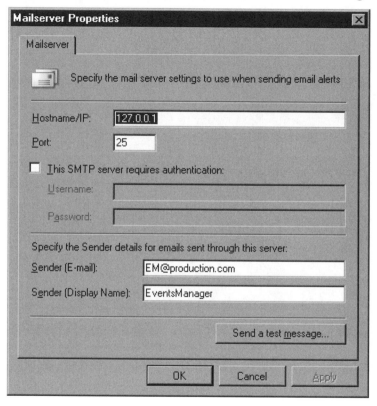

8. When you are done, click the **Send A Test Message** button.

9. A prompt should appear asking you for the recipient's e-mail address. Enter an e-mail address and click **OK**.

10. You should now see a message telling you the mail settings were successfully verified, and that a test message was sent. It is important to check the specified mailbox to make sure the message has actually come through though, because Setup has no way of knowing whether or not the test message was actually received.

11. Once you have confirmed that the test message was received, click **OK**, and you will be returned to the Alerting Options properties sheet. The address 127.0.0.1 should appear in the list of mail servers, as shown in Figure 13.13.

Figure 13.13 The IP Address 127.0.0.1 Now Appears in the List of Mail Servers

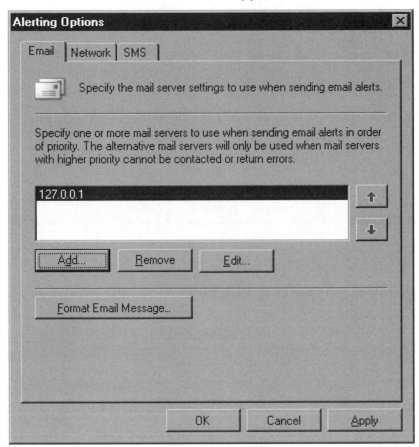

As you look at the figure, you will also notice a Format Email Message button. Clicking this button allows you to customize the messages that GFI EventsManager sends out. Normally though, you should just stick with the default message format unless you have a compelling reason to change it.

One more thing you might have noticed about the screen shown in Figure 13.13 is that the properties sheet also has tabs labeled Network and SMS. These tabs contain other alerting options that I will talk about later in this chapter.

Notes from the Underground…

Mail Relay

You must be careful about how you configure your SMTP server, and how it is used. As it is right now, your SMTP server can transmit mail without requiring authentication. Should this server become compromised, it could easily be turned into a "spam factory" and the resulting spam would be traced back to your IP address, which would likely get you blacklisted.

Configuring GFI EventsManager for Use with Microsoft Exchange Server

Although I am writing this book on GFI security software, I am best known throughout the IT community for my work with Microsoft Exchange Server. That being the case, I wanted to show you an alternate mail settings configuration you can use if you have an Exchange Server organization in place.

As I mentioned earlier, my internal domain name is production.com. I therefore created an Exchange Server mailbox with an e-mail address of Security@production.com. Since I don't actually own the production.com domain name, this e-mail address is only accessible from within my perimeter network.

I won't go through the steps of creating an Exchange Server mailbox because they are performed in a very different manner from one version of Exchange Server to the next. Besides, if your company has an Exchange Server organization in place, then I would think it would be a safe assumption that somebody in the company knows how to create a mailbox. I will at least tell you though, that my Security@production.com mailbox resides on an Exchange 2007 server.

If your company has an Exchange Server organization in place, then the process of configuring the mail settings for GFI EventsManager will be much simpler than what you saw in the previous section. That's because in the previous section, we had to build an SMTP server from scratch. Exchange Server is natively equipped to handle SMTP mail, so we don't have to bother with most of those configuration steps. In fact, all of the configuration takes place through the Alerting Options properties sheet. To configure GFI EventsManager to use your Exchange Server to send e-mail alerts, perform the following steps:

1. Click the **Click Here To Configure** link, found in the **Component Configuration Quick Start** screen's **Configure Alerting Options** section, as shown earlier in Figure 13.3.

2. Windows now displays the **Alerting Options** properties sheet. Verify that the properties sheet's **Email** tab is selected.

3. Click the **Add** button.

4. Enter your Exchange Server's IP address into the **Hostname/IP** field.

5. Verify that the port number is set to **25**.

6. Select the **This SMTP Server Requires Authentication** check box.

7. As you may recall, we created a mailbox called Security@production.com to receive e-mail alerts. We are going to use this mailbox as both the sender and recipient. Of course, you will want to substitute the e-mail address you have configured for Security@production.com in the following steps. With that said, enter **Security@production.com** into the **Username** field (Windows allows you to substitute an e-mail address for a username.

8. Enter the mailbox password into the **Password** field.

9. Enter **Security@Production.com** into the **Sender (E-mail)** field.

10. Enter the words **GFI EventsManager** into the **Sender (Display Name)** field. The Mailserver Properties dialog box should now look something like what you see in Figure 13.14.

Figure 13.14 How the Mailserver Properties Dialog Box Should Look When Fully Populated

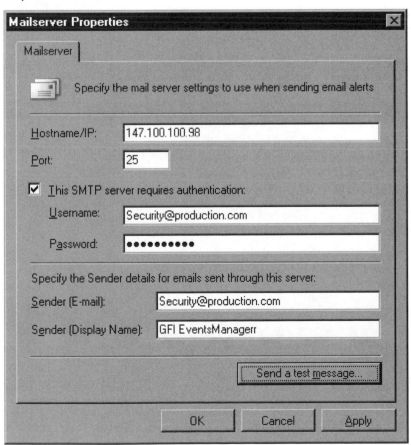

11.   Click the **Send A Test Message** button.

12.   When prompted, enter the recipient's e-mail address. In this case, I am using Security@ production.com as the recipient e-mail address.

13.   Click **OK** to acknowledge that the message was sent.

14.   Open Outlook or Outlook Web Access (OWA) to confirm that the test message has been received. You can see what the test message looks like in Figure 13.15.

Figure 13.15 You Should Receive a Test Message from Setup

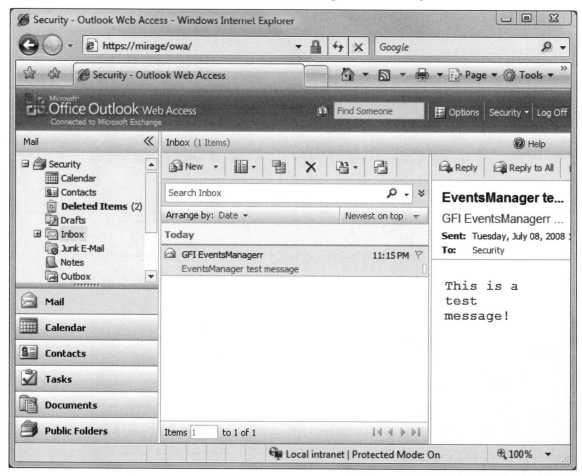

15.   Click **OK** to close the Mailserver properties sheet.

> **NOTE**
>
> It is important to verify that you have actually received the test message. GFI EventsManager is only able to acknowledge that it has attempted to send a message. The software checks for common SMTP error codes, but ultimately it is up to you to make sure the message was delivered.

If you are using Exchange Server 2007, there may be one more thing you need to do before you will be able to receive the test message. Exchange 2007 is designed so the hub transport only allows secure authenticated connections. This means that if you simply specify the IP address of a hub transport server, the Exchange Server is going to reject the test message.

This problem can be circumvented in two ways. The best option is to use the IP address of an edge transport server as the SMTP server address. If you don't have an edge transport server, you will need to allow anonymous connections to the transport pipeline. You can do this by opening the Exchange Management Shell and entering the following command:

```
set-ReceiveConnector "Default <Servername>" -permissiongroups:"ExchangeUsers,
ExchangeServers,ExchangeLegacyServers,AnonymousUsers"
```

As you can see in Figure 13.16, the command doesn't really appear to do anything when executed, but it should allow you to send messages from your GFI EventsManager server to a mailbox on the Exchange 2007 mailbox server.

Figure 13.16 The *Set-ReceiveConnector* Command Doesn't Appear to Do Anything When Executed

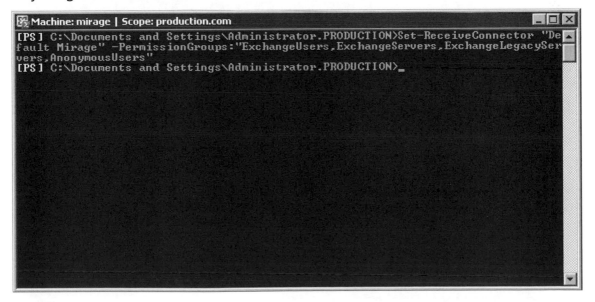

Formatting Your E-Mail Message

Regardless of whether you choose to use an Exchange Server or an SMTP Server, you have the option of customizing the e-mail message that is sent when an alert is triggered. To do so, just click the **Format E-mail Message** button found on the **Alerting Options** properties sheet's **Email** tab, shown earlier in Figure 13.13. GFI EventsManager provides you with a rather nice default e-mail message, but if you want to make modifications to this message, it is easy to do so. Clicking the **Format Email Message** button opens a text editor you can use to compose your message. You can even insert EventsManager-specific tags and rich text.

Network Alerts

Although GFI EventsManager's primary alert mechanism is e-mail, it also uses network messages and SMS text messages as other mechanisms for sending alerts. Notice the Alerting Options properties sheet's Network tab in Figure 13.17. As you can see, there isn't much you can do on this tab, other than format the network message.

Figure 13.17 Compose a Network Message by Clicking the Format Network Message Button

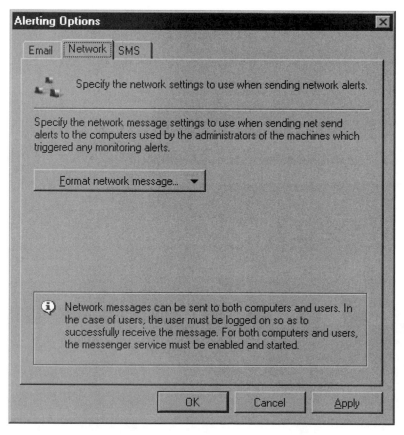

If you click the **Format Network Messages** button though, you will see the several types of network alerts GFI EventsManager uses. An example of this is shown in Figure 13.18. Each of these alert types has its own default messages, but you do have the option of modifying any of the existing messages.

Figure 13.18 GFI EventsManager Uses Several Different Types of Network Alerts

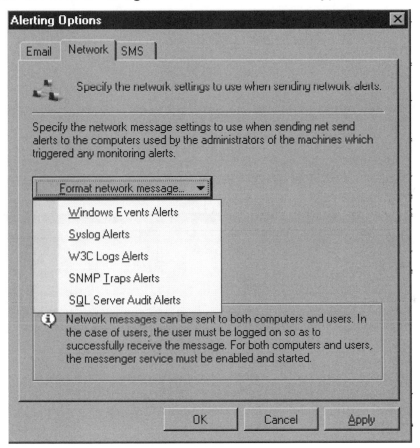

SMS Alerts

As I mentioned earlier, GFI EventsManager also gives you the option of sending SMS text messages to mobile phones. SMS text messages are configured through the properties sheet's SMS tab, which is very similar to the Network tab. The only real difference is that the SMS tab provides the option of choosing the mechanism you want to use for transmitting SMS messages. Normally, you shouldn't have to change the defaults though. Like your network alerts though, you will need to compose the SMS message you want to transmit.

> **NOTE**
>
> Many mobile phones only support very short SMS messages. Therefore, you probably won't be able to provide nearly as much detail in an SMS message as you would in an e-mail alert or network message.

Configuring Events Sources

The last thing you need to configure is the event sources. These are the sources from which event information will be collected. To carry out the configuration process, perform the following steps:

1. Click the **Start** button in the **Configure Event Sources** section. You will be taken to the screen shown in Figure 13.19.

Figure 13.19 The Left Side of the Screen Shows the Categories of Computers Found on Your Network

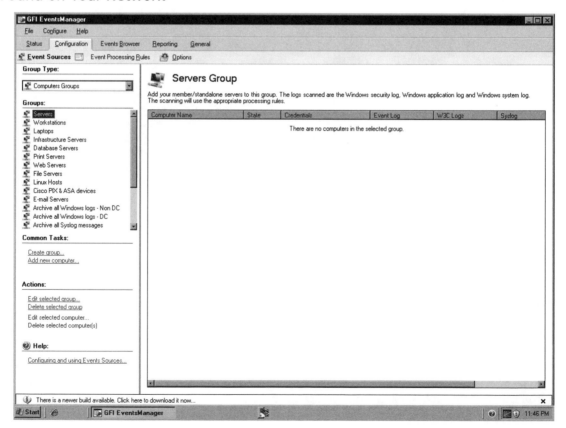

2. As you can see in the figure, the left side of the screen contains several different categories of computers that may appear on your network. To add a computer to a category, right-click the category, and choose the **Add New Computer** command from the resulting shortcut menu. When you do, Windows will display the **Add New Computer** dialog box.

3. Enter the name of the computer you want to add.

4. Click the **Add** button.

5. Click **Finish**.

6. The computer should now be listed within the container you selected earlier, as shown in Figure 13.20.

Figure 13.20 The Computer Should Now Be Listed in the Container You Selected

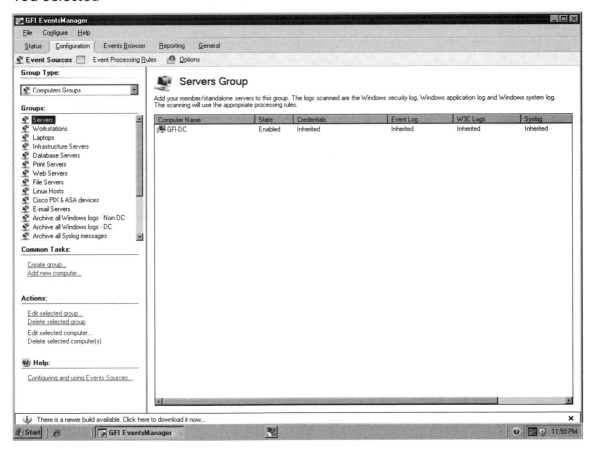

Installing the ReportPack

In the first section of this book, I showed you how to install the ReportPack that went with GFI LANguard Network Security Scanner. However, each of the GFI products that is ReportPack-compatible uses its own version of the ReportPack, containing reports specifically designed for that product. Because of this, I want to go ahead and walk you through the process of installing the GFI EventsManager ReportPack.

1. Download the ReportPack software, and save it to a temporary directory. You can download the ReportPack at www.gfi.com/downloads/downloads.aspx?pid=esm&lid=EN. The download consists of a 12.8MB self-extracting executable file named eventsmanager8rp report pack.exe.

2. Double-click the file you've downloaded.

3. If you receive a Windows security warning, click the **Run** button.

4. Windows will now launch the **GFI EventsManager 8 ReportPack Setup Wizard**. Click **Next** to bypass the wizard's Welcome screen.

5. A screen will appear asking you if you want to check for a newer version of the ReportPack software. Choose the option **Check For A New Version**, and then click **Next**.

6. The next screen you encounter displays the End User License Agreement (EULA). Choose the option to accept the license agreement, and then click **OK**.

7. A screen appears asking you to enter your full name, your company name, and your license key. If you have not yet purchased a GFI EventsManager license, you can enter the word **Evaluation** in place of a license key. Using the evaluation version will let you use the ReportPack and all its features for ten days. I should point out though, that although the ReportPack is a separate download, a ReportPack license is included when you buy a license for GFI EventsManager. If you've already bought a GFI EventsManager, you can use the same license key for the ReportPack that you used for the main product.

8. Click **Next**.

9. Setup will now display a screen asking you which type of database you want to use. As you can see in the Figure 13.21, you have the option of using a sample database or a Microsoft SQL Server database. Although the test database option lets you play with the ReportPack and its features, you will have to use the same SQL Server database that GFI EventsManager is using if the ReportPack is to be of any value in a production environment. Therefore, select the **Use SQL Server Database** option.

Figure 13.21 How the Database Selection Screen Should Look

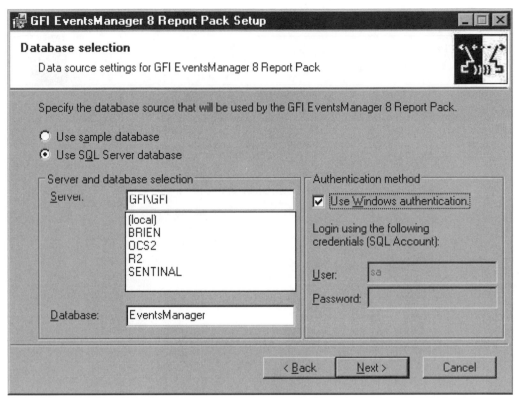

10. Select the server that is hosting your SQL Server database.

11. In the **Database** field, enter the name of the database server and the name of the SQL Server instance that GFI EventsManager is using. The server name and SQL instance name should be entered in SERVER\INSTANCE format, as shown in Figure 13.21.

12. Select the **Use Windows Authentication** check box.

13. Click **Next**.

14. You are now going to see a screen asking you to configure the mail settings for the ReportPack. Unfortunately, I can't tell you exactly what to type here, because it is going to be different for each organization. What I can tell you is that the settings you use should be identical to the settings you used earlier in this chapter when you configured the mail settings for GFI EventsManager. You can see what the Mail Settings for my organization look like in Figure 13.22.

Figure 13.22 How the Mail Settings Screen Will Look for My Organization

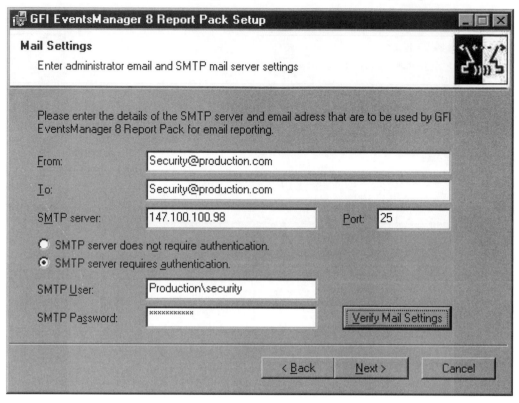

15. After entering your Mail Settings, click the **Verify Mail Settings** button. You should receive a message indicating the test message was sent successfully. Keep in mind that it is possible you will receive this message even if some of your mail settings are wrong! It is very important that you check to make sure the message was actually delivered.

16. Once you have confirmed that your mail settings are functioning properly, click **Next**.

17. A screen should appear asking you to confirm the destination folder. Go ahead and accept the default installation path, and then click **Next**.

18. A message should appear indicating that Setup is ready to install the application. Click **Next** and the Setup wizard will begin copying the necessary files.

19. When the file copy process completes, click **Finish**.

NOTE

It is important to verify that you have actually received the test message. GFI EventsManager is only able to acknowledge that it has attempted to send a message. The software checks for common SMTP error codes, but ultimately it is up to you to make sure that message delivery has occurred.

NOTE

You must use the same database for both the GFI LANguard Network Security Scanner and the ReportPack.

Summary

As you can see, the installation process and initial configuration process for GFI EventsManager tends to be a little tedious. Since so much work is involved, I recommend taking one last look at the Component Configuration Quick Start screen to make sure everything has been configured, as shown in Figure 13.23. We will deal with configuring protection policies in the next chapter.

Figure 13.23 Always Do One Last Check to Make Sure Everything Has Been Configured

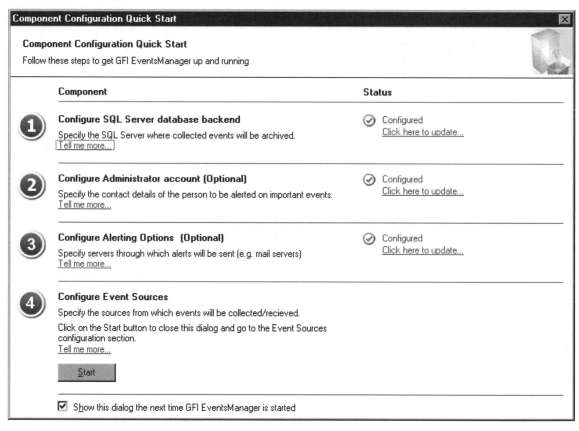

Solutions Fast Track

Installing GFI EventsManager

☑ You must verify that your server meets the minimum hardware and software requirements prior to installation.

☑ Check to make sure you have the most recent version of the software.

Performing the Initial Configuration

☑ You can use either a SQL Server database or an MSDE database, but a SQL Server database is preferred in larger organizations.

☑ You can configure GFI EventsManager to use either a Microsoft Exchange Server or a stand-alone SMTP server. If you have an Exchange Server in your organization, I recommend using it.

Installing the ReportPack

☑ Make sure you configure the ReportPack to use the same database GFI EventsManager is using.

Frequently Asked Questions

Q: Can I use an MSDE database with GFI EventsManager?

A: Sure, but I would only recommend doing so in smaller organizations since MSDE does not scale well.

Q: Does GFI EventsManager support the use of Microsoft Access databases?

A: No. Some GFI products do allow Microsoft Access databases to be used, but this one doesn't.

Q: I don't have an Exchange Server, but I may want to use one later on. Is this possible?

A: Yes. The management console lets you reconfigure your alerting options.

Q: How do I know if I need SQL Server or not?

A: It's not imperative that smaller organizations have SQL Server. If your organization will be monitoring more than 50 servers, I would recommend using SQL Server. Keep in mind that this is just *my* recommendation, not GFI's, and it certainly isn't a requirement.

Q: The installation process seems to be taking forever. Is this normal?

A: On my lab machines, the installation process was fairly quick. Keep in mind though, your server hardware has a lot to do with the speed of the installation.

Q: Can I piggyback GFI EventsManager onto a server that is running other applications?

A: It is possible, but I would recommend using a dedicated server, if possible, for security and performance reasons.

Q: Can I install a SQL Server database onto the same server that will be running GFI EventsManager?

A: Assuming that your server has the resources to run both, yes.

Chapter 14

Browsing the Event Logs

Solutions in this chapter:

- Browsing the Logs
- Customizing the Events Browser View
- Creating Custom Queries
- Exporting Events

☑ Summary

☑ Solutions Fast Track

☑ Frequently Asked Questions

Introduction

Now that the initial installation and configuration is complete, it's time to actually begin using GFI EventsViewer. In this chapter, I want to familiarize you with the software and show you how to locate specific events, as well as specific types of events, within the logs that GFI EventsManager collects.

Browsing the Logs

The first thing I want to show you is how you can use the GFI EventsManager console to view the various event log entries that have been collected. To see the collection of events compiled, select the console's **Events Browser** tab, and then choose the **Windows Events Browser** option located just beneath the tab. A screen should then appear similar to the one in Figure 14.1.

Figure 14.1 This Screen Shows You All the Events Collected

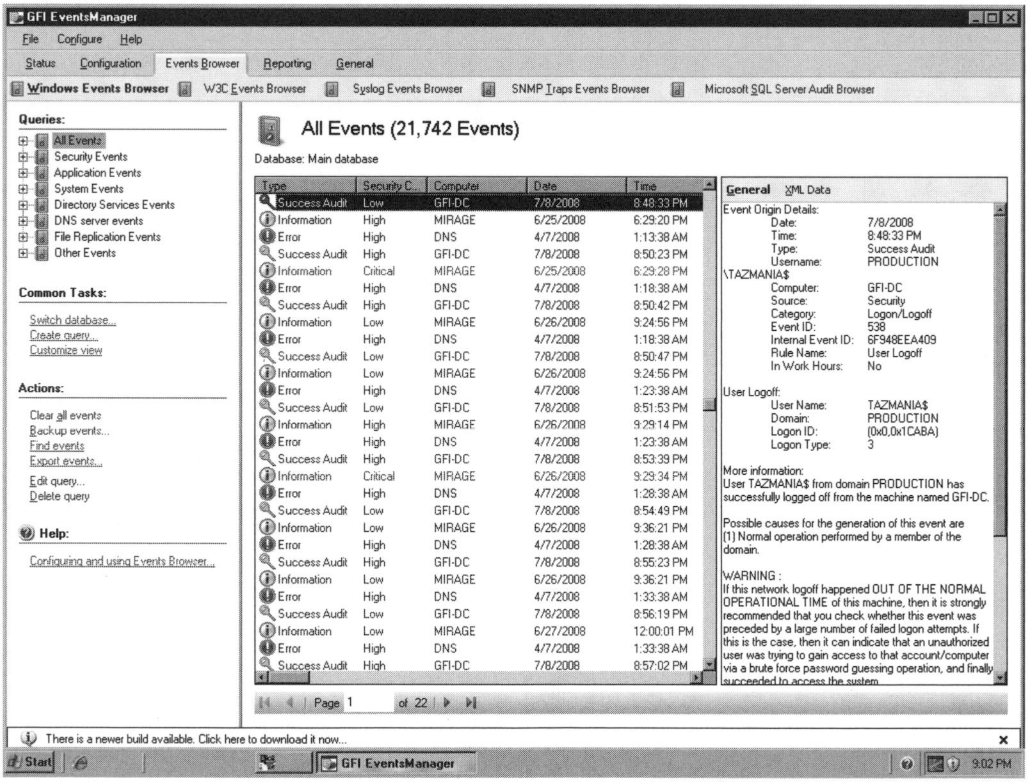

The first thing you will probably notice in Figure 14.1 is that the middle column contains a list of events similar to the ones normally displayed through the Windows Event Viewer. Note, too, that the column on the right contains the details of the event currently selected. A few things might not initially be as obvious though.

First, take a look at the Computer column in the list of events. As you can see, the list of events contains events from all of the computers you have chosen to monitor. Another thing I want to point out is that the list of events is color-coded. Yes, I realize this book is printed in black and white, but you should still be aware of this. The colors are assigned primarily according to the list's Security Category column. Events with a security category of low are listed in green, while those with a security category of high appear in dark red. Critical events are listed in bright red. Later, I'll show you how to view and even change the color-code assignments.

Now, take a look at the column on the left. The Queries section in this column provides you with a number of containers, each of which are linked to dynamic queries of the event logs. These dynamic queries let you filter the events by event type. Most of the containers in Figure 14.1 also contain subcontainers where you can look at even more specific types of log entries. One great benefit of the GFI filters is that they are remembered even after you close GFI Event Manager, whereas the Windows Event Viewer does not retain filter information. For example, suppose you wanted to view log entries related to users logging on to your network. Rather than scroll through thousands of event log entries, you could simply navigate through the console tree to **Security Events | Account Usage**. As you can see in Figure 14.2, selecting the **Account Usage** container causes the console to display events related to successful logons, failed logons, logoff events, and account lockouts.

Figure 14.2 The Console Is Designed to Let You Easily Locate Specific Types of Log Entries

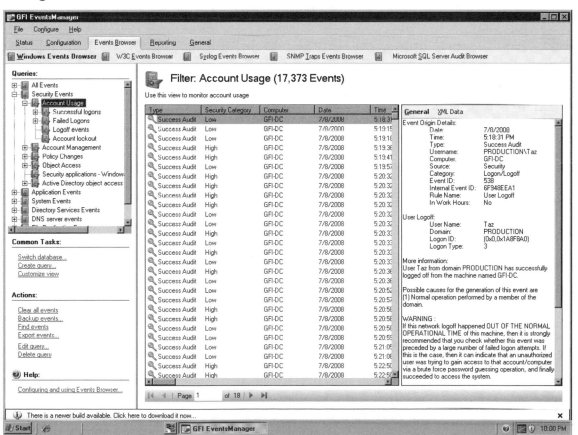

One of the really cool things about the way the console is designed is that sometimes the console is able to apply some intelligence and provide you with information that is not directly available through the Windows event logs. For example, most administrators usually don't pay a lot of attention to the audit log entries related to successful logins unless there is an immediate security concern. After all, the audit log entries for successful logins just show users logging in throughout the day, and don't really tell you anything interesting, right? Well, as you may recall, one of the pieces of information we provided GFI EventsManager with during the initial setup process was the company's normal business hours. GFI EventsManager is able to take this information and tell you who has logged in outside of normal business hours. You can access this information by navigating through the console tree to Security Events | Account Usage | Successful Logins | Successful Logins Outside Work Hours. You can see an example of this in Figure 14.3.

Figure 14.3 The Console Lets You See Who Has Logged in Outside Work Hours

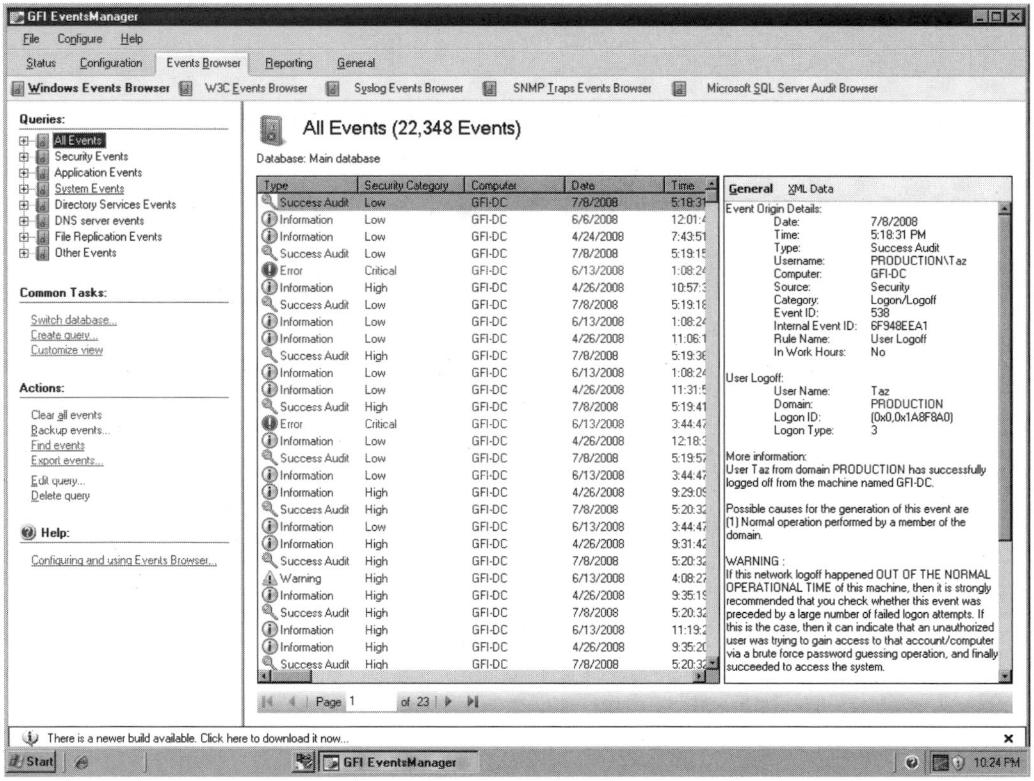

Other Types of Events

In the previous section, I showed you how all of the events that have been compiled can be filtered by event category and type. In a way, this is a bit misleading though. If you look at Figure 14.4, you can see that I have selected the All Events container. Although this container is labeled All Events, it doesn't actually show all of the events GFI EventsManager knows about.

Figure 14.4 The All Events Container Is a Bit Misleading Since It Doesn't Really Show You All the Events

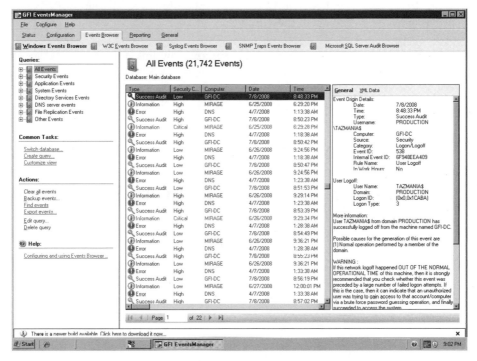

If you take a closer look at Figure 14.4, you'll notice that the Events Browser tab is selected, and that a series of subtabs are located just beneath it. Currently, the Windows Events Browser subtab is selected. Therefore, when I select the All Events container, what the console is really showing me is all the *Windows*-related events—meaning, other types of events exist that the console is also aware of. Table 14.1 describes the various event browsers and their purposes. Since Windows-native Event Viewer does not support logging for Unix/Linux machines, this gives GFI EventsManager a huge advantage in a network of mixed operating systems.

Table 14.1 GFI EventsManager Actually Includes Five Different Events Browsers

Event Browser	Purpose
Windows Events Browser	Monitors the Windows Event Logs
W3C Events Browser	Monitors events related to Internet Information Server (IIS)
Syslog Events Browser	Monitors Syslog events generated by UNIX and Linux servers
SNMP Trap Events Browser	Monitors SNMP (Simple Network Management Protocol) alerts generated by network devices like switches and routers
Microsoft SQL Server Audit Browser	Monitors alerts generated by Microsoft SQL Server

Customizing the Events Browser View

One of the things I like about the Events Browser is that the display is fully customizable. You have the option of changing the way items in the console are arranged, the colors used, and even the types of information displayed.

To customize the Events Browser, click the **Customize View** link, found in the **Common Tasks** area. A screen should appear similar to the one shown in Figure 14.5. As you can see in the figure, the Customize View screen initially gives you the option of how you want to display the event details. You can display them to the right of the list of events (this is the default configuration), display the event details at the bottom of the screen, or turn them off completely.

Figure 14.5 The Customize View Option Lets You Control How Event Details Are Displayed

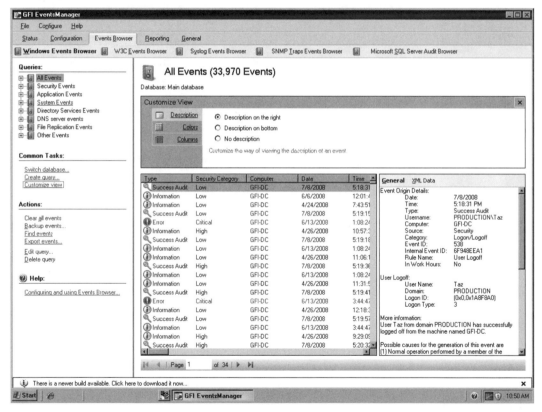

The Colors option, located just beneath the Description option, lets you color-code events. You actually have many more options for color-coding events than you might initially expect based on the colors used by default. Note in Figure 14.6 that you can base color codes on event type, security category, computer, date, time, source, Event ID, and a plethora of other characteristics. A Boolean editor lets you set specific conditions that must be met in order for the color code to be applied. For example, you can apply a color to an event if the event type equates to a successful audit.

Figure 14.6 You Have Many Different Options for Assigning Colors to Events

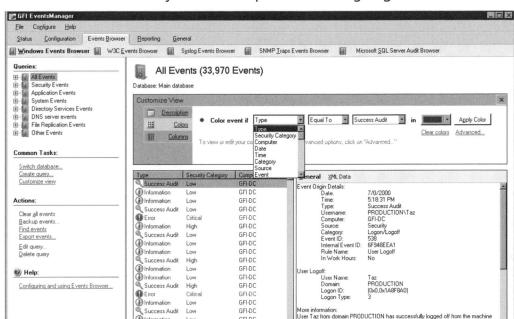

Tools & Traps...

Color-Code Craziness

When I first started playing with the options to assign color codes to events, I thought it was pretty cool that the console gave you a Boolean filter. I was almost immediately let down though when I realized that the filter is only a single-level filter. I'd hoped the Boolean filter would let me create complex multi-level Boolean conditions. For example: Set the color to blue if the event is a successful audit, if the event occurred outside working hours, and the event source was Security.

As I thought about this though, I began to realize that a multi-level Boolean filter would be overkill. GFI EventsManager is designed to process up to six million events per hour. Nobody is going to go through thousands, or even millions of events looking for a specific color. Colors are nice for flagging certain types of events, but if you really need to know about certain types of events, you are usually better off using the alerting feature or creating a custom query. I will talk about custom queries in the next section.

The other customization option available to you is the Columns option. As shown in Figure 14.7, you can configure the console to either display or hide various columns in the list of events by selecting or deselecting the corresponding check boxes. You also have the option of changing the order in which the columns are displayed by selecting a column and then clicking either the up or down arrow icons.

Figure 14.7 You Can Control Which Columns Are Displayed in the List of Events, and the Order in Which Those Columns Are Displayed

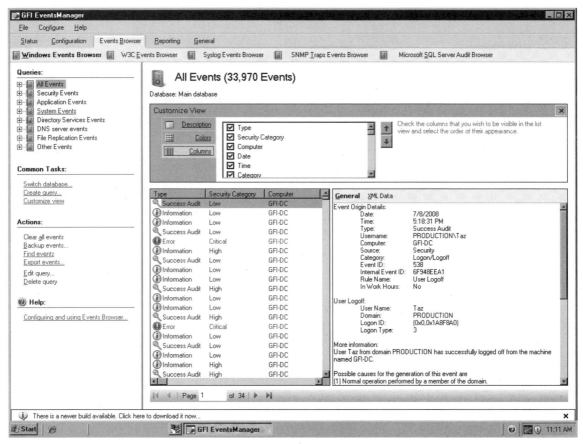

Earlier in this chapter, I said I would show you how you could tell which colors had already been assigned. To do so, perform the following steps:

1. Click the **Customize View** link in the **Common Tasks** section.

2. Click the **Colors** link.

3. Click the **Advanced** link in the **Customize View** window.

4. The Advanced Color Filters screen shows you all the colors currently being used and gives you the chance to add, modify, or remove colors (as shown in Figure 14.8).

Figure 14.8 The Advanced Color Filters Screen Shows You Which Colors Are Currently in Use

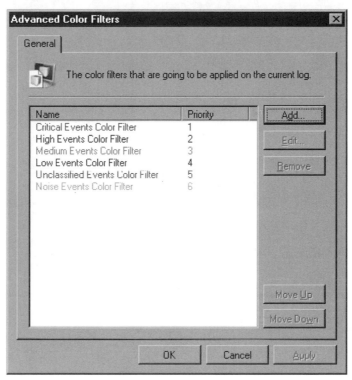

Creating Custom Queries

In the last section, I mentioned that you may have certain types of events that interest you more than others, but that color-coding wouldn't be the best way to find them, because if you use color-codes alone, you would still have to manually hunt through thousands, or even millions, of events. If you are interested in finding specific types of events more easily, then one way of doing so is to create a custom query.

I think that the easiest way to show you how custom queries work is to walk you through a simple exercise. For demonstration purposes, let's create a custom query that displays all the errors that have occurred on a server named Mirage. (If you're wondering about the weird server name, all I can say is that I *love* Las Vegas!) To create this type of custom query, perform the following steps:

1. Click the **Create Query** link in the **Common Tasks** section.
2. Windows opens the **Query Builder** dialog box. Click the **Add** button.
3. Windows opens the **Edit Query Restriction** dialog box. Choose the **Type** option.
4. Set the **Select Field Operator** to **Equal To**.
5. Set the **Enter Field Value** field to **Error**, as shown in Figure 14.9.

Figure 14.9 These Options Tell the Query Builder to Look for Errors

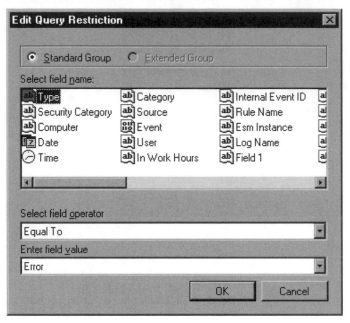

6.   Click **OK**.

7.   Click the **Add** button

8.   Set the **Select Field Name** option to **Computer**.

9.   Set the **Select Field Operator** value to **Equal To**.

10.   Type the word **Mirage** in the **Enter Field Value** text box.

11.   Click **OK**.

12.   Enter a name for your query in the Query Builder's **Name** field.

13.   Enter a description of the query in the **Description** field, as shown in Figure 14.10.

Figure 14.10 The Query Builder Screen Should Look Like This

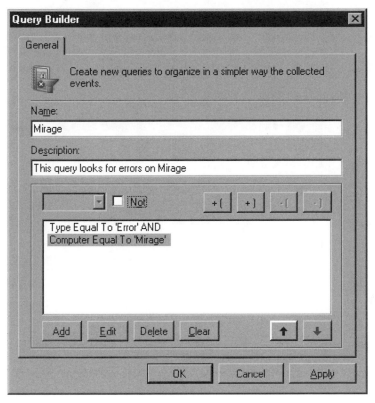

14.   Click **OK**.

You should now see the custom query you have created displayed beneath the All Events container. When you select the custom query, the console will display the event log entries that match your query's parameters, as shown in Figure 14.11.

Figure 14.11 The New Custom Query Is Created Beneath the All Events Container

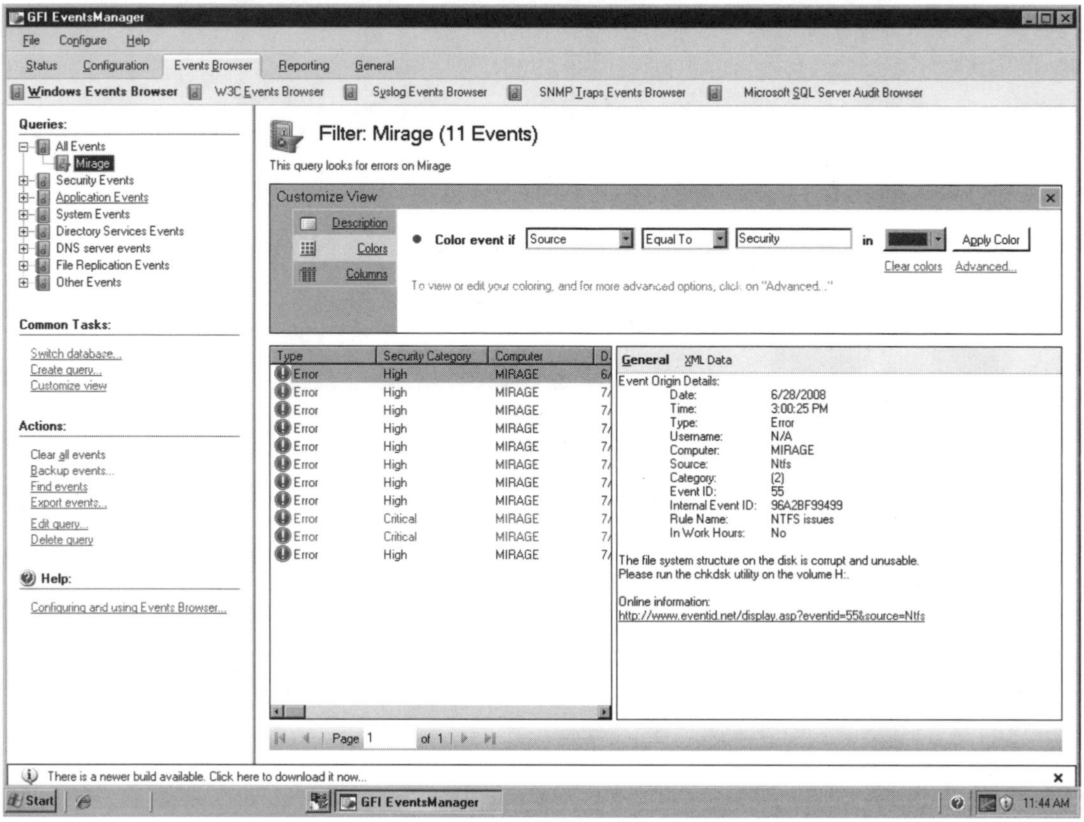

NOTE

In case you are wondering why the new query was placed beneath the All Events container, it's because that's the container that was selected when I created the custom query.

NOTE

If you want to delete a custom query, just right-click it and choose the **Delete** command from the resulting shortcut menu.

Exporting Events

About 15 years ago, I was working as a network administrator for a large corporation. Like any large company, it had its share of problems, but perhaps the biggest problem the IT department had was a network administrator who was on a mission to sabotage the organization. For example, whenever my staff would spend all day on Saturday working on a project, this person would come in on Sunday and completely undo everything we had accomplished. The reason why I'm telling you about something that happened so long ago is because the only way I was able to prove this person's malicious activities was through the events recorded in the Windows event logs.

Back then, Windows NT 3.5 was the network operating system of choice, but the Windows event logs really haven't evolved much since then (at least not until Windows Server 2008 was released anyway). At the time, tools like GFI EventsManager simply didn't exist. In order to build a case against the rogue administrator, I had to sort through hundreds of log entries each day looking for evidence of malicious activity. When I found something, I wrote down the date, time, and other details of the event. When it finally came time to present my case to HR, I had to sit them down at a computer, and manually scroll through thousands of log entries looking for the entries I had recorded. Having date and time stamps kept this from being an impossible task, but it was still tedious and time-consuming. The whole process would have been a lot easier if I had been able to set up a custom query to monitor that user's activity, and then export the events connected with the query to a spreadsheet. Fortunately, GFI EventsManager lets you do just that.

As I said, the Windows Event Viewer was a bit crude back when I was trying to bust that rogue administrator. So, to make the process easier, I adjusted my log settings to help maximize the chances of finding the log files I needed, while reducing "noise" entries. Although this technique worked, it was not an ideal solution. Making changes to the logging options like that meant that if someone else had breached security, the event might have gone unnoticed because my logging efforts were primarily centered around one person.

If the same thing happened today, I could easily create a custom query to log the target user's activity without sacrificing the other logging information. I could then create a nice neat spreadsheet of the activity, which I could e-mail to HR. To see how this works, let's create a custom query that logs all the activity centered around the Administrator. After this is done, we'll create a spreadsheet of all of the Administrator's activity. To do so, perform the following steps:

1. Select the **All Events** container.

2. Click the **Create Query** link.

3. Enter **Admin** as the name of the new query.

4. Click the **Add** button.

5. When the **Edit Query Restriction** dialog box appears, choose the **User** option from the **Select Field Name** section.

6. Set the **Select Field Operator** option to **Equal To**.

7. Enter **your domain\Administrator** into the **Enter Field Value** field.

8. Click **OK**.

9. Select the **Admin** container to view the results of the custom query.

10. Click the **Export Events** link in the **Actions** section.

11. When prompted, enter a path and filename for the CSV file you are creating.

12. Click **OK**.

The query results should now be written to a CSV file. You can double-click this CSV file to open it in Microsoft Excel, as shown in Figure 14.12. Excel lets you perform further analysis of your data by making it easy to organize, sort, or tally the contents of the various columns.

Figure 14.12 Use Microsoft Excel to Open the CSV File You Created

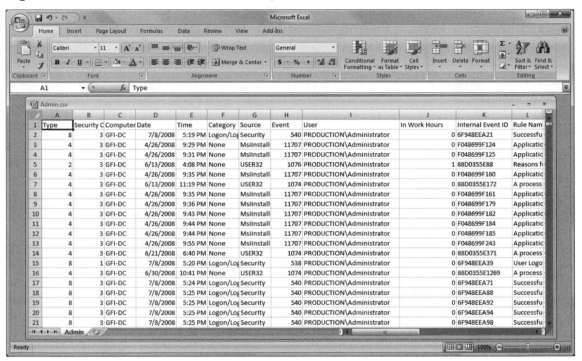

Summary

In this chapter, I described the basic techniques involved in using the GFI EventsManager console. In the next chapter, I will introduce the concept of Event Processing Rules, which lets GFI EventsManager react to certain types of events.

Solutions Fast Track

Browsing the Logs

☑ The management console displays log entries in a single list from all the computers being monitored.

☑ Each of the containers on the left side of the console is linked to a dynamic query.

☑ The All Events container does not actually display all the events collected, but rather only those events concerning the currently selected events browser.

Customizing the Events Browser View

☑ To customize the Events Browser, click the Customize View link, found in the Common Tasks area.

☑ The customization process lets you control where, or if, event details should be displayed.

☑ You can color-code certain types of events.

Creating Custom Queries

☑ You can create custom queries that appear as containers alongside the default queries.

☑ You can remove a custom query by right-clicking it and choosing the Delete command from the shortcut menu.

Exporting Events

☑ If you need to build a case against someone, it is easier to export the pertinent events to a spreadsheet than to sift through log entries.

☑ Exported events are written to a CSV file, which can be opened in Excel.

Frequently Asked Questions

Q: Does the EventsManager console let me view events on a computer-by-computer basis?

A: Yes, but you will have to create a custom query for each computer.

Q: Can I reuse or reassign any of the default color-codes?

A: Absolutely!

Q: Why do my custom queries appear beneath another container?

A: Custom queries are created beneath the container that was selected when you created the query.

Q: Can you export events to an .XLS or .XLSX file?

A: No, but CSV files can be opened in Excel and then saved as an Excel spreadsheet in one of those formats.

Chapter 15

Event Processing Rules

Solutions in this chapter:

- **Default Classification Actions**
- **Event Processing Rules**
- **The Anatomy of a Rule**
- **Making Your Own Rules**

Introduction

So far, I have shown you several different methods for sorting through all of the events that GFI EventsManager collects. In some cases, though, it would be nice to be able to use certain events as triggers to launch various processes. For example, you may want to generate an alert when critical events occur. The good news is that GFI EventsManager contains a comprehensive set of event processing rules you can use as a mechanism for taking action when certain conditions exist. In this chapter, I will show you how.

Default Classification Actions

In the previous chapter, I showed you that GFI EventsManager is configured by default to assign certain color codes to various types of events. Although assigning color codes can be helpful, color-coding events isn't the only action GFI EventsManager takes by default. An entire set of default classification actions exist that perform certain actions in response to event log entries.

To access the default classification actions, select the management console's **Configuration** tab and choose the **Options** icon located just beneath the list of tab names. A screen will appear like that shown in Figure 15.1.

Figure 15.1 The Default Classification Options Are Found on the Configuration Tree

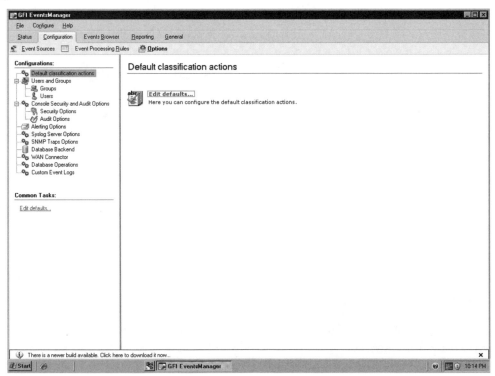

Make sure the **Default Classification Actions** container is selected, and then click the **Edit Defaults** link, shown in Figure 15.1. Windows will display the Default Classification Actions dialog box, shown in Figure 15.2.

Figure 15.2 The Default Classification Actions Dialog Box Lets You Control How GFI EventsManager Responds to Various Types of Events

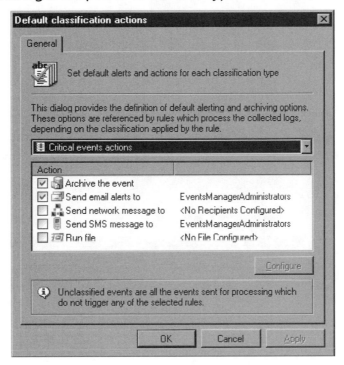

As you can see in Figure 15.2, this dialog box contains a drop-down list you can use to select the event classification level that you want to check the defaults for. The classification levels are Critical, High, Medium, Low, Unclassified, and Noise Events. Simply select a classification level, and then use the check boxes found in the lower portion of the dialog box to set the default response to events that fall into that particular classification. For example, GFI EventsManager is configured by default to archive the event and to send an e-mail alert when critical events occur. You also have the option of sending network messages, sending SMS messages, or running a file.

TIP

It is tempting to write a script that takes corrective action when critical events occur, but I would advise against doing so. Remember that you are setting default options that apply globally to all the events collected from multiple computers. It is unlikely it would be appropriate to run a single corrective script with no regard to the machine the event occurred on.

Event Processing Rules

Although the default classification actions I showed you in the previous section work well, it is important to remember that they are only default settings, and that sometimes responses to events need to be more specific to the actual events that have occurred. This is where event processing rules come into play. Event processing rules are a set of rules that allow GFI EventsManager to react to certain events as they occur.

You can access the events processing rules by clicking the management console's **Configuration** tab, and then selecting the **Event Processing Rules** option, located just beneath the tab. A screen will then appear similar to that shown in Figure 15.3.

Figure 15.3 The Event Processing Rules Screen Lets You Tell GFI EventsManager How to Respond to Various Events

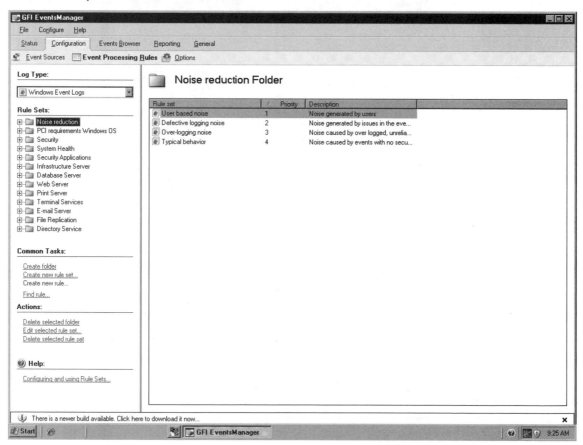

Are You Owned?

Some Alerts Are Worth Paying Attention To

With multiple machines being monitored and every critical event generating an alert, it is easy to lose interest in the alerts and ignore them. After all, the servers on my network generate critical events every day, and it doesn't necessarily mean there is a problem. It is important to remember though that some alerts are more important than others.

When a hacker gains control of a Windows network, they often do a couple of things right off the bat. One is to temporarily disable auditing as a way of covering their tracks. Another thing is that they will often either create a new account that has administrative privileges, or elevate the privileges of the account they are using. If you see alerts that point to either of these types of activities, you need to take them seriously.

Notice at the top of the console's left column that the event processing rules are segregated by log type. The event processing rules you see in the figure apply to the Windows Event Logs, but you *can* choose a different log type.

Just beneath the Log Type drop-down list is the Rule Sets section. The console takes a hierarchical approach to rule sets. As you can see in Figure 15.4, the top level of the hierarchy is a folder. The folder contains one or more rule sets, and each of the rule sets contains one or more rules. For example, in Figure 15.4, I have expanded the Noise Reduction folder. This folder contains several rule sets, all geared toward limiting the impact of noise events in the logs. The GFI Web site defines Noise reduction events as ones that are repeated events (http://support.gfi.com/manuals/en/esm7/esm7manual-1-067.html).

Figure 15.4 The Management Console Takes a Hierarchical Approach to Event Processing Rules

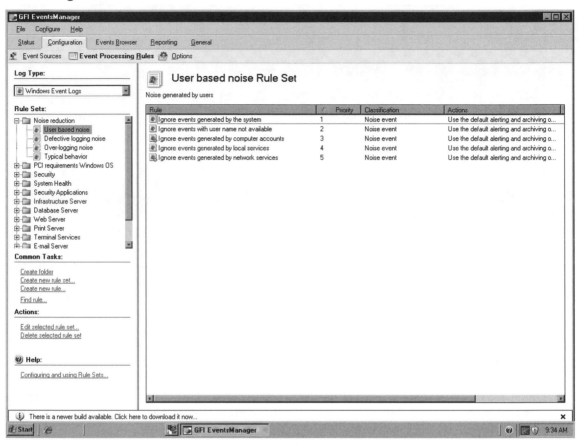

In Figure 15.4, I have selected the User Based Noise rule set, and the column on the right shows all the rules within that rule set. Notice that each of the rules in the rule set is prioritized. This allows GFI EventsManager to resolve situations in which a rule set contains contradictory rules.

The Anatomy of a Rule

GFI EventsManager contains hundreds of built-in rules that serve various purposes. In some cases, the existing rule sets may be all you need. For example, if you look at Figure 15.4, you will notice there is already a rule set for PCI Compliance, so there is no need for you to manually create a set of rules in order to achieve PCI compliance. Even so, you may find that the existing rules are overkill for your organization, or that you need to add some additional rules in order to achieve your organization's goals. In either case, it is critical you understand the anatomy of a rule before you make any modifications to the existing rule sets.

For the sake of demonstration, I am going to dissect rule number 1 in the PCI Primary Requirements rule set. I begin the process by right-clicking the rule. In Figure 15.5, notice that the resulting shortcut menu contains options to delete the rule, to temporarily disable the rule, and to increase or decrease the rule's priority. For now though, let's select **Properties**, which will take us to the rule's properties sheet, shown in Figure 15.6.

Figure 15.5 You Can Access the Rule's Properties Sheet by Selecting the Properties Command From the Rule's Shortcut Menu

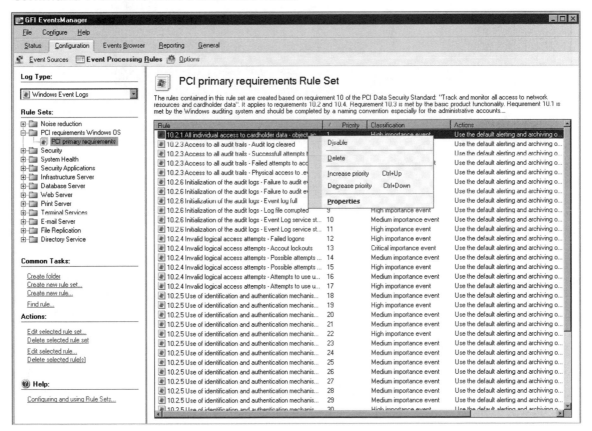

Figure 15.6 The General Tab Contains the Rule's Name and an Optional Description

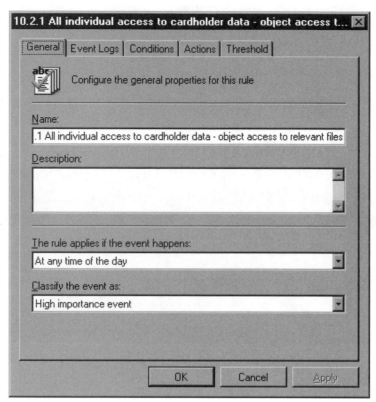

The General Tab

The General tab, shown in Figure 15.6, is where you can find the basic definition for the rule. Normally, this tab will contain a name and a description for the rule. Looking at the figure, you can see that GFI has entered a description as part of the rule name rather than using a separate description.

If you look at the lower portion of the tab, notice that we can set up a condition and an action. The condition refers to the time of day the event occurs. You can set the rule to always apply, or to only apply if the event occurs within or outside of business hours.

The last option on the General tab lets you assign a classification to the event. Remember that every event is classified by default, but this section gives you the option of reclassifying the events that the rule applies to. Keep in mind that the default classification options we looked at earlier will be applied to the events based on the classification you choose here.

The Event Logs Tab

The Event Logs tab, shown in Figure 15.7, lets you tell GFI EventsManager where to look for the events to which the rule will apply. For example, this particular rule is going to apply to Event ID 560. The current settings on the Events tab tell GFI EventsManager that the rule should apply if Event ID 560 occurs within the Windows security log, but to ignore the event ID if it should occur in any of the other Windows event logs.

Figure 15.7 The Event Logs Tab Lets You Choose Which Event Logs to Check for the Specified Event

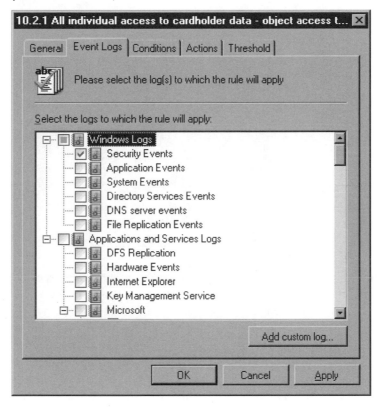

The Conditions Tab

The Conditions tab is the heart and soul of a rule. It lets you specify which conditions must be met for the rule to go into effect. For example, in Figure 15.8, notice that this particular rule goes into effect if Event IDs 560 or 4656 are detected. Remember, though, that we have placed some additional conditions on the rule. The rule only goes into effect if these events occur within the Windows security log. Likewise, the General tab gave us the option of placing time-of-day restrictions on the condition.

Figure 15.8 The Conditions Tab Is the Heart and Soul of the Event Rule

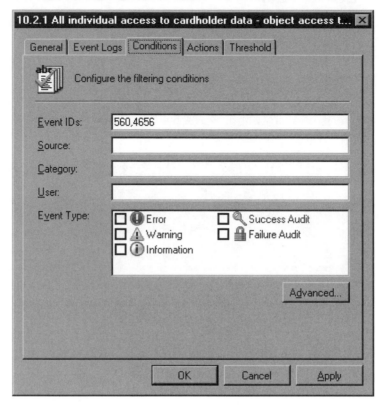

The nice thing about the way the Conditions tab works is that we can specify multiple conditions. The tab already specifies multiple event IDs by separating those IDs by a comma, but we could have entered an event source, an event category, a user, or an event type.

All of the fields on the Conditions tab are optional, so long as you set at least one condition. For example, instead of providing a specific Event ID, you can create a rule that applies to a specific user.

One last thing I want to point out about the Conditions tab is the Advanced button at the bottom of the screen. Normally, you will probably never have to use this, but I think it is important for you to at least realize it exists. The basic idea behind the Advanced button is that sometimes you need to provide some additional criteria for the conditions you are setting. For example, event ID 560 is nothing more than an audit response. Under normal circumstances, this event is triggered when:

- The audit policy states that the type of access requested should be audited.

- The audit result (success or failure) has been enabled for auditing.

- The user who is running a given application is flagged for auditing, or the user belongs to a group that is being audited.

I say all this to make the point that Event ID 560 is just a generic auditing event. As you will recall, though, the rule we are examining is a PCI compliance rule. In order to achieve PCI compliance, only certain events must be audited. If you click the Advanced button, you can see that some advanced filtering restrictions have been added to the condition, as shown in Figure 15.9. That way, the rule will only go into effect if the event references a file containing the %CARDHOLDER% environment variable.

Figure 15.9 You Can Add Advanced Filtering Conditions to a Rule

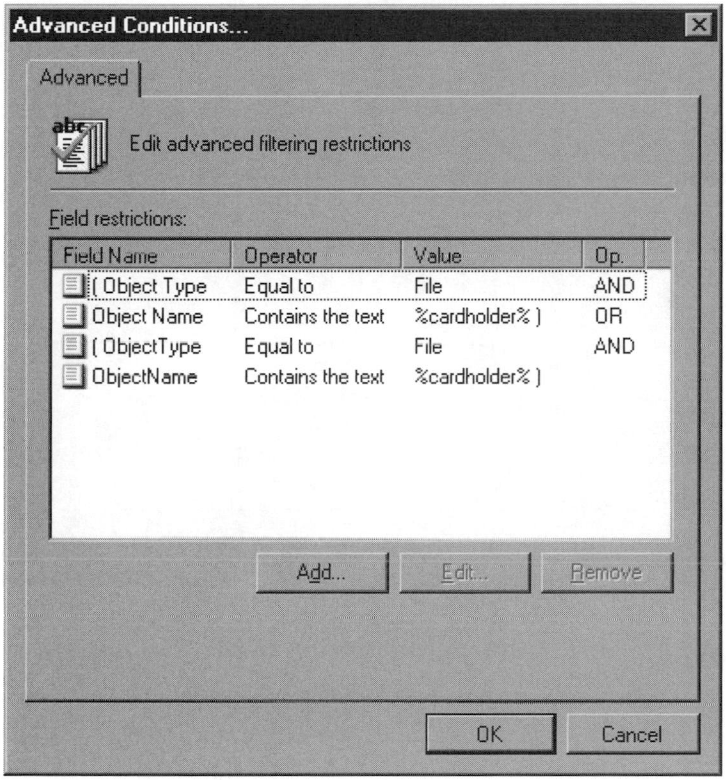

The Actions Tab

The Actions tab, shown in Figure 15.10, lets you control what happens when the rule applies to an event. Almost all of the built-in rules are set to simply apply the default classification action. You can, however, choose to ignore the event or run a different action profile.

Figure 15.10 Most of the Built-in Rules Are Configured to Perform the Default Classification Action

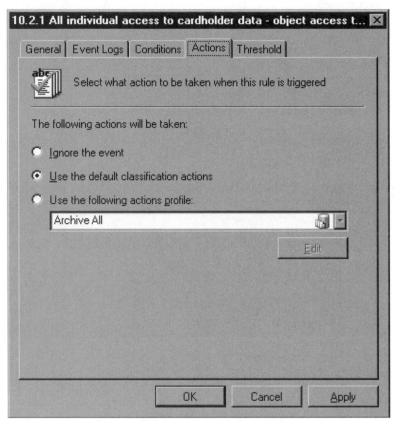

Action Profiles

Only one action profile is built into GFI EventsManager: the Archive All profile. You can, however, create a new action profile. To do so, select the **Use The Following Action Profile** option, and then choose the **New Action Profile** option from the drop-down list. The console will display the New Actions Profile dialog box, shown in Figure 15.11. All you have to do to create a new action profile is to assign a name to the profile, select the actions you want to perform, and click **OK**.

Figure 15.11 GFI EventsManager Lets You Create Your Own Action Profiles

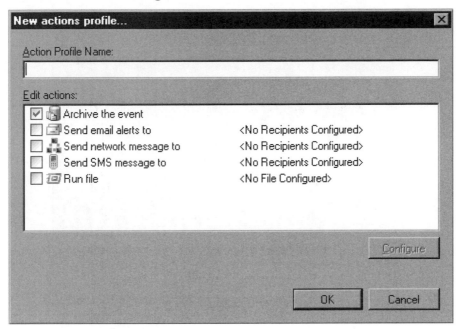

The Threshold Tab

The last tab found on the rule's properties sheet is the Threshold tab, shown in Figure 15.12.
The Threshold tab's purpose is to prevent an excessive number of actions from being taken on
repeated events. Sometimes situations occur that cause the same events to be written to the Windows
event logs over and over again in rapid succession. When this happens, you probably don't want your
Inbox flooded with hundreds of e-mail alerts about the same event.

Figure 15.12 The Threshold Tab Lets You Prevent an Excessive Number of Actions From Being Performed

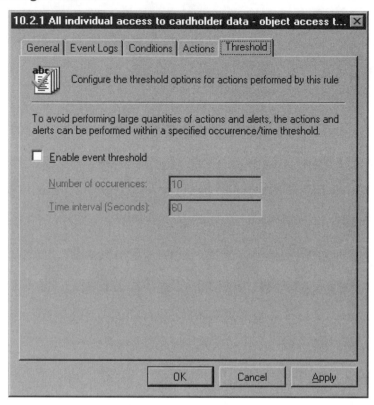

If excessive alerting becomes a problem, you can enable the event threshold. You can then set a number of occurrences for the event, or set a time interval that must pass before you are alerted again.

Making Your Own Rules

Now that you understand how the rules work, you can easily delete or modify any of the existing rules to meet your needs. I don't want to cover the process of making your own rules in great detail, because most of it is a repeat of what I just covered in the previous section. I do want to provide you with some steps to get you started though. To create your own rule, follow these steps:

1. Click the **Create Folder** link.
2. Enter a name for the folder you are creating.
3. With the new folder selected, click the **Create New Rule Set** link.
4. Enter a name and an optional description for the rule set.

5. Click **OK**.

6. With the new rule set selected, click the **Create New Rule** link. This will cause Windows to launch the New Processing Rule Wizard.

Although the rules are created through the wizard, the wizard asks for the same information I just showed you on the rule's properties sheet. If you make a mistake, you can always right-click the rule you just created and then either delete the rule or choose the Properties command to access the rule's properties sheet, which will allow you to modify the rule.

TIP

The preceding steps walk you through the process of creating a new rule in a new rule set within a new folder. You don't have to take this approach though. You can create a new rule set in an existing folder, or even create a new rule within an existing rule set.

Summary

In this chapter, I have explained that while it is nice to be able to sort through the events that have been collected, GFI EventsManager's real power is its ability to act on those events. I then showed you how to create and edit event processing rules that let you do just that. In the next chapter, I will conclude the section on GFI EventsManager by talking about its reporting capabilities.

Solutions Fast Track

Default Classification Actions

- ☑ All events are classified by default.
- ☑ The default classification levels cause messages to be color-coded.
- ☑ Alerting may also occur depending on the severity of the event.

Event Processing Rules

- ☑ Event processing rules let you tell GFI EventsManager how to respond to certain events.
- ☑ Event processing rules are grouped into rule sets, which are grouped together in folders.
- ☑ GFI Events Manager contains hundreds of built-in events processing rules, but you can disable, delete, modify, or augment these rules.

The Anatomy of a Rule

- ☑ Events processing rules are made up of conditions and actions.
- ☑ You can modify a rule through the rule's properties sheet.
- ☑ Keep in mind that not all of the available conditions are found on the properties sheet's Conditions tab. The Time of Day option exists on the General tab, and the Event Logs tab allows you to choose which logs to monitor for the conditions you specify elsewhere.

Making Your Own Rules

- ☑ Although hundreds of rules are built into GFI EventsManager, you can create your own rules.
- ☑ You can create your own folders and rule sets, or you can place new rules within existing rule sets.

Frequently Asked Questions

Q: How many events can GFI EventsManager process?

A: It really depends on your hardware's capabilities, but the GFI Web site claims that the software can process over six million events per hour.

Q: Is there any way to disable the default alerting?

A: By default, the alerting occurs because messages fall into a particular classification. If you want to disable alerting, you should modify the default classifications.

Q: Will creating an excessive number of rules bog down the server?

A: It seems theoretically possible, although my lab server never bogged down except when I was generating an excessive number of log entries.

Q: What are noise reduction rules?

A: Windows creates some event log entries that are practically meaningless. Noise reduction rules are typically designed to prevent these types of events from being archived in the database. This speeds up database access and helps conserve disk space.

Chapter 16

Getting the Big Picture

Solutions in this chapter:

- **Status Reports**
- **Reporting**

☑ **Summary**

☑ **Solutions Fast Track**

☑ **Frequently Asked Questions**

Introduction

So far in this section of the book, I have shown you several different techniques for browsing the event logs and for configuring GFI EventsManager to respond to various events. Ultimately, though, the techniques we've covered up to now are ineffective if you want to use the event log entries to gauge the overall health of the computers on your network. In this chapter, I want to conclude my discussion of GFI EventsViewer by exploring some other ways to get information about what's happening on your network.

Status Reports

The first thing I want to show you is how to check the overall status of the event log entries. To do this, simply open the management console, select the **Status** tab, and click the **General** icon, located just beneath the tab. A screen similar to the one shown in Figure 16.1 will appear.

Figure 16.1 The EventsManager Summary Screen

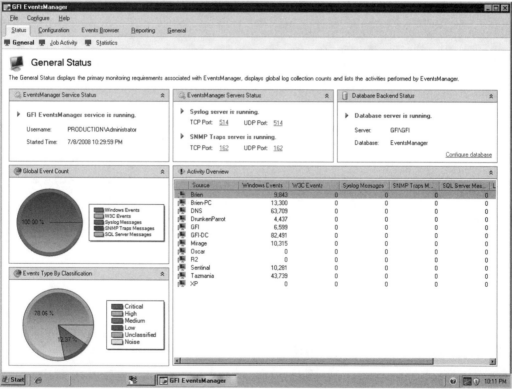

The screen in Figure 16.1 provides you with a brief overview of your network's current state. As you can see, the top left pane simply confirms that the GFI EventsManager service is running, and tells you how long it has been running. The panes in the top middle and top right of the console display the status of the Syslog server and the database server, respectively.

The pane in the middle of the left portion of the console window shows you the distribution of events across your network. In this particular case, all the events are Windows events, but that's only because I'm not actually tracking W3C, SQL Server, or any other types of events.

The pane in the screen's lower-left portion shows the events that have occurred based on their classifications. This gives you an easy way of seeing which percentage of events occurring on your network is critical or of high importance.

The large pane in the lower-right portion of the console shows the systems being monitored, and the number of events that have been logged on each. You may notice that some of the servers have zero events logged in the figure. The reason for this is that I intentionally powered down a few machines because I wanted to see how GFI EventsManager would react to servers that were unavailable.

Job Activity

If you click the **Job Activity** link at the top of the screen, you'll see a screen similar to the one shown in Figure 16.2. The basic idea behind this screen is that events are not collected in real time. Instead, GFI EventsManager queues jobs to collect the most recent events from the target machines. The Job Activity screen lets you see which jobs are in the queue, and which jobs are currently active.

Figure 16.2 The Job Activity Screen Lets You Monitor the Log Collection Process

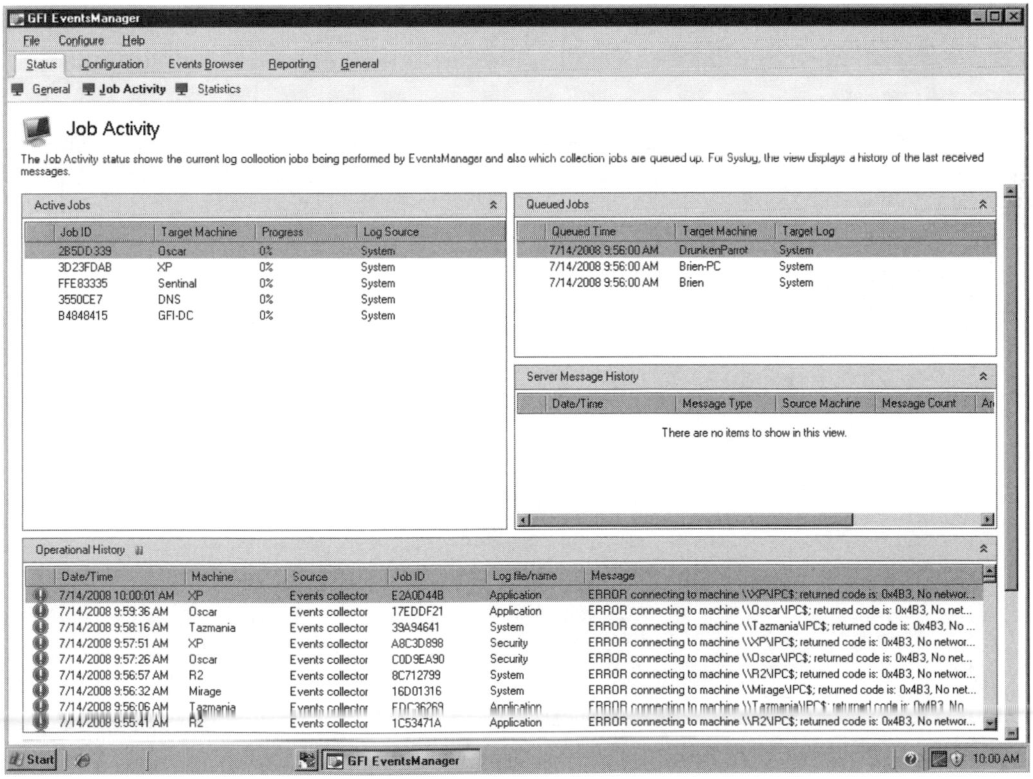

At the bottom of the screen in Figure 16.2, you can see several error messages stating that GFI EventsManager was unable to connect to certain machines. This typically happens when the target machine is powered down, or when the Windows firewall is blocking the log file collection process.

WARNING

By default, GFI EventsManager uses several different TCP and UDP ports for log file monitoring. These ports must be open in the Windows firewall, otherwise the collection process will fail. The following is a list of the ports used:

- Network message alerts – TCP port 135
- Syslog messages – TCP and UDP port 514
- SNMP trap messages – TCP and UDP port 162
- SQL Server Databases – TCP port 1433
- Internal RPC communications – TCP ports 7787 and 7788

Statistics

Another way to get some good information about the overall status of the event logs on your network is by looking at the Statistics screen, shown in Figure 16.3. You can access the Statistics screen by selecting the management console's **Status** tab, and then clicking the **Statistics** link, located just beneath the tabs.

Figure 16.3 The Statistics Screen Displays Information About the Event Collection Process

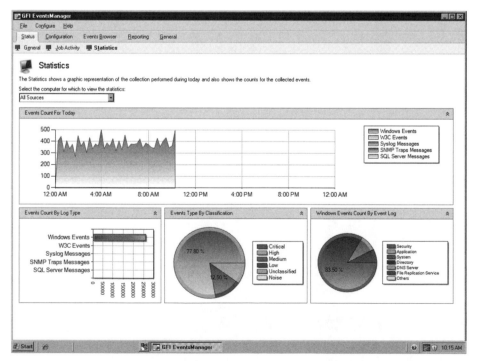

As you can see in Figure 16.3, the top portion of the console screen offers a graphical representation of the number of events collected today. Once again, I am only collecting Windows events, so that's all you'll see in this screen capture; however, the graph will normally show other types of events as well.

The nice thing about this graph is that it shows what your peak periods of activity typically are. Once you get a feel for what is normal on your network, you can easily spot periods of excessive logging, which may indicate a problem.

The lower portion of the console contains three separate panes. The left-most pane shows you the event count based on log type. In the middle is a graph similar to the one seen earlier and displays what percentage of the total number of events collected fall into each classification. The last chart shows you which event logs are generating the most events. For example, in this figure you can see that more than 80 percent of the events I've collected are coming from the Windows Security logs.

Reporting

The last thing I want to show you is how GFI EventsManager can use the ReportCenter to generate reports based on the contents of the logs it has collected. Since I've already talked about the ReportCenter in depth in Chapter 5, I'm not going to show you every single feature, but I wanted to at least give you an idea of what is available to you. If you want to learn more about the ReportCenter, I recommend reading Chapter 5.

Accessing the ReportCenter

You might have noticed in some of the previous figures that the management console contains a Reporting tab. Contrary to what you might expect, you can' not access the ReportCenter through this tab. The tab only contains an advertisement for the ReportPack (of which the ReportCenter is the primary component). To access the ReportCenter, click the Windows **Start** button and then navigate to **All Programs | GFI ReportCenter | EventsManager 8 ReportPack**. Once done, Windows will launch the ReportCenter console, shown in Figure 16.4.

Figure 16.4 The ReportCenter Console Screen

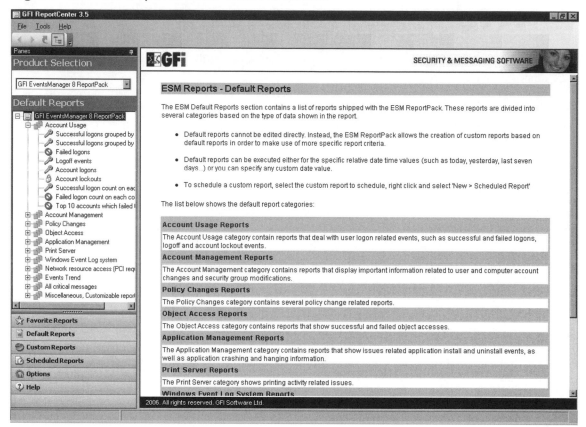

The ReportCenter console is actually very easy to use. The column on the left contains several different tabs, and the Default Reports tab is selected by default. Beneath the Default Reports tab are dozens of built-in reports, all of which have been grouped by category. In Figure 16.4, I've expanded the Account Usage category so you can see the individual reports within it.

The ReportCenter provides you with lots of great reporting options, but a section of reports has been specifically designed to help you achieve PCI compliance. To see how the ReportCenter works, let's generate one of these reports by performing the following steps:

1. Navigate through the console tree to **GFI EventsManager 8 ReportPack | Network Resource Access (PCI Requirement 10) | 10.2.2 All Actions Taken By An Individual With Root Or Administrative Privileges**.

2. When you select the **10.2.2 All Actions Taken By An Individual With Root Or Administrative Privileges** container, a sample report will appear in the column on the right, as shown in Figure 16.5. This sample report shows you what the report will look like and what types of information are included in the report.

Figure 16.5 The Sample Report Shows Which Types of Information Will Be Included in the Real Report

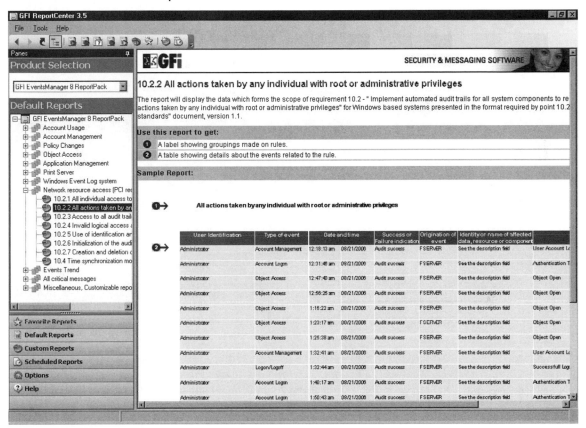

3. Right-click the **10.2.2 All Actions Taken By an Individual With Root or Administrative Privileges** container and then choose the **Run | For Last Month** commands from the resulting shortcut menus, as shown in Figure 16.6.

Figure 16.6 You Can Run a Report for Various Time Periods

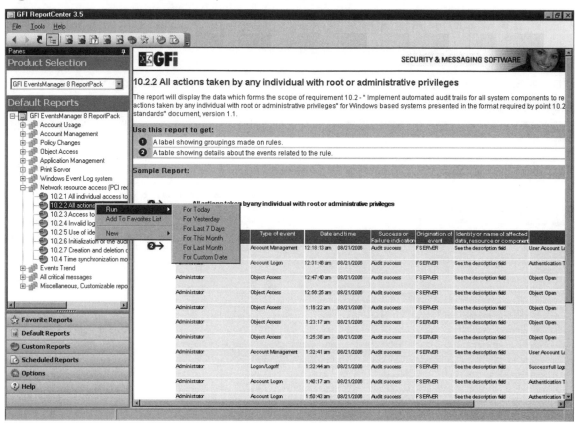

When the report completes, it will be displayed within the console, as shown in Figure 16.7. You can use the icons located above the report window to print, search, export, or delete the report. From this point forward, whenever you select the container that corresponds to the report, the most recently run instance of the report will appear rather than the sample report.

Figure 16.7 The Report as Displayed Within the ReportCenter Console

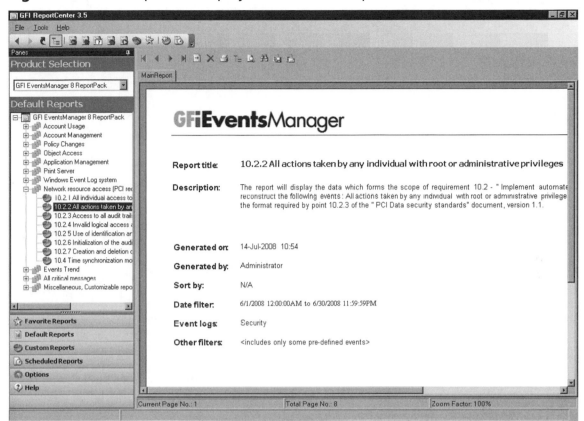

Summary

In this chapter, I've explained that although it's handy to be able to search through the event logs for specific events, it's usually more important to be able to see the big picture rather than a bunch of individual events. We then discussed how to view some statistics regarding the collected events, and how to produce reports based on them.

Solutions Fast Track

Status Reports

- ☑ The General Status screen is a great place to get a feel for which computers are generating the most events.

- ☑ The Job Activity screen shows the logs currently being collected.

- ☑ The Statistics screen offers an overview of today's log file activity.

Reporting

- ☑ You can launch the ReportCenter by clicking the **Start** button and then navigating to **All Programs | GFI ReportCenter | EventsManager 8 ReportPack**.

- ☑ The ReportCenter contains reports specifically geared to PCI compliance.

- ☑ You can run a report by right-clicking it, choosing the **Run** command, and then selecting a time period from the resulting shortcut menus.

Frequently Asked Questions

Q: Is there any way to narrow down the information presented on the Statistics screen?

A: Sure. The screen contains a drop-down list you can use to select an individual computer. When you do this, the console will display information related to that specific machine.

Q: The Operation History section of the Job Activity screen is becoming really large. What can I do about it?

A: Right-click the entries in the section and select the **Clear All Messages** command from the shortcut menu.

Q: Can I change the ports used for log collection?

A: Yes. If you go to the General Status screen, you can click a port number. You will then be given the opportunity to select a different port. Normally, you should use the default port numbers though.

Q: Is there any way to generate a custom report?

A: Yes. The ReportCenter features a Custom Reports tab that lets you create your own reports (but with several limitations). Much more info about this feature can be found in Chapter 5.

Chapter 17

Installing and Configuring GFI Network Server Monitor

Solutions in this chapter:

- **Hardware and Software Requirements**

- **Installing GFI Network Server Monitor**

- **Performing the Initial Configuration**

- **Creating Separate Folders**

☑ **Summary**

☑ **Solutions Fast Track**

☑ **Frequently Asked Questions**

Introduction

The last GFI product I will be covering in this book is GFI Network Server Monitor 7.0. GFI Network Server Monitor is designed to automatically scan the servers on your network for failures or for anomalies that could lead to a failure, and then alert you to the issue before the phones start ringing.

Hardware and Software Requirements

Believe it or not, neither the GFI Web site nor the instruction manual provides any hardware requirements for GFI Network Server Monitor. Therefore, I can't really tell you what it is you are going to need. What I can tell you is that in my lab I am running GFI Network Server Monitor within a virtual server. The physical server has an Intel Core 2 Quad processor and 4 GB of RAM. I have allocated 1 GB of RAM to the virtual machine, and it seems to run fine in spite of the fact that I am also running the host operating system, and at times, two other virtual machines.

Software Requirements for the GFI Network Monitor Server

Although GFI Network Server Monitor's hardware requirements are not stated, its software requirements are. The software requirements are as follows:

- Windows 2000 (with SP4 or later), Windows XP Professional, or Windows Server 2003
- Windows Scripting Host 5.5 or later (This is included in Internet Explorer 5.5 and later.)
- Version 1.1 of the Microsoft .NET Framework

Any servers you plan on monitoring will require an agent to be installed. The software requirements for servers being monitored are:

- WMI
- Windows Scripting Host 5.5 or higher (Included with Internet Explorer 5.5 and higher)

Notice that I did not list any operating systems among the software requirements for machines being monitored. That's because GFI Network Server Monitor can monitor a wide variety of Windows and Linux operating systems. The operating systems that are officially supported are:

- Windows 2000 Professional
- Windows 2000 Server
- Windows XP

- Windows Server 2003
- Windows Vista
- Windows Server 2008
- Suse Linux
- Red Hat Linux
- Mandrake Linux
- Fedora Linux

Installing GFI Network Server Monitor

Now that you have verified that your server meets the various software requirements, it is time to install GFI Network Server Monitor. To do so, follow these steps:

1. Log in to the server with local administrative privileges.

2. Begin the process by downloading GFI Network Server Monitor from the GFI Web site at www.gfi.com/downloads/downloads.aspx?pid=nsm&lid=EN. You can also download the installation manual and the product's user manual from the same location. The file you will be downloading is a 13.4 MB self-extracting executable named NetworkServerMonitor7.exe. Save this file to a temporary directory, and then double-click it to start the installation process.

3. If Windows presents you with a security warning, click the **Run** button to move forward with the installation process.

4. Windows will now launch the product's **Setup Wizard**. Click **Next** to bypass the wizard's Setup screen.

5. At this point, you will be prompted to accept the End User License Agreement (or EULA, as it has come to be known). After doing so, click the **Next** button.

6. On the next screen that appears, enter your name, the name of your company, and your license key. If you are installing GFI Network Server Monitor in trial mode, then enter the word **EVALUATION** (all caps) into the License Key field, as shown in Figure 17.1. Using an evaluation key will give you full use of the product for ten days. After that time expires, you can purchase a license and add a license key to your existing installation without having to reinstall the software.

Figure 17.1 You Can Enter the Word EVALUATION in Place of a License Key

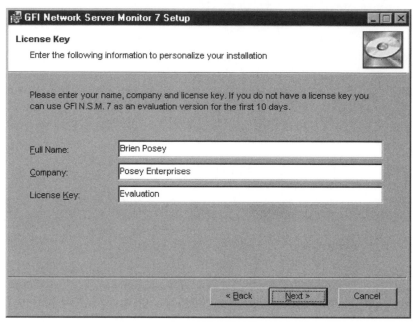

7.   Click **Next**.

8.   A screen appears informing you that in order for the software to be able to monitor target computers, it will need you to provide it with an account it can use to log on to those targets. Go ahead and enter the username and password for an account with administrative credentials, and then click **Next**.

Are You Owned?

Service Account Credentials

By default, the Setup Wizard asks you to enter the domain administrator's password. This isn't usually practical though, because of the frequency with which this account's password is typically changed. Unless you plan on reconfiguring the software every 30 days or so, you are going to need to use an account with a password that doesn't expire. Needless to say, you should assign this account a very strong password.

Because their passwords do not usually change, service accounts are often one of the biggest targets for hackers. As such, I recommend auditing the use of the service account. If you ever see it used for anything other than GFI Network Server Monitor, then you know the account has been compromised.

9. You should now see a screen asking you to enter your SMTP mail server settings. If you have an Exchange Server or another type of SMTP server, you should enter the settings for that server. If not, you can actually configure the GFI Network Server Monitor server to act as an SMTP Server. Once you enter these settings, you should click the **Verify Mail Settings** button. This will cause the Setup Wizard to send an e-mail message using the settings you have provided. It is very important you verify that the test message actually arrives in the recipient's mailbox. If you have trouble getting the Setup Wizard to successfully transmit a test message, or if you need some help with your Exchange Server's settings, or if you want to configure your GFI Network Server Monitor server to act as an SMTP server, then check out the Configure Alerting Options section in Chapter 1.

10. Once you have entered and verified your mail server settings, click **Next**.

11. A screen similar to that in Figure 17.2 will appear. As you can see in the figure, you are given the choice of using either a Microsoft Access, SQL Server, or MSDE (Microsoft Database Engine) database. In case you aren't familiar with MSDE, it is Microsoft's free version of SQL Server. In the time since GFI Network Server Monitor was released, Microsoft has changed MSDE's name to SQL Server 2005 Express Edition. Make your selection, and then click **Next**. For the purposes of this example, I will be using a SQL Server 2005 database.

Figure 17.2 You Can Choose to Use a SQL Server, MSDE, or Microsoft Access Database

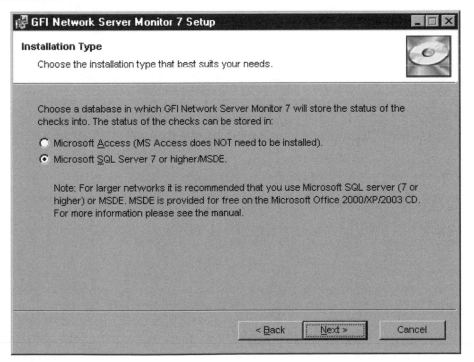

Tools & Traps...

Choose Your Database Carefully

Once you choose your database type, the choice you have made is semi-permanent. It isn't easy to switch database types, so it is important to make the right choice. Generally speaking, MSDE and Microsoft Access are suitable for small to medium-sized organizations. SQL Server offers far better performance and scalability than MSDE or Microsoft Access. If you have a SQL Server in place, and it has the capacity to host an additional database, then I would recommend using it.

12. A screen like that in Figure 17.3 will appear, prompting you to enter the name of the SQL Server database you want to use. Enter the server name and the database instance name in the server\instance format, as shown in the figure.

Figure 17.3 Enter the Database Server and Database Instance Names in the Server\Instance Format

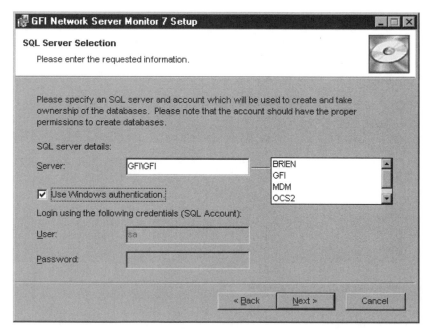

13. Click **Next**.

14. A screen will appear prompting you to enter the installation path. Click **Next** to accept the defaults.

15. You should now see a screen telling you that the installation process is about to begin. Click **Next** to continue.

16. Once the file copy process finishes, click the **Finish** button.

Performing the Initial Configuration

Unlike the other GFI applications I have talked about in this book, GFI Network Server Monitor is made up of several separate applications. This means you are not given a single monolithic console that can be used to control every single aspect of the application. As such, one of the biggest tricks involved in using GFI Network Server Monitor is figuring out which application to use for the task at hand.

The initial configuration process is done through the GFI Network Server Monitor 7 Configuration console. You can access this console by clicking the Windows **Start** button and then clicking the **All Programs | GFI Network Server Monitor 7 | GFI N. S. M. 7 Configuration** menu entries from the Start menu. Having done so, a screen like that in Figure 17.4 will appear.

Figure 17.4 The Main Configuration Screen

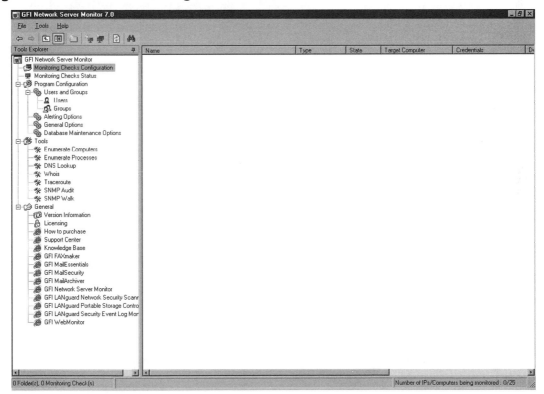

The initial configuration process requires you to configure one target computer at a time. Therefore, you should pick a computer you want to monitor before you begin the initial configuration process. If you want to add additional computers, you can do so by repeating the steps I am about to show you for each computer you want to monitor. Another option is to add similarly configured computers in a single step. To perform the initial configuration, perform the following steps:

1. Right-click the console's **Monitoring Checks Configuration** container, and then choose the **New | Quick Start Wizard** commands from the resulting shortcut menu. When you do, Windows will launch the Quick Start Wizard.

2. Click **Next** to bypass the wizard's Welcome screen.

3. You will now see the screen shown in Figure 17.5. You must specify the operating system that the target computer is running. As you can see in the figure though, several different flavors of Windows and Linux are supported.

Figure 17.5 You Must Specify the Operating System That the Target Computer Is Running

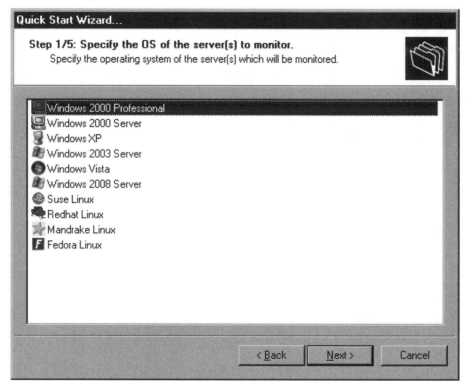

4. After making your selection, click **Next**.

5. At this point, the Quick Start wizard will show you a screen similar to that in Figure 17.6. The basic idea behind this screen is that once you have selected an operating system, the Quick Start Wizard shows you a list of roles the selected operating system could potentially be running. Choose the roles (or services) running on the target computer, and then click **Next**.

Figure 17.6 Select the Roles the Target Server Is Running

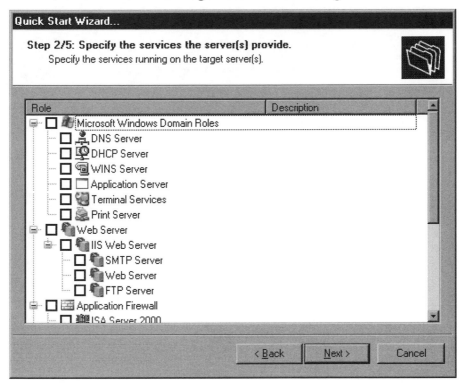

6. Click **Next** and the wizard will display the screen shown in Figure 17.7. This screen gives you the chance to select the third-party applications that could potentially be running on the target machine. Before you get too excited about the idea of monitoring third-party applications, you should know that the list consists primarily of GFI products, but does include a couple of third-party antivirus applications.

Figure 17.7 Select Any Third-Party Applications Running on the Target Server

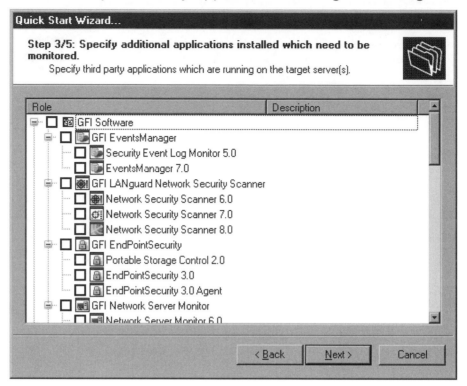

7. Make your selection, and then click **Next**.

8. The wizard will now display a screen that gives you the chance to specify the name of the computer you want to monitor, as shown in Figure 17.8. Just type the computer's name you want to monitor, and then click the **Add** button. If you have other computers running the same operating system, hosting the same roles, and running the same (if any) monitored applications, you can also add them at this time.

Figure 17.8 Type the Name of the Computer You Want to Monitor and
Click Add

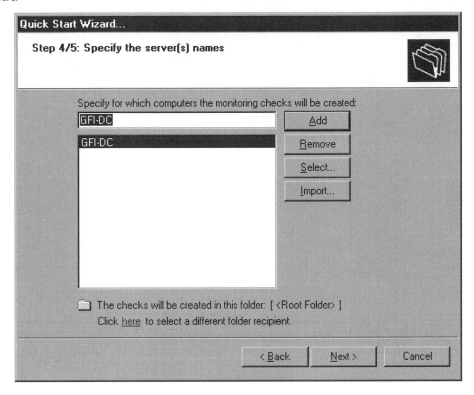

9.   At the bottom of the screen is an option to change the folder the checks will be created in.
      For now, just go with the default option of creating the checks in the root folder, and then
      click **Next**.

10.   Click **Finish** to complete the wizard.

11.   The server you have added will now appear in a folder beneath the Monitoring Checks
      Configuration folder, as shown in Figure 17.9.

Figure 17.9 A Separate Subfolder Is Created for Every Computer You Add

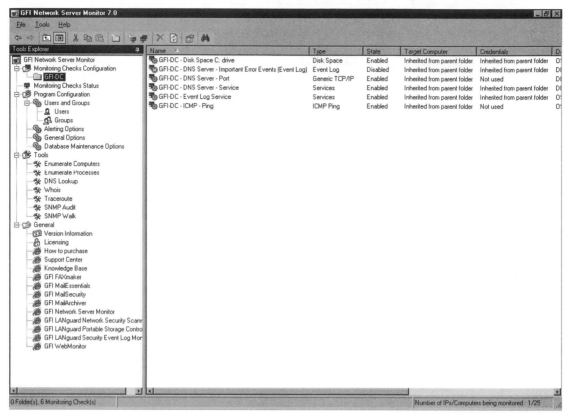

Creating Separate Folders

In the previous section, I briefly mentioned an option to save the monitored computer to a folder other than a root folder. Folders have two primary purposes in GFI Network Server Monitor. The most obvious use for a folder is to help you stay organized. For example, you could put all of your domain controllers into one folder, your Exchange servers into another folder, and so on.

More importantly though, folders allow you to group together computers with similar monitoring needs. For example, earlier in the setup process you provided GFI Network Server Monitor with a set of authentication credentials it could use to authenticate with the computers being monitored. Depending on how your organization is set up, these credentials may not be valid for every computer on your network. If you have some computers that require a different set of authentication credentials, you could place those computers into a separate folder, and then make the folder aware of the required credentials.

Folders can be used to control many different aspects related to the monitoring process. In this section, I want to walk you through the process of creating a new folder. As I do, I will point out some of the configuration options available to you.

To create a new folder, right-click the **Monitoring Checks Configuration** container, and then select the **New | Folder** options from the resulting shortcut menus. When you do, Windows will display the New Folder properties sheet shown in Figure 17.10.

Figure 17.10 The New Folder Properties Sheet Lets You Create and Configure a New Folder

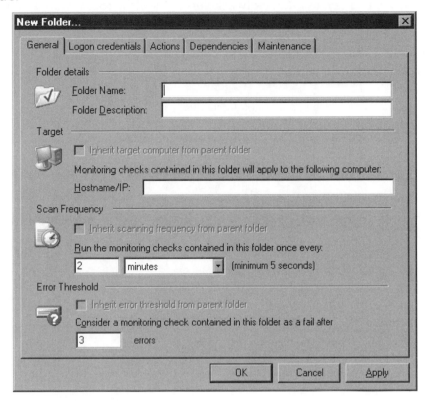

The General Tab

As you can see in the figure, the properties sheet's General tab is selected by default. The only thing you absolutely have to do on this tab is assign the folder a name. I do, however, strongly recommend providing a description for the folder as well.

Just beneath the Folder Details section is the Target section. This section lets you enter the IP addresses or host names of computers that should reside in the folder. Personally, I prefer to add computers to the folder using the technique I showed you in the previous section.

The lower portion of the General tab lets you control how frequently computers within the folder are scanned for errors. By default, computers are checked every two minutes, and a failure is considered to have occurred after three errors are detected.

WARNING

Be careful about adjusting the scan frequency. Setting the scans to occur more frequently can impact the performance of both your GFI Network Server Monitor server and the target server. Configuring scans to occur less frequently means that errors are not detected as quickly. It is important to find the balance that works well for you. Keep in mind though that the scanning frequency is adjusted on a folder-by-folder basis. This means you have the option of scanning less important servers less frequently, which may help GFI Network Server Monitor focus its attention on more important network servers.

The Logon Credentials Tab

Just to the right of the General tab is the Logon Credentials tab, shown in Figure 17.11. As I mentioned earlier, this tab is helpful if you have a subset of servers that require a different set of authentication credentials. This is especially true of Linux servers, for which a certificate-based authentication is required.

Figure 17.11 The Logon Credentials Tab Lets You Provide an Alternate Set of Credentials for Computers in the Folder

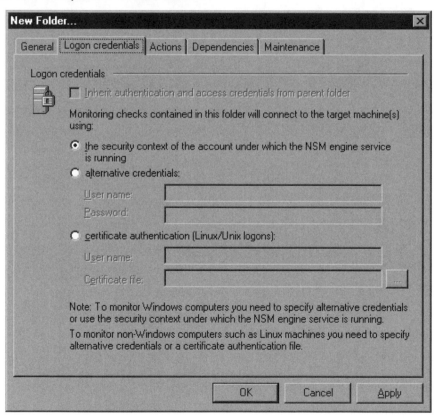

The Actions Tab

The Actions tab, shown in Figure 17.12, lets you decide what needs to happen when GFI Network Server Monitor detects an error on one of the machines in the folder. As you can see in the figure, the Actions tab is divided into three different sections; Alerts, Run External File, and Reboot Computer/Restart Services.

Figure 17.12 The Actions Tab Controls How GFI Network Server Monitor Responds to Various Network Conditions

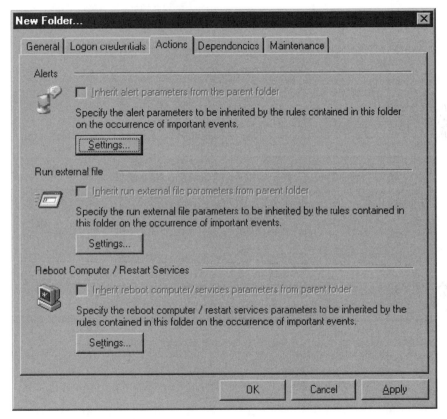

Alerts

The Alerts section lets you control if and how network administrators will be alerted when certain types of conditions are detected. If you click the **Settings** button, you will be taken to the dialog box shown in Figure 17.13.

Figure 17.13 The Settings – Alerts Dialog Box Lets You Configure Various Alerting Options

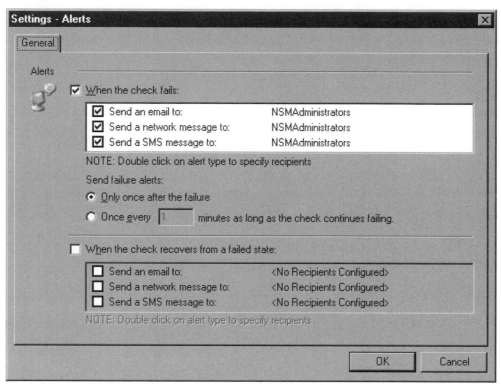

As you can see in the figure, you have the option of generating an alert when a check fails, and/or when a check recovers from a failed state. By default though, check recoveries do not produce alerts. This dialog box also gives you the option of controlling which types of alerts are sent, and whether the alert is generated once per failure, or if the alert is sent constantly until the failure is addressed.

WARNING

Back in the early '90s, I used a similar network monitoring product that would send alerts on a continuous basis until the condition that had triggered the alert was resolved. At that time, the alerts were sent in the form of network messages. This was really a problem though, because the alerts would actually get in my way while I was trying to fix the problem. If you do decide to use constant alerts, you should avoid using network messages, or be very selective about where those messages are sent.

Although it may sometimes be overkill, I would recommend generating an alert when a check recovers from a failed state. Imagine for example that it's 1 A.M. and you receive an SMS alert that a failure has occurred on a critical server. If the failure were the result of a temporary condition, it would be nice to be told that the server has recovered from the failure before you make the drive to the office.

TIP

Notice in Figure 17.13 that alerts are configured to be sent to the NSMAdministrators group. This is not a Windows group, but rather a group that is a part of GFI Network Server Monitor. You can check the group's membership by navigating through the console tree to **Program Configuration | Users and Groups | Groups**.

The Run External File Section

The Run External File section gives you the option of running either a script or an executable file when a check fails. You can tell GFI Network Server Monitor which files you want to run by clicking the **Settings** button, and then populating the dialog box shown in Figure 17.14.

Figure 17.14 You Have the Option of Running a Program or a Script Whenever a Check Fails or When a Check Recovers From a Failed State

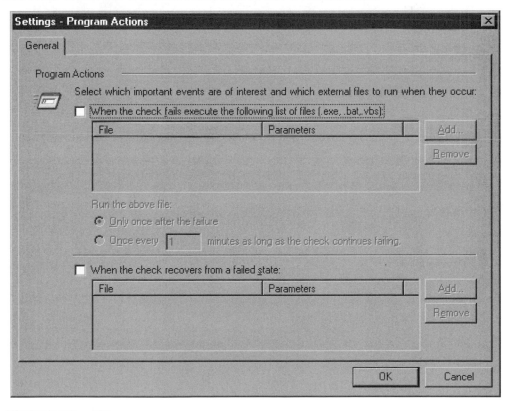

I would tend to recommend that you avoid using this option, because it is a blanket policy. If you tell GFI Network Server Monitor to run a program when a check fails, then the program will be run regardless of which computer the failure occurred on, or which type of check failed. This is fine if you want to write some kind of alerting script, but it is impractical to try to run a remediation script unless you are only checking for a single condition.

Reboot Computer/Restart Services

The last section on the Actions tab is the Reboot Computer/Restart Services section. Once again, you can configure the options associated with this section by clicking the Settings button. Doing so causes GFI Network Server Monitor to display the dialog box shown in Figure 17.15.

Figure 17.15 You Have the Option of Rebooting a Failed Machine or of Restarting the Machine's Services

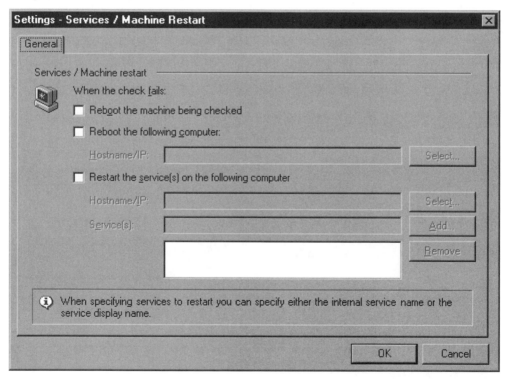

Notice in Figure 17.15 that you have the option of either rebooting the computer being checked, or rebooting a specific computer. You also have the option of restarting a specified set of services on a specific computer, but you don't have the option of restarting the services on the computer being checked.

TIP

If you decide you want services to be restarted, you can enter either the service's internal name or the service's display name.

The Dependencies Tab

The Dependencies tab, shown in Figure 17.16, gives you the option of ensuring that one or more checks succeed prior to running the checks associated with the folder. It is worth pointing out that the dependencies are listed on a per-server basis. For example, if you look at Figure 17.17, you can see that when I click the Add button, the dependencies offered to me are associated with a specific server.

Figure 17.16 The Dependencies Tab Gives You the Option of Ensuring That Specific Checks Succeed Prior to Processing the Checks Associated With the Folder

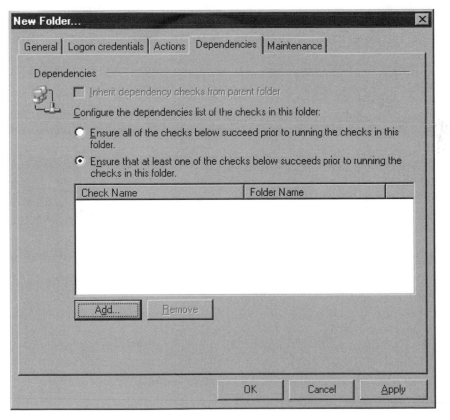

Figure 17.17 All of the Dependencies Are Associated With Specific Servers

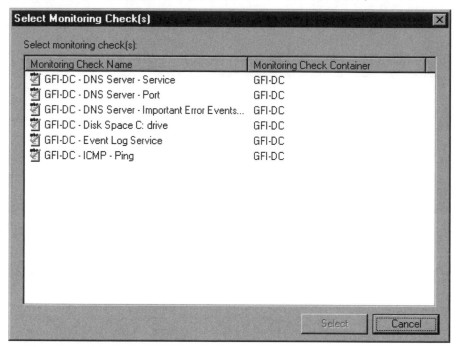

The Maintenance Tab

The last tab on the New Folder properties sheet is the Maintenance tab. As you may recall, the folder had a default maintenance schedule which called for it to perform checks against the servers in the folder every two minutes. However, it may not make sense to check every server, every two minutes, 25 hours a day, seven days a week. For example, maybe you take the servers down on the weekend to do some maintenance of your own. In a situation like that, it wouldn't make sense to monitor the servers on the weekend.

The Maintenance tab, shown in Figure 17.18, is pretty self-explanatory. It lets you deselect any time slots during which you do not want monitoring to occur.

Figure 17.18 The Maintenance Tab Lets You Disable Monitoring for Specific Time Periods

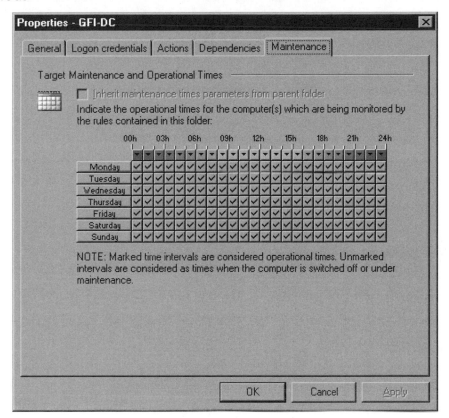

Placing Computers into Folders

Earlier I showed you how the Quick Start Wizard could be used to designate a computer to be placed in a certain folder. You don't have to select a folder in this way though. The next time you are ready to add a computer, you can actually right-click the folder you want to use, and choose the **New | Quick Start Wizard** entries from the succeeding shortcut menus. This will tell the Quick Start Wizard you want to use the selected folder.

Folder Behavior

One last thing that I want to show you is how GFI Network Server Monitor treats the computers within a folder. If you look at Figure 17.19, you can see that I have placed two computers in a folder named Test. If I right-click one of these computers and choose the **Properties** command from the shortcut menu, the console will display the computer's properties sheet. Almost every option on this properties sheet contains a setting that allows the parameters to be inherited from the parent folder. You can see an example of this in Figure 17.20. The screen capture shows the properties sheet's Actions tab, but almost all of the tabs contain options to inherit parameters from the parent folder.

Figure 17.19 How It Looks When Computers Are Placed in a Folder

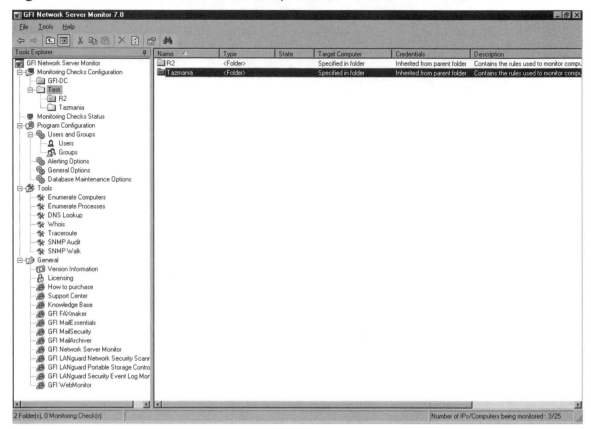

Figure 17.20 Computers Within a Folder Automatically Inherit the Folder's Settings

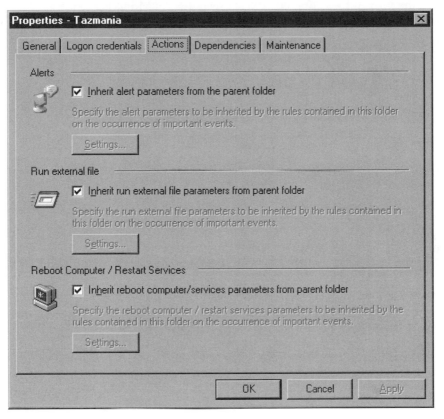

Summary

As you can see, the process for setting up GFI Network Server Monitor is quite a bit less involved than what is required for setting up some of the other GFI products. Now that the initial configuration process is out of the way, I will begin showing you how to use the product in the next chapter.

Solutions Fast Track

Hardware and Software Requirements

- ☑ No hardware requirements are stated.
- ☑ The supported operating systems include Windows 2000 (SP4 or later), Windows XP Professional, or Windows Server 2003.
- ☑ Windows Scripting Host 5.5 or later is required. This is included with Internet Explorer 5.5 and later.
- ☑ Version 1.1 of the .NET Framework is also required.
- ☑ A wide variety of Windows and Linux operating systems are supported on computers that are being monitored.

Installing GFI Network Server Monitor

- ☑ You can use either a SQL Server database, Microsoft Access, or an MSDE database, but a SQL Server database is preferred in larger organizations.
- ☑ You can configure GFI Network Server Monitor to use either a Microsoft Exchange Server or a stand-alone SMTP server for e-mail alerts. If you have an Exchange Server in your organization, I recommend using it.

Performing the Initial Configuration

- ☑ Target computers with similar configurations should be grouped into folders.
- ☑ Computers within a folder inherit the settings from the parent folder.

Creating Separate Folders

- ☑ Folders let you group together servers with similar monitoring needs.
- ☑ Unless you specify otherwise, servers within a folder inherit folder level settings.

Frequently Asked Questions

Q: Can I use an MSDE database with GFI Network Server Monitor?

A: Sure, but I would only recommend doing so in smaller organizations since MSDE does not scale well.

Q: I don't have an Exchange Server, but I may want to use one later on. Is this possible?

A: Yes, the management console lets you reconfigure your alerting options.

Q: How do I know if I need SQL Server or not?

A: Smaller organizations don't have to have SQL Server. If you are planning on monitoring more than 50 servers, I would definitely recommend using a SQL Server database. Keep in mind this is just my recommendation, not GFI's—and it certainly isn't a requirement.

Q: The installation process seems to be taking forever. Is this normal?

A: On my lab machines, the installation process was fairly quick. Keep in mind though that your server hardware has a lot to do with the speed of the installation.

Q: Can I piggyback GFI Network Server Monitor onto a server running other GFI applications?

A: It is possible, but I would recommend using a dedicated server, if possible, for security and performance reasons.

Q: Can I install a SQL Server database onto the same server that will be running GFI Network Server Monitor?

A: Assuming your server has the resources to run both, yes.

Chapter 18

Working with GFI Network Server Monitor's Configuration Console

Solutions in this chapter:

- **Customizing Monitoring Checks**
- **Monitoring Checks Status**
- **Built-in Tools**

- ☑ **Summary**
- ☑ **Solutions Fast Track**
- ☑ **Frequently Asked Questions**

Introduction

In the previous chapter, I explained how to install GFI Network Server Monitor and how to add individual servers to the list of computers being monitored. In this chapter, I want to show you additional aspects of using the Configuration console. I will talk about how you can add some additional monitoring checks to the servers you are monitoring, and how you can check the status of the monitored servers. I will also show you how to use some of the console's built-in tools.

Customizing Monitoring Checks

In Chapter 17, you learned that monitoring checks are performed at the folder level. If you select a folder, you can see the monitoring checks that exist for that particular folder. For example, in Figure 18.1, I have selected a folder named R2, and the column to the right lists three separate monitoring checks bound to the selected folder.

Figure 18.1 Monitoring Checks Are Bound to Individual Folders

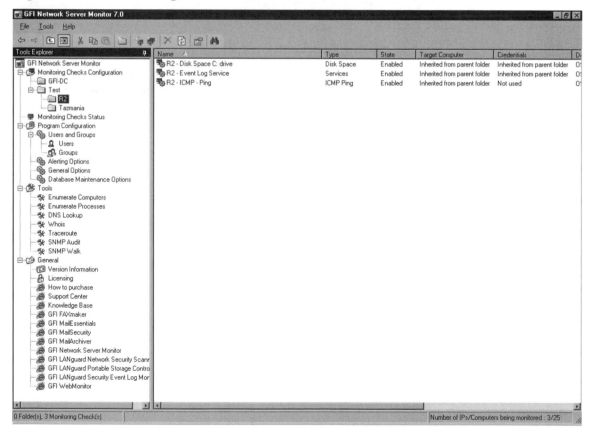

Normally, you probably won't have to make any changes to the individual monitoring checks. GFI Network Server Monitor does a pretty good job of assigning the monitoring checks that make

the most sense for servers associated with a given folder. Sometimes, though, you may have a server whose role changes, or you may want to modify or customize a folder's monitoring checks for other reasons. Fortunately, this isn't hard to do.

Adding a Monitoring Check

You can easily add additional monitoring checks to a selected folder. To do so, perform the following steps:

1. Right-click the folder and choose the **New | Monitoring Check** options from the resulting shortcut menus. The console will display the **New Check** dialog box, shown in Figure 18.2.

Figure 18.2 The New Check Dialog Box Lets You Pick the Individual Monitoring Check You Want to Add to the Folder

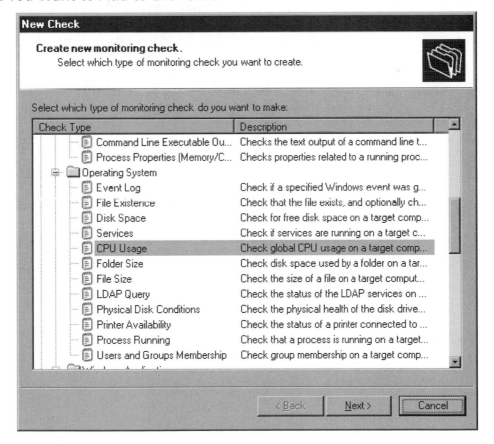

2. Click **Next**.

3. A screen appears asking you to set some parameters for the monitoring check you are adding. The actual contents of this screen vary widely, depending on the type of monitoring

check you have selected. For example, if you choose the CPU Usage check, you will see a screen similar to that in Figure 18.3. This screen asks you what the maximum allowed CPU usage should be.

Figure 18.3 A Screen Appears Asking for Additional Information About the Monitoring Check You Have Chosen

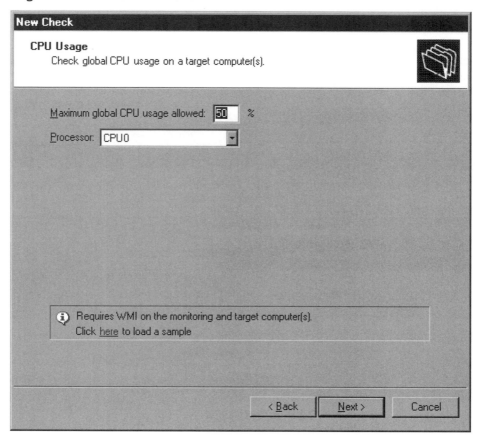

4.   Click **Next**.

5.   A screen appears giving you the choice to either inherit the authentication credentials from the parent folder, or supply a separate set of credentials. Assuming you want to use inherited credentials, click **Next** to accept the defaults.

6.   The next screen asks you to enter a name for the new monitoring check. The name is populated automatically though, so just click **Next**, unless you want to customize the name.

7.   A screen similar to that in Figure 18.4 appears, asking you to specify which computers the new monitoring check will apply to. Normally, you would just select the **Create The Checks In A Dedicated Folder For Every Computer** check box.

Figure 18.4 You Will Be Prompted to Choose Which Computers the New Monitoring Check Will Apply To

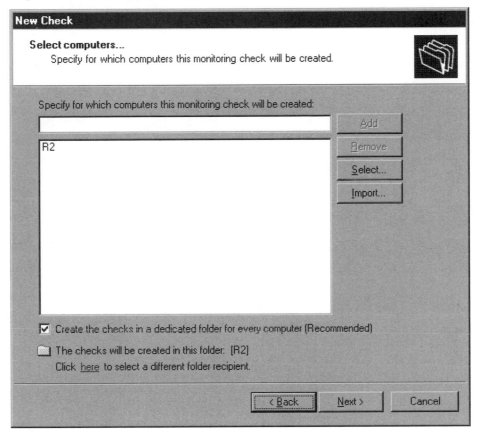

8.   Click **Next**.

9.   You should now see a screen confirming that the monitoring check is about to be created. Click **Finish** to complete the process. The monitoring check should now be added to the folder you specified, as shown in Figure 18.5.

Figure 18.5 The New Monitoring Check Is Added to the Folder

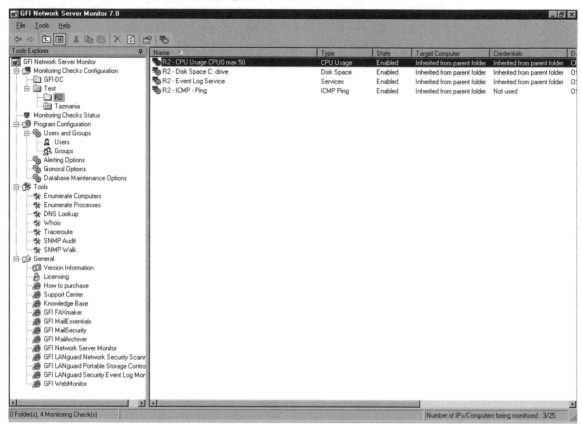

Modifying a Monitoring Check

You have the ability to modify any of the monitoring checks. To do so, just right-click the monitoring check you want to monitor and choose the **Properties** command from the shortcut menu. When you do, the console will display the monitoring check's properties sheet. You can modify any of the properties associated with a monitoring check, but usually you will be most interested in the properties sheet's Check Parameters tab. This is the tab that specifies the monitoring check's threshold value or other monitoring parameters. An example of this tab is shown in Figure 18.6.

Figure 18.6 The Check Parameters Tab Controls the Monitoring Check's
Threshold Values

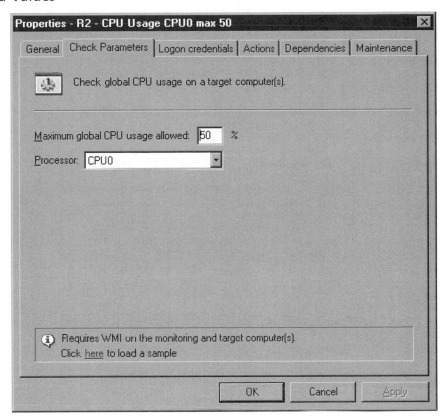

Deleting a Monitoring Check

You can delete a monitoring check by right-clicking it and selecting the **Delete** command from
the resulting shortcut menu. An example of this appears in Figure 18.7.

Figure 18.7 Delete a Monitoring Check by Right-Clicking It and Choosing the Delete Command From the Shortcut Menu

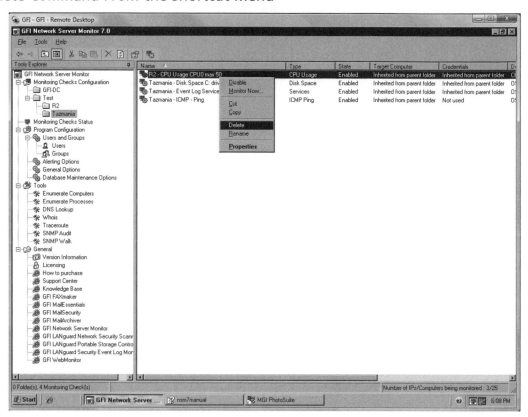

Moving Servers and Monitoring Checks

One thing that seems to be consistent for most organizations is that IT configurations are rarely static. As an organization's needs change over time, so too does its configurations. The good news is that GFI Network Server Monitor makes it simple to move both servers and monitoring checks.

Moving a server is as simple as dragging the server's folder and dropping it in a different location. The same can be said for monitoring checks. You can drag and drop monitoring checks to your heart's content.

WARNING

You should not drag and drop monitoring checks unless the monitoring check is configured to inherit its parameters from the parent folder. Otherwise, you could be in for some unexpected problems. Not all of the monitoring check's properties must be inherited, but you should take some time to review the properties to make sure the monitoring check will still function properly after it has been moved.

Monitoring Checks Status

So far, I have shown you many ways to configure the monitoring process so it will work just the way you want. However, monitoring your servers won't do you much good if you can't occasionally check the server's status. Sure, GFI Network Server Monitor will send you alerts when certain types of failures occur, but you can also check on your servers anytime you want by using the Monitoring Checks Status feature.

The easiest way of accessing the Monitoring Checks Status screen is to select the **Monitoring Checks Status** container in the GFI Network Server Monitor 7 Configuration console. Its screen is shown in Figure 18.8.

Figure 18.8 The Monitoring Checks Status Screen Shows What Is Happening on Your Network

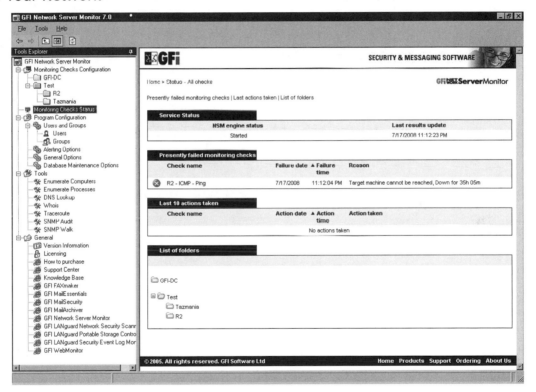

As you can see in the figure, this screen is divided into four separate sections. The top section is the Server Status section. This section basically just confirms that GFI Network Server Monitor is functioning.

The second section is the Presently Failed Monitoring Checks section. This is the area that highlights any errors that have been detected and are currently an issue. For example, I took the server R2 offline a couple of days ago so I could do some maintenance on it. If you look at Figure 18.8, you can see this server has been down about 35 hours.

The third section on this screen is the Last 10 Actions Taken section. This section lets you see at a glance what GFI Network Server Monitor has been up to lately. In this case, this section is empty because I am only monitoring a few servers—two of those servers are healthy, and one is offline.

The bottom section is the List of Folders. If you click any of the folders, you can see any recent errors or warnings produced by recent status checks run against the server associated with the folder. Looking at Figure 18.9, notice some of the errors and warnings I have intentionally triggered.

Figure 18.9 By Selecting a Folder, You Can See Recent Errors and Warnings for the Server Associated with the Folder

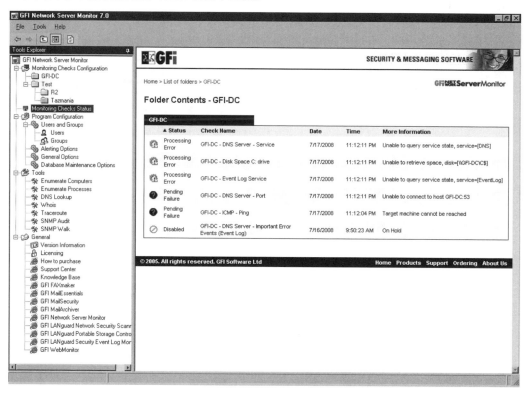

TIP

Ping tests can fail if the server's firewall policy prevents ICMP traffic.

Notice the navigation links at the top of the screen in Figure 18.9. These can return you to the main Status Monitor screen. The main Status Monitor screen also contains some links at the top of the page that you can use to navigate the Network Status screen. These links are shown at the top of Figure 18.8.

In this case, the navigation links probably seem like overkill. But keep in mind that I am only monitoring a few servers. If I were monitoring many servers, then this page could be very long, wherein the navigation links would make it much easier to access the desired part of the page.

Tools & Traps...

What Do the Results Really Mean?

The results displayed on the Monitoring Checks Status screen can sometimes be misleading. Sometimes, conditions occur in which GFI Network Server Monitor is unsure of itself. When this happens, the software treats the condition as a processing error by default. You do have the option of changing this behavior though. To do so, select the Configuration console's **General Options** container, and click the **Properties** link. This will cause the console to display the General Options properties sheet, shown in Figure 18.10. You can use the properties sheet's **Uncertain Results** tab to control how GFI Network Server Monitor deals with these types of situations.

Figure 18.10 Use the Uncertain Results Tab to Control How GFI Network Server Monitor Deals with Situations Where the Monitoring Check Cannot Interpret Its Results

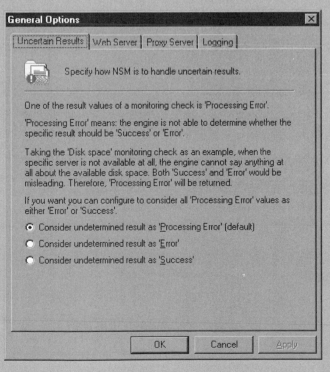

Remote Monitoring

So far, I have shown you how to access the Monitoring Checks Status screen from within the configuration console, but this can be done in other ways, too. One option is to use the stand-alone console provided with GFI Network Server Monitor. You can access this console by clicking the Windows **Start** button, and then choosing the **All Programs | GFI Network Server Monitor 7 | GFI N.S.M. Status Monitor** options from the resulting shortcut menus. As you can see in Figure 18.11, the stand-alone Status Monitor console looks just like the Status Monitor screen, which is accessible from within the Configuration console.

Figure 18.11 You Can Access the Status Monitor Console Outside of the Configuration Console

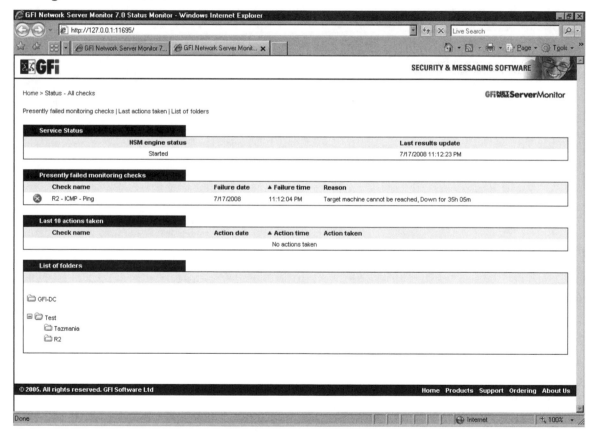

If your GFI Network Server Monitor server is accessible from the outside world, you can also view the Server Monitor console over the Internet. GFI Network Server Monitor contains a built-in Web Server that makes this possible. This Web server is enabled by default, but uses an obscure port number.

You can enable or disable the Web server, or change its port number, by opening the **Configuration** console, selecting the **General Options** container, and then clicking the **Properties** link. When you do so, the console will display the General Options properties sheet. The properties sheet's Web Server tab contains an option to enable or disable the Web server, control access to the Web server, and set the port number. The screen is shown in Figure 18.12.

Figure 18.12 The Web Server Tab Lets You Disable the Web Server, Establish Access Control, or Change the Port Number

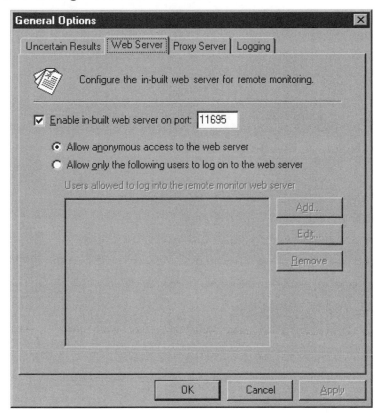

So how do you access the built-in Web server? Well, if you return to Figure 18.11, you will notice that the Status Monitor is actually open in Internet Explorer. In this case, the URL is http://127.0.0.1:11695. In case you are a bit rusty on TCP/IP, 127.0.0.1 is the local host address, and the number after the colon is the port number. If you want to access this Web server from another machine, you simply replace the 127.0.0.1 with the server's IP address.

Built-in Tools

GFI Network Server Monitor contains a number of built-in tools that are exposed directly through the Configuration console. A few of these tools are proprietary to GFI, but most are simply graphical versions of command-line tools that are built into Windows. In the following sections, I will briefly discuss these various tools.

Enumerate Computers

The Enumerate Computers tool lets you create a list of all of the computers in the domain. All you have to do is enter the name of the domain, and click the **Retrieve** button, and the list will be created, as shown in Figure 18.13.

Figure 18.13 The Enumerate Computers Tool Lets You Get a List of the Computers in the Domain

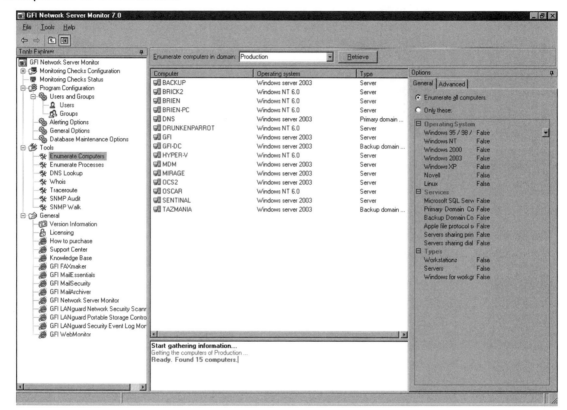

By default, all of the computers in the domain are listed, but notice at the far right side of Figure 18.13 the option of building an enumeration list based on operating system, server role, or machine type.

The far right side of the screen also contains an Advanced tab that can be used to control how the information found on the enumeration list is compiled. By default, the information comes from Windows Explorer, but you do have the option of querying Active Directory instead, as shown in Figure 18.14. In my opinion, querying Active Directory is usually a better option, because Windows Explorer only shows you machines that are online currently. Active Directory–based enumeration is also faster than using Windows Explorer–based enumeration. For example, in Figure 18.13, a Windows Explorer–based enumeration detected 15 computers. However, when I ran an Active Directory–based enumeration, it detected 45 computers. Keep in mind that if you plan on using Active Directory–based enumeration, you must have Domain Admin permissions.

Figure 18.14 Active Directory–Based Enumeration Usually Detects Many More Machines

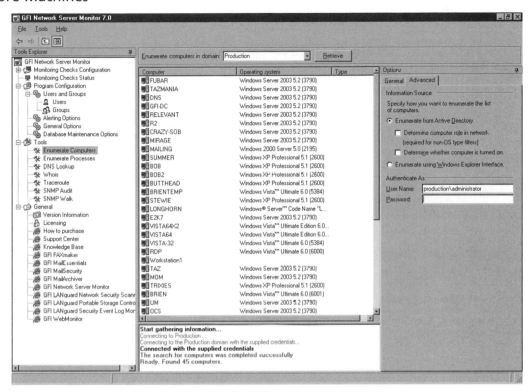

Tools & Traps...

A Huge Difference in the Enumeration Count

In the preceding section, you saw that when I performed a standard enumeration, 15 computers were detected on my network. When I performed the Active Directory–based enumeration, though, the count rose to 45 computers. This is a huge difference. Two thirds of the computers on my network were not detected by the initial enumeration!

The reason for this is simple. A Windows Explorer–based enumeration only lists computers that are online at the moment. I keep about two thirds of the computers

Continued

on my network turned off most of the time. It's a little off topic, but I'll explain why I'm mentioning this.

I work out of my home, and the entire second floor of my house is jam packed with computers. These computers consume a lot of electricity, and give off a tremendous amount of heat. The excessive heat makes the air conditioner run more, which causes even more electricity to be consumed. An astronomical electric bill isn't my only reason for keeping the machines turned off though. It's really more about the heat.

Most major corporations have server rooms with raised floors and dedicated cooling systems. This is tough to come by in a residential setting. That being the case, the computers sometimes give off more heat than the air conditioner can handle.

A few years ago, Troy Thompson (this book's technical editor) spent Fourth of July weekend at my house. At that time, the temperatures outside were hovering around 100 degrees. I made the mistake of powering up all of my systems because I wanted to show Troy some stuff. As a result, it ended up being hotter in my office than it was outside, even with the air conditioning running full blast. We actually had to open the windows on a 100-degree day to cool down my office. Ever since that weekend, I only power up the systems I need.

Enumerate Processes

The Enumerate Processes tool is kind of neat. It gives you an easy way of seeing which processes are currently running on a target system. To perform a process enumeration, just enter the target system's host name or IP address into the space provided, and then click **Start**. As Figure 18.15 shows, you can also select some check boxes if you want to see the current CPU consumption on a per-process basis, or if you want to see the path to each process's executable file.

Figure 18.15 The Enumerate Processes Tool Displays Those Processes Running on a Target Server

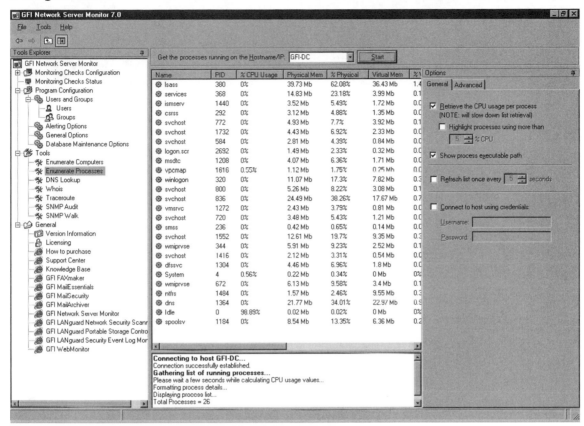

The Enumerate Processes tool offers an Advanced tab, which gives you the option of filtering the processes on the list. You can hide some processes, while highlighting others. Notice in Figure 18.16 that I have highlighted the CSRSS processes and hidden the SVCHOST process.

Figure 18.16 You Can Hide or Highlight Target Processes

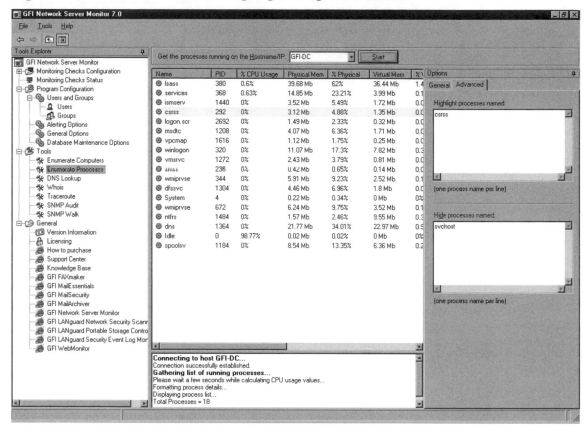

DNS Lookup

The DNS Lookup tool is just a graphical version of the Windows *NSLOOKUP* command. To use it, simply select the check boxes that correspond to the types of DNS records you want to retrieve, enter a hostname or an IP address, and click the **Retrieve** button. You can see an example of how the tool works in Figure 18.17.

Figure 18.17 The DNS Lookup Tool Is a Graphical Version of the Windows *NSLOOKUP* Command

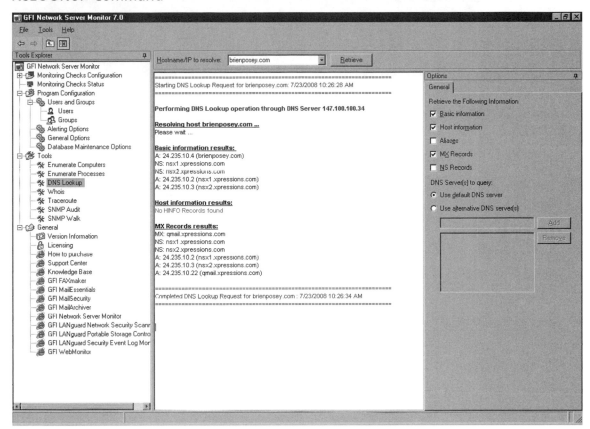

Who Is

The Who Is tool lets you retrieve the registration information for a domain. Simply enter the domain name and click the **Retrieve** button. Figure 18.18 shows the registration information for my domain.

Figure 18.18 The Who Is Tool Retrieves Registration Information for a Domain

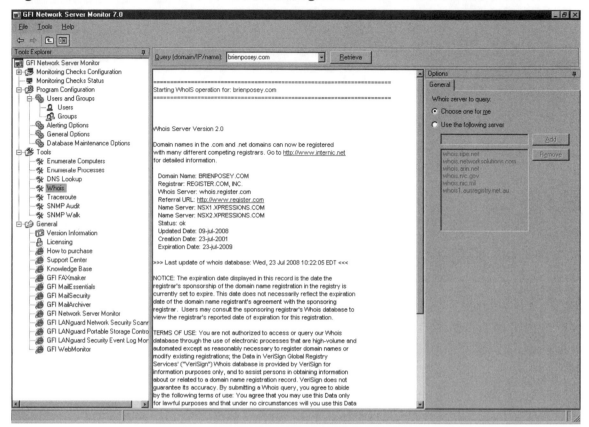

Trace Route

The Trace Route tool is a graphical version of the Windows TRACERT command-line tool. This tool lets you track the path a TCP/IP packet follows en route to its destination. To use this tool, just enter a domain name and click the **Traceroute** button. You can see what the tool's output looks like in Figure 18.19.

Figure 18.19 The Trace Route Tool Is a Graphical Version of the Windows
TRACERT Command-Line Tool

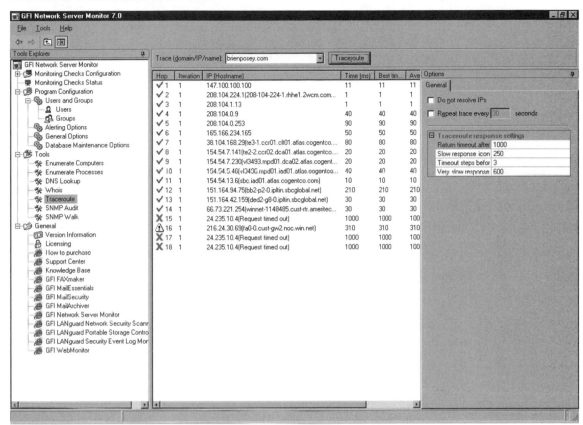

SNMP Tools

GFI Network Server Monitor contains two different SNMP tools: SNMP Audit and SNMP Walk.
Unfortunately, I do not have any SNMP-compatible devices on my network, so I don't have a way
of demonstrating these tools for you, but I wanted to at least mention them.

Summary

As you can see, the configuration console is the primary interface for using GFI Network Server Monitor. You can use this console to define the servers you want to monitor, customize the aspects of those servers you are interested in monitoring, and check each server's status. In the next chapter, I will show you some additional components of GFI network Server Monitor, including the Activity Monitor, the Reporter, and the Troubleshooter.

Solutions Fast Track

Customizing Monitoring Checks

☑ The console lets you add, delete, and modify monitoring checks.

☑ You can drag and drop to move a monitoring check to another folder.

☑ Modify a monitoring check by right-clicking it and choosing the Properties command from the resulting shortcut menu.

Monitoring Checks Status

☑ The Monitoring Checks Status screen lets you view the outcome of the various monitoring checks.

☑ You can access the Monitoring Checks Status screen either directly through the Configuration console or through a Web browser.

Built-in Tools

☑ GFI Network Server Monitor offers a number of built-in tools that are accessible through the Configuration console's Tools container.

☑ Many of the tools are graphical versions of tools built into Windows.

Frequently Asked Questions

Q: Why can't I access the Monitoring Checks Status page over the Internet?

A: GFI Network Server Manager's built-in Web server is configured, by default, to use an obscure TCP port. You must include this port number in the URL and configure your firewall to allow inbound Web traffic through that port.

Q: I am enumerating computers based on the contents of Active Directory, but I see computers that do not even exist on my network. Why is that?

A: If you take a computer off the network without gracefully removing it from your domain, the computer account will remain in Active Directory. You can use the Active Directory Users and Computers console to remove unwanted computer accounts.

Q: Is there a way to interact with the list of enumerated processes?

A: Unfortunately, no. Unlike the Windows Task Manager, the Enumerate Processes tool does not let you kill a process or change its priority.

Q: What do the DNS Lookup, Who Is, and Trace Route tools have to do with monitoring network servers?

A: Nothing. These are just standard troubleshooting tools that GFI threw in as a way of helping you diagnose any problems the monitoring checks might report. These tools are in no way specifically geared toward GFI Network Server Monitor.

Chapter 19

GFI Network Monitor's Additional Components

Solutions in this chapter:

- **The Activity Monitor**
- **The Reporter**
- **The Troubleshooter**

☑ **Summary**

☑ **Solutions Fast Track**

☑ **Frequently Asked Questions**

Introduction

So far, I have shown you most of the basic techniques behind using GFI Network Server Monitor. However, a few additional components are also included with GFI Network Server Monitor, so I wanted to wrap things up by exploring these.

The Activity Monitor

In the previous chapter, I showed you how to use the Configuration console's Monitoring Checks Status screen to get some information about what was going on with the servers you are monitoring. As you probably noticed, the Monitoring Checks Status screen only offers a limited amount of information, however. This is where the Activity Monitor comes into play. The Activity Monitor, shown in Figure 19.1, lets you watch the results of monitoring checks as they complete.

Figure 19.1 The Activity Monitor Lets You Watch Monitoring Checks in Real Time

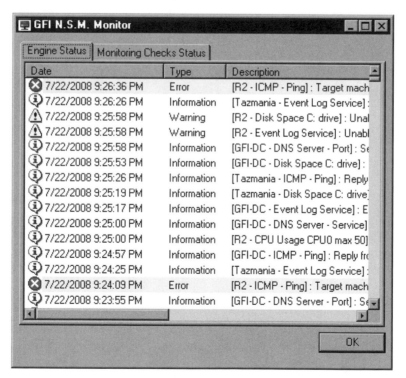

You can access the Activity Monitor by clicking the Windows **Start** button, and then selecting the **All Programs | GFI Network Server Monitor 7 | GFI N.S.M. 7 Activity Monitor** options from the menus that follow.

When the Activity Monitor opens, the Engine Status tab is selected by default. This tab displays the monitoring engine's activity. For example, you can view information such as the type of activity that has occurred (error, warning, and so on), the date and time of an event, and a brief description of the event.

If you click the Activity Monitor's Monitoring Checks Status tab, information specific to the individual monitoring checks appears. This tab shows the most recent monitoring checks, as shown in Figure 19.2.

Figure 19.2 The Monitoring Checks Status Tab Displays the Results of the Most Recent Monitoring Checks

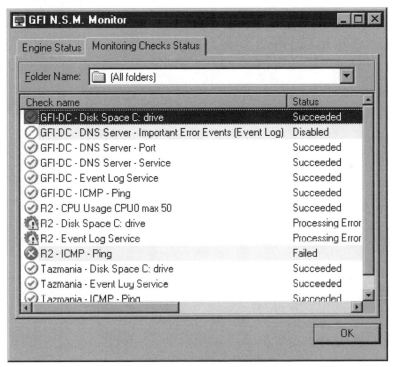

As you can see in Figure 19.2, the Monitoring Checks Status tab displays monitoring check information for every computer being monitored. In a large enterprise environment, this list could end up being really long. Notice at the top of the figure, though, that an option exists to specify an individual folder. This lets you view the monitoring checks for a specific machine rather than for the network as a whole.

Viewing Monitoring Check Status Remotely

In the previous chapter, I mentioned that GFI Network Server Monitor contains a built-in Web server that can be used to remotely access the Status Monitor console. This same Web server can also be used to remotely access the Monitoring Check Status screen. You can access this screen by entering the appropriate URL in your browser. By default, the URL consists of HTTP:// followed by the server's

IP address, a colon, the port number (11695 by default), and /list.html. For example, if your server's IP address was 192.186.1.1, you could access the console by going to http://192.168.1.1:11695/list.html. Figure 19.3 shows what the Monitoring Check Status Web interface looks like.

Figure 19.3 Monitoring Check Status Information Is Available Through a Web Interface

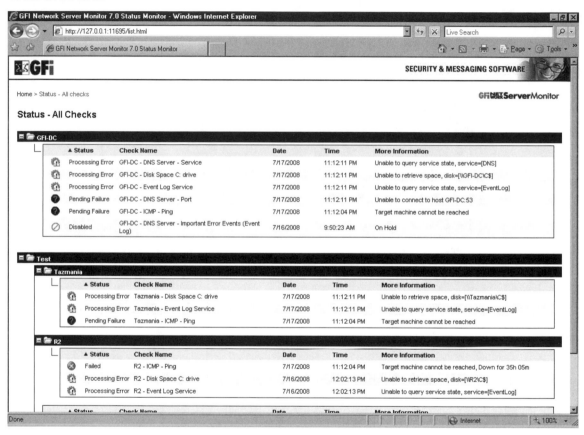

> **TIP**
>
> It is also possible to view the Monitoring Check Status screen from a Windows mobile device. GFI Network Server Monitor even provides a special view that is formatted to fit a mobile device's screen.

Are You Owned?

Don't Give the Hackers Information about Your Network

By default, the Web interface is configured to allow anonymous access. If the Web server is externally accessible, and a hacker knows which port to use, they could use the Web interface to gather information about the servers on your network. At the very least, a hacker could learn your server names, and which servers are performing which roles. This is valuable information to anyone planning a network hack. Therefore, I recommend securing or disabling the Web server. You can learn how in Chapter 18.

The Reporter

GFI Network Server Monitor does offer reporting capabilities, although they are not nearly as comprehensive as what other GFI products provide through the ReportPack. When it comes to generating reports, you really only have two choices: you can generate a detailed report, or you can produce a summary report.

In an effort to show you how the Reporter works, I'm going to walk you through the process of creating a summary report. To create a summary report, perform the following steps:

1. Click the Windows **Start** button, and choose the **All Programs | GFI Network Server Monitor 7 | GFI N.S.M. 7 Reporter** options from the subsequent menus. When finished, Windows will launch the GFI Network Server Monitor Reports Wizard, shown in Figure 19.4.

Figure 19.4 The GFI Network Server Reports Wizard Helps You Generate Availability Reports

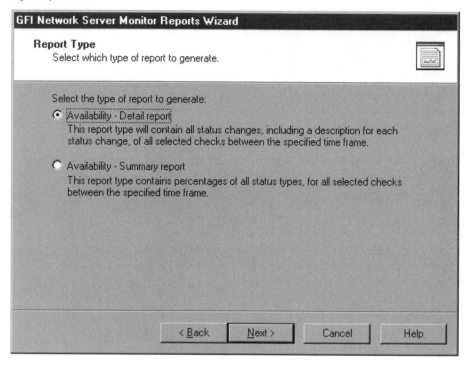

2. As you can see in Figure 19.4, the wizard's initial screen gives you a choice between creating a detailed report and a summary report. Choose the **Availability – Summary Report** option, and then click **Next**.

3. The next screen you encounter asks you to specify a date range for the data that will be included in the report, as shown in Figure 19.5. Select a date range, and then click **Next**.

Figure 19.5 Choose a Date Range for the Data You Want to Include in the Report

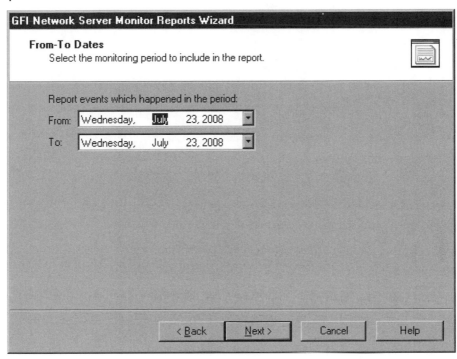

4. A screen appears similar to the one in Figure 19.6. Here, you have the option of either including all of the monitoring checks in the report, or of limiting the report to only include specific monitoring checks. For now, select the **All Checks** option, and then click **Next**.

Figure 19.6 You Can Include All of the Monitoring Checks in the Report or Limit the Report to Only Specific Monitoring Checks

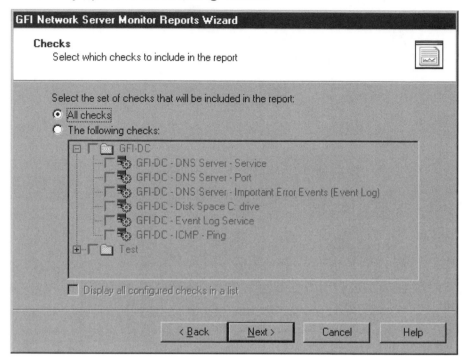

5. A screen like that in Figure 19.7 appears, asking you which format you want to generate the report in. By default, reports are generated in XML format, but you also have the option of creating an HTML report, or of exporting the report to a CSV file. The CSV file option is useful if you want to turn the report data into a spreadsheet. For this example, choose the **HTML** option, and then click **Next**.

Figure 19.7 You Can Create a Report in One of Three Different Formats

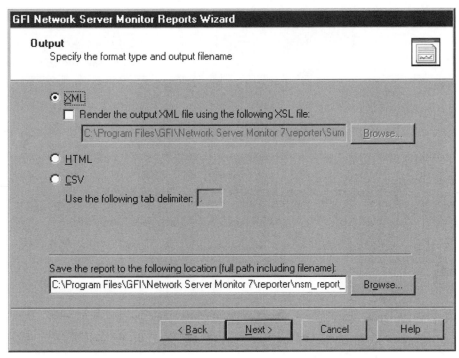

6. A screen appears telling you that the wizard is ready to generate the report. Click **Next** to create the report.

7. When the wizard finishes compiling the report, click **Finish**. Figure 19.8 shows what the report looks like.

Figure 19.8 A Summary Report in HTML Format

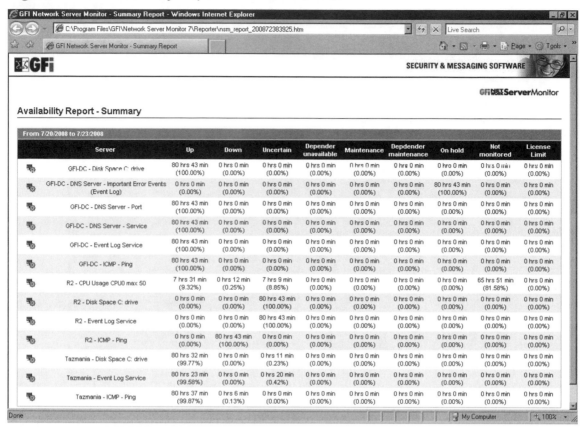

The Troubleshooter

We all need technical support now and then, and this is where the Troubleshooter console comes into play. The Troubleshooter console will not actually diagnose a problem you may be having, but it will let you assemble some diagnostic files and enter some information about the problem you are having, so GFI's technical support department can help you.

Using the Troubleshooter is fairly straightforward, but I will quickly go over the process anyway. If GFI's technical support department instructs you to run the Troubleshooter, you can do so by performing the following steps:

1. Click the Windows **Start** button and choose the **All programs | GFI Network Monitor 7 | GFI N.S.M. 7 Troubleshooter** commands from the Windows Start menu. When you do, Windows will launch the GFI Network Server Monitor 7 Troubleshooter Wizard.

2. Click **Next** to bypass the wizard's Welcome screen.

3. A screen appears similar to that in Figure 19.9, asking you to enter your contact information. Although it is tempting to skip this step, entering the requested information is important and enables GFI to contact you and match the support data with your case.

Figure 19.9 It Is Important You Enter Your Contact Information

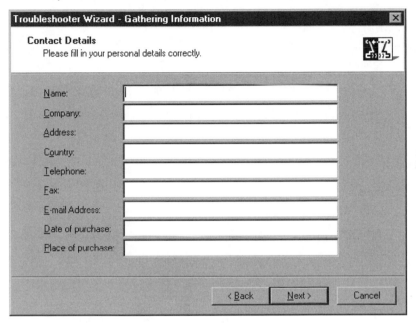

4. Click **Next**.

5. At the next screen, enter an explanation of your problem, and the steps required to reproduce it.

6. Click **Next**. The wizard will now compile some information about your server's configuration. As shown in Figure 19.10, this screen also lets you add any additional details about your server's configuration that may help the technical support staff.

Figure 19.10 You Have the Option of Providing Additional Information About Your Server

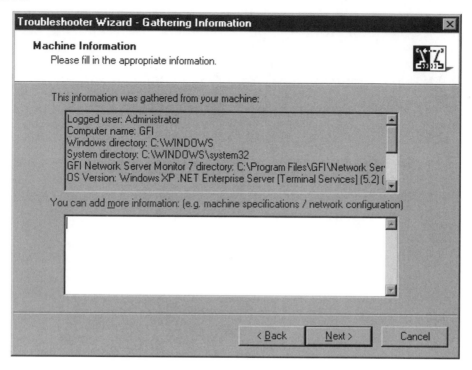

7. Click **Next**.

8. A screen appears telling you some files have been written to the C:\Program Files\GFI\ Network Server Monitor 7\Support folder. It instructs you to zip up these files and e-mail them to Support@GFI.com. As shown in Figure 19.11, the information that has been compiled is written to a series of text files. Click **Finish** to close the wizard.

Figure 19.11 Zip Up the Files You Have Compiled and E-mail Them to support@GFI.com

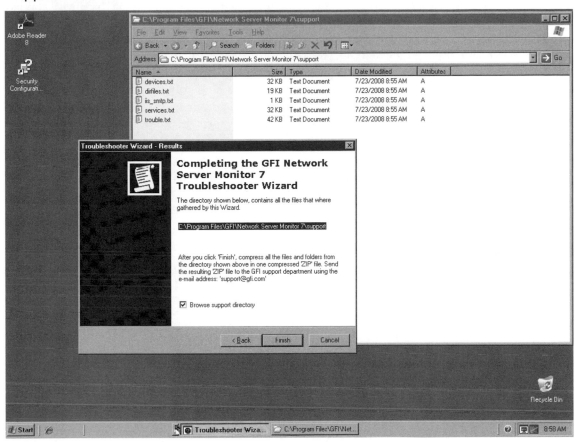

TIP

Many administrators are understandably concerned about the idea of sending data from a network server to an external technical support department. If you have concerns about your organization's privacy, I recommend taking a moment to look through the text files that have been assembled. This way, you can see exactly what information is being sent to GFI.

Summary

As you can see, GFI Network Server Monitor is by far the easiest GFI product to use that I have covered in this book. Even so, that does not in any way reflect negatively on the product's usefulness. While there are definitely more comprehensive server monitoring products on the market, GFI Network Server Monitor is unique in that it is simple to use. An administrator can install the software and begin monitoring their network in only a few hours. Some of the other network monitoring products I have used require a week-long training class and extensive deployment planning prior to installation. GFI Network Server Monitor is ideal for administrators who want to keep things simple, and who do not have the budget for the more comprehensive server monitoring products available, nor the time to deal with their complexities.

Solutions Fast Track

The Activity Monitor

- ☑ The Activity Monitor can display the engine status and the monitoring checks status.

- ☑ If the Monitoring Checks Status screen gets too crowded, consider viewing an individual folder rather than the whole network.

- ☑ The Monitoring Checks Status information is remotely accessible through a Web interface.

The Reporter

- ☑ The Reporter is not nearly as comprehensive as the ReportPack that comes with many other GFI products.

- ☑ You can produce an Activity Summary report or a more detailed report.

- ☑ Reports can be saved in HTML, XML, or CSV format.

The Troubleshooter

- ☑ The Troubleshooter helps the technical support staff at GFI diagnose problems with GFI Network Server Monitor.

- ☑ The Troubleshooter does not perform any actual diagnostics. It only gathers information.

- ☑ You must manually send information gathered by the Troubleshooter to GFI.

Frequently Asked Questions

Q: Why won't the Activity Monitor launch when I select it from the Start menu?

A: If the Activity Monitor won't launch, check your system tray. It may already be running. If so, you can just click its icon to maximize the Activity Monitor window.

Q: What formats can reports be created in?

A: The Reporter can write reports in XML, HTML, and CSV format.

Q: What are .CSV reports good for?

A: .CSV files are text files (comma separated value files) that can be read into Microsoft Excel. This lets you save the report as a spreadsheet. With a little work, you can also import a CSV file into Microsoft Access.

Q: Will the Troubleshooter fix the problem I'm having?

A: No, it only gathers information for the GFI technical support department.

Q: I ran the Troubleshooter, but I haven't heard anything back from GFI. What could be the problem?

A: The Troubleshooter does not automatically send GFI your troubleshooting information. You must zip up the support files yourself and e-mail them to support@GFI.com.

Index

customizing monitoring checks
adding monitoring check, 421–424
deletion, 425–426
modification, 424–425

D
default classification actions, 364–365
Dependencies tab, 411–412
Deploy Microsoft Service Packs, 60
device boot order, 260
device security permissions
adding permissions
Add Permissions dialog box, 241
additional device management, 240
device access control, 242
USB and FireWire ports access, 244–245
write access control, 243
control access level, 236–237
Device Block Access, 238
Devices View and Users View, 238–239
Device Statistics, 310–311
device usage monitoring
alert options
Access Deny Events, 297
Configuration tab, 294
e-mail and network message alerts, 295–296
protection policy, 294
configuring alert recipients, 297–299
Deployment Status screen, 308
e-mail and network message alerts, 295–296
Filter tab, 294
GFI EndPointSecurity reports
General Status screen, 306–307
GFI ReportCenter, 299–301
report creation, 301–305
log options, 292–294
Configuration tab, 292
Filter tab, 293–294
protection policy, 292
statistics, 310–311
updating agents, 307–309
domain name system (DNS) lookup, 36, 436–437

E
e-mail notification configuration, GFI LANguard
Microsoft Exchange Server, 19–23
standalone SMTP server, 13–18
end user experience
agent uninstalling steps, 277–281
temporary access
access denied message, 277
applet, 281–282
Deploy Agent option, 281
GFI EndPointSecurity, 285, 288
Grant Temporary Access Link, 284
Grant Temporary Access wizard, 286–287
hidden mechanism, 282
long term effects, 283
No Menu option, 280
Request Code, 283–284
Time Restriction screen, 286
unlock code, 287
Universal Serial Bus devices, 276–277
End User License Agreement (EULA), 196
event collection process, 384–385
Event ID 560, 372–373
event processing rules
GFI EventsManager response, 366
hierarchical approach, 368
noise reduction events, 367
Events Log tab, 372

F
file type restrictions
blocking files, 269
creation of file type filter, 267–269
Main File-Type Filter screen, 271
preventing executable files, 268
full scan, 45
fully qualified domain name (FQDN), 16, 20, 203

G
General tab, 370
GFI EndPointSecurity
advanced security configurations
blacklisting and whitelisting devices, 266–267

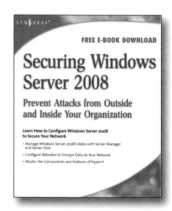